Kaplan Publishing are constantly finding new
difference to your studies and our exciting or
offer something different to students looking

CW00546286

This book comes with free MyKaplan online r
study anytime, anywhere. **This free online resource is not sold separately and is included in the price of the book.**

Having purchased this book, you have access to the following online study materials:

CONTENT	ACCA (including FBT, FMA, FFA)		FIA (excluding FBT, FMA, FFA)	
	Text	Kit	Text	Kit
Electronic version of the book	✓	✓	✓	✓
Check Your Understanding Test with instant answers	✓			
Material updates	✓	✓	✓	✓
Latest official ACCA exam questions*		✓		
Extra question assistance using the signpost icon**		✓		
Timed questions with an online tutor debrief using clock icon***		✓		
Interim assessment including questions and answers	✓		✓	
Technical answers	✓	✓	✓	✓

* Excludes BT, MA, FA, FBT, FMA, FFA; for all other papers includes a selection of questions, as released by ACCA

** For ACCA SBL, SBR, AFM, APM, ATX, AAA only

*** Excludes BT, MA, FA, LW, FBT, FMA and FFA

How to access your online resources

Kaplan Financial students will already have a MyKaplan account and these extra resources will be available to you online. You do not need to register again, as this process was completed when you enrolled. If you are having problems accessing online materials, please ask your course administrator.

If you are not studying with Kaplan and did not purchase your book via a Kaplan website, to unlock your extra online resources please go to www.mykaplan.co.uk/addabook (even if you have set up an account and registered books previously). You will then need to enter the ISBN number (on the title page and back cover) and the unique pass key number contained in the scratch panel below to gain access. You will also be required to enter additional information during this process to set up or confirm your account details.

If you purchased through the Kaplan Publishing website you will automatically receive an e-mail invitation to MyKaplan. Please register your details using this email to gain access to your content. If you do not receive the e-mail or book content, please contact Kaplan Publishing.

Your Code and Information

This code can only be used once for the registration of one book online. This registration and your online content will expire when the final sittings for the examinations covered by this book have taken place. Please allow one hour from the time you submit your book details for us to process your request.

Please scratch the film to access your unique code.

Please be aware that this code is case-sensitive and you will need to include the dashes within the passcode, but not when entering the ISBN.

KAPLAN PUBLISHING

ACCA Certificate in Taxation
(RQF Level 4)

FTX (FA2021)

Foundations in Taxation

STUDY TEXT

For June and December 2022 examination sittings

British Library Cataloguing-in-Publication Data

A catalogue record for this book is available from the British Library.

Published by:

Kaplan Publishing UK
Unit 2 The Business Centre
Molly Millars Lane
Wokingham
RG41 2QZ

ISBN: 978-1-78740-852-4

Printed and bound in Great Britain.

The text in this material and any others made available by any Kaplan Group company does not amount to advice on a particular matter and should not be taken as such. No reliance should be placed on the content as the basis for any investment or other decision or in connection with any advice given to third parties. Please consult your appropriate professional adviser as necessary. Kaplan Publishing Limited and all other Kaplan group companies expressly disclaim all liability to any person in respect of any losses or other claims, whether direct, indirect, incidental, consequential or otherwise arising in relation to the use of such materials.

Acknowledgements

These materials are reviewed by the ACCA examining team. The objective of the review is to ensure that the material properly covers the syllabus and study guide outcomes, used by the examining team in setting the exams, in the appropriate breadth and depth. The review does not ensure that every eventuality, combination or application of examinable topics is addressed by the ACCA Approved Content. Nor does the review comprise a detailed technical check of the content as the Approved Content Provider has its own quality assurance processes in place in this respect.

We are grateful to the Association of Chartered Certified Accountants, the Chartered Institute of Management Accountants and the Institute of Chartered Accountants in England and Wales for permission to reproduce past examination questions. The answers have been prepared by Kaplan Publishing. The copyright to the questions remains with the examining body.

We are grateful to HM Revenue and Customs for the provision of tax forms, which are Crown Copyright and are reproduced here with kind permission from the Office of Public Sector Information.

CONTENTS

Quality and accuracy are of the utmost importance to us so if you spot an error in any of our products, please send an email to mykaplanreporting@kaplan.com with full details, or follow the link to the feedback form in MyKaplan.

Our Quality Co-ordinator will work with our technical team to verify the error and take action to ensure it is corrected in future editions.

INTRODUCTION

This is the new edition of the FIA study text for FTX (FA2021) – *Foundations in Taxation*, approved by the ACCA and fully updated for changes in legislation and the FIA syllabus.

Tailored to fully cover the syllabus, this study text has been written specifically for FIA students. Clear and comprehensive style, numerous examples and highlighted key terms help you to acquire the information easily. Plenty of activities and self-test questions enable you to practise what you have learnt.

At the end of most of the chapters you will find practice questions. These are examination-style questions and will give you a very good idea of the way you will be tested.

An examining team review by ACCA ensures that this text covers the syllabus in the appropriate breadth and depth.

ACCA SUPPORT

For additional support with your studies please also refer to the ACCA Global website.

SYLLABUS AND STUDY GUIDE

Position of the examination in the overall syllabus

The Certified Accounting Technician (CAT) Qualification consists of nine exams which include seven of the FIA examinations, at all three levels, plus two examinations from three of the specialist options. The CAT qualification also requires the completion of the Foundations in Professionalism (FiP) module and 12 months relevant work experience, including the demonstration of 10 work based competence areas. Exemptions can be claimed from a maximum of the first four FIA exams for relevant work experience.

FTX is one of the three specialist option examinations. Its aim is to develop the ability to prepare computations of tax liability for both individuals and businesses resident in the UK for the purposes of income tax, corporation tax, capital gains tax and value added tax. In addition, to develop knowledge and understanding of the manner in which dealings must be conducted with HM Revenue and Customs, including knowledge of the statutory timescales for the submission of claims and returns and the due dates for the payment of tax liabilities.

DETAILED SYLLABUS

A Introduction to the UK tax system

1 Principal sources of revenue law and practice
2 Different types of taxes

B Adjusted profit / loss computations for trades and professions

1 Adjustment of trading profits/losses for tax purposes
2 Capital allowances
3 Basis of assessments
4 Relief for trading losses
5 Partnerships
6 National insurance contributions for self-employed
7 Prepare relevant pages of a tax return

C Income tax liabilities

1 Introduction to personal taxation
2 Income from employment and class 1 national insurance contributions
3 Income from property, savings and investments
4 The comprehensive computation of taxable income and income tax liability
5 The use of pension contributions in deferring and minimising income tax liabilities
6 Income tax administration

D Capital gains tax

1 The scope of the taxation of capital gains for individuals
2 The basic principles of computing gains and losses
3 Gains and losses on the disposal of shares and securities
4 Gains and losses on the disposal of movable and immovable property
5 The computation of capital gains tax payable by individuals and the completion of the self-assessment tax return.
6 The use of exemptions and reliefs in deferring and minimising tax liabilities arising on the disposal of capital assets

E Corporation tax liabilities

1 The scope of corporation tax
2 Taxable total profits
3 The comprehensive computation of corporation tax liability
4 Chargeable gains for companies
5 Relief for losses
6 The use of exemptions and reliefs in deferring and minimising corporation tax liabilities
7 Complete the corporation tax return
8 Corporation tax administration

F Value Added tax (VAT)

1 The scope of value added tax (VAT)
2 The VAT registration requirements
3 The basic principles of VAT
4 VAT invoices and records
5 Administration of VAT
6 The effect of special schemes
7 Preparing and completing VAT returns
8 Communicate VAT information

G Employability and technology skills

1 Use computer technology to efficiently access and manipulate relevant information
2 Work on relevant response options, using available functions and technology, as would be required in the workplace
3 Navigate windows and computer screens to create and amend responses to exam requirements, using the appropriate tools
4 Present data and information effectively using the appropriate tools

Study Guide

A INTRODUCTION TO THE UK TAX SYSTEM

1 Principal sources of revenue law and practice — Chapter 1

(a) Describe the overall structure of the UK tax system.

(b) Identify the main sources of UK tax legislation.

(c) Identify the key reference sources for UK tax legislation.

(d) Describe the organisation HM Revenue & Customs (HMRC) and its terms of reference including the appeals system.

(e) Describe the appeals process for income tax First and Upper Tier Tribunals.

(f) Explain the system of income tax and its background (how the legislation does not define income but defines taxable sources).

2 Different types of taxes — Chapter 1

(a) Identify the different types of capital and revenue tax.

(b) Explain the difference between direct and indirect taxation.

Excluded topics

- *Anti-avoidance legislation.*

B ADJUSTED PROFIT / LOSS COMPUTATIONS FOR TRADES AND PROFESSIONS

1 Adjustment of trading profits / losses for tax purposes — Chapter 3, 4

(a) Recognise the basis of assessment for self-employment income.

(b) Explain the principles of deductible and non-deductible expenditure.

(c) Recognise the relief that can be obtained for pre-trading expenditure.

(d) Prepare adjusted profit computations.

(e) Illustrate the use of capital allowances on commencement and cessation of business.

Excluded topics

- *Badges of trade.*
- *Successions.*
- *Change of accounting date.*
- *Personal service companies.*
- *Farmers averaging of profit.*
- *The averaging of profits for authors and creative artists.*
- *Remoteness and duality tests for profit deduction.*
- *Post cessation receipts and expenses.*
- *Cash basis for small businesses.*

2 Capital allowances — Chapter 4

(a) Explain the principles relating to capital allowances on plant & machinery
  - (i) definition of plant
  - (ii) cars
  - (iii) private use assets
  - (iv) short life assets
  - (v) hire purchase and leasing
  - (vi) special rate pool.

(b) Prepare capital allowance computations for plant & machinery
  - (i) writing down allowances
  - (ii) annual investment allowance
  - (iii) restrictions.

(c) Compute structures and buildings allowance.

Excluded topics

- *Long life assets.*
- *The 100% allowance for expenditure on renovating business premises in disadvantaged areas, flats above shops and water technologies.*
- *Apportionment in order to determine the amount of annual investment allowances where a period of account spans 1 January 2022.*
- *Knowledge of the annual investment allowance limits of £200,000 applicable from 1 January 2022.*

3 Basis of assessments — Chapter 5

(a) Explain the basis of assessment for a continuing sole trader's business.

(b) Explain and demonstrate the calculations of the basis of assessment for commencement and cessation of business.

(c) Calculate overlap relief, explain and demonstrate how it can be used on cessation.

4 Relief for trading losses — Chapter 6

(a) Explain the alternative loss reliefs available to a sole trader
  - (i) s64 current and prior years
  - (ii) s83 carry forward.

(b) Demonstrate the best use of a loss relief claim
  - (i) save the highest amount of tax
  - (ii) timing
  - (iii) protection of personal allowances.

Excluded topics

- *The special rules for losses in the opening years of a trade (s72 ITA 2007).*
- *The special rules for losses in the closing years of a trade (terminal losses under s89 ITA 2007).*

- *The special rules for the use of trade losses against capital gains (s261B TCGA 1992).*
- *Loss relief for shares in unquoted trading companies.*
- *For class 4 NIC: the offset of trading losses against non-trading income.*
- *The temporary extension of the carry back of trading losses incurred in the tax years 2020/21 and 2021/22 from one year to three years.*

5 Partnerships **Chapter 7**

(a) Explain how the trading profit rules are adapted for partnerships.

(b) Explain and show the effect of capital allowances on partnerships.

(c) Demonstrate the effect of changes in partnerships

(i) change in profit sharing ratios

(ii) new partners

(iii) departing partners.

(d) Illustrate the loss relief claims available to individual partners.

Excluded topics

- *Notional profits / losses for partnerships.*
- *Limited liability partnerships.*
- *The temporary extension of the carry back of trading losses incurred in the tax years 2020/21 and 2021/22 from one year to three years.*

6 National insurance contributions for self-employed **Chapter 11**

(a) Calculate national insurance contributions (NIC) for self-employed and contrast with employees

(i) class 2

(ii) class 4.

Excluded topics

- *Carry forward of trade losses which have been used against other income.*

7 Prepare relevant pages of a tax return **Chapter 8**

(a) Complete the self-employed or partnership supplementary pages of the tax return for individuals, and submit them within the statutory time limits.

C INCOME TAX LIABILITIES

1 Introduction to personal taxation **Chapters 2, 14**

(a) Identify the tax year.

(b) Outline the scope of income tax: chargeable persons, chargeable income.

(c) Identify sources of taxation information for individuals.

(d) Distinguish between income and capital profits/losses.

(e) Outline the key elements of a personal income tax computation

(i) earned income

(ii) non-savings income

(iii) savings income

(iv) dividend income

(v) net income

(vi) taxable income.

Excluded topics

- *Child benefit income tax charge.*
- *Residence status.*
- *Allowances for miscellaneous income.*

2 Income from employment and class 1 national insurance contributions **Chapters 9, 10, 11**

(a) Identify assessable income

(i) salaries

(ii) commissions

(iii) bonuses

(iv) benefits.

(b) Define and illustrate the basis of assessment for:

(i) directors

(ii) others.

(c) Identify the principal categories of deductions and illustrate their scope (no detail on pension contributions at this point)

(i) payroll giving

(ii) subscriptions

(iii) travelling expenses

(iv) expenses incurred wholly, exclusively and necessarily in the performance of duties.

(d) Identify the information required on a P11D.

(e) Identify and calculate benefits.

(f) Compute aggregate income

(i) all income

(ii) benefits

(iii) expenses.

(g) Identify source documents required to complete tax returns

(i) interest statements

(ii) receipts for expenses

(iii) form P11D

(iv) form P60.

(h) Compute basic class 1 national insurance contributions

(i) employees

(ii) employers (including class 1A)

(iii) weekly/monthly computations.

(i) Understand the annual employment allowance.

Excluded topics

- *The difference between employment and self-employment.*
- *Tax free childcare scheme.*
- *The calculation of car benefit where the car was registered before 6 April 2020.*
- *The calculation of a car benefit for cars which have emissions below 50g/km and are neither electric nor hybrid.*
- *The charge applicable to zero emission company vans.*
- *Detailed operation of the PAYE system (including calculations of code numbers).*
- *PAYE settlement agreements.*
- *Automatic exemption for reimbursed expenses.*
- *Payrolling of benefits.*
- *Share incentive schemes.*
- *Termination payments.*
- *Real time reporting late filing penalties.*
- *The calculation of directors' national insurance on a month by month basis.*
- *Classes 1(b) and 3 national insurance contributions.*
- *The restriction on the employment allowance where a director is the sole employee.*
- *Group aspects of the annual employment allowance.*

3 Income from property, savings and investments — Chapters 12, 13

(a) Identify property income assessable
 (i) furnished and unfurnished property
 (ii) premiums from short leases.

(b) Outline the deductions allowable
 (i) revenue expenses
 (ii) capital allowances
 (iii) replacement furniture relief
 (iv) repairs and renewals
 (v) restriction for private use.

(c) Describe rent-a-room relief.

(d) Explain the treatment of furnished holiday lettings.

(e) Understand how relief for a property business loss is given.

(f) Identify tax-free investments.

(g) Identify the source documents used to complete the tax return and complete the relevant pages of a self-assessment tax return.

Excluded topics

- *Savings income paid net of tax.*
- *Tax planning involving the transfer of savings income between spouses to utilise the savings income nil rate band.*
- *Dividend tax planning between spouses, civil partners and the impact on the decision to incorporate or extract funds from a company.*
- *The enterprise investment scheme, the seed enterprise investment and venture capital trusts.*
- *Trust income.*
- *Detailed knowledge of the rules and limits for individual savings accounts (ISA) other than that income from such accounts is exempt from tax.*
- *Junior ISAs.*
- *Premiums for granting subleases.*
- *The tax reduction scheme for gifts of pre-eminent objects.*
- *Accrued income scheme.*
- *The restriction on property income finance costs.*
- *Non-deductible capital expenditure under the cash basis for property income other than motor cars, land and buildings.*

4 The comprehensive computation of taxable income and income tax liability — Chapter 14

(a) Explain the entitlement to and the amount of the personal allowance.

(b) Identify and explain the use of eligible interest.

(c) Illustrate the allocation of tax bands and tax rates against taxable income
 (i) non-savings
 (ii) savings
 (iii) dividends.

(d) Explain and illustrate the difference between tax liability and tax payable for the deduction of PAYE.

(e) Explain and illustrate charitable payments:
 (i) payroll giving
 (ii) gift aid and the extension of basic rate and higher rate bands.

(f) Prepare examples of income tax computations
 (i) standard layout
 (ii) net income
 (iii) use of rates and bands
 (iv) basic rate and higher rate band extension
 (v) tax liability and tax payable.

Excluded topics

- *Consideration of the most beneficial allocation of the personal allowance to different categories of income.*
- *The transferable amount of personal allowance for spouses and civil partners.*
- *Tax reducers.*
- *Foreign income and double tax relief.*
- *The calculation of under/overpaid or late paid tax.*
- *Maintenance payments.*
- *The income of minor children.*
- *Cap on income tax reliefs.*
- *Child benefit income tax charge.*

5 The use of pension contributions in deferring and minimising income tax liabilities **Chapter 15**

(a) Identify the schemes available
  (i) occupational pension schemes
  (ii) private pension plans.
(b) Define net relevant earnings.
(c) Explain the maximum contributions allowed for tax relief
  (i) occupational schemes
  (ii) personal pension plans
  (iii) stakeholder plans
  (iv) employee, employer and self-employed.
(d) Show how the relief is given
  (i) deductions from salary
  (ii) basic rate tax withheld at source
  (iii) higher rate tax relief given via basic rate band extension
  (iv) additional rate tax relief given via higher rate band extension.
(e) Show the tax effects of employer contributions
  (i) on the employer
  (ii) on the employee.

Excluded topics

- *Excess charges for exceeding annual and lifetime allowances.*
- *The carry forward of unused annual allowance.*
- *The tapered annual allowance.*
- *Receiving income from pension arrangements.*

6 Income tax administration **Chapters 9, 16**

(a) Explain and apply the features of the self- assessment system as it applies to individuals.
(b) Detail the responsibilities that individuals have for disclosure of income and payment of tax to the relevant authorities.
(c) Describe the duties and responsibilities of a tax practitioner.
(d) Compute payments on account and balancing payments/repayments.
(e) List the information and records that taxpayers need to retain for tax purposes.
(f) Pay As You Earn (PAYE) forms and deadlines for submission
  (i) P11D
  (ii) P60
  (iii) P45.
(g) Explain the tax authority's filing and payment process in relation to all personal income.
(h) Explain the system of penalties and interest as it applies to income tax and capital gains.

Excluded topics

- *HM Revenue & Customs compliance checks, determinations and discovery assessments.*
- *Reducing payments on account.*
- *General Anti-Abuse rule.*
- *Calculation of late payment and repayment interest.*
- *Calculation of payment on account on disposals of residential property (knowledge of the payment on account due date is examinable).*

D CAPITAL GAINS TAX

1 The scope of the taxation of capital gains for individuals **Chapter 17**

(a) Define chargeable persons, chargeable disposals and chargeable assets
  (i) individuals
  (ii) exempt disposals
  (iii) exempt assets.
(b) Outline the administrative framework for capital gains tax
  (i) individuals
  (ii) payment.
(c) Outline the basic calculation including the deduction of expenses of purchase and sale.
(d) Explain the entitlement to the annual exempt amount.

2 The basic principles of computing gains and losses **Chapters 17, 18, 19**

(a) Compute capital gains for individuals.
(b) Explain the circumstances when market value may be used for the transfer value
  (i) bargains not at arm's length
  (ii) gifts.

(c) Demonstrate the calculation of market value for quoted shares and securities.

(d) Calculate disposals of post 31 March 1982 assets including enhancement expenditure.

(e) Explain the use of capital losses for individuals

  (i) current year

  (ii) brought forward.

(f) Compute the amount of allowable expenditure for a part disposal.

Excluded topics

- *Assets held at 31 March 1982.*
- *Losses in the year of death.*
- *Connected persons and transfers between spouses.*
- *Partnership capital gains.*
- *Negligible value claims.*
- *Relief for losses incurred on loans made to traders.*
- *Assets transferred to and from trading stock.*
- *CGT questions involving the effects of pension contributions and gift aid payments on income tax reliefs.*

3 Gains and losses on the disposal of shares and securities Chapter 19

(a) Outlining the matching rules for individuals

  (i) same day

  (ii) next 30 days

  (iii) share pool.

(b) Compute gains and losses on disposals by individuals.

(c) Illustrate the impact of bonus and rights issues on shareholdings.

(d) Identify exempt disposals

  (i) gifts

  (ii) qualifying corporate bonds (individuals only).

Excluded topics

- *Disposals of rights issues.*
- *Employee shareholders.*

4 Gains and losses on the disposal of movable and immovable property

Chapter 18

(a) Define chattels

  (i) non-wasting

  (ii) wasting.

(b) Explain and demonstrate the calculation of gains on chattel disposals

  (i) exemptions

  (ii) marginal relief

  (iii) deemed proceeds for losses

  (iv) awareness of the interaction with capital allowances.

(c) Calculate gains on part disposals.

(d) Calculate gains where compensation or insurance proceeds are received for assets lost or destroyed.

Excluded topics

- *Small part disposals of land.*
- *Wasting assets (other than chattels) and leases.*
- *Damaged assets.*

5 The computation of capital gains tax payable by individuals and the completion of the self-assessment tax return

Chapter 17

(a) Compute the amount of capital gains tax payable.

(b) Record relevant details of gains and the capital gains tax payable legibly and accurately in the tax return.

6 The use of exemptions and reliefs in deferring and minimising tax liabilities arising on the disposal of capital assets

Chapter 20

(a) Private residence relief (PRR)

  (i) outline the rules governing PRR

  (ii) explain and calculate the exemption

  (iii) explain and calculate the relief for absences

(b) Gift holdover relief

  (i) outline availability

  (ii) explain and calculate the relief

  (iii) calculate the restriction as a result of a sale at undervalue.

(c) Roll-over relief

  (i) outline availability

  (ii) explain and calculate the relief

  (iii) calculate the relief available on the partial reinvestment of sale proceeds

  (iv) depreciating assets.

(d) Explain and apply business asset disposal relief as it applies to individuals.

Excluded topics

- *Reinvestment relief.*
- *Letting relief.*
- *Business asset disposal relief for associated disposals.*
- *CGT questions involving both business asset disposal relief and other reliefs.*
- *Expanded definition of the 5% shareholding condition for business asset disposal relief.*

- *Availability of business asset disposal relief where shareholding is diluted below the 5% qualifying threshold.*
- *Business asset disposal relief lifetime limit prior to 6 April 2020.*
- *Investor's relief.*
- *Incorporation relief.*

E CORPORATION TAX LIABILITIES

1 The scope of corporation tax Chapter 21

(a) Identify the scope of corporation tax
  (i) chargeable entities
  (ii) chargeable income
  (iii) chargeable gains.

(b) Identify accounting periods, including periods longer and shorter than 12 months.

(c) Identify the basis of assessment for all sources of income
  (i) trading income
  (ii) profits from loan relationships and interest
  (iii) property business income
  (iv) chargeable gains.

Excluded topics

- *Close companies.*
- *Groups and consortia.*
- *Foreign income and double tax relief.*
- *Investment companies and companies in receivership or liquidation.*
- *The purchase by a company of its own shares.*
- *Personal service companies.*
- *Completion of forms CT61.*
- *Non-corporate dividends.*
- *Freeports.*

2 Taxable total profits Chapter 21

(a) Recognise the expenditure that is allowable in calculating the tax-adjusted trading profit.

(b) Explain how relief can be obtained for pre-trading expenditure.

(c) Compute capital allowances
  (i) as for income tax
  (ii) the main pool super deduction of 130% and special rate pool first year allowance of 50% for expenditure incurred from 1 April 2021 to 31 March 2023.

(d) Compute property business profits.

(e) Explain the treatment of interest paid and received under the loan relationship rules.

(f) Explain the treatment of qualifying charitable donations.

(g) Compute taxable total profits.

Excluded topics

- *Interest paid and received net of tax.*
- *Research and development expenditure.*
- *Non-trading deficits on loan relationships.*
- Relief for intangible assets.
- *Patent box.*
- *Apportionment in order to determine the amount of main pool super deduction where a period of account straddles 1 April 2023.*
- *Disposals of assets for which a 130% main pool super deduction or 50% special rate pool first year allowance claim was made.*

3 The comprehensive computation of corporation tax liability Chapter 22

(a) Identify the financial year(s) relevant to an accounting period.

(b) Calculate the corporation tax liability.

Excluded topics

- *Accounting periods that span two financial years if there is a change in the rate of tax.*
- *Marginal relief.*
- *51% group companies.*
- *Franked investment income.*
- *The corporate venturing scheme.*

4 Chargeable gains for companies Chapters 17, 19, 20

(a) Compute chargeable gains for companies.

(b) Calculate indexation allowance up to the date of sale using a given indexation factor.

(c) Explain the use of capital losses for companies
  (i) current year
  (ii) brought forward.

(d) Outline the matching rules for companies
  (i) same day
  (ii) last 9 days
  (iii) share pool (construction of a basic pool, including the calculation of indexation allowance up to the date of sale will be required).

(e) Compute gains and losses on disposals.

(f) Roll-over relief
  (i) outline availability
  (ii) explain and calculate the relief
  (iii) calculate the relief available on the partial reinvestment of sale proceeds
  (iv) depreciating assets.

Excluded topics

- *Substantial shareholdings.*
- *Assets held at 31 March 1982.*
- *Calculation of indexation factors.*

5 **Relief for losses** **Chapter 23**

(a) Explain the loss reliefs available for both trade and non-trade losses.

(b) Illustrate the use of the loss reliefs in a basic calculation

(i) trade losses
- CTA 2010 s37 current period
- CTA 2010 s37 carry back (including cessation)
- CTA 2010 s45A carry forward

(ii) non-trade losses
- property business loss relief
- capital losses
- explain the impact of cessation of trade on trade and non-trade losses.

(c) Compute corporation tax repayable following a loss relief claim.

Excluded topics

- *The carry back of a loss involving periods of less than 12 months.*
- *Restriction on carried forward trading losses and capital losses for companies with profits over £5 million.*
- *The temporary extension to the carry back of trading losses incurred in accounting periods ending between 1 April 2020 and 31 March 2022 from one year to three years.*

6 **The use of exemptions and reliefs in deferring and minimising corporation tax liabilities:**

(a) The use of such exemptions and reliefs is implicit within all of the above sections 1 to 5 of part E of the syllabus, concerning corporation tax.

7 **Complete the corporation tax return** **Chapters 21, 22**

(a) Complete corporation tax returns correctly and submit them within statutory time limits.

8 **Corporation tax administration** **Chapter 22**

(a) Explain and apply the features of the self-assessment system as it applies to companies, including the use of iXBRL.

(b) Explain the system of penalties and interest as it applies to corporation tax.

(c) Recognise the time limits that apply to the filing of returns and the making of claims.

(d) Recognise the due dates for the payment of corporation tax under the self-assessment system.

(e) Explain how large companies are required to account for corporation tax on a quarterly basis.

(f) List the information and records that taxpayers need to retain for tax purposes.

Excluded topics

- *HM Revenue & Customs compliance checks, determinations and discovery assessments.*
- *Calculations of corporation tax instalments for short periods.*
- *The effect of dividend income received from non-group companies on determining if corporation tax instalments are due.*
- *Calculation of late payment and repayment interest.*
- *The quarterly instalment payment dates for very large companies.*

F **VALUE ADDED TAX** **Chapter 24**

1 **The scope of value added tax (VAT)**

(a) Describe the scope of VAT and identify sources of information on VAT.

(b) Explain the relationship between the organisation and the relevant government agency.

2 **The VAT registration requirements**

(a) Recognise the circumstances in which a person must register for VAT.

(b) Explain the advantages of voluntary VAT registration.

(c) Explain the circumstances in which a person may request exemption from registration.

(d) Explain how and when a person can deregister for VAT.

Excluded topics

- *Group registration.*
- *Intending trader registration.*
- *The consequences of deregistration.*
- *Disaggregation.*

3 **The basic principles of VAT**

(a) Explain and contrast the types of supply

(i) standard

(ii) zero-rated

(iii) exempt.

4 **VAT invoices and records**

(a) Explain the detail required on VAT invoices.

5 Administration of VAT

(a) Detail the basic VAT administration requirements

- (i) records
- (ii) late registration penalties.

Excluded topics

- *Substantial traders.*

6 The effect of special schemes

(a) Describe the following schemes

- (i) annual accounting scheme
- (ii) cash accounting scheme
- (iii) flat rate scheme.

Excluded topics

- *The second hand goods scheme.*
- *The capital goods scheme.*
- *The special schemes for retailers.*

7 Preparing and completing VAT returns

(a) Computing VAT liabilities

- (i) input tax
- (ii) output tax
- (iii) impaired debts
- (iv) discounts
- (v) irrecoverable VAT.

(b) Make adjustments and declarations for any errors or omissions identified in previous VAT returns.

(c) Accounting for VAT

- (i) return periods
- (ii) tax point
- (iii) VAT return.

Excluded topics

- *VAT periods where there is a change in VAT rate.*
- *Partial exemption.*
- *Penalty for an incorrect VAT return.*
- *Default interest.*
- *Explain the treatment of imports, exports and trade outside the UK.*
- *The reverse charge for building and construction services.*
- *Postponed accounting for VAT on imports.*

8 Communicate VAT information

(a) Inform managers of the impact that the VAT payment may have on the company cash flow and financial forecasts.

(b) Advise relevant people of the impact that any changes in VAT legislation, including the VAT rate, would have on the organisations recording systems.

(c) Communicate effectively with the relevant tax authority when seeking guidance.

G EMPLOYABILITY AND TECHNOLOGY SKILLS

1 Use computer technology to efficiently access and manipulate relevant information.

2 Work on relevant response options using available functions and technology, as would be required in the workplace.

3 Navigate windows and computer screens to create and amend responses to exam requirements, using the appropriate tools.

4 Present data and information effectively using the appropriate tools.

THE EXAMINATION

Format of the examination

		Number of marks
Section A	15 compulsory objective test (OT) questions worth 2 marks each	30
Section B	Eight compulsory questions	
	Two questions (15 marks each)	30
	Two questions (10 marks each)	20
	Four questions (5 marks each)	20
		100

Total time allowed: 2 hours

Section B

One of the 15-mark questions will focus on income tax.

One of the 15-mark questions will focus on corporation tax.

The remaining questions will examine topics from any area of the syllabus and this means there will be a wide coverage of the syllabus in every examination. It is therefore vital to study the entire syllabus and not just the basic principles.

Additional information

Examinations falling in the year 1 April 2022 to 31 March 2023 will examine the Finance Act 2021 and any examinable legislation, which is passed outside of the Finance Act before 31 May 2021.

The latest Finance Act that will be examined at the June and December 2022 sessions is the Finance Act 2021.

Tax rates and allowance tables will be provided in the examination.

Calculations should be made to the nearest month and the nearest £.

Knowledge of section numbers will not be needed to understand questions in this examination, nor will students be expected to use them in their answers. If students wish to refer to section numbers in their answers they may do so and will not be penalised if old, or even incorrect, section numbers are used.

Examination tips

- Spend time reading the questions carefully, particularly in section B, where questions will be longer than in section A.

- Stick to the timing principle of 1.2 minutes per mark that applies for FTX (120 minutes/100 marks). For example, this means that Section A (30 marks) should take 36 minutes.

- Note that each examination will include broad coverage of the syllabus and trying to 'question spot' is unlikely to result in success.

- Spend time learning the rules and definitions.

- Practice plenty of questions to improve your ability to apply the techniques and perform the calculations.

- Spend the last five minutes reading through your answers and making any additions or corrections.

Computer Based Exam (CBE)

In addition to reading the tips contained here, we recommend that you review the resources available on the ACCA Global Website before sitting the CBE. Here you will find guidance documents, videos and a link to the CBE question practice platform.

Before the exam starts – You will be given 10 minutes to read the introductory page and the four pages of instructions. These will be the same for each FTX exam and therefore it is important that you familiarise yourself with these (using the ACCA practice exams) during your revision. The exam time (2 hours) will start automatically at the end of the 10 minutes or earlier if requested by you.

Section A

- **Make sure you answer all the objective test questions.**

- Read the question thoroughly, starting with the prompt (the actual question that is to be answered) and try to figure out the answer without referring to the options available.

- Take note of words such as never/always or least/most, which can change the meaning of the question.

- The question should be answered based on the information provided – you should not need to make any assumptions.

- Work out the answer on paper or on the CBE Scratch Pad, not just in your head or on your calculator, as you are less likely to skip steps in the calculation this way. However, your workings will not be marked, and you do not need to waste time making them legible to anyone but yourself. For remote invigilated exams you will not be able to use scrap paper, but will have to do workings in the on-screen scratchpad. It is therefore essential to practice using this functionality prior to your exam.

- Work steadily. Rushing leads to careless mistakes and questions are designed to include answers that result from careless mistakes.

- When you have an answer, compare it to the choices given and (hopefully) pick the correct one. If your answer does not match any of the choices given, try to rework your answer. Remember, that the wrong answers (or 'distracters') have been deliberately calculated to provide answers students will calculate if they make simple mistakes such as forgetting to apply an exemption.

- If you are unsure try to eliminate the answers you are sure are incorrect and see if the answer becomes more obvious.

- Remember that only one answer to an objective test question can be right and you will not have marks deducted for putting the wrong answer. After you have eliminated the options that you know to be wrong, if you are still unsure, guess.

Section B

- In section B, each question will require a typed response rather than being multiple choice. Therefore, different techniques need to be used to score well.

- Make sure you answer **all** parts of **every** question.

- Unless you know exactly how to answer the question, spend some time **planning your answer**. Stick to the question and tailor your answer to what you are asked.

- Do not write out the question or repeat the requirement in your answer.

- **Fully explain all your points** but be concise.

- Set out all workings with a logical and well laid out structure, and state briefly what you are doing. Remember that any workings done on paper or in the CBE Scratch Pad will not be marked – you must include all workings in the answer area. You can copy and paste from the Scratch Pad.

- You should do everything you can to make things easy for the marker. The marker will find it easier to identify the points you have made if your answers are clear.

- If you leave something out of a calculation, perhaps because it is tax free, state why you have left it out. The examining team has stated that where a question requires you to identify and state why an item is excluded, then simply leaving out a figure will not score a mark, even if the final answer is 100% correct.

- If you do not understand what a question is asking, **state your assumptions**. Even if you do not answer precisely in the way the examining team hoped, you should be given some credit for reasonable assumptions.

- **If you get stuck** with a question, move on and return to it later. It is easy to navigate between questions in the CBE software from the Navigator or Item Review screens.

- **Computations**: It is essential to include all your workings in your answers.

  Many computational questions require the use of a standard format: computation of taxable income, capital allowance computation, computation of taxable total profits, for example. Be sure you know these formats thoroughly before the examination and use the layouts that you see in the answers given in this book and in model answers.

  Adopt a logical approach and cross reference workings to the main computation to keep your answer tidy.

  If you are asked to comment or make recommendations on a computation, you must do so. There are important marks to be gained here. Even if your computation contains mistakes, you may still gain marks if your reasoning is correct.

- **Reports, memos and other documents:** Some questions ask you to present your answer in the form of a report or a memo or other document. Use the correct format – there could be easy marks to gain here.

STUDY SKILLS AND REVISION GUIDANCE

Preparing to study

Set your objectives

Before starting to study decide what you want to achieve – the type of pass you wish to obtain.

This will decide the level of commitment and time you need to dedicate to your studies.

Devise a study plan

Determine when you will study.

Split these times into study sessions.

Put the sessions onto a study plan making sure you cover the course, course assignments and revision.

Stick to your plan!

Effective study techniques

Use the **SQR3** method

Survey the chapter – look at the headings and read the introduction, contents list and learning outcomes. Get an overview of what the text deals with.

Question – during the survey, ask yourself the questions that you hope the chapter will answer for you.

Read through the chapter thoroughly, answering the questions and meeting the learning outcomes. Attempt the activities and questions and work through all the examples.

Recall – at the end of the chapter, try to recall the main ideas of the chapter without referring to the text. Do this a few minutes after the reading stage.

Review – check that your recall notes are correct.

Use the **MURDER** method

Mood – set the right mood.

Understand – issues covered and make note of any uncertain bits.

Recall – stop and put what you have learned into your own words.

Digest – go back and reconsider the information.

Expand – read relevant articles and newspapers.

Review – go over the material you covered to consolidate the knowledge.

While studying…

Summarise the key points of the chapter.

Make linear notes – a list of headings, divided up with sub-headings listing the key points. Use different colours to highlight key points and keep topic areas together. Use plenty of space to make your notes easy to use.

Try mind-maps – put the main heading in the centre of the paper and put a circle around it. Then draw short lines radiating from this to the main sub-headings, which again have circles around them. Continue the process from the sub-headings to sub-sub-headings, etc.

Revision

The best approach to revision is to **revise the course as you work through it**.

Also, try to leave **four to six weeks before the examination for final revision**.

Make sure you **cover the whole syllabus**.

Pay special attention to **those areas where your knowledge is weak**.

If you are stuck on a topic, find somebody (a tutor) to explain it to you.

Read around the subject – read good newspapers and professional journals, especially ACCA's *Student Accountant* – this can give you an advantage in the examination.

Read through the text and your notes again. Maybe put key revision points onto index cards to look at when you have a few minutes to spare.

Practise examination standard questions under timed conditions. Attempt all the different styles of questions you may be asked to answer in your examination.

Review any assignments you have completed and look at where you lost marks – put more work into those areas where you were weak.

Ensure you **know the structure of the examination** – how many questions and of what type they are.

TAX RATES AND ALLOWANCES

Throughout this study text:

1 **Calculations and workings need only to be made to the nearest £.**

2 **All apportionments should be made to the nearest month.**

3 **All workings should be shown when answering section B.**

Income tax

		Normal rates	Dividend rates
		%	%
Basic rate	£1 – £37,700	20	7.5
Higher rate	£37,701 – £150,000	40	32.5
Additional rate	£150,001 and over	45	38.1

Savings income nil rate band	– Basic rate taxpayers	£1,000
	– Higher rate taxpayers	£500
Dividend nil rate band		£2,000

A starting rate of 0% applies to savings income where it falls within the first £5,000 of taxable income.

Personal allowance

Personal allowance	£12,570
Income limit	£100,000

Where adjusted net income is £125,140 or more, the personal allowance is reduced to zero.

Car benefit percentage

The relevant base level of CO_2 emissions is 55 grams per kilometre.

The percentage rates applying to petrol-powered motor cars (and diesel-powered motor cars meeting the RDE2 standard) with CO_2 emissions up to this level are:

51 grams to 54 grams per kilometre	14%
55 grams per kilometre	15%

The percentage for electric-powered motor cars with zero CO_2 emissions is 1%.

For hybrid-electric motor cars with CO_2 emissions between 1 and 50 grams per kilometre, the electric range of a motor car is relevant:

Electric range

130 miles or more	1%
70-129 miles	4%
40-69 miles	7%
30-39 miles	11%
Less than 30 miles	13%

Car fuel benefit

The base figure for calculating the car fuel benefit is £24,600.

Company van benefits

The company van benefit scale charge is £3,500, and the van fuel benefit is £669.

Pension scheme limits

Annual allowance	£40,000

The maximum contribution that can qualify for tax relief without any earnings is £3,600.

Approved mileage allowances: cars

Up to 10,000 miles	45p
Over 10,000 miles	25p

Capital allowances: rates of allowance

Plant and machinery	
Main pool	18%
Special rate pool	6%
Motor cars	
New motor cars with zero CO_2 emissions	100%
CO_2 emissions between 1 and 50 grams per kilometre	18%
CO_2 emissions over 50 grams per kilometre	6%
Annual investment allowance	
Rate of allowance	100%
Expenditure limit	£1,000,000
Enhanced capital allowances for companies	
Main pool super deduction	130%
Special rate pool first year allowance	50%
Structures and buildings allowance	
Straight-line allowance	3%

Corporation tax

Rate of tax	19%
Profit threshold	£1,500,000

Value added tax

Standard rate	20%
Registration limit	£85,000
Deregistration limit	£83,000

Capital gains tax

	Normal rates	Residential property
Rate of tax – Lower rate	10%	18%
– Higher rate	20%	28%

Annual exempt amount		£12,300
Business asset disposal relief		
	– Lifetime limit	£1,000,000
	– Rate of tax	10%

National insurance contributions

Class 1	Employee	£1 – £9,568 per year	Nil
		£9,569 – £50,270 per year	12%
		£50,271 and above per year	2%
Class 1	Employer	£1 – £8,840 per year	Nil
		£8,841 and above per year	13.8%
		Employment allowance	£4,000
Class 1A			13.8%
Class 2		£3.05 per week	
		Small profits threshold	£6,515
Class 4		£1 – £9,568 per year	Nil
		£9,569 – £50,270 per year	9%
		£50,271 and above per year	2%

Where weekly or monthly calculations are required the class 1 limits shown above should be divided by 52 (weekly) or 12 (monthly) as applicable.

Official rate of interest (assumed)

2.00%

Standard penalties for errors

Taxpayer behaviour	Maximum penalty	Minimum penalty – unprompted disclosure	Minimum penalty – prompted disclosure
Deliberate and concealed	100%	30%	50%
Deliberate but not concealed	70%	20%	35%
Careless	30%	0%	15%

Chapter 1

INTRODUCTION TO THE UK TAX SYSTEM

INTRODUCTION

This chapter looks at the administration of the tax system. It will give you an understanding of the main sources of UK tax legislation and the mechanism by which the UK tax system operates. It also looks at the categories into which income is divided for tax purposes. This chapter covers syllabus areas A1 and A2.

CONTENTS	LEARNING OUTCOMES
1 Overall structure of the UK tax system **2** Identify the main sources of UK tax legislation **3** Identify the key reference sources for UK tax legislation **4** Describe the organisation of HM Revenue and Customs (HMRC) **5** Describe the appeals process – reviews and the Tax Tribunal **6** Taxable sources of income	At the end of this chapter, you should be able to: • describe the overall structure of the UK tax system • identify the main sources of UK tax legislation • identify the key reference sources for UK tax legislation • describe the organisation HM Revenue and Customs (HMRC) and its terms of reference including the appeals system • describe the appeals process for income tax First and Upper Tier Tribunals • explain the system of income tax and its background (how the legislation does not define income but defines taxable sources) • identify the different types of capital and revenue tax • explain the difference between direct and indirect taxation.

1 OVERALL STRUCTURE OF THE UK TAX SYSTEM

Taxation is the raising of money by the State from the general public.

- The UK Parliament passes tax legislation.
- The Treasury is the ministry responsible, under the Chancellor of the Exchequer (a government minister), for the imposition and collection of taxation.
- The Treasury appoint permanent civil servants, as the Board of Revenue and Customs, to administer the UK's taxation system.
- See Section 4 for more details of the organisation of HM Revenue and Customs (HMRC).

2 IDENTIFY THE MAIN SOURCES OF UK TAX LEGISLATION

2.1 SCOPE

The principal taxes which are examinable are:

Tax	**Suffered by**	**On**
Income tax	Individuals	Employment income Self-employed income Investment income
National insurance contributions (NICs)	Individuals Businesses (sole traders, partnerships and companies)	On earnings from employment or self-employment On employee earnings
Capital gains tax	Individuals	On disposal of capital assets like shares, land and buildings and antiques
Corporation tax	Companies	On their income and gains
Value added tax (VAT)	Consumers	On the purchase of goods and services from registered businesses

2.2 DIRECT OR INDIRECT TAXATION

All these taxes, except VAT, are **DIRECT** taxes. This means that they are paid directly to HMRC by the persons or companies on whom the tax is charged. They are based on income/profits and the more that is earned/received, the more tax is paid.

VAT is an **INDIRECT** tax. This is a tax which is collected from the taxpayer by an intermediary such as a retail shop. The intermediary then pays the VAT collected over to HMRC.

2.3 CAPITAL OR REVENUE TAXES

CAPITAL taxes apply to capital assets whereas **REVENUE** taxes apply to income.

Capital gains tax is a capital tax. Note that companies do not pay capital gains tax but pay corporation tax on their gains calculated under capital gains tax rules.

2.4 SOURCES OF TAX LAW

The basic rules of the UK tax system are contained in various statutes – the main ones are:

- Income and Corporation Taxes Act 1988 (ICTA 88)
- The Taxation of Chargeable Gains Act 1992 (TCGA 92)
- Capital Allowances Act 2001 (CAA 01)
- Taxes Management Act 1970 (TMA 70)
- The Income Tax (Employment and Pensions) Act 2003 (ITEPA 03)
- Income Tax (Trading and Other Income) Act 2005 (ITTOIA 05)
- Income Tax Act 2007
- Corporation Tax Act 2009 (CTA 2009) and Corporation Tax Act 2010 (CTA 2010)
- Annual Finance Acts

Amendments and additions to the law are given effect by means of the annual Finance Act. Each Finance Act is the vehicle by which the annual taxes are reimposed. Each provides that it shall be construed as one with all previous legislation, so that the total body of tax law is brought into force each year.

You do not need to learn this list for the examination.

3 IDENTIFY THE KEY REFERENCE SOURCES FOR UK TAX LEGISLATION

Legislation can be given effect, or interpreted, in the following ways:

Statutory Instruments

Acts of Parliament confer powers on Ministers to make more detailed orders, rules or regulations by means of statutory instruments. An Act will often contain a broad framework and statutory instruments are used to provide the necessary detail that would be too complex to include in the Act itself.

Case law

Judges cannot make law relating to taxation, but they can be required to interpret the law which applies to the circumstances of the particular case. These rulings are binding and therefore provide guidance on the interpretation of tax legislation.

Extra-Statutory Concessions

In cases where there is doubt as to the meaning of the law, or where a strict application of the law produces an unacceptable result, HMRC does not always seek to apply the law strictly but instead makes an Extra-Statutory Concession.

HMRC Guidance

HMRC issues various types of guidance, setting out its interpretation of the legislation, both on its website and in publications such as Briefs, Statements of Practice, Notices and Guidance notes. They have no legal force and do not remove the taxpayer's right of appeal.

4 DESCRIBE THE ORGANISATION OF HM REVENUE AND CUSTOMS (HMRC)

4.1 OVERVIEW

- HMRC is the body that controls and administers all areas of UK tax law.
- Commissioners head up HMRC and their main duties are to implement statute law and to oversee the process of UK tax administration.
- Staff who work for HMRC are known as officers of Revenue and Customs.

4.2 DEALING WITH HMRC

- HMRC have offices located all over the UK, many of which have specialist functions such as dealing with international businesses or large companies.
- Most taxpayers will never deal directly with a local tax office as HMRC encourage taxpayers to file tax returns online, use their website (www.gov.uk/government/organisations/hm-revenue-customs) to answer queries or telephone or email a number of specialist helplines (e.g. the self-assessment helpline).
- Taxpayers are encouraged to file their tax returns online and pay by electronic means. Companies have to file returns and pay tax electronically but individual taxpayers can still send their returns and payments by post if they wish.
- Under self-assessment the responsibility for reporting the correct amount of taxable income and paying the correct amount of tax has been delegated to the taxpayer to 'self-assess'. However, the officers of Revenue and Customs can still be requested to do the calculation of tax payable based on the income reported for individual taxpayers (but not companies).

5 DESCRIBE THE APPEALS PROCESS – REVIEWS AND THE TAX TRIBUNAL

5.1 INTRODUCTION

When taxpayers disagree with a decision made by HMRC they must appeal against it within 30 days. An appeal simply means that the taxpayer (or their agent) must write to HMRC saying they disagree with the decision. Most appeals will then be settled by discussion between the taxpayer and HMRC. If taxpayers are not satisfied with the outcome of these discussions they can proceed in one of two ways:

- request a review by a different HMRC officer from the one who made the decision or

- have their case heard by an independent Tax Tribunal.

If taxpayers opt to have their case reviewed but disagrees with the outcome, they can still send their appeal to the Tax Tribunal.

Taxpayers must also apply to postpone all or part of the tax charged. Otherwise they will have to pay the disputed amount.

5.2 REVIEW

A taxpayer can choose whether or not to have a review of a disputed appeal decision.

Once a taxpayer has requested a review, HMRC should normally complete it within 45 days. A taxpayer cannot ask the tribunal to hear their case until either this time limit has expired or HMRC have told the taxpayer the outcome of the review.

The review is carried out by different HMRC staff to those involved in the original disputed decision. After completing their review they will inform the taxpayer who can either accept the decision or ask the tribunal to hear their case. If the taxpayer chooses the latter he or she must do it within 30 days of the review conclusion letter.

The review process has two advantages for the taxpayer.

- It is a simple and low cost procedure.

- The taxpayer does not lose anything by asking for a review as he or she can still appeal to the Tax Tribunal afterwards if they are not satisfied.

5.3 TAX TRIBUNAL

The Tax Tribunal is an independent body administered by the Tribunals Service of the Ministry of Justice. It hears appeals by taxpayers. Cases are heard by independently appointed expert tax judges and/or panel members.

It is divided into two tiers:

- First-tier Tribunal (Tax) – most cases will be dealt with at this level

- Upper Tribunal (Tax and Chancery Chamber) – will deal directly with more complex cases.

All appeals are placed into one of four categories.

- Default Paper cases: simple appeals (e.g. against a fixed penalty), which will usually be disposed of without a hearing provided both sides agree.
- Basic cases: straightforward appeals involving a minimal exchange of paperwork in advance of a short hearing.
- Standard cases: appeals involving more detailed consideration of issues and a more formal hearing.
- Complex cases that will usually be dealt with by the Upper Tribunal.

If the dispute is not resolved at the First-tier level then the appeal can go to the Upper Tribunal and from there to the Appeal Court.

In general, hearings are held in public and decisions are published.

6 TAXABLE SOURCES OF INCOME

The legislation does not define income, but instead defines taxable sources.

Income is classified for income tax purposes according to its nature and source.

According to its category, income will be taxable on either an actual or a current year basis. The actual basis of assessment is where the taxable amount is the actual income arising in the tax year. The current year basis of assessment is where the taxable amount is the profits of an accounting period ending in the tax year.

The categories of income which are examinable are summarised below:

Type of income	**Normal basis of assessment**
Property income	Actual
Trading income	Current year
Savings income	Actual
Dividend income	Actual
Employment income	Actual

KEY TERMS

Statutory Instruments – allow government ministers to make an order giving effect to legislation.

Extra-Statutory Concession – used by HMRC to deal with cases where a strict application of the law produces an unacceptable result.

Statements of Practice – public announcements of HMRC's interpretation of the legislation. They have no legal force.

Officer of Revenue and Customs – an employee of HMRC who is responsible for (among other things) issuing tax returns, examining completed returns and checking the taxpayer's calculations.

Appeal – the process by which a taxpayer formally disagrees with a decision made by HMRC.

Tax Tribunal – independent tribunal that hears appeals against HMRC decisions.

Actual basis of assessment – means that the taxable amount is the actual income arising in the tax year.

Current year basis of assessment – means that the taxable amount is the profits of an accounting period ending in the tax year.

SELF TEST QUESTIONS

		Paragraph
1	What are the main sources of UK tax legislation?	2.4
2	What is a Statutory Instrument?	3
3	What is the function of the Tax Tribunal?	5.3
4	Identify the main sources of taxable income.	6

MULTIPLE CHOICE QUESTIONS

1 Which of the following is statutory legislation?

- **A** Case law
- **B** Extra statutory concession
- **C** HMRC statement of practice
- **D** Income Tax Act 2007

2 When a taxpayer requests a review of a decision made by HMRC it is initially carried out by whom?

- **A** The Tax Tribunal
- **B** The existing officer of Revenue and Customs
- **C** A different officer of Revenue and Customs
- **D** The Court of Appeal

3 Which of the following is an indirect tax?

- **A** Corporation tax
- **B** Capital gains tax
- **C** Income tax
- **D** Value added tax

4 Which of the following taxes is NOT paid by a company?

- **A** Capital gains tax
- **B** Corporation tax
- **C** National insurance contributions
- **D** Value added tax

For suggested answers, see the 'Answers' section at the end of the book.

Chapter 2

INTRODUCTION TO PERSONAL TAXATION

INTRODUCTION

This chapter is a brief guide to income tax and the types of income charged. It also shows how income is brought together in the personal income tax computation in order to calculate an individual's income tax liability for the year. Detailed calculations of income tax are dealt with in Chapter 14. This chapter helps to set the scene for your studies of the different sources of income in Chapters 3 to 13. This chapter covers syllabus area C1.

CONTENTS	LEARNING OUTCOMES
1 Identify the tax year 2 Outline the scope of income tax: chargeable persons, chargeable income 3 Identify sources of taxation information 4 Distinguish between income and capital profits/losses 5 Outline the key elements of a personal income tax computation	At the end of this chapter, you should be able to: • identify the tax year • outline the scope of income tax: chargeable persons, chargeable income • identify sources of taxation information for individuals • distinguish between income and capital profits/losses • outline the key elements of a personal income tax computation.

1 IDENTIFY THE TAX YEAR

Liability to income tax is computed by reference to income for a tax year. This is a year ended on 5 April. It is referred to by the calendar years it straddles. Thus, the year from 6 April 2021 to 5 April 2022 is referred to as the tax year 2021/22.

2 OUTLINE THE SCOPE OF INCOME TAX: CHARGEABLE PERSONS, CHARGEABLE INCOME

2.1 CHARGEABLE PERSONS

Chargeable persons are:

- individuals who live in the UK. They have to pay UK tax on all their income wherever it arises throughout the world, or
- individuals living abroad who have income arising in the UK. They have to pay UK tax on their UK income.

2.2 EXEMPT PERSONS

The following persons are exempt from UK income tax:

- charities
- registered pension funds and personal pension schemes.

2.3 INDEPENDENT TAXATION

Individual taxpayers, married, in a civil partnership or single, are taxed separately on their own income.

Each individual is separately responsible for:

- making a tax return
- declaring all their income to HMRC
- claiming their own allowances and reliefs
- paying any tax due on their own income (and chargeable gains) or receiving any repayments due.

2.4 CHARGEABLE INCOME

Income is chargeable to UK income tax if it falls within one of the categories listed in Chapter 1 (e.g. employment income or savings income) and it is not specifically exempt (see below).

The basis of calculating the amount of chargeable income to be included in an individual's income tax computation for a tax year is different for each category of income and is covered in Chapters 3 to 13. However, in all cases it is the **gross** amount of income that must be included in the income tax computation.

Income received gross

For the purpose of the FTX examination all categories of income are received gross apart from employment income. Income received gross has had no tax deducted. Any tax due is collected through the self-assessment system (see Chapter 16).

Deduction at source

- HMRC collects income tax at source on employment income – that is immediately as the income arises.

- This avoids the necessity of collecting the tax subsequently from each individual taxpayer receiving the income. The employer acts like an agent for HMRC, deducting income tax and paying over that tax to HMRC. The recipient will, therefore, receive only the net income.

- Deduction at source is a method of collecting tax. It does not necessarily represent the final liability of the recipient. The gross income must be brought into the taxpayer's income tax computation. Once the total liability has been calculated, the amount of income tax already deducted at source is offset against that total liability. Any overpayment may be reclaimed from HMRC.

- The method of deduction at source on employment income is the Pay As You Earn (PAYE) system. Under this system the employer is liable to account to HMRC for the tax deducted, which is calculated by reference to the employee's tax code number.

2.5 EXEMPT INCOME

The following are the main categories of exempt income:

- interest and terminal bonus on NS&I savings certificates

- interest on repayments of overpaid income tax or capital gains tax

- certain redundancy payments

- scholarship income and bursaries

- interest and dividends from individual savings accounts (ISAs)

- betting and gaming winnings.

3 IDENTIFY SOURCES OF TAXATION INFORMATION

Individuals can obtain information regarding the taxation system from various sources, including contacting HMRC (via phone, email etc.), accessing the HMRC website and using taxation advisers.

Information required to complete the individual's tax return can be obtained from sources such as interest statements, records received from the employer (see Chapter 9) and dividend vouchers.

4 DISTINGUISH BETWEEN INCOME AND CAPITAL PROFITS/LOSSES

4.1 INCOME AND CAPITAL

An individual is only charged income tax on his or her sources of income. Profits from capital transactions are chargeable to capital gains tax. It is therefore necessary to distinguish between income and capital transactions. Types of income have been detailed earlier in this chapter. Capital transactions arise from the sale or gift of capital assets, which include items such as:

- buildings
- shares
- paintings
- antique furniture.

4.2 PROFITS AND LOSSES

Certain sources of income may produce a loss rather than a profit. This arises when expenses exceed the income. For example, a trader may find that the costs of running his or her business are greater than the income he or she has derived from it. Relief is generally given for losses by either reducing future profits from the same source or reducing other types of income. The rules for relieving each type of loss are dealt with in future chapters.

Capital assets may be disposed of for less than cost, which produces a capital loss. Relief is usually given for capital losses by reducing capital profits made on other disposals. The specific rules are covered in future chapters.

5 OUTLINE THE KEY ELEMENTS OF A PERSONAL INCOME TAX COMPUTATION

5.1 LAYOUT OF A PERSONAL INCOME TAX COMPUTATION

An individual's income tax computation includes the gross amount of income from all chargeable sources of income. Then reliefs (qualifying interest payments and losses) are deducted from this total income figure, in order to compute net income. A personal allowance is then deducted to arrive at a figure of taxable income.

An example of the calculation of taxable income follows. Much of the terminology is explained in later chapters.

Taxpayer's name:

Income tax computation – 2021/22

	Non-savings income	**Savings income**	**Dividend income**	**Total income**
	£	£	£	£
Trading income	X			X
Employment income	X			X
Property income	X			X
Savings income		X		X
UK dividends			X	X
Total income	X	X	X	X
Less: Reliefs	(X)			(X)
Net income	X	X	X	X
Less: Personal allowance (Note)	(X)			(X)
Taxable income	X	X	X	X

Note: Entitlement to personal allowance is reduced once net income exceeds £100,000 (see Chapter 14).

In the FTX examination, the personal allowance **should always** be deducted from the taxpayer's income in the following order:

1 Non-savings income

2 Savings income

3 Dividend income

Columns are used to divide total income into non-savings income, savings income and dividend income as different rates of tax can apply to each of these.

Tax rates apply to the different types of income as follows:

- Non-savings income – 20%, 40% and 45%.
- Savings income – 0%, 20%, 40% and 45%.
- Dividend income – 0%, 7.5%, 32.5% and 38.1%

This is explained in more detail in Chapter 14.

5.2 NON-SAVINGS INCOME

Non-savings income comprises both earned and unearned income. The distinction is important when considering relief for pension contributions (see Chapter 15).

The following are the **main** sources of **earned** income:

- **Trading income**
- **Employment income** which includes:
  - wages and salaries
  - taxable benefits (e.g. the use of a company car)
  - bonuses, commissions and expense allowances
  - pensions arising from past employment.
- **Property income** from the commercial letting of furnished holiday accommodation.

Unearned income included within non-savings income is:

- **Property income** – from the commercial letting of UK property generally.

5.3 SAVINGS INCOME

This includes bank, building society and other forms of taxable interest.

5.4 DIVIDEND INCOME

Dividends received are taxed at different rates to non-savings and savings income.

The layout above shows separate columns for non-savings income, savings income and dividends. However, provided you can identify the amount of interest and the amount of dividends remaining in taxable income, you can combine the three different types of income in one column.

5.5 RELIEFS

There are two main reliefs that you are expected to know about:

- Qualifying interest paid – certain interest payments made by an individual are allowable deductions for income tax purposes. Some are deductible from a specific source of income. Others are deductible from **total** income using the same order of deductions as for the personal allowance. Relief from total income is given in a tax year for payments **made** in that same year.

  See Chapter 14 section 2 for further information.

- Loss relief – when traders make a loss in their business they may be able to deduct that loss from their total income.

  See Chapter 6 for further information.

KEY TERMS

Tax year – runs from 6 April to the following 5 April.

Chargeable person – an individual who either lives in the UK, or who has income arising in the UK.

Exempt persons – persons such as charities and pension funds which are exempt from UK income tax.

Chargeable income – income is chargeable to UK income tax if it falls within one of the categories of taxable income.

Capital transactions – the sale or gift of a capital asset such as a building or shares.

Earned income – income such as trading profits and employment income.

Non-savings income – taxable income other than savings income and dividend income, e.g. employment income, trading income, property income.

Savings income – interest from bank and building society accounts.

Total income – income from all sources.

Net income – income from all sources, less loss relief and qualifying interest payments.

Taxable income – net income less the personal allowance.

SELF TEST QUESTIONS

		Paragraph
1	What is a tax year?	1
2	Who is liable to UK income tax?	2.1
3	Give two examples of exempt persons.	2.2
4	Give four examples of income which is exempt from tax.	2.5
5	Which tax applies to profits arising from capital transactions?	4.1
6	What are the main sources of earned income?	5.2

MULTIPLE CHOICE QUESTIONS

1 Which of the following sources of income is exempt from income tax?

- **A** Property income
- **B** Salary
- **C** Dividends from shares held in an ISA
- **D** Building society interest

2 Which one of the following sources of income is received net of tax?

- **A** Dividends
- **B** Building society interest
- **C** Employment income
- **D** Property income

3 An individual buys some shares for £2,000 and sells them 5 years later for £10,000. The profit of £8,000 is a capital profit.

- **A** True
- **B** False

For suggested answers, see the 'Answers' section at the end of the book.

PRACTICE QUESTION

KATE

Kate has the following income, outgoings and personal allowance for the year ended 5 April 2022.

		£
Salary (gross amount)		41,970
Investment income	– bank interest	1,520
	– building society interest	890
Rents from UK lettings		1,890
Personal allowance		12,570
Qualifying interest payments		2,160

Required:

Calculate her taxable income for the tax year 2021/22. **(6 marks)**

For a suggested answer, see the 'Answers' section at the end of the book.

Chapter 3

TRADING INCOME

INTRODUCTION

Earned income arises from employment or self-employment. Later chapters will consider employment income. This chapter deals with trading income (i.e. income from self-employment).

In this chapter we consider the principles of deductible and non-deductible expenditure; so that the trading profit shown in the accounts can be converted into the tax adjusted trading profit. This chapter covers syllabus areas B1 (a) to (d).

CONTENTS	LEARNING OUTCOMES
	At the end of this chapter, you should be able to: • recognise the basis of assessment for self-employment income • explain the principles of deductible and non-deductible expenditure • recognise the relief that can be obtained for pre-trading expenditure • prepare adjusted profit computations (before capital allowances).

1 INTRODUCTION

1.1 ADJUSTMENTS TO PROFIT

Trading profit for tax purposes is rarely the same figure as the profit shown in a trader's statement of profit or loss, although the accounting profit is the starting point for the series of adjustments that are normally necessary. The adjustments that need to be made to move from accounting profit to tax adjusted trading profit are of four types, as follows:

Reason for adjusting profits	Adjustment required to arrive at tax adjusted trading profit
Expenditure that has been charged in the statement of profit or loss but which tax law prevents from being an allowable deduction	**Add back** to the accounting profit
Taxable trading income that has not been included in the statement of profit or loss	**Add** to the accounting profit
Expenditure that is deductible for tax purposes, but which has **not** been charged in the statement of profit or loss	**Deduct** from accounting profit
Income included in the statement of profit or loss that is **not** taxable as trading income	**Deduct** from accounting profit

Before considering the adjustments in detail, two important points need to be emphasised.

- It is only the tax adjusted trading profit of the business that is being calculated. The fact that an item of income (such as interest received) is excluded does not mean that it is not taxable; only that it is not taxable as trading profit.

- The accounts of the business must follow the principles of normal commercial accountancy. These apply unless overridden by tax law (derived either from statute or decided cases).

Pro forma – tax adjusted trading profit

		£	£
Net profit per the accounts		X	
Add:	Expenditure not allowed for taxation purposes	X	
	Expenditure allowable for taxation purposes	0	
	Taxable trading income not credited in the accounts	X	
Less:	Expenditure not charged in the accounts but allowable for taxation		X
	Income included in the accounts that is not taxable as trading income		X
	Income included in the accounts that is taxable as trading income (e.g. trade related patent royalties)		0
	Capital allowances (see Chapter 4)		X
		X	Y
		(Y)	
Tax adjusted trading profit		X	

It is important to follow the instructions provided in the examination question. If the requirement specifies that unadjusted items should be included in your answer, it is important that, in addition to the adjustments required, you also show all items that **do not** require adjustment, and indicate by the use of a 0 that these items are allowable.

1.2 BASIS OF ASSESSMENT

Once the profits have been adjusted, they are taxed in the appropriate tax year for an individual. (Companies include the tax adjusted trading profits in their corporation tax computation and this is explained further in Chapter 21).

For a continuing unincorporated business, the appropriate tax year is the one in which the period of account ends. The period of account is the period for which the trader prepares accounts.

Example

Josiah prepares accounts to 31 December each year. For the tax year 2021/22 he is taxed on the profits of the year ending 31 December 2021.

2 DEDUCTIBLE AND NON-DEDUCTIBLE EXPENDITURE

Generally, in order to be deductible, expenditure must be incurred **'wholly and exclusively' for the purpose of the trade.**

Non-deductible expenditure (also known as disallowable expenditure) is the most common form of adjustment to the accounting profit. The necessary adjustments reflect a series of principles which are examined below.

2.1 EXPENDITURE NOT INCURRED 'WHOLLY AND EXCLUSIVELY' FOR TRADING PURPOSES

If expenses are incurred partly for private, and partly for business use, then the strict application of this rule would disallow the whole expense.

In practice, if the business and private parts of the expense can be identified then the expense can be split. The business proportion will be allowed whereas the private proportion will be disallowed.

Example

Tanni's telephone and motor expenses were as follows:	£
Telephone rental	55
Calls (2,500 minutes of which 2,000 minutes were for business calls)	250
Motor expenses (Tanni travelled 10,000 miles of which 6,400 were for business)	2,400

In the adjustment of profits computation:

Telephone rental – disallow £55 as not exclusively for business
Calls – disallow 500/2,500 × £250 = £50 as for private use

Motor expenses – Tanni has travelled 3,600 miles privately (10,000 – 6,400)
Disallow 3,600/10,000 × £2,400 = £864 as for private use

2.2 SUBSCRIPTIONS AND DONATIONS

Trade or professional association subscriptions are normally deductible since they are made wholly and exclusively for the purposes of the trade. Other subscriptions are generally not deductible.

Subscriptions and donations to political parties are never deductible.

A charitable donation must meet three tests to be allowable:

- it must be 'wholly and exclusively' for trading purposes (for example promoting the business's name)
- it must be reasonable in size in relation to the donor's business
- it must be made to a registered charity.

In practice, this means that small donations to local charities will be allowable; all others will not.

If not an allowable deduction, charitable donations may be relieved under the gift aid scheme (see Chapter 14).

2.3 CAPITAL EXPENDITURE

Expenditure on capital assets is not allowed in computing trading profits.

- Any amount charged in the form of depreciation, loss on sale of non-current assets or lease amortisation must therefore be added back to the accounting profit for tax purposes.
- Any profit on the sale of a non-current asset should be deducted from the accounting profits.

It is necessary to distinguish between **repairs** expenditure (treated as revenue expenditure and so allowable) and **improvement** expenditure (treated as capital expenditure and so disallowed). The distinction between repairs and improvement expenditure for tax purposes is based on a few important cases.

- The cost of initial repairs to an asset is not deductible where they are necessary to make it serviceable for the trade.

  For example, a taxpayer failed to obtain a deduction for repair work on a newly bought ship, which was incurred in order to make the ship seaworthy prior to use.

- However, the cost of initial repairs is deductible if the assets can be put into use before the repairs are carried out, if they are to make good normal wear and tear and the purchase price was not reduced to take account of the necessary repair work.

  For example, a taxpayer obtained a deduction for the cost of renovating newly acquired cinemas. The work was to make good normal wear and tear and the purchase price was not reduced to take account of this work. The cinemas continued to be in operation while the repairs were carried out.

- Other than initial repairs, the principal source of dispute is the treatment of restoration costs. Here the principle to be applied is whether the restoration renews a subsidiary part of an asset (in which case it is an allowable repair to the larger asset) or whether it is the replacement of a separate asset (in which case it is treated as disallowable capital expenditure).

  For example, the replacement of a factory chimney was held to be a repair to the factory. However, the replacement of an old stand with a new one at a football club was held to be expenditure on a new asset and thus disallowable capital expenditure.

Expenditure on certain categories of capital assets, such as plant and machinery attracts tax allowances known as capital allowances (see Chapter 4). Capital allowances are deductible as if they were a trading expense.

2.4 ENTERTAINING AND GIFTS

Gifts to customers or suppliers are allowable provided that:

- the cost is no more than £50 per recipient
- the gift is not food, drink, tobacco or vouchers exchangeable for goods
- the gift carries a conspicuous advertisement for the donor.

The cost of gifts which do not meet these restrictive conditions are disallowed unless they are to charities or to employees. Gifts to employees will normally be allowable deductions for an employer, but may result in an income tax charge to an employee under the benefits rules (see Chapter 10).

Entertainment expenditure is disallowed. The only exception is expenditure relating to employees, unless it is merely incidental to the entertainment of others.

2.5 LEGAL AND PROFESSIONAL CHARGES

Legal and professional charges are allowable provided they are incurred in connection with the trade and are not related to capital items. So, for example, the following common types of professional charge are allowed:

- legal fees to collect trade debts
- charges incurred in defending title to non-current assets.

Using the same principle, the following are not deductible:

- fees incurred when buying new non-current assets
- fees arising as a result of issuing new share capital.

The principle of allowing or disallowing professional fees by relating them to the type of expenditure with which they are connected is broken in the case of fees incurred in obtaining loan finance. Fees and other incidental costs of obtaining loan finance in relation to the trade are specifically allowable.

2.6 APPROPRIATIONS

Appropriations are the withdrawal of funds from a business's profits rather than expenses incurred in earning them. The obvious examples are

- a business owner's salary
- drawings made by a sole trader or partner in a partnership
- interest paid to the owner on capital invested in the business
- any private element of expenditure relating to the owner's car, telephone and so on.

Any salary paid to a member of the family of the business owner will be allowable as long as it is not excessive, i.e. at the commercial rate for the work performed. Any excess is disallowed.

2.7 IMPAIRMENT LOSSES

Impairment losses relate to the write off or impairment of debts. Those losses that are not in relation to trade debts are not allowable, for example, write offs of loans to former employees or suppliers.

In contrast, writing off a trade debt or changes to an allowance or provision for receivables (debtors) calculated in accordance with UK Generally Accepted Accounting Practice (UK GAAP) or International Financial Reporting Standards (IFRS® Standards), is allowable on the grounds that they represent a best estimate of an actual cost to the business.

Example

Albert Green has a net profit per the accounts of his sole trader business of £25,829.

You are given the following information about impairment losses

	£
Increase in specific receivables provision (£5,194 – £4,185)	1,009
Amounts written off:	
Trade debt	8,129
Former employee debt	50
Trade debts previously written off now recovered	(6,023)
Impairment loss expense charged in accounts	3,165

Identify the allowable and disallowable items and calculate the tax adjusted trading profit figure for the year ended 30 April 2021.

Solution

	£	**Allowed/ (Taxable)?**
Increase in specific receivables provision (£5,194 – £4,185)	1,009	Yes
Amounts written off:		
Trade debt	8,129	Yes
Former employee debt	50	No
Trade debts previously written off now recovered (Note)	(6,023)	Yes
Impairment loss expense charged in accounts	3,165	

	£
Profit per the accounts	25,829
Add: Non-trade debt (former employee) written off	50
Tax adjusted trading profit	25,879

Note: An allowable deduction was available when the trade debts of £6,023 were originally written off. The amount received is therefore taxable income when the debts are subsequently recovered. As income of £6,023 has been included in the accounting profit no adjustment for tax purposes is required.

2.8 INTEREST PAYABLE

Interest payable on loans, business account overdrafts, credit cards or hire purchase contracts is for a trading purpose and allowable on an accruals basis. Therefore no adjustment is needed to the accounting profit.

Interest on late paid tax is not allowable for an individual and likewise repayment interest on overpaid tax is not taxable. These will therefore need adjusting if they are included in the accounting profit.

2.9 PRE-TRADING EXPENDITURE

Pre-trading expenditure incurred in the seven years before the trade begins is deductible, provided that the expense is of a kind that would have been deductible had the trade been carried on at the time. The expenditure is treated as though it had been incurred on the first day of trade.

Example

Mateo plans to start a business. On 1 January 2021 he rents premises for £10,000 per annum, spends £1,500 on advertising and £450 on entertaining prospective customers. He starts to trade on 1 April 2021.

His allowable pre-trading expenditure is:

	£
Rent (3/12 of £10,000)	2,500
Advertising	1,500
Entertaining (not an allowable expense)	0
	4,000

2.10 LEASING OF CARS

The private use portion of any rental charges payable for leasing a car is disallowed.

In addition, if the car has CO_2 emissions of more than 50 grams per kilometre, there is a disallowance of 15% of the leasing charges.

Example

Roy entered into a leasing contract for a car with emissions of 56 grams per kilometre. He pays £8,000 per year in rental charges. His business use amounts to 80%.

The allowable amount is:

£8,000 × 80% = £6,400 less 15% = £5,440

Hence the disallowable amount is:

£8,000 – £5,440 = £2,560

2.11 OTHER ITEMS

The items dealt with above are the more important ones that you are likely to meet in the course of adjusting expenditure charged in a trader's accounts. Set out below is a list of some other items you may meet and a brief description of how to treat them.

Although most are items that appear to fall foul of the 'wholly and exclusively' rule or 'revenue not capital' rule, they may nevertheless be allowable due to a specific statutory or case law rule.

Type of expenditure	Treatment in computation	Notes
Compensation for loss of office paid to an employee	Allow	Only if for benefit of trade
Counselling services provided in the UK for redundant employees	Allow	
Cost of registering patents and trademarks	Allow	
Cost of seconding employees to charities	Allow	
Damages paid	Allow	Only if paid in connection with trade matter

Type of expenditure	**Treatment in computation**	**Notes**
Defalcations (i.e. losses due to theft)	Allow	Only if by employee, not a director or proprietor
Educational courses	Allow	Only if for trade purposes
Fines	Disallow	Unless parking fines incurred on business by employee (not director or proprietor)
Patent and copyright royalties paid in connection with trade	Allow	
Payment that constitutes a criminal offence e.g. a bribe	Disallow	
Payments made in response to threats, menaces, blackmail and other forms of extortion	Disallow	
Provisions for future costs (e.g. provision for future warranty costs)	Allow	Provided they are calculated in accordance with UK GAAP or IFRS and their estimation is sufficiently accurate
Contributions to a registered pension scheme	Allow	Provided paid (not merely accrued) by the year end
Redundancy payments if business is continuing	Allow	
Redundancy payments if business ceases	Allow	Up to 4 times the statutory redundancy payment
Removal expenses	Allow	Provided not an expansionary move or expenses relating to personal move of proprietor
Restrictive covenants (i.e. amounts paid to former employees who have agreed not to set up in competition)	Allow	Provided the former employee is taxed on the amount as employment income.
Salaries accrued at year end	Allow	Provided paid not more than nine months after year end
Travelling expenses to trader's place of business	Disallow	Unless trader has no fixed place of business
Waste disposal site preparation or restoration costs	Allow	

3 TAXABLE TRADING INCOME NOT INCLUDED IN THE ACCOUNTS

This adjustment is normally needed only when a trader removes goods from the business for his or her own use.

- The trader is treated as making a sale to himself based on the selling price of the goods concerned.

The adjustment required depends on the treatment in the accounts:

- Item already charged to trader at cost price – add profit element to adjusted profit.
- No entry yet made for the drawing of goods – add full selling price to adjusted profit.

Example

Aroha, a car dealer, removes a vehicle from inventory for her own personal use. It had originally cost the business £10,000 and has a market value of £12,500. No entries have been made in the accounts to reflect this transaction, other than the original purchase.

What adjustment, if any, should be made to the car dealer's accounts, for tax purposes, to reflect the above transaction?

Solution

The tax adjusted trading profit must reflect the transaction as if the owner has sold the vehicle to herself based on the selling price of the goods concerned.

In determining the adjustment required it is important to identify the entries made in the accounts to date. In this example, only the original cost has been recorded, therefore the adjustment is to add the market value of £12,500 to the accounting profit to arrive at the tax adjusted trading profit.

4 DEDUCTIBLE EXPENDITURE NOT CHARGED IN THE ACCOUNTS

4.1 INTRODUCTION

Common types of expenditure falling in this category include:

- the premium paid on the grant of a short lease (see 4.2 below)
- business costs paid for personally by the trader and not charged in the accounts e.g. use of home as office
- capital allowances (see Chapter 4).

4.2 LEASE PREMIUMS

When a trader pays a landlord for the grant of a short lease, a portion of the premium is taxed on the landlord as property income (see Chapter 12) and a portion as capital (not examinable).

- A trader is entitled to deduct from his or her trading profits a proportion of the amount taxable on his or her landlord as property income. This will not be reflected in his or her accounts, however, since the cost of the lease will be reflected in an annual amortisation charge.
- The adjustments for the lease are to
  - add back the amortisation charged in the accounts (disallowable as capital) and
  - deduct the proportion of the lease premium charge (which does not feature in the accounts at all).

The property income taxable on the landlord in respect of the lease premium is:

	£
Premium	X
Less: 2% × (n – 1) × premium	(X)
Landlord's property income charge	X

where n = duration of lease in years

The allowable deduction is the landlord's property income charge spread evenly over the period of the lease.

Example

Aroha prepares accounts to 31 March. On 1 April 2021 she paid a premium of £25,200 for the grant of a 21 year lease on business premises.

Calculate the deduction Aroha can claim in calculating her tax adjusted trading profit.

Solution

The amount of the lease premium paid that is assessed on the landlord as property business income is:

	£
Premium	25,200
Less: (£25,200 × 2% × (21 – 1))	(10,080)
	15,120

The trading deduction for Aroha is therefore £720 (£15,120 ÷ 21) each year. This would have been time apportioned for the year ended 31 March 2022, if the premium had not been paid at the start of the accounting period.

5 PROFITS RECOGNISED IN THE ACCOUNTS BUT NOT CHARGED AS TRADING INCOME

These tend to fall into three categories as follows.

- Capital receipts (which may be subject to capital gains tax for individuals or corporation tax for companies). This includes any profit on the sale of a capital asset or insurance proceeds for destruction of a capital asset. Note that insurance proceeds received to cover loss of trade are a taxable receipt.
- Income falling into a different category, such as rents taxable as property income, interest taxable as savings income or dividends.
- Income that is exempt from tax (notably repayment interest received on tax repaid).

Deduct these receipts from the accounting profit. Amounts that are subject to income tax must then be included elsewhere in an individual's personal income tax computation.

6 APPROACH FOR ADJUSTED PROFIT COMPUTATIONS IN THE EXAMINATION

- Read carefully through the statement of profit or loss given and note which items must be added or deducted.
- Read through the notes and decide which items must be adjusted.
- Write out your computation. Note any items that do not need adjustment with a 0 as there will be marks for these.

Example

Benabi's business has the following statement of profit or loss for the year ended 31 March 2022:

	£	£
Revenue		424,800
Cost of sales		(280,900)
Gross profit		143,900
Wages and salaries (Note 1)	22,400	
Rent, rates and insurance	8,100	
Repairs to machinery	3,456	
Advertising and entertaining (Note 2)	6,098	
Accountancy and legal costs	2,400	
Motor expenses (Note 3)	20,555	
Depreciation	8,001	
Telephone and office costs	3,699	
Other expenses (Note 4)	35,702	
		(110,411)
Net profit		33,489

Notes:

		£
1	Wages and salaries include:	
	Benabi	6,000
	Benabi's wife who works in the marketing department and is paid a market rate	8,000
2	Advertising and entertaining includes:	
	Gifts to customers – boxes of chocolate costing £5 each	1,250
	Gifts to customers – calendars with the business logo £10 each	400
3	Motor expenses include:	
	Sales manager's car	820
	Benabi's car – used for 80% private mileage	1,375
4	Other expenses include:	
	Cost of staff training	490
	Cost of meals with customers	220
5	Capital allowances have been calculated at £9,955	

Calculate Benabi's tax adjusted trading profit for the year ended 31 March 2022.

Your computation should start with the net profit for the period of £33,489 and should list all the items in the statement of profit or loss and notes indicating with a zero (0) any items that do not require adjustment.

Solution

		£	£
Net profit per accounts		33,489	
Add:	Benabi's salary	6,000	
	Wife's salary (Note 1)	0	
	Rent, rates and insurance	0	
	Repairs to machinery	0	
	Boxes of chocolates (Note 2)	1,250	
	Calendars (Note 2)	0	
	Accountancy and legal costs	0	
	Sales manager's car	0	
	Benabi's motor expenses (£1,375 × 80%)	1,100	
	Depreciation	8,001	
	Telephone and office costs	0	
	Staff training	0	
	Meals with customers (Note 3)	220	
Less:	Capital allowances		9,955
		50,060	9,955
		(9,955)	
Tax adjusted trading profit		40,105	

Notes:

1 Salaries paid to family members are allowable provided they represent reasonable remuneration for the services provided to the business. Benabi's wife is earning the market rate.

2 Gifts to customers costing no more than £50 per person and carrying a conspicuous advertisement for the business are tax allowable. However, gifts of food, drink, tobacco and vouchers are not allowable.

3 Entertaining customers is not allowable and neither are personal expenses, such as the cost of Benabi's own meals.

ACTIVITY 1

You are presented with the accounts of Mariya for the year to 31 December 2021, as set out below. Mariya runs a small printing business and wishes to know the amount of her tax adjusted trading profits.

		£	£
Gross profit on trading account			25,620
Profit on sale of premises (Note 1)			1,073
Building society interest received			677
			27,370
Advertising		642	
Staff wages (Note 2)		12,124	
Rates		1,057	
Repairs and renewals (Note 3)		2,598	
Car expenses (Note 4)		555	
Impairment losses (Note 5)		75	
Telephone		351	
Heating and lighting		372	
Miscellaneous expenses (Note 6)		347	
Depreciation	– printing presses	1,428	
	– office equipment	218	
	– Mr Cornelius' car	735	
			(20,502)
Net profit			6,868

Notes:

1 The profit on the sale of premises relates to the sale of a small freehold industrial unit in which Mariya used to store paper before building her extension.

2 Staff wages includes an amount of £182 for a staff Christmas lunch.

3 Repairs and renewals comprise the following expenditure:

	£
Refurbishing second-hand press before it could be used in the business	522
Redecorating administration offices	429
Building extension to enlarge paper store	1,647
	2,598

4 Car expenses all relate to Mariya's car which is used 75% for business purposes and 25% for private purposes.

5 The charge for impairment losses was made up as follows:

	£
Write off of specific trade debts	42
Increase in allowance for impaired debts	50
	92
Less: recovery of impaired debt previously written off	(17)
Charge to statement of profit or loss	75

6 Miscellaneous expenses include:

		£
Subscription to Printers' Association		45
Subscription to Chamber of Commerce		50
Gifts to customers	– calendars costing £7.50 each	75
	– two food hampers	95

7 Capital allowances have been calculated as £1,700.

Calculate Mariya's tax adjusted trading profit. Your answer should start with the net profit of £6,868 and should list all the items in the statement of profit or loss and notes indicating with a zero (0) any items that do not require adjustment.

For a suggested answer, see the 'Answers' section at the end of the book.

KEY TERMS

Appropriations – the withdrawal of funds from a business's profits, such as a proprietor's salary, or interest on capital invested in the business.

SELF TEST QUESTIONS

		Paragraph
1	What are the four types of adjustment needed to convert the accounting profit into the tax adjusted trading profit?	1.1
2	Which subscriptions and donations are allowable?	2.2
3	In what circumstances is expenditure on gifts and entertainment allowable?	2.4
4	What types of legal and professional charges are allowable?	2.5
5	When is pre-trading expenditure deductible?	2.9
6	What is the tax treatment of goods taken from the business by a trader for his or her own use?	3
7	Give two examples of income/profits which may be recognised in the accounts but which are not charged to tax as trading profits.	5

MULTIPLE CHOICE QUESTIONS

1 Xander has included a deduction in his accounting profit of £4,800 in respect of the annual leasing cost for a car for use by an employee, which has CO_2 emissions of 223g/km. The car has been used for the whole of the year ended 31 March 2022.

What amount must Xander add back to the accounting profit when calculating the adjusted trading profit for tax purposes for the year ended 31 March 2022?

A £0

B £720

C £4,080

D £4,800

2 Jada runs her own business, selling hand-made greetings cards. Which of the following costs is NOT deductible in arriving at her tax adjusted trading profits?

A Repairs to her shop premises, two weeks after she opened the shop

B Advertising in the local paper

C Cost of writing off inventory obtained from the previous owner

D Parking fine incurred by Jada for parking outside the shop

3 Anya is a sole trader who operates a business as a wine merchant. Her accounts for the year ended 31 March 2022 include the following items:

	£
Impaired trade debts written off	1,200
Subscription to Decanter magazine	500
Late payment interest in respect of the tax on the business profits for the year ended 31 March 2021	275
Legal fees in respect of the acquisition of a new shop	2,500

What amount must be added back in respect of the above items when calculating the adjusted trading profits for the year ended 31 March 2022?

A £275

B £2,775

C £3,000

D £4,475

4 Which of the following receipts is not taxable as trading income?

A Insurance proceeds for loss of trade

B Impaired trading debt recovered

C Repayment interest received on a tax repayment

D Sales proceeds for selling inventory

For suggested answers, see the 'Answers' section at the end of the book.

PRACTICE QUESTION

HOLLY

The following is the statement of profit or loss of Holly who has carried on business for many years in the UK as a wholesale supplier of consumer goods for the home market.

Statement of profit or loss – year ended 30 November 2021

	£	£	£
Gross profit			85,353
Sale proceeds for computer			240
Interest on Government securities			1,540
			87,133
Less: Expenses			
Wages		33,500	
NI contributions (staff)		5,000	
Rent (Note 1)		2,343	
Business rates		496	
Insurance (premises & inventory)		243	
Light and heat (Note 1)		1,101	
Motor car expenses – Holly (Note 2)		1,380	
Advertising		840	
Holly – speeding fine		150	
Depreciation			
Equipment	866		
Motor car	1,200		
		2,066	
Impairment losses (Note 3)		623	
Trade expenses (Note 4)		11,549	
Holly's income tax		12,800	
Professional charges (Note 5)		2,284	
			(74,375)
Net profit			12,758

Notes:

1 Holly lives over the business premises and ⅓ of rent and light and heat relates to private use.

2 Holly has calculated that 25% of the car mileage relates to private use.

3 Impairment losses:

	£		£
Impaired trade debts written off as irrecoverable	438	Allowance for receivables at 1 December 2020	535
Allowance for receivables at 30 November 2021	720	Statement of profit or loss	623
	1,158		1,158

4 Trade expenses:

	£
Stationery	2,250
Printing	3,350
Subscriptions	
Political party	200
Trade association	500
Entertaining customers	2,249
Redecoration of offices	3,000
	11,549

5 Professional charges:

	£
Accountancy	1,712
Debt collecting	572
	2,284

6 Holly has taken goods from the business for her own use during the year, but no entry has been made in the books of account. The goods cost £1,350. Holly's normal mark-up on such goods is 40% on cost.

Required:

Compute the tax adjusted trading profit for the year ended 30 November 2021. Your answer should start with the net profit of £12,758 and should list all the items in the statement of profit or loss and notes indicating with a zero (0) any items that do not require adjustment.

(15 marks)

For a suggested answer, see the 'Answers' section at the end of the book.

Chapter 4

CAPITAL ALLOWANCES

INTRODUCTION

The previous chapter dealt with the adjustment of a trader's statement of profit or loss to arrive at the profits adjusted for tax purposes.

Depreciation is disallowed for tax purposes; instead capital allowances are calculated and deducted as a trading expense.

This chapter is concerned with capital allowances available to traders and others on the purchase of plant and machinery. There are, however, a number of preliminary points that need to be considered. Is the person who has incurred the expenditure eligible for capital allowances? Does the asset count as plant or machinery? If it does qualify, what allowances are available and for which tax year(s) are they given?

Once the rules for deciding these questions are appreciated, the arithmetical calculations are fairly straight forward. Provided that the computations are laid out clearly and with an appropriate structure, the resulting figures should readily fall into place.

This chapter also looks at the rules relating to structures and buildings allowances (SBAs). This chapter covers syllabus areas B2 and B1 (e).

CONTENTS	LEARNING OUTCOMES
1 Eligibility 2 Meaning of plant and machinery 3 Calculating the allowances 4 Assets acquired by hire purchase and leased assets 5 Cars 6 Private use of an asset by the owner 7 Election for depooling of short life assets 8 Special rate pool 9 The small pool WDA 10 VAT 11 Approach to computational questions 12 Structures and buildings allowance (SBA)	At the end of this chapter, you should be able to: • explain the principles relating to capital allowances on plant and machinery • prepare capital allowance computations for plant and machinery • illustrate the use of capital allowances on commencement and cessation of business. • compute structures and buildings allowances.

1 ELIGIBILITY

1.1 QUALIFYING ASSETS

Capital allowances are given at statutory rates on qualifying expenditure on certain non-current assets. The allowances are not only given on original cost, but also on all subsequent qualifying expenditure of a capital nature, which has been disallowed in the adjusted profits computation (e.g. improvements).

For examination purposes, these capital allowances are only available for expenditure on plant and machinery. However, there is also a separate structures and buildings allowance available for expenditure on some buildings – see section 12 of this chapter.

1.2 WHO MAY CLAIM CAPITAL ALLOWANCES?

Capital allowances are available to persons who buy and use plant and machinery:

- in their trade or profession
- in their employment
- in their property business (in limited circumstances – see Chapter 12).

They are given as an expense in calculating taxable income. They are calculated for each period of account (i.e. the period for which accounts are prepared) instead of for a tax year.

2 MEANING OF PLANT AND MACHINERY

2.1 INTRODUCTION

There is no statutory definition of plant. The most informative definition was given in the case of Yarmouth v France (1887). Plant was said to include:

> 'Whatever apparatus is used by a businessman for carrying on his business – not his stock-in-trade which he buys or makes for sale – but all goods and chattels, fixed or movable, live or dead, which he keeps for permanent employment in his business.'

2.2 THE COURTS' INTERPRETATION OF 'PLANT'

The Courts have refined the definition of plant and machinery to a **function test**:

Does the asset perform:	**This means that the asset is:**	**Plant and machinery?**
An active function	Apparatus **with which** the business is carried on	Yes
A passive function	The setting **in which** the business is carried on	No

The dividing line between an asset that is functional and one that is merely setting is not always clear. Examples below show how the Courts have reacted to claims for capital allowances in these circumstances.

- A canopy covering petrol filling pumps was held to be part of the setting and not plant and machinery. (It did not assist in serving petrol to customers.)
- False ceilings in a restaurant were not plant. (All they did was hide pipes.)
- Swimming pools at a caravan park were held to be plant and machinery – the caravan park as a whole was the setting.
- Movable partitioning in an office was held to be plant and machinery.

2.3 ASSETS DEEMED TO BE PLANT

There are various types of expenditure that would not be thought of as plant using the function test, but which are treated as plant by specific legislation. These are:

- the cost of alterations to buildings needed for the installation of plant
- expenditure on acquiring computer software.

2.4 CLARIFICATION ON THE MEANING OF PLANT

The Capital Allowances Act 2001 states that land, buildings and structures cannot be plant. However, expenditure on buildings and structures that has been held to be plant by the courts still qualifies as plant.

2.5 SUMMARY

Determining what is and what is not plant can be difficult in practice. In the examination the most common examples of plant and machinery are:

- computers and software
- machinery
- cars and lorries
- office furniture and carpets
- movable partitions

- air-conditioning and heating installations
- lifts
- alterations to buildings needed to install plant and machinery such as reinforced floors or air conditioning systems for computers.

3 CALCULATING THE ALLOWANCES

3.1 POOLING EXPENDITURE

The cost of all plant and machinery purchased by a trader usually becomes part of a *pool of expenditure* on which capital allowances may be claimed. This is known as the general or main pool. When a purchase is made, it is added to the pool; on disposal the pool is reduced.

Exceptionally, certain items are not included in the main pool. They are:

- cars with CO_2 emissions of more than 50g/km
- assets with private use by the proprietor
- expenditure incurred on short life plant where an election to depool is made
- expenditure incurred on items that form part of the special rate pool.

These exceptional items are dealt with later in the chapter.

3.2 THE ANNUAL INVESTMENT ALLOWANCE (AIA)

The annual investment allowance (AIA) is a 100% allowance for expenditure incurred by a business on plant and machinery. The maximum allowance in a year is £1,000,000. The reduction in AIA to £200,000 from 1 January 2022 is outside the scope of this syllabus and will not be examined, even for periods ending after 31 December 2021.

The key rules for the allowance are as follows:

- available to all businesses
- available on acquisitions of plant and machinery in the main and special rate pools
- not available on **any** cars (regardless of CO_2 emissions)
- limited to a maximum of £1,000,000 expenditure incurred in each accounting period of 12 months in length
- for long and short accounting periods, the allowance is increased/reduced to reflect the length of the accounting period (important when a business starts up)
- not available in the accounting period in which trade ceases.

Where a business spends more than £1,000,000 in a 12 month accounting period on assets qualifying for the AIA the expenditure above the £1,000,000 limit qualifies for writing down allowances (WDA) in the same accounting period.

Note also that:

- the taxpayer does not have to claim all/any of the AIA if he or she does not want to
- any unused AIA cannot be carried forward or carried back; the benefit of the allowance is just lost.

Example

Michael commenced trading on 1 April 2021. In his first year of trading he made the following purchases:

- plant and machinery for the factory he rented £970,000
- office furniture £115,000

(a) Assuming Michael claims the maximum annual investment allowance (AIA) for the year ended 31 March 2022 state how much AIA he will claim and how much of his expenditure is eligible for writing down allowances.

(b) What if Michael only purchased the office furniture and did not purchase the plant and machinery?

(c) What would be the answer to part (a) if Michael's accounting period was the eight months to 30 November 2021?

Solution

(a) Year ended 31 March 2022

	£
Additions:	
Qualifying for AIA	
Plant and machinery	970,000
Office furniture	115,000
	1,085,000
AIA (maximum)	(1,000,000)
Eligible for WDA	85,000

(b) If Michael did not purchase the plant and machinery

	£
Additions:	
Qualifying for AIA	
Office furniture	115,000
AIA (Note)	(115,000)
Eligible for WDA	0

Note: The unused AIA of £885,000 (£1,000,000 – £115,000) is lost.

(c) If the accounting period was eight months ended 30 November 2021

	£
Additions:	
Qualifying for AIA	
Plant and machinery	970,000
Office furniture	115,000
	1,085,000
AIA (maximum) (W)	(666,667)
Eligible for WDA	418,333

Working:

Maximum AIA is £666,667 (£1,000,000 × 8/12)

3.3 WRITING DOWN ALLOWANCES (WDA)

An annual WDA of 18% is given on a reducing balance basis by reference to the unrelieved expenditure in the main pool brought forward at the beginning of the year, after adjustment for additions that do not qualify for the AIA or first year allowances (FYA – see section 3.4) or that exceed the amount of the AIA, and adjustment for disposals during the year.

Example

Georgina commenced trading on 1 April 2021. Her trading profits, adjusted for tax purposes but before capital allowances, are as follows:

	£
Year ended 31 March 2022	25,500
Year ended 31 March 2023	30,000

On 9 November 2021 she bought plant and machinery for £20,000 and a motor car for £6,000 with CO_2 emissions of 40g/km.

Calculate Georgina's tax adjusted trading profit for both years, assuming the capital allowance rules for the tax year 2021/22 continue into the future.

Solution

Capital allowances computation

	£	Main pool £	Allowances £
Year ended 31 March 2022			
Additions:			
Not qualifying for AIA:			
Car		6,000	
Qualifying for AIA:			
Plant and machinery	20,000		
AIA	(20,000)		20,000
Balance to pool		0	
		6,000	
WDA (18% × £6,000)		(1,080)	1,080
TWDV c/f		4,920	
Total allowances			21,080
Year ended 31 March 2023			
WDA (18% × £4,920)		(886)	886
TWDV c/f		4,034	
Total allowances			886

Tax adjusted trading profit

Year ended	Adjusted trading profit £	Capital allowances £	Tax adjusted trading profit £
31 March 2022	25,500	(21,080)	4,420
31 March 2023	30,000	(886)	29,114

ACTIVITY 1

Gabrielle commenced trading on 1 April 2021. Her trading profits, adjusted for tax purposes but before capital allowances, are as follows:

	£
Year ended 31 March 2022	60,500
Year ended 31 March 2023	54,000

On 1 May 2021, Gabrielle acquired plant and machinery for £27,000 and a new motor car for £10,000 with CO_2 emissions of 45g/km.

Calculate Gabrielle's tax adjusted trading profit for both years assuming the capital allowance rules for the tax year 2021/22 continue into the future.

For a suggested answer, see the 'Answers' section at the end of the book.

- No WDA may be claimed in the final period of trade.
- If the period of account of the business is less than 12 months long, the WDA is scaled down proportionately. Similarly, if the period of account is more than 12 months' long, the WDA is scaled up. This often happens when a business starts. (Remember that the maximum AIA is also scaled up or down for periods more or less than 12 months.)
- A person may claim the whole or only part of the allowance to which he or she is entitled. If a partial claim is made in one year, WDAs in subsequent years will be calculated on a higher figure of written down value than if the allowances had previously been claimed in full. However, as a consequence, relief for the expenditure will be delayed. In the examination, you will always be asked to calculate the maximum capital allowances available.
- The WDA is never restricted by reference to the length of ownership of an asset in the basis period.

Example

Yiwan commenced trading on 1 April 2021. Her trading profits, adjusted for tax purposes but before capital allowances, are as follows:

	£
14 month period ended 31 May 2022	74,000
Year ended 31 May 2023	65,000

On 1 November 2021, she bought plant and machinery for £45,000 and a motor car for £19,000 with CO_2 emissions of 45g/km.

Calculate her tax adjusted trading profit for each of the periods of trading, assuming the capital allowance rules for the tax year 2021/22 continue into the future.

Solution

Yiwan – Capital allowances computation

	£	**Main pool** £	**Allowances** £
Period ended 31 May 2022			
Additions:			
Not qualifying for AIA:			
Car		19,000	
Qualifying for AIA:			
Plant and machinery	45,000		
AIA (Note)	(45,000)		45,000
Balance to pool		0	
		19,000	
WDA (18% × £19,000 × 14/12)		(3,990)	3,990
TWDV c/f		15,010	
Total allowances			48,990

Year ended 31 May 2023		
WDA (18% × £15,010)	(2,702)	2,702
TWDV c/f	12,308	
Total allowances		2,702

Note: The maximum AIA for the 14 month period is proportionately increased to £1,166,667 (£1,000,000 × 14/12).

Both the AIA and the WDA are time apportioned to reflect the 14 month period.

	Adjusted trading profit	Capital allowances	Tax adjusted trading profit
	£	£	£
Period ended 31 May 2022	74,000	(48,990)	25,010
Year ended 31 May 2023	65,000	(2,702)	62,298

ACTIVITY 2

Gavin commenced trading on 1 April 2021. His trading profits, adjusted for tax purposes but before capital allowances, are as follows:

	£
4 month period ended 31 July 2021	395,000
Year ended 31 July 2022	145,000

On 1 May 2021, he bought plant and machinery for £356,666 and a motor car for £11,500 with CO_2 emissions of 50g/km.

Calculate the tax adjusted trading profit for each of the periods of trading.

For a suggested answer, see the 'Answers' section at the end of the book.

3.4 FIRST YEAR ALLOWANCES (FYA)

The AIA is not available on cars, however a 100% first year allowance (FYA) is available on the purchase of new zero emissions cars (i.e. CO_2 emissions of 0g/km).

The 100% FYA is given as follows:

- In the period of acquisition, a 100% FYA is given instead of the WDA (i.e. cannot have both the FYA and WDA on that expense in the first year).
- Unlike the AIA and WDA, the FYA is never time apportioned for periods of account greater or less than 12 months.
- Unlike the AIA, there is no overall limit to the amount of FYA that can be given in a period.
- FYAs are not given in the final period of trading.
- If the zero emission car is not new (i.e. second hand) it is treated in the same way as a car with CO_2 emissions of between 1 – 50g/km.
- A disposal of a zero emission car on which FYA has been claimed is treated as a disposal from the main pool.

Example

Amira commenced trading on 1 January 2021. Her trading profits, adjusted for tax purposes but before capital allowances, are as follows:

	£
Year ended 31 December 2021	1,520,770
Year ended 31 December 2022	1,525,000

On 9 May 2021 she bought plant and machinery for £1,250,000, a second hand motor car for £6,500 with CO_2 emissions of 40g/km and a new motor car with zero CO_2 emissions for £13,600.

Calculate Amira's tax adjusted trading profit for both years, assuming the capital allowance rules for the tax year 2021/22 continue into the future.

Solution

Capital allowances computation

		Main pool	Allowances
y/e 31 December 2021	£	£	£
Additions:			
Not qualifying for AIA or FYA:			
Car (CO_2 1-50g/km)		6,500	
Qualifying for AIA:			
Plant and machinery	1,250,000		
AIA	(1,000,000)		1,000,000
		250,000	
		256,500	
WDA (18% × £256,500)		(46,170)	46,170
Additions qualifying for FYA:			
New zero emission car	13,600		
FYA (100%)	(13,600)		13,600
		0	
TWDV c/f		210,330	
Total allowances			1,059,770
y/e 31 December 2022			
WDA (18% × £210,330)		(37,859)	37,859
TWDV c/f		172,471	
Total allowances			37,859

Tax adjusted trading profit

	Adjusted trading profit	Capital allowances (W)	Tax adjusted trading profit
	£	£	£
y/e 31 December 2021	1,520,770	(1,059,770)	461,000
y/e 31 December 2022	1,525,000	(37,859)	1,487,141

3.5 SALE OF PLANT AND MACHINERY

Where an asset is sold during an accounting period, a disposal value is deducted from the balance of unrelieved expenditure in the pool. The deduction is made after bringing in acquisitions in the same period (except those qualifying for FYA), but **before** calculating the WDA. The WDA for the year is then calculated on the remaining figure.

The disposal **value deducted** from the pool is the **lower** of:

- sales proceeds and
- original cost.

An excess of proceeds over original cost may be charged to capital gains tax.

ACTIVITY 3

Sandy prepares accounts to 31 March annually. In the year to 31 March 2022 the following transactions took place.

30 December 2021	Plant sold (originally purchased for £4,000) for £800
20 February 2022	Plant purchased for £20,000

Compute the capital allowances for the year ended 31 March 2022 assuming that the pool balance on 1 April 2021 was £4,900.

For a suggested answer, see the 'Answers' section at the end of the book.

If an asset is traded-in as part exchange, the transaction is treated as two separate events:

- the asset traded-in is treated as a disposal at the trade in value and
- the new asset is treated as purchased for the total of the trade in value plus any additional amount paid.

Example

Joseph had a tax written down value brought forward on the main pool of £10,500 as at 1 April 2021.

On 1 June 2021 he bought a new car (CO_2 emissions 50g/km) which cost £12,400. He traded in an old car and paid the garage the balance of £9,400. The old car cost £10,000 in 2018 and had been allocated to the main pool on purchase.

He had no other additions or disposals.

Calculate the capital allowances for the year ended 31 March 2022.

Solution

The trade in allowance for the old car is £3,000 (£12,400 – £9,400) which is less than the original cost.

	Main pool	Allowances
	£	£
TWDV b/f	10,500	
Addition not qualifying for AIA or FYA	12,400	
Disposal (lower of cost and proceeds)	(3,000)	
	19,900	
WDA at 18%	(3,582)	3,582
TWDV c/f	16,318	
Total allowances		3,582

3.6 BALANCING CHARGES

If, on disposal of an asset in the pool, the disposal value exceeds the pool balance brought forward plus any pool additions in the year, the excess allowances previously given will be recovered and charged to tax by means of a balancing charge.

A balancing charge is added to the trading profits.

3.7 BALANCING ALLOWANCES

Balancing allowances will not be given on the main or special rate pool during the life of the business. They will be given when an asset is disposed of from a single asset pool, such as a private use asset (section 6) or a short life asset (section 7).

3.8 CESSATION OF TRADE

The basic idea underlying capital allowances is that, over the life of a business, traders will obtain relief for the total cost less subsequent sale proceeds of their assets. Where the trade is permanently discontinued and there is still a balance of unrelieved expenditure in the pool (i.e. a balance after deducting the final sale proceeds), the trader is entitled to claim relief for that unrelieved balance by means of a balancing allowance (it is effectively a final year allowance).

On cessation the capital allowances are calculated as follows:

- Acquisitions in the final period are added to the pool, however, **no AIA, FYA or WDA** are available for the final period of account.
- The balancing allowance is the pool balance at the end of the final period of account after deducting the sale proceeds received from the disposal of the assets in the pool (or the cost of the asset if it is lower than sale proceeds).
- If an asset is retained for the private use of the owner of the business, the market value at the date of cessation will be brought into the pool as disposal proceeds (or the original cost if lower).
- The only time a balancing allowance will arise in the main pool is in the period of account at the end of which the trade is permanently discontinued.

Example

Joad prepares accounts to 5 April annually. He ceased to trade on 5 April 2022, on which date he sold all the assets in the main pool for £10,000 (none sold for more than cost). The balance in the pool at the beginning of the final period of account (i.e. on 6 April 2021) was £14,000 and he had purchased plant in June 2021 for £5,000.

Compute the balancing allowance for the year ended 5 April 2022.

Solution

	£
Pool balance b/f	14,000
Addition during year	5,000
Less: Disposals	(10,000)
	9,000
Balancing allowance for the year ended 5 April 2022	(9,000)

4 ASSETS ACQUIRED BY HIRE PURCHASE AND LEASED ASSETS

The essence of a **hire purchase** contract is that, on making the final payment, the payer becomes the asset's legal owner. Although the payer only hires the asset beforehand, this is effectively ignored for capital allowances purposes and he or she is treated as though he or she had bought the asset in the first place. Consequently:

- the hire purchase interest is treated as a trading expense of the period of account in which it accrues (and is deductible in computing tax adjusted trading profits)
- the full cash price of the asset is brought into the pool in the period of first use
- capital allowances are given on the full cash price irrespective of the actual instalments paid in the period of account.

Legal title to **leased assets** remains with the lessor. The lessee (the user of the asset) is hiring it and this is reflected in the tax treatment. Lease payments are treated as deductible, on an accruals basis, in computing tax adjusted trading profits and no capital allowances are available to the lessee. Note if a car with emissions of more than 50g/km is leased – 15% of the lease payment is added back in computing trading profits (see Chapter 3).

5 CARS

The treatment of motor cars depends on their CO_2 emissions as follows:

CO_2 emissions	Description	Treatment in capital allowances computation
0g/km (or electric)	Zero emission	100% FYA in the year of purchase if new (otherwise treat as 1 – 50g/km)
1 – 50g/km	Standard emission	Include in main pool as an addition not qualifying for AIA – WDA 18%
> 50g/km	High emission	Include in the special rate pool (see section 8) as an addition not qualifying for AIA – WDA 6%

Example

Joist prepares accounts to 31 March each year. In the year ended 31 March 2022 he purchased the following new cars:

1 New car costing £16,000 with CO_2 emissions of 48g/km

2 New car costing £20,000 with CO_2 emissions of 100g/km

3 New car costing £32,000 with zero emissions

The tax written down value brought forward on the main pool was £21,480.

Calculate the capital allowances for the year ended 31 March 2022.

Solution

Joist – Capital allowances computation

		Main pool	Special rate pool	Allowances
		£	£	£
Year ended 31 March 2022				
TWDV b/f		21,480		
Additions not qualifying for AIA or FYA				
Car – emissions 1 – 50g/km		16,000		
Car – emissions >50g/km			20,000	
		37,480		
WDA at 18%		(6,746)		6,746
WDA at 6%			(1,200)	1,200
Addition qualifying for FYA				
Car – new zero emissions	32,000			
FYA at 100%	(32,000)			32,000
Total allowances				39,946
TWDV c/f		30,734	18,800	

6 PRIVATE USE OF AN ASSET BY THE OWNER

Where an asset is used **by the owner** (not an employee) of a business partly for business and partly for private purposes (e.g. a motor car), only a proportion of the available allowances is given. This proportion is computed by reference to the percentage of business use to total use.

The cost of the privately used asset must **not** be pooled, but must be included in a separate column. A separate column should be set up for each private use asset.

The **full cost** is added to the private use asset column and the **full AIA, FYA or WDA** is calculated, but only the **business proportion** is actually deducted in calculating trading profits, therefore the business proportion is shown in the allowances column.

- If the private use asset is a car, the WDA will be 6% or 18%, or an FYA of 100% will be given, depending on the CO_2 emissions. These are the most common private use assets in examinations.
- If the private use asset is not a car then AIA will be available, unless it is set against other additions in the year.
- Note that, if applicable, the business can choose the expenditure against which the AIA is matched.
- It will therefore be most beneficial for the AIA to be allocated against the main pool expenditure rather than any private use asset as only the business proportion of any AIA available can be claimed.

On disposal of the asset, a balancing adjustment is **always** computed by comparing the sale proceeds (or cost if lower) with the tax written down value (if a profit, there is a balancing charge and vice versa). Having calculated the balancing adjustment, the amount assessed or allowed is then reduced to the business proportion, which is shown in the allowances column.

Private use by an employee of an asset owned by the business has **no effect** on the business's entitlement to capital allowances (although there will normally be a benefit charge on the employee – see Chapter 10).

Example

Khadija is a sole trader whose business year end is 31 March. As at 1 April 2021 the tax written down values are as follows:

Main pool	£17,400
Car with 40% private use by Jonas (CO_2 emissions 145g/km)	£11,600

There are no additions or disposals in the year ended 31 March 2022.

Solution

Capital allowances computation

	Main pool	**Private use asset**	**Business use %**	**Allowances**
	£	£		£
TWDV b/f	17,400	11,600		
WDA – 18%	(3,132)			3,132
WDA – 6%		(696)	× 60%	418
TWDV c/f	14,268	10,904		
Total allowances				3,550

Note how the WDA in the private use car column in the last example is the full allowance. The restriction for private use only happens when the allowance is added to the total allowances column.

ACTIVITY 4

Gerald runs a small business and prepares his accounts to 31 March. As at 1 April 2021, the tax written down values are as follows:

Main pool	£11,700
Motor car (used 60% for private purposes by Gerald)	£11,600

The following transactions took place during the year ended 31 March 2022:

- Purchased plant for £8,800.
- Purchased a motor car for £9,400 with CO_2 emissions of 35g/km.
- Sold the motor car owned at 1 April 2021 for £5,500.
- Purchased a motor car for £16,000 (used 45% for private purposes by Gerald). This car has CO_2 emissions of 95g/km.

Calculate the capital allowances for the year to 31 March 2022.

For a suggested answer, see the 'Answers' section at the end of the book.

7 ELECTION FOR DEPOOLING OF SHORT LIFE ASSETS

7.1 THE ELECTION

The election is designed to enable traders to **accelerate** capital allowances on certain short life machinery or plant, where it is the intention to sell or scrap it within eight years of the end of the accounting period in which the asset was acquired.

An election for a company must be made within two years of the end of the accounting period in which the asset was purchased. An election for an unincorporated business must be made within 12 months of 31 January following the tax year in which the period of account in which the expenditure was incurred ends. The election is irrevocable.

Example

Blessing prepares her accounts to 31 March annually. If she purchases an asset on 1 September 2021 and wishes to make a short life asset election, she must do so by 31 January 2024.

This date is arrived at as follows. The asset is purchased in the accounting year ended 31 March 2022. Those accounts end in the tax year 2021/22. The 31 January following 2021/22 is 31 January 2023. 12 months after that date gives 31 January 2024.

Any plant and machinery can constitute a short life asset, except motor cars and assets with private use.

7.2 COMPUTATIONS

The treatment of short life assets is as follows:

- Each short life asset is the subject of a separate computation.
- AIAs and WDAs are given under the normal rules. However, note that the business can choose the expenditure against which the AIA is matched.
- If eligible for the AIA, there will be no expenditure left to 'depool' and the short life asset election will not be made.
- If there is expenditure in excess of the maximum AIA, it is better for the AIA to be allocated against the main pool expenditure rather than a short life asset and for the short life asset election to be made.
- On disposal within eight years of the end of the accounting period of purchase a separate balancing allowance is given or balancing charge arises. The election therefore will benefit the business if it is expected that a balancing allowance will arise.

However, if no disposal has taken place by the eighth anniversary of the end of the period of account in which the acquisition took place, the unrelieved balance is transferred back to the main pool in the first period of account following that anniversary. This ensures that no tax advantage arises from making the election where it ought not, in retrospect, to have been made.

In the examination, if an asset is purchased with a useful economic life of less than 8 years and the question states that all beneficial elections have been made, you should calculate the allowances assuming a short life asset election has been made.

ACTIVITY 5

Gemma has traded for many years preparing accounts to 31 March each year. The TWDV on the main pool was £25,000 on 1 April 2021.

In May 2021, she acquired a new machine costing £15,000. She anticipated that the machine would last two years and she eventually sold it on 30 June 2023 for £1,750.

In August 2021, she acquired plant and machinery for £1,005,000.

Calculate the allowances available for each year, assuming:

1 No short life election is made

2 An election to treat the new machine as a short life asset is made

Advise Gemma which of these options gives the higher amount of capital allowances for the three years ended 31 March 2022, 2023 and 2024.

Assume that the capital allowance rules for future years remain the same as for 2021/22.

Note: A comparison of these two scenarios will not be required in the examination. A question will always state whether the election has been made or not. However, this activity is helpful to demonstrate the benefit of the short life asset election.

For a suggested answer, see the 'Answers' section at the end of the book.

8 SPECIAL RATE POOL

8.1 INTRODUCTION

The special rate pool is a pool of qualifying expenditure that operates in the same way as the main pool except that the WDA is 6% for a 12 month period (rather than 18%).

Note that:

- the AIA is available against this expenditure (except on high emission cars) and
- the business can choose the expenditure against which the AIA is matched.

It will therefore be most beneficial for the AIA to be allocated against expenditure in the following order:

1 the special rate pool (because these assets are only eligible for WDA at 6%)

2 the main pool

3 short life assets

4 private use assets.

8.2 QUALIFYING EXPENDITURE

The special rate pool groups together expenditure incurred on the following types of assets:

- long life assets (not examinable in FTX)
- 'integral features' of a building or structure
- thermal insulation of a building
- high emission cars (CO_2 emissions > 50g/km).

Examples of integral features are given below but note that in the examination you will be told if an asset falls into one of these categories.

8.3 INTEGRAL FEATURES OF A BUILDING OR STRUCTURE

Integral features of a building or structure include:

- electrical (including lighting) systems
- cold water systems
- space or water heating systems
- powered systems of ventilation, air cooling or air purification
- lifts and escalators.

Thermal insulation in all business buildings is also included in the special rate pool.

Example

Aspel runs a manufacturing business and prepares accounts to 31 March each year.

During the year ending 31 March 2022 Aspel incurred the following expenditure:

1 May 2021	Spent £495,000 on a new air conditioning system for the factory. This qualifies as an integral feature in a building.
1 June 2021	Purchased new machinery for £540,000.
15 July 2021	Purchased a new car for £18,000, which will be used by a member of the sales staff. CO_2 emissions are 110g/km.

In addition on 1 July 2021 Aspel sold an old machine for £10,000 (original cost £15,000).

As at 1 April 2021 the tax written down values were as follows:

Main pool	£73,000
Special rate pool	£90,000

Calculate Aspel's capital allowances for the year ended 31 March 2022.

Solution

Aspel – Capital allowances computation for the year ending 31 March 2022

		Main pool	**Special rate pool**	**Allowances**
	£	£	£	£
TWDV b/f		73,000	90,000	
Additions:				
Not qualifying for AIA or FYA:				
Car – emissions exceeding 50g/km			18,000	
Qualifying for AIA:				
Air conditioning	495,000			
AIA	(495,000)			495,000
Balance to special rate pool	0		0	
Qualifying for AIA:				
Machine	540,000			
AIA (£1,000,000 – £495,000)	(505,000)			505,000
Balance to main pool	35,000	35,000		
Disposal proceeds (lower of cost and sale proceeds)		(10,000)		
		98,000	108,000	
WDA at 18%		(17,640)		17,640
WDA at 6%			(6,480)	6,480
TWDV c/f		80,360	101,520	
Total allowances				1,024,120

9 THE SMALL POOL WDA

The WDA of 18% or 6% is claimed each accounting period and if there are no additions in an accounting period to be added to the pool, the WDA will be claimed on an ever decreasing amount for many years.

To prevent the inconvenience of keeping records of small balances of expenditure, a 'small pool WDA' can be claimed.

The small pool WDA available:

- applies to the main pool and special rate pool
- does not apply to depooled assets
- is any amount up to £1,000, and
- is time apportioned for long or short accounting periods. (Watch out for this in questions.)

Therefore, an allowance of up to £1,000 can be claimed on the main and/or special rate pool where the unrelieved expenditure on the pool (after dealing with additions qualifying for WDAs and disposals in the period) is £1,000 or less. This allows the balance on a small pool to be written off at once.

The claim is optional. However, it is likely that the taxpayer will want to claim as much as possible and reduce the remaining balance on the pool to nil.

Example

Annabelle is in business as a sole trader and prepares accounts to 31 March. During the year ending 31 March 2022 she incurred the following expenditure:

15 May 2021	Purchased new office furniture for £13,800.
2 June 2021	Purchased a new car for £10,000 which Annabelle will use 20% of the time for private purposes. This car has CO_2 emissions of 42g/km.
10 June 2021	Installed a new computer system in her business premises at a cost of £9,200.

In addition on 1 July 2021 she sold office equipment for £10,000 (original cost £18,000).

As at 1 April 2021 the tax written down value on her main pool was £10,800.

Calculate Annabelle's maximum capital allowances for the year ended 31 March 2022.

Solution

Annabelle – Capital allowances computation

		Main pool	**Private use car (B.U. 80%)**	**B.U. %**	**Allowances**
	£	£	£		£
Year ended 31 March 2022					
TWDV b/f		10,800			
Additions:					
Not qualifying for AIA or FYA					
Car (emissions 1 – 50g/km)			10,000		
Qualifying for AIA:					
Computer system	9,200				
Furniture	13,800				
	23,000				
AIA	(23,000)				23,000
Balance to main pool		0			
Disposal proceeds		(10,000)			
		800	10,000		
Small pool WDA		(800)			800
WDA (18% × £10,000)			(1,800)	× 80%	1,440
TWDV c/f		0	8,200		
Total allowances					25,240

10 VAT

In some (**but not all**) examination questions you are given the figures for additions and disposals including value added tax (VAT). VAT is charged by businesses on most sales and hence when another business buys the item its cost will include VAT.

If a business is registered for value added tax (VAT) it can reclaim any VAT it has been charged on the purchase of tangible non-current assets. The only exception is cars, for which VAT can only be recovered if the car is used 100% for business (such as a driving school car).

If the business can reclaim the VAT then the cost of the asset in the capital allowances computation must be NET of VAT.

When the assets are sold, the business must charge VAT on the sale proceeds of any asset on which VAT was reclaimed on the purchase. Since the business must pay over any VAT it collects to HMRC, the actual proceeds kept by the business are the proceeds excluding VAT.

If the business has charged VAT on the sale, the proceeds figure in the capital allowances computation must be NET of VAT.

VAT is charged at 20%. You will find detailed coverage of VAT in Chapter 24.

Example

Kiran has a business manufacturing computers. She is registered for VAT. In the year ended 31 March 2022 she bought machinery costing £27,000 and a car for herself costing £12,780. She will use the car 60% for business. She also sold an old piece of machinery for £1,200.

All these figures **include** VAT at 20%.

Solution

In her capital allowances computation the additions will be:

Machinery £ 22,500 (£27,000 × 100/120)

Car £12,780 (VAT is not recoverable therefore capital allowances are claimed on the VAT inclusive price)

The disposal proceeds will be:

Machinery £1,000 (£1,200 × 100/120)

11 APPROACH TO COMPUTATIONAL QUESTIONS

For plant and machinery capital allowances for sole traders, adopt the following step-by-step approach. The approach is similar for companies but slightly adapted (see Chapter 21).

1 Read the information in the question and decide how many columns/pools you will require.

2 Draft the layout and insert the TWDV b/f (does not apply in a new trade).

3 Insert additions not eligible for the AIA or FYA into the appropriate column taking particular care to allocate cars into the correct columns according to their CO_2 emissions.

4 Insert additions eligible for the AIA in the first column, and then allocate the AIA to the additions.

Allocate the AIA to special rate pool additions in priority to additions of plant and machinery in the main pool or short life asset columns.

Remember to time apportion the AIA if the accounting period is not 12 months.

5 Any special rate pool additions in excess of the AIA must be added to the special rate pool column to increase the balance available for 6% WDA.

Any main pool expenditure, in excess of the AIA, should be added to the main pool to increase the balance qualifying for 18% WDA.

6 Deal with any disposal by deducting the lower of cost and sale proceeds.

7 Work out any balancing charge where a balance has become negative or balancing allowance for assets in single asset columns.

Remember to adjust for any private use by the owner if an unincorporated business.

8 Consider whether the small pool WDA applies to the main and/or special rate pools and time apportion the limit if the accounting period is not 12 months.

9 Calculate the WDA on each of the pools at the appropriate rate (18% or 6%).

Remember to:

- time apportion if the accounting period is not 12 months
- adjust for any private use by the owner if an unincorporated business.

10 Insert additions eligible for the FYA (new zero emission cars) in the first column and give the FYA. Remember this is not time apportioned.

11 Calculate the TWDV to carry forward to the next accounting period and add the allowances column.

12 Deduct the total allowances from the tax adjusted trading profits.

Pro forma capital allowances computation – sole traders

		Main pool	Special rate pool	Short life asset	Private use asset	Allowances
	£	£	£	£	£	£
TWDV b/f		X	X	X		
Additions:						
Not qualifying for AIA or FYA:						
Cars (1 – 50g/km or second hand zero emission)		X				
Cars (over 50g/km)			X			
Car with private use					X	
Qualifying for AIA:						
Special rate pool expenditure	X					
AIA (Max £1,000,000 in total)	(X)					X
	——					
Balance to special rate pool			X			
Plant and machinery	X					
AIA (balance) (Max £1,000,000 in total)	(X)					X
	——					
Balance to main pool		X				
Disposals (lower of original cost and sale proceeds)		(X)	(X)	(X)		
		——	——	——	——	
		X	X	X	X	
BA/(BC)				X/(X)		X/(X)
				——		
Small pools WDA (if applicable)						
WDA at 18%		(X)				X
WDA at 6%			(X)			X
WDA at 6%/18% (depending on emissions)					(X) × BU%	X
Qualifying for FYA						
New zero emissions cars	X					
FYA at 100%	(X)					X
	——					
		0				
		——	——		——	
TWDV c/f		X	X		X	
		——	——		——	——
Total allowances						X
						——

ACTIVITY 6

On 1 October 2021, Gordon commenced in self-employment running a music recording studio. He prepared his first set of accounts for the three months to 31 December 2021.

Gordon purchased the following assets:

		£
1 October 2021	Recording equipment	277,875
15 October 2021	Motor car with CO_2 emissions of 79g/km (used by Gordon – 60% business use)	15,800
20 October 2021	Motor car with CO_2 emissions of 48g/km (used by employee – 20% private use)	10,400
4 December 2021	Recording equipment (expected to be scrapped in 2 years)	3,250

Calculate Gordon's capital allowances for the period ended 31 December 2021 assuming all beneficial claims have been made. Ignore VAT.

For a suggested answer, see the 'Answers' section at the end of the book.

12 STRUCTURES AND BUILDINGS ALLOWANCE (SBA)

12.1 INTRODUCTION

The following expenditure qualifies for a 3% straight line **SBA** for a 12 month accounting period, if it is used in a trade or property letting:

- Buildings including offices, retail and wholesale premises, factories and warehouses.
- Structures including walls, bridges and tunnels.
- Costs of converting, renovating or improving the property also qualify for a separate allowance from the original purchase price (if that also qualified).
- When an unused building is purchased from a builder or developer the qualifying cost is the price paid less the value of the land.

The building must have been constructed or renovated on or after 6 April 2020 to qualify for SBAs in the FTX exam. The construction date will be provided in the exam questions. If the building is purchased (rather than constructed), you should assume that the SBA is not available unless the question states otherwise.

The following expenditure does not qualify:

- land and professional fees
- residential property or buildings that function as dwellings.

Unlike the AIA, FYA and WDA, the SBA can only be claimed from when the asset is bought into use and must be **time apportioned** if that is part way through the accounting period. SBAs will also be time apportioned for short or long periods.

Capital allowances are not available on the cost of structures and buildings but would be available on any qualifying plant and machinery purchased as well. Expenditure can never qualify for both capital allowances for plant and machinery and SBAs.

12.2 DISPOSAL OF THE ASSET

On disposal the following steps should be followed:

- There is no balancing adjustment for the seller.
- The buyer takes over the remainder of the life of the SBA (33⅓ years) and receives a 3% SBA based on the original cost of the structure or building.
- The seller adds the SBAs claimed to the sales proceeds when calculating the capital gain on disposal (see Chapter 17).

Example

Helen purchased a building for £270,000 (excluding the value of land) from a property developer to use in her trade. She purchased the building on 1 June 2021, but the property was not used in the trade until 1 September 2021.

On 1 November 2022, Helen sold the building to Amina for £375,000. Amina immediately started to use the building for trading purposes.

Both Helen and Amina prepare accounts to 31 December.

Calculate Helen and Amina's capital allowances for the years ended 31 December 2021, 2022 and 2023.

Solution

Helen

Year ended 31 December 2021	Helen will be entitled to a 3% straight line SBA from when the building is brought into use on 1 September 2021. (3% × £270,000 × 4/12) = £2,700
Year ended 31 December 2022	Helen will be able to claim allowances up to the date of disposal. (3% × £270,000 × 10/12) = £6,750

Amina

Year ended 31 December 2022	Amina will be able to claim allowances for the last two months to 31 December 2022. (3% × £270,000 × 2/12) = £1,350
Year ended 31 December 2023	Amina will be able to claim SBA for the whole period. (3% x £270,000) = £8,100

Note There is no balancing adjustment on disposal. The price Amina paid for the building does not affect the SBA available, which is always based on original cost.

KEY TERMS

Capital allowances – a standardised version of depreciation for tax purposes.

Plant – an item **with which** the trade is carried on as opposed to an item which is merely part of the premises **in which** the trade is carried on.

Annual investment allowance – a 100% allowance for expenditure incurred by a business on plant and machinery. The maximum allowance is £1,000,000 in each 12 month accounting period.

Writing down allowance – an annual allowance that writes off part of the cost of an asset for tax purposes.

First year allowance – an allowance on new zero emissions cars only. Never apply pro rata.

Balancing charge – a negative capital allowance that can arise on any pool (including a single asset pool) at any time when the disposal proceeds exceed the tax written down balance on the pool. The balancing charge recovers the excess allowances given.

Balancing allowance – the allowance given in the final period of ownership of an asset (for a single asset pool) or on the cessation of the business. It is the amount necessary to make the total allowances equate exactly to the net cost of the asset.

Hire purchase – a method of purchasing an asset over a period of time. The asset is effectively hired until the final payment is made.

Short life asset – an asset that will be sold or scrapped within eight years of the end of the accounting period in which the asset was acquired.

Structures and buildings allowance – an annual allowance that writes off part of the cost of a structure or building for tax purposes.

SELF TEST QUESTIONS

		Paragraph
1	Who may claim capital allowances?	1.2
2	What distinction does the function test make in determining whether an asset qualifies as plant or not?	2.2
3	State two assets that are specifically deemed to be plant by legislation.	2.3
4	How is the WDA affected if the accounting period is less than 12 months long?	3.3
5	On which cars can FYAs be given?	3.4
6	When plant is sold what amount is deducted from the pool?	3.5
7	In what circumstances do balancing allowances arise?	3.7
8	Which allowances are given in the period to cessation?	3.8
9	What is the treatment of an asset bought on hire purchase?	4
10	What is the rate of WDA that can be claimed in respect of a car with CO_2 emissions of 60g/km?	5
11	How are allowances calculated on assets used partly for private purposes by the trader?	6
12	How does the calculation of capital allowances on short life assets differ from that of 'normal' assets?	7
13	A retail premises, used in the trade, is purchased and brought into use three months later, which date should be used when calculating the structures and building allowance?	12

MULTIPLE CHOICE QUESTIONS

1 Kelly runs a small business, which she started on 1 May 2021. She prepared her first set of accounts for the nine months to 31 January 2022. On 1 June 2021, she purchased a car for £12,500 which she uses 30% for business purposes. The car has CO_2 emissions of 40g/km.

What are the capital allowances available to her for the period ended 31 January 2022?

A £3,750

B £1,688

C £675

D £506

2 Gideon draws up accounts to 30 June each year. On 5 August 2022 he sold a car for £17,200, which had originally been purchased on 1 September 2021 for £18,000. This car has CO_2 emissions of 90g/km and was not used privately by Gideon. On 1 July 2021 Gideon had balances of nil on his capital allowance pools.

For the year ended 30 June 2023, this transaction results in capital allowances of:

A £280 balancing charge

B £280 balancing allowance

C £2,440 balancing charge

D £2,440 balancing allowance

3 Which one of the following would not qualify for capital allowances?

A Movable partitions in an office

B Swimming pools at a caravan park

C False ceilings in a restaurant installed to cover pipes

D Costs of altering factory to install new machinery.

4 Ernie has a business and draws up accounts to 31 October each year. He purchases an office building, for use in his trade, on 1 February 2021 for £500,000. It is brought into use the same day. How much structures and building allowance could Ernie claim for the year ended 31 October 2021?

A £11,250

B £15,000

C £500,000

D £67,500

For suggested answers, see the 'Answers' section at the end of the book.

PRACTICE QUESTIONS

1 BORIS

Boris has been trading for many years, preparing accounts to 31 March annually.

His main pool of unrelieved expenditure on plant and machinery brought forward on 1 April 2021 was £7,000.

In the two years ended 31 March 2023 the following transactions took place.

Year ended 31 March 2022

1 June 2021	Sold two lorries (purchased for £8,450 each) for £2,750 each. Purchased two replacement lorries for £5,250 each.
1 Oct 2021	Purchased plant costing £9,000.
1 Dec 2021	Purchased two cars costing £6,600 each. One of the cars is used 30% for private purposes by Boris. Both have CO_2 emissions of 45g/km.

Year ended 31 March 2023

1 May 2022	Purchased plant costing £1,000
18 Nov 2022	Purchased two new cars costing £5,200 each (used wholly for business purposes). One car has CO_2 emissions of 48g/km and the other has zero emissions.
1 January 2023	Sold both cars purchased on 1 December 2021 for £2,000 each.

Required:

Compute the capital allowances available to Boris for the years ended 31 March 2022 and 31 March 2023. Assume capital allowance rules for the tax year 2021/22 continue into the future. Ignore VAT. **(15 marks)**

2 CHARLIE CEASING

Charlie Ceasing, who prepares his accounts to 5 August in each year, ceases to trade on 5 August 2022.

The tax written down value of the main pool after computing the capital allowances for the year ended 5 August 2020 was £1,210. Capital expenditure in the later periods of account was as follows:

Year ended 5 August 2021

		£
11 April 2021	Purchased motor car with 80% business use by Charlie (CO_2 emissions 45g/km)	16,100
30 April 2021	Purchased office equipment	450
1 May 2021	Sold office equipment	100
2 June 2021	Purchased delivery van	2,550 (second-hand)
10 June 2021	Sold plant and machinery	250

Year ended 5 August 2022

5 March 2022	Purchased office equipment (deposit paid £200 – balance £1,000 paid over 12 months from 5 April 2022)	1,200 (on HP)
10 July 2022	Sold office equipment	100

Following the cessation of trading, the remaining plant and equipment was sold for £2,250 (no item being sold for more than cost), the delivery van for £2,663 and Charlie kept the motor car for his own use. The market value of the motor car at 5 August 2022 was £5,455.

Required:

Calculate the capital allowances computations for Charlie for the years ended 5 August 2021 and 5 August 2022. Assume capital allowance rules for the tax year 2021/22 continue into the future. Ignore VAT. **(15 marks)**

3 CORDELIA

The following is the statement of profit or loss of Cordelia who has carried on her business for many years.

Statement of profit or loss – Year ended 30 June 2022

	£	£	£
Gross profit			75,862
Sale proceeds for plant (lower than cost)			2,000
Bank interest received			750
			78,612
Less: Expenses			
Wages (Note 1)		15,820	
Light and heat		870	
Telephone		543	
Motor expenses (Note 2)		752	
Depreciation			
Equipment	2,440		
Motor car (Note 2)	4,500		
		6,940	
Trade expenses (Note 3)		7,580	(32,505)
Net profit			46,107

Notes:

1 Wages includes Cordelia's drawings of £5,200.

2 Cordelia bought a car on 1 August 2021 for £17,000. Cordelia has calculated that 30% of the car's mileage relates to private use. She did not own a car before this purchase in August 2021. The car has CO_2 emissions of 40g/km.

3 Trade expenses

			£
Stationery			1,320
Entertaining customers			1,670
Subscriptions	–	political party	200
	–	Chamber of Commerce	250
Printing			4,140
			7,580

4 The tax written down value of the main pool at 1 July 2021 was £15,000.

Required:

Calculate Cordelia's tax adjusted trading profit for the year ended 30 June 2022.

(15 marks)

For suggested answers, see the 'Answers' section at the end of the book.

Chapter 5

BASIS PERIODS

INTRODUCTION

In Chapter 3 you learned how to take the accounting profit of a business and adjust it for the purposes of calculating tax adjusted trading profit. In Chapter 4, you learned how to calculate capital allowances. Capital allowances are deducted from the adjusted profit of a business to give the tax adjusted trading profit. This chapter now deals with the tax years in which those tax adjusted trading profits are taxed. This is referred to as the basis of assessment.

This chapter covers syllabus area B3.

CONTENTS	LEARNING OUTCOMES
1 Basis periods and tax years **2** The current year basis **3** Opening year rules **4** Overlap profits **5** Closing year rules	At the end of this chapter, you should be able to: • explain the basis of assessment for a continuing sole trader's business • explain and demonstrate the calculations of the basis of assessment for commencement and cessation of business • calculate overlap relief, explain and demonstrate how it can be used on cessation.

1 BASIS PERIODS AND TAX YEARS

Income tax is charged for tax years (also known as years of assessment) that run from 6 April to the following 5 April. Since traders normally do not make up their statements of profit or loss to coincide with the tax year, there needs to be a system for allocating profits earned in a period of account to a particular tax year.

The period of account that is attributed to a particular tax year is known as the 'basis period' for that tax year.

2 THE CURRENT YEAR BASIS

The basic rule is that the assessable profits for a tax year are the tax adjusted profits for the period of account ending in that year. This is known as the current year basis (or CYB for short).

In the examination, this basis should be used if a business is described as 'on-going' or 'trading for many years'.

Example

Erfan prepares accounts to 30 September annually. His profits for the two years to 30 September 2021 were:

	£
Year to 30 September 2020	20,000
Year to 30 September 2021	22,000

These form the basis periods for the tax years 2020/21 and 2021/22:

Tax year	**Basis of assessment**	**Assessable profits**
2020/21	Year to 30 September 2020	£20,000
2021/22	Year to 30 September 2021	£22,000

3 OPENING YEAR RULES

In order to ensure that there is an assessment for each tax year that a business is trading, assessments must commence in the tax year in which the business starts trading. This would not be the case if the current year basis was applied from the very start of a business. Therefore, the basis of assessment in the opening years is normally as follows:

Tax year	**Basis of assessment**
First tax year (tax year in which trade starts)	From: Date of commencement To: Following 5 April ('Actual basis')
Second tax year The period of account ending in the tax year is:	
(i) 12 months	That period of account (CYB)
(ii) less than 12 months	The first 12 months of trade
(iii) more than 12 months	12 months to the accounting date ending in the second tax year (i.e. last 12 months of long period of account)

There is **no period of account** ending in the second tax year	Actual profits in the second tax year: From: 6 April To: 5 April
Third tax year	12 months to the accounting date ending in the third tax year – normally CYB – if a long period of account = last 12 months of long period
Fourth tax year onwards	CYB

Note that whichever scenario applies, from tax year two onwards the basis period will always be exactly 12 months long.

The following examples and activities illustrate the four possible situations that can arise in tax year two.

Note that in examinations any apportionments are made on a monthly basis, with the last 5 days of the tax year being ignored. In the examination, you should also always state the tax year (just stating year 1 for example is insufficient) as well as the actual dates of the basis period.

Example

Arthur commenced trading on 1 July 2019. He prepared accounts to 30 June each year. His adjusted trading profits for the first two years were as follows:

	£
Year ended 30 June 2020	24,000
Year ended 30 June 2021	28,000

Calculate the trading profit assessments for the first three tax years of trading.

Solution

The assessable amounts of trading profit are as follows:

		£
2019/20		
(1 July 2019 – 5 April 2020)	(£24,000 × 9/12)	18,000
2020/21 (see note)		
(12 m/e 30 June 2020)		24,000
2021/22		
(12 m/e 30 June 2021)		28,000

Note: Because there is a period of account ending in 2020/21 that is 12 months long, the assessment is the 12 months ending on that accounting date.

> **Example**
>
> Raoul started to trade on 1 September 2019 and prepared his first accounts to 30 June 2020 and annually thereafter.
>
> His tax adjusted trading profits for the first two periods were as follows:
>
> | | |
> |---|---|
> | Period ended 30 June 2020 | £22,000 |
> | Year ended 30 June 2021 | £60,000 |
>
> Calculate the trading income assessments for the first three tax years.

Solution

The assessable amounts of trading profit are as follows:

		£
2019/20		
(1 September 2019 – 5 April 2020)	(£22,000 × 7/10)	15,400
2020/21 (see note)		
(First 12 months – 1 September 2019 – 31 August 2020)		
(£22,000 + £60,000 × 2/12)		32,000
2021/22		
(12 m/e 30 June 2021)		60,000

Note: The period of account ending in the second tax year, 2020/21, is less than 12 months long. Hence, the assessment must be based on the first 12 months of trading.

> **Example**
>
> Rafael started to trade on 1 May 2019 and prepared his first accounts to 31 July 2020 and annually thereafter.
>
> His tax adjusted trading profits for the first two periods were as follows:
>
> | | |
> |---|---|
> | Period ended 31 July 2020 | £45,000 |
> | Year ended 31 July 2021 | £37,000 |
>
> Calculate the trading income assessments for the first three tax years.

Solution

The assessable amounts of trading profit are as follows:

		£
2019/20		
(1 May 2019 – 5 April 2020)	(£45,000 × 11/15)	33,000
2020/21 (see note)		
(12 months ending on the normal accounting date)		
(£45,000 × 12/15)		36,000
2021/22		
(12 m/e 31 July 2021)		37,000

Note: The period of account ending in the second tax year, 2020/21, is more than 12 months long. Hence, the assessment is based on the 12 months ending on the normal accounting date in 2020/21, i.e. 12 months to 31 July 2020.

ACTIVITY 1

Edwina commenced trading on 1 July 2019. She prepared accounts to 31 March 2021 and annually thereafter. Her adjusted trading profits for the first two periods were as follows:

	£
21 months ended 31 March 2021	42,000
Year ended 31 March 2022	27,000

Calculate the trading profit assessments for the first three tax years of trading.

For a suggested answer, see the 'Answers' section at the end of the book.

Example

Maria started to trade on 1 December 2019 and prepared her first accounts to 30 April 2021 and annually thereafter.

Her tax adjusted trading profits for the first two periods were as follows:

Period ended 30 April 2021	£51,000
Year ended 30 April 2022	£37,000

Calculate the trading income assessments for the first three tax years.

Solution

The assessable amounts of trading profit are as follows:

		£
2019/20		
(1 Dec 2019 – 5 Apr 2020)	(£51,000 × 4/17)	12,000
2020/21 (see note)		
(Profits from 6 Apr 2020 to 5 Apr 2021)		
	(£51,000 × 12/17)	36,000
2021/22		
(12 m/e 30 Apr 2021)	(£51,000 × 12/17)	36,000

Note: There is no period of account ending in the second tax year, 2020/21. Hence, the assessment is based on the actual profits in the second tax year i.e. from 6 April 2020 to 5 April 2021.

ACTIVITY 2

Pattie commenced trading on 1 September 2019. She prepared accounts to 30 June 2020 and annually thereafter. Her adjusted trading profits for the first two periods were as follows:

	£
10 months ended 30 June 2020	30,000
Year ended 30 June 2021	48,000

Calculate the trading profit assessments for the first three tax years of trading.

For a suggested answer, see the 'Answers' section at the end of the book.

ACTIVITY 3

Caroline commenced trading on 1 July 2019. She prepared accounts to 30 April 2021 and annually thereafter. Her adjusted trading profits for the first two periods were as follows:

	£
22 months ended 30 April 2021	55,000
Year ended 30 April 2022	32,000

Calculate the trading profit assessments for the first three tax years of trading.

For a suggested answer, see the 'Answers' section at the end of the book.

4 OVERLAP PROFITS

In each of the above four opening year examples and in two of the three activities, it can be seen that some of the profits have been included in the assessable amounts for more than one tax year. The portion of profits that were assessed in more than one year are known as the '**overlap profits'**.

- The overlap profits are carried forward and **deducted** from the assessable amount for the tax year in which the business ceases.

- This ensures that the total adjusted profit earned over the life of the business is the same as the total trading profit assessed.

This did not apply in Activity 1, as the accounts were prepared to 31 March each year. There will be no overlap profits when the accounting date coincides with the tax year.

Remember that in examinations we ignore the 5 days from 31 March to 5 April and always perform calculations to the nearest month.

Example

The assessable amounts for the first two tax years in the above example involving Arthur were:

			£
2019/20	(1 July 2019 – 5 April 2020)	£24,000 × 9/12 =	18,000
2020/21	(12 m/e 30 June 2020)		24,000

The overlap profits which were assessed twice are those of the period 1 July 2019 – 5 April 2020 i.e. £24,000 × 9/12 = £18,000.

ACTIVITY 4

Calculate the overlap profits for Caroline in Activity 3.

For a suggested answer, see the 'Answers' section at the end of the book.

5 CLOSING YEAR RULES

The final tax year is the tax year in which the business ceases trading. In the final tax year, the assessment is based on the profit(s) from the end of the basis period of the previous tax year until the date of cessation.

Any unrelieved overlap profits are deducted in the final tax year.

Example

Moaz decided to retire from his carpet cleaning business and ceased trading on 31 December 2021.

His adjusted trading profits for the last few years of trading are as follows:

	£
Year ended 30 June 2019	18,000
Year ended 30 June 2020	22,000
Year ended 30 June 2021	21,000
Period ended 31 December 2021	12,000

Moaz had overlap profits of £7,350 brought forward.

What are his trading income assessments for the tax years 2019/20 to cessation?

Solution

When looking at a closing year's computation, it is important to determine the final tax year of trading. In this case the business ceases on 31 December 2021, which is in the tax year 2021/22. This means that the assessments up to that year are normal current year basis. The final tax year will tax all the remaining profits less overlap relief brought forward.

		£	£
2019/20	Year ended 30 June 2019		18,000
2020/21	Year ended 30 June 2020		22,000
2021/22	Year ended 30 June 2021	21,000	
	Period ended 31 December 2021	12,000	
		33,000	
	Less: Overlap profits	(7,350)	
			25,650

ACTIVITY 5

Michael commenced trading on 1 May 2011. After trading profitably for some years, he ceased trading on 31 March 2022. His adjusted trading profits for the final three periods are as follows:

	£
Year ended 30 April 2020	40,000
Year ended 30 April 2021	42,000
Period ended 31 March 2022	38,000

(a) Calculate Michael's trading profit assessments for each tax year to the date of cessation. Assume his overlap profits from commencement were £27,000.

(b) Assuming Michael delayed the cessation of trade until 30 April 2022 (but his profit figures were unchanged), how would Michael's trading profit assessments differ?

For a suggested answer, see the 'Answers' section at the end of the book.

ACTIVITY 6

Lucy started in business as a magician on 6 April 2021. She prepared accounts for the 15 months to 30 June 2022 and then annually thereafter.

Before capital allowances, her results, as adjusted for tax purposes, were:

Fifteen months to 30 June 2022	£27,360
Year to 30 June 2023	£21,660

She bought equipment as follows:

1 July 2021	£6,900
1 August 2021	£5,100
1 May 2022	£1,600

She bought a car on 10 June 2022 for £8,000 (40% private use). She sold it on 20 June 2023 and replaced it with one costing £16,000 (again, with 40% private use). The garage gave her a trade in allowance of £4,000 on her old one. Both cars have CO_2 emissions of 40g/km.

Calculate:

(a) the capital allowances for the two periods of account ending 30 June 2022 and 30 June 2023. (Assume capital allowance rules for the tax year 2021/22 continue into the future.)

(b) the trading profit assessments for the tax years 2021/22, 2022/23 and 2023/24.

(c) the overlap profits.

Note: All aspects of this question are examinable in FTX, however, since the maximum marks in any one question is 10 (excluding the income tax and corporation tax questions), there would not be as much detail as this within one question. It has been included here as it is useful practice on this topic.

For a suggested answer, see the 'Answers' section at the end of the book.

CONCLUSION

It is important to remember that the opening and closing year rules detailed above are applied to the trading profits **after** the deduction of capital allowances. Where a question requires you to compute capital allowances and apply the opening or closing year rules, it is essential that you tackle the answer in the following order:

- Calculate the capital allowances for the periods of account produced by the business. Remember that if a period of account is less/(more) than 12 months' long, any WDA and AIA will need to be scaled down/(up) proportionately.
- Deduct the capital allowances from the adjusted profits. This will give you the tax adjusted trading profits.
- Apply the opening or closing year rules as appropriate.

KEY TERMS

Basis period – the period of account that is attributed to a particular tax year.

Current year basis – the system of taxing profits according to the period of account ending in the tax year.

Overlap profits – profits that are taxed in more than one tax year.

Period of account – the period for which a set of accounts is prepared.

SELF TEST QUESTIONS

		Paragraph
1	What is the normal basis of assessment for a continuing business?	2
2	How is a business assessed in its opening years?	3
3	What are overlap profits and how are they relieved?	4
4	What is the basis of assessment in the closing years of a business?	5

MULTIPLE CHOICE QUESTIONS

1 Rihanna has been a sole trader for many years preparing her accounts to 31 August each year. She ceased to trade on 31 January 2022. Rihanna's most recent adjusted profits for tax purposes have been:

Year ended 31 August 2020	£19,200
Year ended 31 August 2021	£16,800
5 months ended 31 January 2022	£8,400

She has overlap profits brought forward from commencement of trade amounting to £4,800.

What is Rihanna's taxable trading profit figure for the tax year 2021/22?

A £25,200

B £20,400

C £16,800

D £3,600

2 Hardeep started to trade on 1 June 2021. His tax adjusted profits for the year ended 31 May 2022 are £50,000.

What is Hardeep's taxable trading profit for the tax year 2021/22?

A £37,500

B £41,667

3 Xosé commenced trading on 1 February 2021 and prepared his first set of accounts to 30 June 2022. The period upon which his profits will be assessed for the second tax year of trading is:

A 1 February 2021 to 5 April 2021

B 1 February 2021 to 31 January 2022

C 6 April 2021 to 5 April 2022

D 12 months ended 30 June 2022

For suggested answers, see the 'Answers' section at the end of the book.

PRACTICE QUESTIONS

1 GRACE (PART ONE)

Grace started business on 1 January 2022. She prepared accounts to 31 October 2022 and annually thereafter. Her adjusted trading profits for the first two periods were as follows:

	£
10 months ended 31 October 2022	31,786
Year ended 31 October 2023	45,954

She bought equipment as follows:

	£
1 July 2022	7,480
1 August 2022	2,600

She bought a car on 1 January 2022 for £16,000. Private use was calculated at 20%. The car has CO_2 emissions of 45g/km.

She sold equipment on 1 April 2023 for £560. The equipment had been purchased on 1 July 2022 for £1,120 and is included within the purchases above.

Required:

Calculate the capital allowances for the two periods of account ending 31 October 2022 and 31 October 2023. (Assume capital allowance rules for the tax year 2021/22 continue.) **(10 marks)**

2 GRACE (PART TWO)

For this question, use the details provided in question one above.

Required:

Calculate the trading profit assessments for the tax years 2021/22 2022/23 and 2023/24. Your answer should include the amount of overlap profits and state how they will be relieved. **(6 marks)**

For a suggested answer, see the 'Answers' section at the end of the book.

Chapter 6

TRADING LOSSES

INTRODUCTION

So far in this text we have concentrated on situations where traders have made profits. However, we need to know how to deal with losses incurred by traders and this is the subject of this chapter.

A trading loss arises when the accounting profit or loss as adjusted for tax purposes is negative. Where the tax adjusted result for a period of account is a loss, there are two effects:

1 the trading income assessment based on that loss is nil and

2 the loss can be used to reduce taxable income.

This chapter explains the methods of doing this.

Although you are not required to learn the sections of legislation for your examination, loss reliefs can be referred to by their section number. The section numbers are from the Income Tax Act (ITA) 2007.

This chapter covers syllabus area B4.

CONTENTS	LEARNING OUTCOMES
1 Loss reliefs for businesses **2** Loss relief by carry forward **3** Loss relief against total income	At the end of this chapter you should be able to: • explain the alternative loss reliefs available to a sole trader • demonstrate the best use of a loss relief claim.

1 LOSS RELIEFS FOR BUSINESSES

The two examinable reliefs available for a trading loss, as explained in the following sections, are as follows:

- s83 ITA 2007 – carry forward against future trading profits
- s64 ITA 2007 – relief against total income.

Section numbers are not required in the examination and will not be used further in this text.

2 LOSS RELIEF BY CARRY FORWARD

A trading loss may be carried forward and set against the **first** future taxable trading profits arising in the **same** trade.

Example

Jenna carries on two trades, umbrella manufacture and ice-cream sales. She makes a loss in her ice-cream business.

She cannot carry the ice-cream business loss forward and deduct it from the profits of the umbrella manufacture trade. She can only carry it forward and deduct it from the profits of the ice-cream business.

The loss may be carried forward indefinitely, but must be set off as soon as possible. You cannot miss a year out or choose to deduct the loss from only part of the profits.

- A claim must be made to establish the amount of the loss to be carried forward within four years from the end of the tax year in which the loss arose.
- Once the claim has been established, the loss will be used automatically against the future trading profits without the need for a further claim.

When dealing with the set off of losses it is useful to adopt a columnar layout, presenting each tax year in a separate column. It is important to state the tax years, rather than, for example, year 1 and year 2 or year ended 31 March 2022.

Keep a separate working to show when, and how much of, the loss has been used up. This working is usually referred to as a loss memorandum. This working should also show how much loss (if any) is carried forward at the end of the period.

The trading income in the tax year of the loss should always be shown as £0.

Example

Michael has been trading for many years as a retailer. His recent tax adjusted trading profits are as follows:

		£
Year ended 31 August 2019	Loss	(9,000)
Year ended 31 August 2020	Profit	6,000
Year ended 31 August 2021	Profit	19,000

Calculate Michael's net taxable trading income for the tax years 2019/20 to 2021/22, assuming he carries the loss forward.

Solution

	2019/20	2020/21	2021/22
	£	£	£
Trading income	0	6,000	19,000
Less: Loss relief b/f	0	(6,000)	(3,000)
Net trading income	0	0	16,000

Working – loss memorandum

Trading loss in year ended 31 August 2019	9,000
Less: Relief in 2020/21	(6,000)
	3,000
Less: Relief in 2021/22	(3,000)
Loss carried forward to 2022/23	0

Note that the loss arises in the tax year 2019/20, i.e. the tax year in which the period of account ends. Losses are allocated to tax years in the same way as tax adjusted profits (see Section 3). The 2019/20 assessment, i.e. the one based on the loss making period, is £0.

The loss is set off first against the trade income of 2020/21 and then 2021/22.

It must be used against the first available trade profits which means you cannot miss a year or make partial claims.

ACTIVITY 1

Manraj has the following tax adjusted trading results:

		£
Year to 31 December 2019	Loss	(5,000)
Year to 31 December 2020	Profit	3,000
Year to 31 December 2021	Profit	10,000

Assuming that Manraj wishes to claim loss relief only by carrying the loss forward, calculate his taxable trading profits for the tax years 2019/20 to 2021/22 inclusive.

For a suggested answer, see the 'Answers' section at the end of the book.

3 LOSS RELIEF AGAINST TOTAL INCOME

3.1 INTRODUCTION

If a business makes losses for several years or has a period of low profits, then obtaining relief by carrying the loss forward may take a long time. Consequently, there is another loss relief option available to taxpayers.

They may claim to relieve trading losses against **their total income of the tax year of the loss and/or the previous one**.

- Total income is the individual's income from all sources for the tax year, before the personal allowance.

- This relief allows a trading loss to be deducted from income not obtained from the trade.
- This reduces the amount of tax payable and may lead to a tax repayment.
- The personal allowance is deducted from net income (i.e. total income after deducting reliefs). Therefore, a claim against total income may involve wasting the personal allowance. The personal allowance for 2021/22 is £12,570.

There is a temporary extension to the period for which losses can be carried back, but this is not covered in this chapter as it is not examinable.

3.2 CALCULATING THE LOSS

The loss is calculated, and allocated to tax years, in the same way as profits. Therefore, a loss for the year ended 31 March 2022 arises in the tax year 2021/22 and may therefore be relieved against total income of the tax year 2021/22 and/or 2020/21.

Capital allowances are treated as an expense in arriving at the tax adjusted trading profit or loss, so they are relieved as an integral part of the loss.

ACTIVITY 2

Graham prepares accounts to 31 December annually. His recent tax adjusted results are as follows:

		£
Year to 31 December 2020	Profit	10,000
Year to 31 December 2021	Loss	(6,000)
Year to 31 December 2022	Profit	12,000

In which tax years can a claim be made to deduct the loss from total income?

For a suggested answer, see the 'Answers' section at the end of the book.

3.3 LOSS PRO FORMA

When answering examination questions on losses, it is useful to remember the following pro forma which shows how the losses are dealt with in the computation of taxable income.

This pro forma is based on a business making a trading loss in 2021/22 which is used against total income in 2021/22 and 2020/21, before the balance is carried forward to 2022/23 and deducted from trading income only.

	2020/21	2021/22	2022/23
	£	£	£
Trading income	X	0	X
Less: Loss b/f			(X)3
			X
Other income	X	X	X
Total income	X	X	X
Loss relief against total income	(X)2	(X)1	–
Net income	0	0	X
Less: PA	Wasted	Wasted	(X)
Taxable income	0	0	X

3.4 OBTAINING RELIEF FOR THE LOSS

- The taxpayer can relieve the loss against total income of:
  - the tax year of the loss, followed by a claim against total income of the previous year, or
  - the previous tax year, followed by a claim against total income of the current year, or
  - either tax year in isolation.
- In each case, any unrelieved loss is carried forward to deduct from future trading profits.

The key point to note is that the taxpayer cannot decide to set only part of his or her loss against total income; it must be set off to the maximum possible extent for a given year.

Other points to note:

- The two years available for potential claims are treated separately and thus a claim is required for each year.
- A written claim must be made within 12 months of 31 January following the end of the tax year of loss. For a 2021/22 loss this would be by 31 January 2024.
- A taxpayer may have losses for two consecutive tax years and wish to relieve both against total income. In these circumstances the total income of a year is relieved by the loss of that year, in priority to the loss carried back from the following year.

3.5 CHOICE OF LOSS RELIEF

As you have seen, a taxpayer has a choice of loss relief claims. In deciding which claims are most beneficial, the following three points should be considered:

- Where possible, the taxpayer should avoid wasting the personal allowance. As it is not possible to restrict a loss relief claim in order to use the full amount of personal allowance, it might be better to omit a loss relief claim in a year if income only just exceeds the personal allowance.

- If possible, a taxpayer should also avoid offsetting losses against income which is taxed at 0%, i.e. savings or dividend income in the starting or nil rate bands (see Chapter 14). Loss relief should be claimed against income taxable at the higher or additional rate of tax if possible.

- If the taxpayer is liable at the same rate of tax in all the years in which it is possible to relieve the loss, relief should be claimed against the earliest year possible.

If an examination question states that losses should be claimed as early as possible, this means a prior year claim should be made, followed by a current year claim if there is sufficient loss, regardless of whether it wastes the personal allowance.

If an examination question states to assume that all beneficial claims are made, this means that a claim should not be made against a tax year where either the income against which it is set would be taxed at 0% or would be covered by the personal allowance. In both these cases the loss would be used without there being a saving of tax.

Example

Fernando prepares accounts annually to 30 April each year. His recent results are:

		£
Year ended 30 April 2020	Profit	34,000
Year ended 30 April 2021	Loss	(42,000)
Year ended 30 April 2022	Profit	21,000

Fernando receives other income of £5,000 each year.

Show how relief for the loss would be given against total income, assuming all beneficial claims are made. Assume the personal allowance for all tax years is £12,570.

Solution

The loss is for the year ended 30 April 2021 i.e. a 21/22 loss. This may be set off against net income of 2021/22 and/or 2020/21.

	2020/21	**2021/22**
	£	£
Trading income:		
Year ended 30 April 2020	34,000	
Year ended 30 April 2021		0
Other income	5,000	5,000
Total income	39,000	5,000
Loss relief against total income (Note)	(39,000)	0
Net income	0	5,000
Less: PA (max)	0	(5,000)
Taxable income	0	0

Note: It is not beneficial to deduct the loss from the 2021/22 income as this is covered by the personal allowance. It would use £5,000 of the loss but save no tax.

The personal allowance for 2020/21 is wasted as the loss **cannot** be restricted to protect the personal allowance. However, without the loss relief claim taxable income, after the personal allowance would be £26,430 (£39,000 - £12,570) so even with the loss of the personal allowance it would still be beneficial to make the claim as a significant amount of tax has been saved.

Working: Loss memorandum

	£
Trading loss in year ended 30 April 2021	42,000
Less: Used in current year claim	0
Used in claim against prior year	(39,000)
Loss remaining to carry forward against future trading profits	3,000

ACTIVITY 3

Adrian prepares accounts annually to 31 December. His recent results have been:

		£
Year ended 31 December 2020	Profit	31,200
Year ended 31 December 2021	Loss	(48,000)
Year ended 31 December 2022	Profit	62,000

Adrian has other income of £5,000 for the tax year 2020/21 and £3,500 for the tax year 2021/22.

Show how relief for the loss would be given against total income, assuming that Adrian makes all claims to the extent that they are beneficial.

What loss, if any, is available for carry forward against trading profits after all claims against total income have been made?

For a suggested answer, see the 'Answers' section at the end of the book.

3.6 CAPITAL ALLOWANCES

Capital allowances can increase a trading loss or turn a profit into a loss.

It is not necessary for a business to claim the full amount of capital allowances. Any part of the allowances that is not claimed is added back to the TWDV to increase the WDA in the future. Such a reduced claim can be used to reduce a loss.

However, in the FTX examination, since tax planning is not in the syllabus, questions on capital allowances will always require a calculation of the maximum allowances available.

3.7 CHARGEABLE GAINS

For FTX, trading loss claims against chargeable gains will not be made.

Do not combine chargeable gains with income for individuals – they are always dealt with separately.

KEY TERMS

Carry forward relief – involves carrying a trading loss forward and setting it against the first available trading profits of the same trade.

Claim against total income – involves setting the trading loss against total income of the tax year of the loss and/or the preceding year.

SELF TEST QUESTIONS

		Paragraph
1	What is the time limit for making a claim to establish the amount of loss that may be carried forward?	2
2	Against the income of which tax years can a loss relief claim against total income be made?	3.1
3	What is the time limit for a claim against total income?	3.4
4	Can a claim against total income be restricted in order to avoid wasting the personal allowance?	3.4
5	What are the three principles that should be considered in deciding which loss relief to claim?	3.5

MULTIPLE CHOICE QUESTIONS

1 Heeya has been trading for many years and incurred a tax adjusted trading loss for the period ended 31 October 2021.

Which of the following statements is correct with regard to the use of the loss?

A The loss may be carried forward and set against trading income for the tax year 2021/22 arising from the same trade

B The loss can be set against total income for the tax year 2021/22, but only after the loss is set against total income for the tax year 2020/21

C The loss can be set against total income for the tax year 2020/21, irrespective of whether the loss has been set against total income for the tax year 2021/22

D The loss can be set against taxable income for the tax year 2020/21 and/or 2021/22

2 Janice has been trading as a picture framer for many years. Her recent results have been as follows:

Year ended 30 June 2019	£30,000
Year ended 30 June 2020	£25,000
Year ended 30 June 2021	(£45,000)

Janice's only other income is bank interest of £5,000 each year.

Assuming that Janice claims relief for her loss in the most efficient way, how much loss, if any, is available to carry forward to the tax year 2022/23?

A £0

B £15,000

C £20,000

D £10,000

3 Which of the following statements about losses is true?

A A trade loss can only be carried forward for a maximum of two years.

B A trade loss carried forward must be deducted from future profits of the same trade.

C A claim against total income must be made for the tax year of loss first before carrying it back to the previous year.

D When a loss is deducted from total income it can be restricted to allow the personal allowance to be relieved in full.

For suggested answers, see the 'Answers' section at the end of the book.

PRACTICE QUESTION

THANAYI

Thanayi commenced trading as a part-time pleasure boat operator on 1 April 2011. Recent results have been as follows:

	Trading profit/(loss)
	£
Year ended 31 March 2021	12,055
Year ended 31 March 2022	(13,375)

Thanayi's other income comprises

	Years ended 5 April	
	2021	2022
	£	£
Thanayi:		
Part-time salary from Deephaven Docks Ltd	6,600	6,825
Property income	3,520	4,000

Required:

Calculate the taxable income of Thanayi for the tax years 2020/21 and 2021/22 assuming loss relief is taken at the earliest opportunity.

Assume the personal allowance is £12,570 for both years. **(6 marks)**

For a suggested answer, see the 'Answers' section at the end of the book.

Chapter 7

TAXATION OF PARTNERSHIPS

INTRODUCTION

Although a partnership is a single trading entity, for tax purposes each individual partner is effectively treated as trading in his or her own right.

The partnership profit is firstly adjusted for tax purposes, this is then divided between the partners according to the profit sharing arrangements and each partner is individually taxed on his or her share of trading profit.

This chapter covers syllabus area B5.

CONTENTS	LEARNING OUTCOMES
	At the end of this chapter, you should be able to: • explain how the trading profit rules are adapted for partnerships • explain and show the effect of capital allowances on partnerships • demonstrate the effect of changes in partnerships • illustrate the loss relief claims available to individual partners.

1 TRADING PROFIT ASSESSMENTS FOR INDIVIDUAL PARTNERS

1.1 INTRODUCTION

The partnership is not itself liable to income tax. Instead, the tax adjusted trading profits of the partnership are divided between the individual partners. Each partner is taxed on his or her share of profits.

The basic steps in dealing with partnerships are:

- Calculate capital allowances for the partnership's period of account.
- Adjust the partnership's accounting profit and deduct the capital allowances from it to arrive at the figure of tax adjusted trading profits.
- Allocate the tax adjusted trading profit between the partners.
- Apply the basis period rules to each partner individually to allocate his or her share of the partnership profit to a tax year.

1.2 THE COMPUTATION OF PARTNERSHIP PROFITS AND LOSSES

The principles of computation of a partnership's tax adjusted trading profit or loss are the same as those for a sole trader.

Partners' salaries and interest on capital are not deductible, since these are an allocation of profit rather than an expense of the business.

1.3 THE ALLOCATION OF THE PROFIT OR LOSS

The tax adjusted trading profit or loss is allocated between the partners according to their profit sharing arrangements for that period of account.

Partners may be entitled to salaries (a fixed allocation of profit) and interest on capital. These are allocated first and deducted from the total profit for the period. The **balance** is allocated in the profit sharing ratio.

Example

Harriet, Jacqui and Kylie have been in business for many years. They share profits as follows:

Interest on fixed capital	10%
Salaries	
Harriet	£3,000 per annum
Jacqui	£4,000 per annum
Kylie	£3,000 per annum
Share of balance	
Harriet	60%
Jacqui	20%
Kylie	20%

Capital account balances were as follows :

Harriet	£10,000
Jacqui	£5,000
Kylie	£5,000

The tax adjusted trading profit of the partnership for the year ended 31 December 2021 was £80,000.

Show how this profit is allocated between the partners.

Solution

Profits are allocated as follows:

	Total	**Harriet**	**Jacqui**	**Kylie**
	£	£	£	£
Interest on capital				
(10% × Capital balance)	2,000	1,000	500	500
Salaries	10,000	3,000	4,000	3,000
	12,000			
Balance (60:20:20)	68,000	40,800	13,600	13,600
	80,000	44,800	18,100	17,100

Even though there is reference to salaries and interest it is important to remember that this is just a way of allocating profits. For example, Harriet is treated as having £44,800 of tax adjusted trading profits, **not** employment income.

2 COMPUTATION OF CAPITAL ALLOWANCES FOR A PARTNERSHIP

2.1 PARTNERSHIP ASSETS

Capital allowances are deducted as an expense in calculating the tax adjusted trading profit or loss. The profit allocated between the partners is therefore **after** capital allowances.

Example

Edwina and Charles have been in partnership for many years. Their profit, as adjusted for tax purposes but before capital allowances, for the year ended 31 March 2022 is £62,600.

The tax written down value on the main pool at 1 April 2021 was £20,000.

The following purchase of plant was made in the year:

1 June 2021 £8,400

The profits were shared between Edwina and Charles in the ratio 4:3 after paying salaries of £8,000 and £6,000.

Show the assessable trading income for each of the partners for the tax year 2021/22.

Solution

Capital allowance computation for y/e 31 March 2022

		Main pool	Allowances
	£	£	£
TWDV b/f		20,000	
Addition qualifying for AIA	8,400		
AIA	(8,400)		8,400
Balance to main pool		0	
		20,000	
WDA (18%)		(3,600)	3,600
TWDV c/f		16,400	
Total allowances			12,000

Tax adjusted trading profit for y/e 31 March 2022

	£
Adjusted profit before capital allowances	62,600
Capital allowances	(12,000)
Tax adjusted trading profit	50,600

Allocation of partnership profit for y/e 31 March 2022

	Total	Edwina	Charles
	£	£	£
Salaries	14,000	8,000	6,000
Balance (4:3)	36,600	20,914	15,686
	50,600	28,914	21,686

Taxable trading income for 2021/22

For the tax year 2021/22 Edwina and Charles are taxed on the current year basis on trading profits of £28,914 and £21,686 respectively (i.e. their share of the adjusted profit for the year ended 31 March 2022).

2.2 ASSETS OWNED INDIVIDUALLY BY PARTNERS

Individual partners cannot claim capital allowances on their own behalf. Instead, the partnership as a whole must claim.

3 CHANGE IN THE PROFIT SHARING ARRANGEMENTS

If a partnership changes its basis of profit sharing during a period of account, then the profit or loss must be time apportioned accordingly, prior to allocation between the partners.

Any salaries or interest on capital must also be time apportioned.

After the two time apportioned profit allocations have been calculated the profit allocation for each partner for the full accounting period should be totalled.

Example

Irmak and Tyanna are in partnership preparing accounts to 31 October each year. Their tax adjusted trading profit for the year to 31 October 2021 was £96,000.

Until 1 January 2021 they shared profits equally. From that date it was decided that Irmak should receive an annual salary of £24,000 with the balance of profits being shared 2:3 (Irmak: Tyanna).

Show the allocation of the profits for the year ended 31 October 2021 and state in which tax year these profit shares will be taxed.

Solution

Allocation of profits for the year ended 31 October 2021

	Total	**Irmak**	**Tyanna**
	£	£	£
1 November 2020 – 31 December 2020 (2 months)			
(Profits £96,000 × 2/12 = £16,000)			
Balance 1: 1	16,000	8,000	8,000
1 January 2021 – 31 October 2021 (10 months)			
(Profits £96,000 × 10/12 = £80,000)			
Salary (£24,000 × 10/12)	20,000	20,000	
Balance (2:3)	60,000	24,000	36,000
	80,000	44,000	36,000
Total allocation – taxable in 2021/22	96,000	52,000	44,000

ACTIVITY 1

David and Peter are in partnership. Their tax adjusted trading profit for the year ended 30 September 2021 was £16,500.

Up to 30 June 2021 profits were shared between David and Peter in the ratio 3:2, after paying annual salaries of £3,000 and £2,000.

From 1 July 2021 profits were shared in the ratio 2:1 after paying annual salaries of £6,000 and £4,000.

Show the allocation of profits and the partners' trading income assessments for the tax year 2021/22.

For a suggested answer, see the 'Answers' section at the end of the book.

4 NEW PARTNERS, ONGOING PARTNERS AND RETIRING PARTNERS

4.1 PARTNERSHIP COMMENCING OR CEASING

- The normal commencement and cessation basis of assessment rules apply upon the commencement and the cessation of a partnership. The rules are applied **after** the allocation of the profit or loss between the partners.
- Each partner is effectively taxed as a sole trader in respect of his or her share of the profit or loss. The trade commences for a partner when that partner joins the partnership and ceases when the partner leaves the partnership.
- Each partner will have his or her own overlap relief on cessation of the partnership.

4.2 A CHANGE IN THE MEMBERSHIP

The membership of a partnership may change as the result of the admission, death or retirement of a partner.

- Provided that there is at least one partner common to the business before and after the change, the partnership will automatically continue. Ongoing partners are therefore taxed as carrying on an ongoing business, i.e. the normal current year basis of assessment is used to determine the profits assessable for the tax year.
- The commencement rules apply to the individual partner who is joining the partnership. New partners will generate overlap profits when they join the partnership.
- The cessation rules apply to the individual partner who is leaving the partnership (on retirement or death). A partner who leaves the partnership is entitled to overlap relief. Continuing partners will carry their overlap relief forward until they eventually leave the partnership or the partnership ceases.

Example

Picard and Riker are in partnership and have been in business for many years preparing accounts to 31 December each year. On 1 January 2021 Worf joined the partnership.

Until 1 January 2021 profits were shared equally. From 1 January 2021 the profits are shared 40% each to Picard and Riker and 20% to Worf.

The partnership's tax adjusted trading profits are as follows:

Year ended 31 December 2020	£65,000
Year ended 31 December 2021	£80,000
Year ended 31 December 2022	£94,000

Show the amounts taxed on each partner for the tax years 2020/21 to 2022/23.

Solution

Profits are allocated between the partners as follows:

	Total	Picard	Riker	Worf
	£	£	£	£
Y/e 31 Dec 2020 Equal shares	65,000	32,500	32,500	–
Y/e 31 Dec 2021 40%:40%:20%	80,000	32,000	32,000	16,000
Y/e 31 Dec 2022 40%:40%:20%	94,000	37,600	37,600	18,800

Picard and Riker have been in business for many years and are assessed on the current year basis as follows:

		£
2020/21	Year ended 31 December 2020	32,500
2021/22	Year ended 31 December 2021	32,000
2022/23	Year ended 31 December 2022	37,600

Worf is assessed as follows, based upon a commencement date of 1 January 2021:

			£
2020/21	1 January 2021 to 5 April 2021	£16,000 × $^3/_{12}$	4,000
2021/22	Year ended 31 December 2021		16,000
2022/23	Year ended 31 December 2022		18,800

Worf has overlap profits carried forward of £4,000.

ACTIVITY 2

Malika and Khadija have been in partnership since 1 July 2018 making up their accounts to 30 June each year. On 1 July 2020 Dania joined the partnership and Khadija left.

The partnership's tax adjusted trading profits are as follows:

	£
Year ended 30 June 2019	10,000
Year ended 30 June 2020	13,500
Year ended 30 June 2021	18,000

Profits are shared equally.

Show the amounts taxed on the individual partners for the tax years 2018/19 to 2021/22 and the amount of any overlap profits.

Note: Make sure you allocate the profits between the partners first, and then consider the commencement and cessation rules individually for each partner.

All aspects of this question are examinable in FTX, however, since the maximum marks in one question is 10, there would not be this much detail within one question. It has been included as it is useful practice on this topic.

For a suggested answer, see the 'Answers' section at the end of the book.

4.3 SOLE TRADERS

If a sole trader takes someone into partnership, the commencement rules will apply to the new partner, whereas the sole trader will be treated as continuing.

Similarly, when a business goes from a partnership to a sole trader, the sole trader will be treated as continuing, while the other partner(s) will be treated as ceasing to trade.

5 LOSS RELIEF

A loss is allocated between the partners in the same way as a profit. The loss relief claims available to partners are the same as those for sole traders – see Chapter 6.

Each partner has his or her own share of the loss and can make his or her own decision as to how it is to be relieved. Therefore, for example, it is possible for one partner to carry his or her loss forward against his or her share of future partnership profits, whilst another partner may claim against total income of the tax year of loss and/or the preceding tax year.

Note that it is not possible for a partner to pass his or her share of a partnership loss to another partner.

Example

Dhoni and Kumar are in partnership sharing profits and losses in the ratio 60:40. In the year ended 31 December 2021 the partnership made a tax adjusted trading loss of £80,000.

Dhoni has other income of £40,000 per year. Kumar's only income is from the partnership.

The loss is allocated in the same way as a profit:
Dhoni has 60%, £48,000 and Kumar has 40%, £32,000

Dhoni decides to claim his loss against his total income for 2020/21 and the balance in 2021/22.

Kumar decides to carry his loss forward against his share of profits in 2022/23 and future years.

KEY TERMS

Profit sharing ratio – the agreed method of dividing a partnership's profit or loss between the partners.

SELF TEST QUESTIONS

		Paragraph
1	Why are the partners' salaries not a deductible expense for trading profit purposes?	1.2
2	How are profits allocated between partners?	1.3
3	If a partnership changes its profit sharing ratio during a period of account, what must be done prior to the allocation of profit between the partners?	3
4	When will the commencement rules apply to a partner?	4.2
5	When can a partner claim overlap relief?	4.2
6	Must all partners make the same loss relief claim?	5
7	Can a partner pass his or her share of a loss to another partner?	5

MULTIPLE CHOICE QUESTIONS

1 Desmond and Elijah started trading on 6 April 2021 and made a tax adjusted trading profit for the year ended 5 April 2022 of £72,000. They agreed to split the profits equally.

Fatima joined the partnership on 6 January 2022, at which point the profit sharing arrangement was changed and Desmond, Elijah and Fatima agreed to share profits in the ratio 3:2:1.

What is Fatima's trading income assessment for 2021/22?

A £18,000

B £12,000

C £6,000

D £3,000

2 Aaqib, Bob and Caroline have been in partnership since 1 April 2018. The partnership draws up accounts to 31 December each year.

On 1 November 2021, Aaqib retired from the partnership and the profit sharing arrangements were changed from that date onwards.

Which of the following statements is correct?

A The partnership is deemed to cease on Aaqib's retirement and the partners will operate closing year rules to calculate their trading income assessments for the final year

B The final tax year of trading for Aaqib, Bob and Caroline is 2021/22

C Bob and Caroline will operate the opening year rules to calculate their trading income assessments for the tax year 2021/22

D Aaqib will operate the closing year rules in order to calculate his trading income assessment for the tax year 2021/22

3 Nick and David are in partnership sharing profits in the ratio 3:2 respectively after a salary of £15,000 per year to David.

On 1 January 2022 the partners agree to share profits equally in the future with no salaries.

The tax adjusted trading profit for the year ended 30 June 2022 is £92,000.

What is David's share of the profits for the year ended 30 June 2022?

A £46,000

B £41,400

C £45,900

D £50,400

For suggested answers, see the 'Answers' section at the end of the book.

PRACTICE QUESTION

LILY, MAUD AND NINA

Lily and Maud have been in partnership since 1 January 2019 making up their accounts to 31 December each year. On 1 January 2021 Nina joined the partnership.

The partnership's tax adjusted profits are as follows:

	£
Year ended 31 December 2019	88,000
Year ended 31 December 2020	98,000
Year ended 31 December 2021	120,000

Profits are shared equally.

Required:

Show the amounts taxed on the individual partners for the tax years 2018/19 to 2021/22 and state the amount of overlap profit to carry forward. **(10 marks)**

For a suggested answer, see the 'Answers' section at the end of the book.

Chapter 8

TAX RETURNS FOR THE SELF-EMPLOYED

INTRODUCTION

This chapter deals with the supplementary pages of the tax return that deal with the self-employed individual and with a partnership.

This chapter covers syllabus area B7.

CONTENTS	LEARNING OUTCOMES
1 Self-employed individual 2 Partnership tax return	At the end of this chapter, you should be able to: • Complete the self-employed or partnership supplementary pages of the tax return for individuals, and submit them within the statutory time limits.

1 SELF-EMPLOYED INDIVIDUAL

1.1 SELF-EMPLOYMENT SUPPLEMENTARY PAGES

An individual may be required to complete a tax return.

There is a main return (SA100) and several supplementary pages to be completed as appropriate. One of the sets of supplementary pages consists of six pages on self-employment (SA103).

The first three pages of the SA103 are set out on the following pages. One of these pages or an extract from a page may appear in your examination.

1.2 PAGE SEF1

The first part of this page is used to gather details of the business, including the date of the accounting period (this was looked at in detail in Chapter 5).

The second part of the page is used to record the income of the business.

Box 16 will include other income received by the business (e.g. bank interest), but this must then be entered into Box 62 (page SEF3) and deducted at Box 63 to arrive at trading profit.

Box 16.1 is not examinable.

1.3 PAGE SEF2

This page records the expenses of the business. The detailed section on expenses need only be completed if the annual turnover of the business is at least equal to the VAT registration threshold (currently £85,000). Otherwise it is only necessary to enter a total expenses figure in Box 31.

- The left hand column includes all expenses shown in the accounts (analysed as appropriate) and any allowable expenses which are not included in the accounts.
- The right hand column shows the disallowable expenditure included within the expenses figures.

It is possible that boxes in both columns could include the same figure; for example, if depreciation in the accounts is £3,000 then:

- Box 29 will show £3,000, and
- Box 44 will show £3,000.

Usually the boxes will show different figures; for example, if wages and salaries of £50,000 included the owner's drawings of £20,000 then:

- Box 19 will show £50,000, and
- Box 34 will show £20,000.

1.4 PAGE SEF3

Boxes 47 and 48 give the net profit or net loss as shown in the accounts.

The second part of the page is used to record the capital allowances claimed by the business.

The final section of this page is the equivalent of the adjustment of profits pro forma shown in Chapter 3. Note however, that capital allowances and balancing charges are not netted off but must be shown separately in the tax return.

Outline pro forma for adjustment of profits computation

		Box	£	£
Net profit (or loss) per accounts		47(48)		X
Add:	Disallowable expenditure	46	X	
	Income not included in the accounts but taxable as trading income	60	X	
	Balancing charges	59	X	
		61		X
				X
Less:	Income included in the accounts but not taxable as trading income	62	X	
	Expenditure not in the accounts but allowable as a trade deduction	*	X	
	Capital allowances	57	X	
		63		(X)
Tax adjusted trading profit (or loss)		64(65)		X

* Expenses which are allowable as a trade deduction should be included in the relevant expense box (depending on the type of expense) on page 2 of the return, even if they do not appear in the accounts.

When completing the tax return form in the examination it is important to:

- complete the return with accuracy and
- enter figures in the correct boxes.

Note that in the examination you will not have to complete all pages and may only have to complete an extract from a return or list out the entries required for a return.

1.5 DUE DATE FOR SUBMISSION OF THE RETURN

Paper returns – 31 October following the tax year end.

Electronic returns – 31 January following the tax year end.

More details of filing of returns are given in Chapter 16.

HM Revenue & Customs

Self-employment (full)

Tax year 6 April 2021 to 5 April 2022 (2021–22)

Please read the 'Self-employment (full) notes' to check if you should use this page or the 'Self-employment (short)' page.

For help filling in this form, go to www.gov.uk/taxreturnforms and read the notes and helpsheets.

Your name

Your Unique Taxpayer Reference (UTR)

Business details

1 **Business name** – unless it's in your own name

2 **Description of business**

3 **First line of your business address** – unless you work from home

4 **Postcode of your business address**

5 **If the details in boxes 1, 2, 3 or 4 have changed in the last 12 months, put 'X' in the box and give details in the 'Any other information' box**

6 **If your business started after 5 April 2021, enter the start date** DD MM YYYY

7 **If your business ceased after 5 April 2021 but before 6 April 2022, enter the final date of trading**

8 **Date your books or accounts start** – the beginning of your accounting period

9 **Date your books or accounts are made up to or the end of your accounting period** – read the notes if you have filled in box 6 or 7

10 **If you used cash basis, money actually received and paid out, to calculate your income and expenses, put 'X' in the box**

Other information

11 **If your accounting date has changed permanently, put 'X' in the box**

12 **If your accounting date has changed more than once since 2016, put 'X' in the box**

13 **If special arrangements apply, put 'X' in the box**

14 **If you provided the information about your 2021–22 profit on last year's tax return, put 'X' in the box**

Business income

15 **Your turnover** – the takings, fees, sales or money earned by your business

£ · 0 0

16 **Any other business income (include coronavirus support payments such as CJRS, but not SEISS)**

£ · 0 0

16.1 **Trading income allowance** – read the notes

£ · 0 0

SA103F 2021 Page SEF 1 HMRC 12/20

Business expenses

Please read the 'Self-employment (full) notes' before filling in this section.

Total expenses If your annual turnover was below £85,000, you may just put your total expenses in box 31	**Disallowable expenses** Use this column if the figures in boxes 17 to 30 include disallowable amounts
17 Cost of goods bought for resale or goods used £ • 0 0	32 £ • 0 0
18 Construction industry – payments to subcontractors £ • 0 0	33 £ • 0 0
19 Wages, salaries and other staff costs £ • 0 0	34 £ • 0 0
20 Car, van and travel expenses £ • 0 0	35 £ • 0 0
21 Rent, rates, power and insurance costs £ • 0 0	36 £ • 0 0
22 Repairs and maintenance of property and equipment £ • 0 0	37 £ • 0 0
23 Phone, fax, stationery and other office costs £ • 0 0	38 £ • 0 0
24 Advertising and business entertainment costs £ • 0 0	39 £ • 0 0
25 Interest on bank and other loans £ • 0 0	40 £ • 0 0
26 Bank, credit card and other financial charges £ • 0 0	41 £ • 0 0
27 Irrecoverable debts written off £ • 0 0	42 £ • 0 0
28 Accountancy, legal and other professional fees £ • 0 0	43 £ • 0 0
29 Depreciation and loss or profit on sale of assets £ • 0 0	44 £ • 0 0
30 Other business expenses £ • 0 0	45 £ • 0 0
31 Total expenses (total of boxes 17 to 30) £ • 0 0	46 Total disallowable expenses (total of boxes 32 to 45) £ • 0 0

SA103F 2021 Page SEF 2

Net profit or loss

47 **Net profit** – if your business income is more than your expenses (if box 15 + box 16 minus box 31 is positive)

£ · 0 0

48 **Or, net loss** – if your expenses are more than your business income (if box 31 minus (box 15 + box 16) is positive)

£ · 0 0

Tax allowances for vehicles and equipment (capital allowances)

There are 'capital' tax allowances for vehicles, equipment and certain buildings used in your business (do not include the cost of these in your business expenses). Please read the 'Self-employment (full) notes' and use the examples to work out your capital allowances.

49 **Annual Investment Allowance**

£ · 0 0

50 **Capital allowances at 18% on equipment, including cars with lower CO2 emissions**

£ · 0 0

51 **Capital allowances at 6% on equipment, including cars with higher CO2 emissions**

£ · 0 0

52 **Zero-emission goods vehicle allowance**

£ · 0 0

53 **The Structures and Buildings Allowance**
(you must hold a valid allowance statement – read the notes for details on how much you can claim per year)

£ · 0 0

54 **Electric charge-point allowance**

£ · 0 0

55 **100% and other enhanced capital allowances**

£ · 0 0

56 **Allowances on sale or cessation of business use (where you've disposed of assets for less than their tax value)**

£ · 0 0

57 **Total capital allowances (total of boxes 49 to 56)**

£ · 0 0

Box 58 is not in use

59 **Balancing charge on sales of assets or on the cessation of business use (including where Business Premises Renovation Allowance has been claimed) for example, where you've disposed of assets for more than their tax value**

£ · 0 0

Calculating your taxable profit or loss

You may have to adjust your net profit or loss for disallowable expenses or capital allowances to arrive at your taxable profit or your loss for tax purposes. Please read the 'Self-employment (full) notes' and fill in the boxes below that apply.

60 **Goods and services for your own use**

£ · 0 0

61 **Total additions to net profit or deductions from net loss (box 46 + box 59 + box 60)**

£ · 0 0

62 **Income, receipts and other profits included in business income or expenses but not taxable as business profits**

£ · 0 0

63 **Total deductions from net profit or additions to net loss (box 57 + box 62)**

£ · 0 0

64 **Net business profit for tax purposes (if box 47 + box 61 minus (box 48 + box 63) is positive)**

£ · 0 0

65 **Net business loss for tax purposes (if box 48 + box 63 minus (box 47 + box 61) is positive)**

£ · 0 0

SA103F 2021 Page SEF 3

Example

Manuel Costa

Manuel Costa is a self-employed wholesale clothing distributor. His summarised accounts for the year ended 30 June 2021 are as follows:

	£	£
Sales		400,000
Opening inventory	40,000	
Purchases	224,000	
	264,000	
Closing inventory	(32,000)	
Cost of sales		(232,000)
Gross profit		168,000
Wages and National Insurance (Note 1)	84,655	
Motor car running expenses (Manuel's car) (Note 2)	2,000	
Lighting and heating	4,250	
Rent and business rates	31,060	
Repairs and renewals (all allowable)	3,490	
Legal expenses (Note 3)	1,060	
Depreciation	3,570	
Profit on sale of office furniture	(60)	
Sundry expenses (all allowable)	5,770	
		(135,795)
Net profit		32,205

Notes to the accounts

1 Wages

Included in wages are Manuel's drawings of £300 per week, his class 2 national insurance contributions of £159 for the year and wages and national insurance contributions in respect of his wife totalling £16,750. His wife worked full time in the business as a secretary.

2 Motor car running expenses

Manuel estimates that one-third of his mileage is private. Included in the charge is £65 for a speeding fine incurred by Manuel whilst delivering goods to a customer.

3 Legal expenses

	£
Defending action in respect of alleged faulty goods	357
Defending Manuel in connection with speeding offence	613
Debt collection	90
	1,060

4 Capital allowances on main pool plant and machinery for the year to 30 June 2021 are £2,480, which includes £1,200 annual investment allowance.

His tax adjusted trading profits for the accounting period to 30 June 2021 are as follows:

Manuel Costa

Adjustment of profits for 12 months ended 30 June 2021

		£
Net profit per accounts		32,205
Manuel's drawings (£300 × 52)		15,600
Manuel's NIC (personal expense)		159
Speeding fine		65
Motor expenses (1/3 of balance) (£2,000 – £65) × $^{1}/_{3}$		645
Legal expenses in connection with speeding offence		613
Depreciation		3,570
		52,857
Less:	Profit on sale of office furniture	(60)
	Capital allowances	(2,480)
Tax adjusted trading profits		50,317

Required:

State the detail or amounts that would be entered in the relevant boxes on the first three pages of Manuel's tax return supplementary pages.

It is not necessary to include any boxes which will be left blank in your answer.

Manuel's self-assessment tax return entries

Your name	Manuel Costa	
Box 2	Wholesale clothing distribution	
Box 8	1 July 2020	
Box 9	30 June 2021	
Box 15	£400,000	
Box 17	£232,000	
Box 19	£84,655	
Box 20	£2,000	
Box 21	£35,310	(£4,250 + £31,060)
Box 22	£3,490	
Box 28	£1,060	
Box 29	£3,510	(£3,570 – £60)
Box 30	£5,770	
Box 31	£367,795	
Box 34	£15,759	(£15,600 + £159)
Box 35	£710	(£645 + £65)
Box 43	£613	
Box 44	£3,510	(£3,570 – £60)
Box 46	£20,592	
Box 47	£32,205	
Box 49	£1,200	
Box 50	£1,280	
Box 57	£2,480	
Box 61	£20,592	
Box 63	£2,480	
Box 64	£50,317	

2 PARTNERSHIP TAX RETURN

2.1 INTRODUCTION

A partnership does not pay its own tax liability. However the partnership must file a tax return for the partnership as a whole and individual partners must complete partnership supplementary pages of the tax return. It is these supplementary pages that you may be required to complete.

The pages cover details of the partner's share of the partnership income and related information.

There are two supplementary pages.

2.2 SUPPLEMENTARY PARTNERSHIP PAGES – PAGE 1

Page 1 starts with the partner's name and unique taxpayer reference.

Boxes 1 – 4 cover partnership information and the dates that a partner joins or leaves the partnership if this is during the year.

Boxes 6 – 7 are for the basis period of the partner.

Box 8 is an important box as it includes the partner's share of the partnership profits.

Boxes 13 and 14 include details of overlap relief used and overlap profits carried forward.

Box 16 will be the same as Box 8 unless overlap profits are to be deducted.

Box 17 is for losses brought forward and utilised against the partnership profits in the current year.

Boxes 18 and 20 are likely to be the same figures, i.e. profits for the year from Box 16 less losses brought forward if any.

Boxes 5, 9 – 12 and 19 will not normally be needed.

2.3 SUPPLEMENTARY PARTNERSHIP PAGES – PAGE 2

On page 2 Boxes 21 – 24 deal with losses.

Boxes 25 – 27 deal with aspects of class 2 and 4 NIC and are not examinable.

Box 28 on the form below is for interest received. In the examination the partner's share of any partnership interest received is entered in this box.

Boxes 30 – 31 are not examinable.

2.4 COMPLETING THE TAX RETURN

When completing the tax return form in the examination it is important to note that:

- The return is expected to be completed with accuracy.
- Figures should be entered in the correct boxes.

The key relevant pages 1 and 2 are shown overleaf.

2.5 DUE DATE FOR SUBMISSION OF THE RETURN

Paper returns – 31 October following the tax year end.

Electronic returns – 31 January following the tax year end.

More details of filing of returns are given in Chapter 16.

HM Revenue & Customs

Partnership (short)

Tax year 6 April 2021 to 5 April 2022 (2021–22)

Your name

Your Unique Taxpayer Reference (UTR)

Complete a 'Partnership' page for each partnership of which you were a member and for each partnership business.
For help filling in this form, go to www.gov.uk/taxreturnforms and read the notes and helpsheets.

Partnership details

1 **Partnership reference number**

2 **Description of partnership trade or profession**

3 **If you became a partner after 5 April 2021, enter the date you joined the partnership** DD MM YYYY

4 **If you left the partnership after 5 April 2021 and before 6 April 2022, enter the date you left**

5 **If the partnership used cash basis, money actually received and paid out, to calculate its income and expenses, put 'X' in the box** – read the notes

Your share of the partnership's trading or professional profits

Please refer to the Partnership Statement to complete these pages and if you need any help, read the 'Partnership (short) notes'.
If you want to enter a loss, or an adjustment needs to be taken off, put a minus sign (–) in the box next to the £ sign.

6 **Date your basis period began** DD MM YYYY

7 **Date your basis period ended** DD MM YYYY

8 **Your share of the partnership's profit or loss** – from box 11 or box 12 on the Partnership Statement

£ . 0 0

9 **If your basis period is not the same as the partnership's accounting period, enter the adjustment needed to arrive at the profit or loss for your basis period**

£ . 0 0

9.1 **Self-Employment Income Support Scheme grant**

£ . 0 0

10 **Adjustment for change of accounting practice** – from box 11A on the Partnership Statement

£ . 0 0

11 **Averaging adjustment** – only for farmers, market gardeners and creators of literary or artistic works

£ . 0 0

12 **Foreign tax claimed as a deduction** – only if Foreign Tax Credit Relief is not being claimed on the 'Foreign' pages

£ . 0 0

13 **Overlap relief used this year**

£ . 0 0

14 **Overlap profit carried forward**

£ . 0 0

15 **If box 8 includes any disguised remuneration income, put 'X' in the box** – from box 12A on the Partnership Statement

16 **Adjusted profit for 2021–22** – see the working sheet in the notes

£ . 0 0

17 **Losses brought forward from earlier years set off against this year's profit (up to the amount in box 16)**

£ . 0 0

18 **Taxable profits after losses brought forward (box 16 minus box 17)**

£ . 0 0

19 **Any other business income not included in the partnership accounts**

£ . 0 0

20 **Your share of total taxable profits from the partnership's business for 2021–22 (box 18 + box 19)**

£ . 0 0

SA104S 2021 Page SP 1 HMRC 12/20

Your share of the partnership's trading or professional losses

21 **Adjusted loss for 2021–22** – see the working sheet in the notes

£ .00

22 **Loss from this tax year set off against other income for 2021–22**

£ .00

23 **Loss to be carried back to previous year(s) and set off against income (or capital gains)**

£ .00

24 **Total loss to carry forward after all other set-offs** – including unused losses brought forward

£ .00

Class 2 and Class 4 National Insurance contributions (NICs)

If your total profits from all self-employments and partnerships for 2020–21 are less than £6,475 you do not have to pay Class 2 NICs, but you may want to pay voluntarily (box 25) to protect your rights to certain benefits. Read the Partnership (short) notes.

25 **If your total profits for 2021–22 are less than £6,515 and you choose to pay Class 2 NICs voluntarily, put 'X' in the box**

26 **If you're exempt from paying Class 4 NICs, put 'X' in the box**

27 **Adjustment to profits chargeable to Class 4 NICs**

£ .00

Your share of the partnership's untaxed interest

28 **Your share of untaxed interest** – from box 13 on the Partnership Statement

£ .00

Your share of the partnership's tax paid and deductions

Box 29 is not in use

30 **Your share of Construction Industry Scheme deductions made by contractors** – from box 24 on the Partnership Statement

£ .00

31 **Your share of any tax taken off trading income (not contractor deductions)** – from box 24A on the Partnership Statement

£ .00

Any other information

32 **Please give any other information in this space**

SA104S 2021 Page SP 2

ACTIVITY 1

Brothers Petra and Nathalie Flannery have traded in partnership as Superhero Supplies for many years, trading in books and comics.

Their tax adjusted trading profits for the year ended 30 September 2021 were £130,400, and the partnership received interest of £16,210.

Petra and Nathalie have always shared the profits of their business in the ratio 4:3.

Petra and Nathalie have overlap profits of £4,000 and £3,000 respectively, brought forward from the start of the business.

The partnership made a tax adjusted loss in the year ended 30 September 2020 and Petra has a loss brought forward of £15,400.

State the detail or amounts that would be entered in the relevant boxes on the partnership supplementary pages of the tax return for Petra Flannery in respect of the year ended 30 September 2021. It is not necessary to include any boxes which will be left blank in your answer.

For a suggested answer, see the 'Answers' section at the end of the book.

KEY TERMS

Supplementary pages – additional pages to accompany the income tax return.

SELF TEST QUESTIONS

		Paragraph
1	Which part of the self-assessment tax return is used for self-employed individuals?	1.1
2	What is the turnover limit which requires completion of the detailed self-employed expenses details?	1.3
3	What are the filing dates for the self-assessment tax return?	1.5
4	What is included on the partnership supplementary pages of the tax return for each partner?	2.2, 2.3

PRACTICE QUESTION

CAPONE

You are given the following statement of profit or loss for Capone for the year ended 30 June 2021.

	£	£
Revenue		292,031
Cost of sales		(227,452)
Gross profit		64,579
Rent and business rates	9,740	
Light and heat	120	
Office salaries	35,110	
Repairs to premises	2,620	
Motor expenses	740	
Depreciation		
– Motor vans	3,400	
– Equipment	750	
Loss on sale of equipment	40	
Impairment losses	6,030	
Professional charges	375	
Interest on bank overdraft	240	
Sundry expenses	770	
		(59,935)
Net profit		4,644

Capone's adjusted profit computation is as follows:

Adjustment of profits for 12 months ended 30 June 2021

	£
Net profit per accounts	4,644
Salary – Capone (included in salaries expense)	14,000
Repairs – alterations to flooring	1,460
Depreciation of vans and equipment	4,150
Loss on sale of equipment	40
Impairment losses	
Increase in provision not in accordance with UK GAAP	3,350
Loan to former employee written off	400
Professional charges	
Costs re defending Capone against speeding fine	130
Sundry expenses	
Speeding fine for Capone	250
Donation	20
Gift of chocolates to customers	300
Adjusted trading profit	28,744

Required:

Using the above information you are required to state the detail or amounts that would be entered in the relevant boxes on page 2 of the self-employed supplementary pages of the income tax return included below. It is not necessary to include any boxes which will be left blank in your answer. **(10 marks)**

For a suggested answer, see the 'Answers' section at the end of the book.

Business expenses

Please read the 'Self-employment (full) notes' before filling in this section.

Total expenses	Disallowable expenses
If your annual turnover was below £85,000, you may just put your total expenses in box 31	Use this column if the figures in boxes 17 to 30 include disallowable amounts
17 Cost of goods bought for resale or goods used £ .00	32 £ .00
18 Construction industry – payments to subcontractors £ .00	33 £ .00
19 Wages, salaries and other staff costs £ .00	34 £ .00
20 Car, van and travel expenses £ .00	35 £ .00
21 Rent, rates, power and insurance costs £ .00	36 £ .00
22 Repairs and maintenance of property and equipment £ .00	37 £ .00
23 Phone, fax, stationery and other office costs £ .00	38 £ .00
24 Advertising and business entertainment costs £ .00	39 £ .00
25 Interest on bank and other loans £ .00	40 £ .00
26 Bank, credit card and other financial charges £ .00	41 £ .00
27 Irrecoverable debts written off £ .00	42 £ .00
28 Accountancy, legal and other professional fees £ .00	43 £ .00
29 Depreciation and loss or profit on sale of assets £ .00	44 £ .00
30 Other business expenses £ .00	45 £ .00
31 Total expenses (total of boxes 17 to 30) £ .00	46 Total disallowable expenses (total of boxes 32 to 45) £ .00

SA103F 2021 Page SEF 2

Chapter 9

EMPLOYMENT INCOME

INTRODUCTION

This chapter deals with the basis of assessment of employment income and explains the employer's responsibility to collect tax from employees. This chapter covers syllabus areas C2 (a) to (c) and (g), and C6 (f).

CONTENTS	LEARNING OUTCOMES
1 Employment and self-employment **2** The basis of assessment **3** Allowable deductions **4** PAYE forms and deadlines for submission **5** Source documents required to complete tax returns	At the end of this chapter, you should be able to: • identify assessable employment income • define and illustrate the basis of assessment for directors and others • identify the principal categories of deductions and illustrate their scope • list the main PAYE forms and the deadlines for their submission • identify source documents required to complete tax returns.

1 EMPLOYMENT AND SELF-EMPLOYMENT

The difference between employment and self-employment is:

- an employee is taxable under the employment income provisions
- a self-employed person is taxed on the profits derived from his or her trade, profession or vocation under the trading income provisions.

You will not be examined on the tests to distinguish between employment and self-employment.

2 THE BASIS OF ASSESSMENT

2.1 ASSESSABLE EARNINGS

Directors and employees are taxed on the amount of earnings **received** in the tax year.

The term 'earnings' includes not only cash wages or salary, but bonuses and commission and benefits made available by the employer. The detailed rules for benefits are dealt with in Chapter 10. Earnings also include tips.

2.2 THE GENERAL RULE

Because employment income assessments are on a receipts basis, the time that the earnings are received is of critical importance. Earnings are treated as received on the **earlier** of the following events:

- actual payment of, or on account of, earnings, or
- becoming entitled to such a payment.

Example

Sabine is an employee with an annual salary of £25,000.

She is entitled to a bonus based on the company's profits. This is paid as follows:

Based on profits of year ended 31 December 2020	£4,575 paid 15 April 2021
Based on profits of year ended 31 December 2021	£6,100 paid 29 April 2022

Sabine's employment income for the tax year 2021/22 is:

	£
Salary	25,000
Bonus (paid during 2021/22)	4,575
Total	29,575

Note: The accounting period on which the bonus is based is irrelevant.

ACTIVITY 1

Stephen is employed at a salary of £30,000 per annum.

His employer determined that he was entitled to a bonus of £5,000 on 31 March 2021 and Stephen was paid the bonus on 10 April 2021.

In which tax year is the bonus taxed?

For a suggested answer, see the 'Answers' section at the end of the book.

2.3 DIRECTORS

In the case of directors, who are in a position to manipulate the timing of payments, there are extra rules. They are deemed to receive earnings on the earliest of four dates; the two general rules set out above and the following two rules:

- when sums on account of earnings are credited to an account in their name in the accounts
- where earnings are determined (determined usually means approved by the Board of directors or the shareholders)
  - **before** the end of a period of account – the end of that period
  - **after** the end of a period of account – date the earnings are determined.

Example

Rom is a director of Quark Ltd. The company prepares accounts to 30 June each year.

Rom is entitled to a bonus based on the company's profits. For the year ended 30 June 2021 the bonus is agreed at £40,000 and is approved at a board meeting on 10 September 2021. Rom is entitled to the bonus on 31 December 2021; however, as the company has cash flow problems Rom does not actually receive the bonus until 3 May 2022.

The bonus is treated as received on the earliest of the following.

(a) Date of payment – 3 May 2022

(b) Date becoming entitled – 31 December 2021

(c) When the bonus is determined after the end of the period of account – the date of determination, which in this case is 10 September 2021.

The bonus is therefore treated as received on 10 September 2021 and is taxed in 2021/22.

ACTIVITY 2

Shaun is a director of Frogham Ltd, a company which prepares accounts to 31 December each year.

Shaun's bonus for the year ended 31 December 2021 was determined on 10 December 2021; he became entitled to payment of the bonus on 20 February 2022 and was paid the bonus on 10 April 2022.

In which tax year is the bonus taxed?

For a suggested answer, see the 'Answers' section at the end of the book.

2.4 EXCEPTIONS

- The above rules do not deal with the timing of when benefits are taxable, which is dealt with under separate legislation (e.g. the provision of an asset as a benefit would normally be assessed initially when first made available).
- Similarly pensions received are taxed on an accruals rather than receipts basis, i.e. when they are due rather than when received.

3 ALLOWABLE DEDUCTIONS

3.1 EXPENSES SPECIFICALLY PERMITTED BY STATUTE

Certain specific types of expenditure are expressly permitted by statute. The most important of these are:

- Contributions to registered occupational pension schemes (see Chapter 15).
- Fees and subscriptions to professional bodies, provided that the recipient is approved by HMRC and its activities are relevant to the employment.
- Payments to charity made under an approved payroll deduction scheme operated by an employer. The employer deducts the donations from wages or salary before calculating the PAYE deductions, and pays them to an approved agent. The agent then distributes the funds to charities selected by the employee. The scheme is also referred to as a 'Give As you Earn' (GAYE) Scheme, or Payroll Giving Scheme. There are no minimum or maximum payments.

Example

Juanita earns a salary of £50,000 per year as an accountant. She pays a subscription of £350 to her professional body the ACCA, a contribution to her employer's pension scheme of 5% of her salary and pays Oxfam £50 per month through a GAYE Scheme.

Juanita's annual taxable employment income is:

	£
Salary	50,000
Less: Pension contribution (5% × £50,000)	(2,500)
Professional subscription	(350)
Payroll giving (12 × £50)	(600)
Taxable employment income	46,550

3.2 TRAVEL EXPENSES

Travel expenses may be deducted where they are incurred:

- necessarily
- in the performance of the duties of the employment.

In deciding whether travel expenses are necessarily incurred, the Courts look to whether it is the **requirements of the job** that make the expense necessary, or **the circumstances of the individual**. If it is the former the 'necessarily' test is passed, but otherwise it is not.

The Courts have looked at the phrase, 'in the performance of the duties of the employment' in many cases. With regard to travel expenses, the following principles have emerged:

- The costs of travelling from home to an employee's normal place of work are not deductible, except in the rare case when it can be shown that the duties are started before leaving home.
- Costs of travelling from one employment to another are not deductible.
- If an employee has more than one place where the duties have to be performed, travel expenses between them are allowable.
- Travel expenses are also allowed for journeys an employee makes to or from a place he or she has to attend in the performance of his or her duties, other than normal commuting journeys. For example, where Jenna lives in Swindon and normally works at her employer's office in London (her permanent workplace) she will be allowed tax relief for the travel and subsistence expenses of travelling from her home to a temporary work location in Manchester (temporary workplace).

  Travel and subsistence costs are allowed for 'site-based' employees and employees required to work at a temporary workplace provided that attendance at the site/temporary workplace is not expected to last more than 24 months.

3.3 OTHER EXPENSES

The rule covering the deductibility of non-travel expenses is very strict. In addition to being 'necessarily' incurred, such expenses must also be incurred 'wholly and exclusively in the performance of the duties'.

- The test that expenditure must be incurred **'in the performance** of the duties' means that there is no deduction for expenditure incurred beforehand to gain the requisite knowledge or experience to do the work. So, for example, the cost of attending evening classes by a schoolteacher has been disallowed.
- For expenditure to be 'necessarily' incurred it must be something that the job itself requires, not something imposed by the employee's circumstances. Thus an employee with poor eyesight was unable to deduct the cost of spectacles. In other words, to be necessary expenditure, each and every person undertaking the duties would have to incur it.

For expenditure to be incurred 'wholly and exclusively' it must be with the **sole** objective of performing the duties of the employment. Two examples show this distinction.

- If an employee is required to wear clothes of a high standard, and so purchases them, the expenditure is **not** deductible. The employee's clothes satisfy both professional and personal needs.

- On the other hand, expenditure on a home telephone can be partly deductible. Business calls are made 'wholly and exclusively' and so are deductible. But, on the same reasoning as applied to the clothes, no part of the line rental for a home phone may be deducted.

4 PAYE FORMS AND DEADLINES FOR SUBMISSION

4.1 INTRODUCTION

PAYE is the system of collecting income tax at source from the earnings of employed individuals.

Earnings taxable as employment income are subject to deduction of tax under the PAYE system. The employer is required to deduct the appropriate amount of tax from each payment (or repay over-deductions) by reference to PAYE Tax Tables and the taxpayer's tax code. These tables are designed to ensure that the tax deducted from the earnings equals the tax liability of the employee.

Tax returns and formal self-assessments will not normally be required in cases where both the tax code and the deduction of tax under it are correct.

4.2 REAL TIME INFORMATION (RTI)

All employers must submit to HMRC the following details online every payday (weekly or monthly). The information must be submitted on or before the day they pay their employees:

- amount paid to employees

- deductions such as income tax and national insurance contributions

- starter and leaver dates if applicable.

All employers must use RTI enabled software packages to run their payroll which will automatically generate the reports needed.

4.3 NET PAY SCHEME

PAYE is calculated based on the amount of pay paid to the employee in the relevant tax week or month. If the employee contributes to the employer's occupational pension scheme, or makes donations under a payroll giving scheme, the employer will deduct these amounts from the employee's pay **before** calculating PAYE.

This method of deducting pension contributions and donations to charity is referred to as the 'net pay scheme'. Note that this procedure does **not** extend to tax deductible expenses. These are dealt with through the employee's PAYE code.

4.4 PAYMENTS OF TAX

The amounts of tax and national insurance that the employer was **liable** to deduct during each tax month are due for payment not later than 14 days after the month ends. A tax month ends on the 5th of the month; therefore the payments are due by the 19th of each month.

If payments are made electronically this deadline is extended to the 22nd of each month.

Employers with 250 or more employees must pay electronically.

4.5 PROCEDURE TO BE ADOPTED WHEN EMPLOYEE LEAVES

When an employee leaves an employment, the PAYE system is interrupted. A form P45 must be completed for an employee that leaves to give him or her a summary of his or her pay, tax deducted and NIC for the tax year to date. If necessary the employee can use the form to claim a tax repayment and/or jobseeker's allowance.

4.6 END OF YEAR PROCEDURE

There are two returns which need to be completed by the employer at the end of each tax year.

P11D

Form P11D provides details of expenses and benefits. It must be submitted to HMRC by 6 July following the tax year. It is completed in respect of each employee who receives taxable benefits during the tax year (see Chapter 10).

P60

The P60 is an end of year summary. It must be given to an employee by 31 May following the tax year. The form must contain the following details for each employee:

- personal details including national insurance number
- total earnings for the year
- final PAYE code
- total net tax deducted for the year
- total national insurance contributions
- employer's name and address.

5 SOURCE DOCUMENTS REQUIRED TO COMPLETE TAX RETURNS

An employee can find much of the information he or she needs to complete his or her tax return from the forms provided to him by his or her employer.

- The amount of income paid to the employee during the tax year can be found on the P60 (or P45 or payslips).
- In addition, details of any payments which are not included on the P60 are required, for example tips. These amounts should be recorded through the year when the money is received.
- Details of taxable expenses and benefits are shown on form P11D. A copy of this form should be provided to the employee by the employer by 6 July after the end of the tax year.
- If the employee wishes to claim a deduction for any expenses incurred wholly, exclusively and necessarily in the performance of his or her duties, he or she should ensure that he or she has retained the relevant receipts.
- Individuals should also obtain details of other income, for example interest received in the tax year can be determined from interest statements (see Chapter 13).

KEY TERMS

Earnings – includes not only cash wages or salary, but bonuses and commission and benefits made available by the employer.

Give As You Earn scheme – a means of making payments to charity through the payroll.

PAYE system – the system of collecting income tax and national insurance at source from the earnings of employees.

P45 – a form given to an employee when he or she leaves the employment. It shows his or her PAYE code number, total pay and tax and NIC to the date of cessation.

P11D – a form listing the benefits provided to directors and employees.

P60 – an end of year summary form given to an employee.

Real time information (RTI) – a system of reporting employees' pay, tax and other details electronically during the year.

SELF TEST QUESTIONS

		Paragraph
1	What earnings are assessed as employment income?	2.1
2	When are earnings treated as received?	2.2
3	What statutory deductions are allowed from employment income?	3.1
4	When are travel expenses deductible from employment income?	3.2
5	What test must be satisfied for other expenses to be deductible from employment income?	3.3
6	How is tax on employment income collected?	4.1
7	What deductions are allowed under the 'net pay scheme'?	4.3
8	When must tax deducted under the PAYE scheme be paid to HMRC?	4.4
9	What form must an employer complete when an employee leaves?	4.5
10	By what date must form P11D be submitted to HMRC?	4.6
11	By what date must form P60 be given to an employee?	4.6

MULTIPLE CHOICE QUESTIONS

1 Jim receives a salary of £50,000 per annum and has the use of a company flat on which he has a taxable benefit of £5,600 in the tax year 2021/22.

Which form should Jim's employer use to report the benefit to HMRC and by when must the form be submitted?

A Form P60 by 31 May 2022

B Form P60 by 6 July 2022

C Form P11D by 31 May 2022

D Form P11D by 6 July 2022

2 Shakera earns £45,000 p.a. as a graphic designer for Commercial Ltd, which prepares accounts to 31 March each year. For the last two years, Shakera has earned bonuses from her employer as follows:

	Paid	£
Year ended 31 March 2021	1 June 2021	8,000
Year ended 31 March 2022	1 June 2022	11,000

In addition, Shakera incurred expenses in travelling to client's offices of £2,000 in 2021/22, which are not reimbursed by Commercial Ltd.

What is Shakera's taxable employment income for the tax year 2021/22?

A £51,000

B £53,000

C £54,000

D £56,000

3 Henry is the finance director of a large company and incurred the following costs during the tax year 2021/22.

Which is deductible from his employment income?

A Subscription to the local health club where he frequently meets clients

B Travel between the two offices of his employer. He splits his time equally between the two centres

C Tips given to taxi drivers if he chooses to take a taxi home from work

D Cost of two new suits bought to impress clients

For suggested answers, see the 'Answers' section at the end of the book.

PRACTICE QUESTION

SAHAR

Sahar, managing director of Pemberley Ltd, is paid an annual salary of £103,000 and also bonuses based on the company's performance. Pemberley Ltd's accounting year ends on 31 December each year and the bonuses are normally determined and paid on 31 May thereafter. In recent years bonuses have been

Year to 31 December 2019	£4,000
Year to 31 December 2020	£8,000
Year to 31 December 2021	£4,000

Sahar pays 5% of her annual salary to charity through payroll giving. She has also spent £1,500 on courses to improve her computer skills.

Required:

Compute Sahar's taxable employment income for the tax year 2021/22. Briefly give reasons for your treatment of items included or excluded in arriving at her employment income.

(6 marks)

For a suggested answer, see the 'Answers' section at the end of the book.

Chapter 10

BENEFITS

INTRODUCTION

This chapter continues with employment income and looks at how benefits are taxed.

Benefits are a very likely examination topic. This chapter covers syllabus area C2 (d) to (f).

CONTENTS	LEARNING OUTCOMES
	At the end of this chapter, you should be able to: • identify and calculate benefits • compute aggregate employment income • identify the information required on a P11D.

1 GENERAL RULE FOR BENEFITS

There are two types of benefit.

	Exempt	Taxable
General rule	Not taxable	Taxed on marginal cost to employer of providing benefit
Special rules apply to these benefits	N/A	• Vouchers • Living accommodation • Use and gift of assets • Motor cars • Private fuel • Vans • Beneficial loans

2 EXEMPT BENEFITS

2.1 MISCELLANEOUS

The following are the more important exempt benefits:

- Trivial benefits (except cash or cash vouchers), which cost no more than £50 per gift per employee and are not provided in recognition of services provided by the employee. This exemption applies to low value benefits given for non-work reasons, such as birthday gifts.

- The employer's contribution to a registered pension scheme.

- The use of subsidised on-site restaurant or canteen facilities provided such facilities are available for all employees and not provided as part of a salary sacrifice scheme.

- Entertainment provided for an employee, by reason of his or her employment, by a genuine third party, e.g. a ticket or seat at a sporting or cultural event provided by a business contact or client to generate goodwill. Note that HMRC have long accepted that, in practice, no tax liability will arise on the typical working lunch or dinner.

- Gifts received by reason of employment from genuine third parties, provided the cost from any one source does not exceed £250 in a tax year.

- Long service awards, which are not in cash (e.g. gold watches), are exempt up to a cost of £50 for each year of service of 20 years or more.

- Employee liability insurance paid by an employer.

- Medical insurance for treatment and medical services where the need for treatment arises while abroad in the performance of the duties. Note that normal subscriptions to private health providers (such as BUPA) are taxable under the general rule (see section 3.1).

- Work related training costs.

- Christmas parties or other annual events for staff provided the cost is not more than £150 per head per year.
- Provision of one mobile phone (including smart phones) for private use by an employee.
- Homeworker's additional household expenses of up to £6 per week can be paid tax free without the need for any supporting evidence.
- Recreational and sporting facilities available to employees generally and not to the general public.
- Up to £8,000 of removal expenses for employees who move to take up a new job or where their existing job is relocated.
- Counselling provided to redundant employees to assist them in finding a new job.
- Awards of up to £5,000 under a staff suggestion scheme.
- Loans totalling no more than £10,000 throughout the year (see section 3.9).
- Medical treatment of up to £500 per employee per tax year, which is paid to assist them in returning to work.
- Up to £500 per employee per tax year for relevant pensions advice.

2.2 TRAVEL EXPENSES

There are a number of travel related exempt benefits, namely the provision of:

- A car parking space at or near the place of work, including the reimbursement of the cost of such a parking place.
- Bicycles and safety equipment for home to work travel and workplace parking for bicycles.
- Travel, accommodation and subsistence during public transport disruption caused by industrial action.
- Travel home where an employee normally travels under car-sharing arrangements with other employees, but these arrangements break down on a particular occasion due to unforeseen and exceptional circumstances.

2.3 SECURITY ASSETS AND SERVICES

No benefit arises where a security asset or security service is provided by reason of employment, or where reimbursement is made for the cost of such measures. Relief is not, however, available where the employee himself bears the cost.

The asset or service must meet a special threat to the employee's personal physical safety, as opposed to his or her property.

- Security assets include such things as intruder alarms, bullet-resistant glass and floodlighting.
- Security services include such things as bodyguards and specially trained chauffeurs.

2.4 EMPLOYER-PROVIDED CHILDCARE

Nurseries run by the employer (who must be responsible for finance and management) at the workplace or at other non-domestic premises are not a taxable benefit. The exemption includes facilities run jointly with other employers or local authorities and similar facilities for older children after school or during school holidays.

Employees may also receive other types of support for childcare costs such as childcare vouchers from their employer or through the Government Tax-Free Childcare Scheme. Neither of these forms of support is examinable in FTX.

2.5 EXPENSES INCURRED BY EMPLOYEES WHILST AWAY OVERNIGHT ON COMPANY BUSINESS

Where employers pay personal expenses, such as telephone calls home, laundry and so on, for employees who stay away from home on business, these expenses are not a taxable benefit, provided that they fall below the maximum limit of £5 per night in the UK and £10 per night overseas.

This exemption applies regardless of how the employer meets the expenses. For instance, the employer may:

- pay hotel bills directly
- provide a nightly allowance
- reimburse the employee with the actual expenses incurred.

If an amount above the limit is paid, the **whole amount** is taxable.

2.6 APPROVED MILEAGE ALLOWANCES

No benefit arises where an employer pays an allowance for business mileage incurred by an employee in his or her own transport, provided HMRC's approved mileage rates are not exceeded:

Form of transport	**On the first 10,000 miles in the tax year**	**On mileage in excess of 10,000 miles in the tax year**
Cars and vans	45p	25p

If the employer pays less than the approved rates, the employee can claim tax relief for the deficit. If the employer pays more than the approved rates, only the excess is taxable.

An employer can pay up to 5p per mile tax free for each passenger that the employee carries in his or her car or van, provided the passenger is a fellow employee. Note, however, that relief cannot be claimed for passengers if the employer does not pay an allowance.

Example

Linda is employed by Weller Ltd as a sales representative. Her employer pays her 32p per mile for business miles driven in her own car. In the tax year 2021/22 she drives a total of 21,000 business miles.

	£	£
Cash received (21,000 × 32p)		6,720
Allowable per the approved mileage allowance		
10,000 × 45p	4,500	
11,000 × 25p	2,750	
		(7,250)
Allowable expense		(530)

Linda receives less from her employer than the approved mileage allowance allows. The deficit is allowed as a deduction from Linda's employment income.

3 TAXABLE BENEFITS

3.1 GENERAL RULE

The general rule is that the taxable amount of the benefit is the **cost of providing** the benefit.

Under case law this has been held to mean the **additional or marginal cost** incurred by the employer – not a proportion of the total cost. This is particularly relevant where employers provide in-house benefits.

Example

A bus company provides free travel for employees on existing bus services. There is no additional cost to the employer of letting employees travel on an existing bus service so there is no taxable benefit.

In addition, there are specific rules that specify how certain benefits are taxed.

- Vouchers and credit tokens
- Living accommodation
- Use of assets
- Gifts of assets
- Cars
- Car fuel
- Vans
- Beneficial loans.

These are covered in the remainder of the chapter.

Rules applicable to all taxable benefits

There are two rules that must be applied in relation to **all** taxable benefits. The taxable benefit is:

- **reduced** by any contributions made by the employee towards the cost of the benefit (however, see exception in relation to private fuel).
- **time apportioned** if it was only available for part of the tax year.

Note that:

- An employee is deemed to be provided with a benefit, not only when it is provided to him or her directly, but also when it is provided to a member of his or her family or household.
- To be taxed under these principles, a benefit must be provided to the employee by reason of his or her employment.

3.2 VOUCHERS AND CREDIT TOKENS

Vouchers are documents that an individual can use to obtain goods and services.

- Cash vouchers are subject to PAYE when given to an employee. No further benefit arises on them since tax has already been paid.
- Non-cash vouchers are taxed as a benefit on the employee at the cost of providing them.

Example

X plc provides all its employees with Marks and Spencer vouchers worth £100. However, X plc only paid £95 for each voucher.

Employees are only taxed on £95, the cost to the employer of providing the benefit.

Credit tokens (such as a company credit card) are taxable on the value of goods and services bought with them for non-business use.

No taxable benefit arises where the employee can show that the use of either vouchers or credit tokens was wholly, exclusively and necessarily in the performance of the duties of his or her employment.

3.3 LIVING ACCOMMODATION

The basic charge

Where an employee is provided with living accommodation as a result of his or her employment, he or she is taxed on the higher of:

- the accommodation's annual value (given in the examination)
- the rent actually paid by the employer, where the employer rents, rather than owns the accommodation.

The benefit is reduced for:

- Business use
- Rent paid by the employee to the employer
- Any periods when the property was not available to the employee during the tax year.

Example

Claudia is provided with a house by her employer. The house is rented by her employer for £10,000 per year. Claudia moved in on 6 July 2021.

The annual value of the house is £6,400.

Claudia pays her employer rent of £250 per month.

What is Claudia's taxable benefit in respect of the house for the tax year 2021/22?

Solution

Basic charge

	£	£
Higher of:		
Annual value	6,400	
Rent paid by employer	10,000	
£10,000 × 9/12 (available from 6 July 2021)		7,500
Less: Rent paid by Claudia (£250 × 9)		(2,250)
Taxable benefit for 2021/22		5,250

The additional charge

There is an additional benefit assessed on 'expensive' living accommodation. It applies in addition to the basic charge where the employer owns the accommodation and it cost in excess of £75,000.

The benefit is calculated as follows:

(Cost of provision – £75,000) × the appropriate percentage

This formula is **not** given in the examination.

The cost of provision is:

- the purchase price of the property plus expenditure on improvements incurred **before the start** of the tax year.
- Where the accommodation has been owned by the employer throughout the six years preceding the employee taking up residence in it, the calculation of the benefit uses the property's market value when **first used** by the employee rather than the purchase price.

The appropriate percentage is the official rate of interest used for beneficial loans in force at the start of the tax year. This will be provided on the rates and allowances sheet in the examination and is 2% for 2021/22.

Deductions from the taxable benefit are available both for business use of the accommodation and for rent paid by the employee to the employer for the use of the accommodation.

Example

Vanske plc provides a company house for use by an employee Tomas. Vanske plc bought the house for £100,000 in June 2006. An extension was built in May 2012 for £40,000 and a conservatory added in July 2021 at a cost of £25,000.

What is the cost of provision for the tax year 2021/22 assuming Tomas moved in during:

(a) December 2010 when the market value of the house was £130,000 or

(b) January 2017 when the market value was £220,000.

Solution

(a) £140,000 (£100,000 cost + £40,000 extension). The conservatory added in July 2021 is ignored as it was added after the start of the tax year.

(b) £220,000. As the house was purchased by the company more than 6 years before Tomas moved in, the market value at the date of moving in is used to replace the costs (purchase and extension) incurred before that date. As with part (a) the conservatory is ignored for the tax year 2021/22.

Job-related accommodation

There is no taxable benefit if the accommodation is job-related. To qualify as such it must be:

- necessary for the proper performance of the employee's duties (e.g. a caretaker), or
- provided for the better performance of the employee's duties and, for that type of employment, it is customary for employers to provide living accommodation (e.g. hotel-worker), or
- provided due to a special threat to the employee's security and the employee resides in the accommodation as part of special security arrangements.

A director can only claim one of the first two exemptions if:

- he or she has no material interest in the company, and
- he or she is a full time working director or the company is a non-profit making organisation.

ACTIVITY 1

Jason was provided with a house to live in by his employer in November 2018. It cost the employer £200,000 in June 2015 and has an annual value of £3,000.

Calculate the taxable benefit for the tax year 2021/22 assuming the accommodation is not job-related.

For a suggested answer, see the 'Answers' section at the end of the book.

ACTIVITY 2

Sacha is provided with a house by his employer, the details of which are as follows.

The house cost £90,000, when acquired in June 2016. It has an annual value of £1,700. Since this time the following improvements have taken place:

Date of expenditure	Type of expenditure	£
February 2017	Conservatory	15,000
August 2018	Redecoration	2,000
September 2021	Garage extension	10,000

Its market value was as follows:

June 2021	£165,000
April 2021	£200,000

The accommodation is not job-related and Sacha pays a rent of £100 per month to his employer.

(a) Calculate the taxable benefit for the tax year 2021/22 in the following situations:

(i) Sacha moved in on 6 June 2021.

(ii) Sacha moved in on 6 June 2021, but the property was actually acquired by his employer in June 2011, not June 2016.

(b) For each of the scenarios above and assuming Sacha remains in the property, with no improvements other than the ones referred to above, what will be the cost of provision of the accommodation for calculating the expensive accommodation charge for the tax year 2022/23.

For a suggested answer, see the 'Answers' section at the end of the book.

Expenses and furnishings connected with living accommodation

- Expenses connected with living accommodation, such as lighting and heating, are taxed on an employee where the cost is met by the employer.
- Furnishings provided are also taxed. The benefit is calculated as 20% of the market value of the furnishings at the date they were first provided, which is the normal use of assets rule set out in section 3.4 below.

Expenses re job-related accommodation

When the living accommodation is job-related there is no benefit for the provision of the accommodation itself, but the expenses and furnishings are still taxable, subject to a limit.

The taxable limit is **10% of net emoluments** (salary plus benefits, other than the accommodation expenses in question, less any expenditure deductible against employment income).

3.4 USE OF ASSETS

The general rule

- If an asset is given to an employee, the employee is taxed on the cost incurred by the employer.
- However, if an asset is loaned to an employee, while its legal ownership remains with the employer, the general rule is that an employee is taxed on an annual benefit amounting to 20% of the asset's market value at the time it is first provided.

Example

Asja is provided with a television costing £500.

She is subject to a benefit charge of £100 (£500 × 20%). The benefit is assessed for each tax year in which it is provided (not just the one in which it was first made available).

Where the employer rents the asset made available to the employee instead of buying it, the employee is taxed on the higher of

– the rental paid by the employer and

– 20% of the market value.

So if the annual rental for the television mentioned above is £120, Asja would be assessed on £120 rather than £100.

ACTIVITY 3

Sushil's employer, KP Ltd, purchased a computer for his personal use on 1 January 2021 for £1,800. Sushil pays his employer £5 per month for the use of the computer.

Calculate the benefit taxable on Sushil for the tax year 2021/22.

For a suggested answer, see the 'Answers' section at the end of the book.

3.5 GIFTS OF ASSETS

If an employer purchases a new asset and gives it to an employee immediately, the employee is taxed on the cost to the employer.

Where an asset has been used by an employee and is then given to the employee, the employee is taxed on the **higher** of:

	£	£
Asset market value when gifted		X
Asset market value at the time it was **first made available** to the employee	X	
Less: Benefits assessed on the employee during the time he or she had the use of it, but did not own it	(X)	X

Any payment made to the employer by the employee for the asset is deducted in either case.

The purpose of the special rule for gifts of used assets is to prevent employees gaining from gifts of assets that depreciate in value rapidly once they are used.

A different rule applies in respect of **cars and vans**. Where an employee is given a car or van which he or she has previously had the use of, he or she will only be assessed on its **market value at the date of the gift** (less any payment made by the employee to the employer).

Example

A suit costing £400 was purchased for Henri's use by his employer on 6 April 2020. On 6 August 2021 the suit was purchased by Henri for £20 when the market value was £30.

What is the taxable benefit for Henri for the tax years 2020/21 and 2021/22?

Solution

In 2020/21 Henri is taxed on £80 (£400 × 20%).

In 2021/22 Henri is taxed on two amounts.

- Use of the suit – £27 (£400 × 20% × 4/12)
- Sale of suit – higher of:

	£	£
1 Asset market value when gifted		30
2 Asset market value at the time it was **first made available** to the employee	400	
Less: Benefits assessed on Henri during the time he had the use of it, but did not own it (£80 + £27)	(107)	
		293
Take the higher value £293 and deduct the price Henri paid of £20		273

ACTIVITY 4

Brian's employer, X Ltd, purchased a dishwasher for his use on 1 June 2020, costing £600. On 6 April 2021 it gave the dishwasher to Brian (its market value then being £150).

(a) Calculate the taxable benefit for Brian in the tax year 2021/22 assuming he paid X Ltd £100 for the dishwasher.

(b) How would your answer differ for the tax year 2021/22 if the asset provided had been a car?

For a suggested answer, see the 'Answers' section at the end of the book.

3.6 CARS

Overview

The company car is one of the most widely provided benefits for employees. Where a company car is available to an employee for private use, a taxable benefit arises calculated as follows:

	£
List price when new × appropriate %	X
Less: Employee contributions for private use of the car	(X)
Taxable benefit	X

- The car benefit charge covers the running expenses of the vehicle, so there is no additional taxable benefit when the employer pays for insurance, road fund licence, maintenance, etc.
- If a chauffeur is provided with the car, however, the cost of the chauffeur constitutes an additional benefit.
- A separate benefit charge is made for car fuel (see below).

Pool cars

There is no benefit for the use of a 'pool car'. To qualify as a 'pool car' **all** of the following conditions must be met during the tax year in question:

- The car must be used by more than one employee (and not usually by one employee to the exclusion of the others).
- It must not normally be kept overnight at or near the residence of any of the employees making use of it.
- Any private use by an employee must be merely incidental to his or her business use of it.

It should be noted that if any employee breaks these conditions he or she exposes all other users of the car to a benefit charge, not just himself.

List price

- The list price of a car is the published inclusive price (i.e. including taxes) appropriate for the car on the assumption that it is sold in the UK as an individual sale in the retail market.
- Consequently, employees of large companies cannot benefit from bulk discounts their employer might negotiate. It is the list price on the day before the car's first registration that is used.

Where the car is fitted with accessories when the car is first provided, the list price of these (or market value where there is no list price) is added to the list price of the car. If the accessories are fitted later, they are added to the list price if they cost £100 or more.

An employee may reduce the list price on which his or her car benefit is calculated by making a capital contribution. The list price is reduced by the lower of:

- the capital contribution towards the cost of the car and its accessories
- £5,000 (this figure is **not** provided in the examination).

Appropriate percentage

The car benefit is calculated by applying a percentage to the list price of the car. The percentage depends on the amount of carbon dioxide (CO_2) emission as recorded on the vehicle's registration certificate.

For 2021/22 a rate of 55 grams per kilometre attracts a minimum percentage of 15%. For every **complete** additional 5 grams there is a 1% increase up to a maximum percentage of 37%, i.e. if the CO_2 emissions do not end in zero or five, round down.

A 4% supplement applies to diesel cars unless they meet the real driving emissions 2 (RDE2) standards. Diesel cars that meet the RDE2 standard are treated in the same way as petrol cars. You will be told in the question if a diesel car meets the RDE2 standard. The maximum percentage for a diesel car (including the supplement) remains 37%.

Neither the diesel supplement nor the maximum percentage are provided in the examination.

Example

A petrol car with an emission rate of 138g/km has an appropriate percentage of 31% i.e. 15% + ((135 – 55)/5) in the tax year 2021/22.

If the car used diesel, the percentage for the tax year 2021/22 would be 35%, unless it meets the RDE2 standard, in which case the percentage would be 31% (the same as for a petrol car).

If the car has an emissions rate of 51-54g/km the relevant percentage is 14%. The 4% diesel supplement is added to this special lower percentage, unless the car meets the RDE2 standard.

These rates all apply to cars registered on or after 6 April 2020 – in the exam you should assume that all cars are registered after this date. The previous rules are not examinable.

Zero emission and hybrid-electric cars

A 1% percentage applies to electric-powered motor cars with zero CO_2 emissions.

For hybrid-electric motor cars with CO_2 emissions between 1 and 50 grams per kilometre, the electric range of a motor car is relevant:

Electric range	
130 miles or more	1%
70 to 129 miles	4%
40 to 69 miles	7%
30 to 39 miles	11%
Less than 30 miles	13%

Reductions in benefit

- Where the car is unavailable for part of the tax year, because it was first provided or ceased to be provided part way through a tax year, the benefit is reduced proportionately.
- The car may also be unavailable for a period during the tax year, for instance if it was under repair after a crash. The benefit charge that would otherwise apply is proportionately reduced provided that it was unavailable for a continuous period of at least 30 days. (Note that this reduction is dependent on the car being unavailable. It is not given if the car was available, but the employee was unable to drive it, for example due to being abroad.)
- A reduction is made where the employee makes a financial contribution as a condition of the car being available for his or her private use. (This should not be confused with a capital contribution made towards the purchase cost of the car, which is deducted from the list price.)

Example

Bernard, Pauline and Lenka are employed by PC Ltd and are provided with company cars.

Bernard's car cost the company £21,000 although it has a list price of £22,600. Bernard contributed £3,000 towards the capital cost. The car has CO_2 emissions of 112g/km. It was first provided to Bernard in January 2021. The company pays all expenses except petrol. Bernard pays the company £10/month for the private use of the car.

Pauline's car has CO_2 emissions of 119g/km and has a list price of £29,750. She contributed £7,000 towards its cost. It was first provided to Pauline on 5 June 2021 and has a diesel engine. Pauline's car meets the RDE2 standard.

Lenka's hybrid-electric car has a list price of £20,000 and CO_2 emissions of 46g/km. The electric range of the car is 37 miles. The car was first provided to her on 5 October 2021.

Calculate the car benefits for Bernard, Pauline and Lenka for the tax year 2021/22.

Solution

Bernard's car benefit

	£
List price	22,600
Less: Capital contribution	(3,000)
	19,600
Relevant % (15% + (110 – 55)/5)	26%
Car benefit is £19,600 × 26%	5,096
Less: Contribution towards running costs (£10 × 12)	(120)
	4,976

Pauline's car benefit

	£
List price	29,750
Less: Capital contribution –	
Lower of: Amount paid (£7,000) or £5,000	(5,000)
	24,750
Relevant % (15% + (115 – 55)/5) (no diesel supplement as meets the RDE2 standard)	27%
Car benefit is £24,750 × 27% × 10/12	5,569

Lenka's car benefit

	£
List price	20,000
Less: Capital contribution	NIL
	20,000
Relevant % (Based on electric range)	11%
Car benefit is £20,000 × 11% × 6/12	1,100

3.7 CAR FUEL

- If fuel is provided for private mileage, there is a separate car fuel charge. This charge is calculated using the same percentage as for the car benefit. The percentage is applied to the figure of £24,600.
- The fuel charge is scaled down when the provision of fuel starts part way through the tax year, or is permanently discontinued during the year. However, no reduction will be made for temporary periods of unavailability of private fuel.

- No reduction is made in the fuel charge for payments made by the employee unless he or she pays for all fuel used for private motoring, in which case, the charge is cancelled.
- Since the fuel charge applies only to vehicles for which there is a car benefit charge, it does not apply to 'pool cars'.

ACTIVITY 5

Charles took up employment with Weavers Ltd on 1 July 2021. His remuneration package included a petrol-driven car, list price £24,000 with a CO_2 emission rate of 147g/km recorded on its registration certificate. He took delivery of the car on 1 August 2021 and during the remainder of the tax year drove 15,000 miles on business and 18,000 miles for private purposes. As a condition of the car being made available to him for private motoring, Charles paid £100 per month for the car and £50 per month for petrol.

Weavers Ltd incurred the following expenses in connection with Charles' car:

	£
Servicing	450
Insurance	780
Fuel (of which £1,150 was for business purposes)	2,500
Maintenance	240

Calculate Charles' taxable benefits for the tax year 2021/22 in connection with his private use of the car.

For a suggested answer, see the 'Answers' section at the end of the book.

3.8 VANS

Where an employer makes a van available to an employee for his or her private use, a benefit scale charge applies.

- The scale charge is £3,500.
- There is an additional benefit of £669 if fuel is provided for private mileage.
- Proportionate reductions in the scale charges are made where a van is unavailable for part of the tax year (in the same way as for cars).
- Again, following the car benefit principle, a reduction is made for payments made by the employee for private use of the van.
- Where employees share the private use of a van, the scale charge is divided between them on a just and reasonable basis.

Note that a benefit charge does not apply where an employee uses a company van for journeys between home and work, provided any other private use is insignificant.

The benefit figures for vans are provided in the tax tables in the examination.

3.9 BENEFICIAL LOANS

Beneficial loans are those made to an employee below the **official rate of interest**. In the examination, it will be assumed that 2% applies throughout 2021/22. This percentage is provided in the rates and allowances sheet in the examination.

Employees are liable to a benefit charge on:

	£
Interest that would be payable on the loan (had interest been charged at the official rate)	X
Less: Interest actually paid in respect of the tax year	(X)
Taxable benefit	X

- An exemption for small loans applies where all of the employee's cheap or interest free loans, excluding loans that qualify for tax relief (see Chapter 14), total no more than £10,000 throughout the tax year.

- There are two methods of calculating the benefit, the average method and the precise method.

  – The average method uses the average of the loan outstanding at the beginning and end of the tax year. If the loan was taken out or redeemed during the tax year, that date is used instead of the beginning or end of the tax year (and the benefit is time apportioned).

  – The precise or accurate method calculates the benefit day by day on the balance actually outstanding. However, note that in the examination this calculation would only be performed to the nearest month.

Either the taxpayer or HMRC can decide that the precise method should be used.

Example

Daniz is given an interest free loan of £15,000 by his employer on 1 July 2021. He repays £3,000 of the loan on 1 January 2022.

(a) The taxable benefit using the averaging method is:

Average loan is ½ (£15,000 + £12,000) = £13,500
Benefit is £13,500 × 9/12 × 2% = £203

(b) Using the precise method:

£15,000 of the loan is outstanding for 6 months and £12,000 for the next 3 months.

Benefit is (£15,000 × 2% × 6/12) + (£12,000 × 2% × 3/12) = £210

HMRC could elect for the precise method.

ACTIVITY 6

Daniel was granted a loan of £35,000 by his employer on 31 March 2021 to help finance the purchase of a yacht. Interest is payable on the loan at 1.75% p.a. On 1 June 2021 Daniel repaid £4,000 and on 1 December 2021 he repaid a further £15,000. The remaining £16,000 was still outstanding on 5 April 2022.

Calculate the taxable benefit for the tax year 2021/22 under:

(a) the averaging method

(b) the precise method.

For a suggested answer, see the 'Answers' section at the end of the book.

Loans written off

If all or part of a loan to an employee is written off, the amount written off is treated as a benefit and charged to income tax.

Where an employee dies with a loan outstanding, no benefit accrues after the date of death and there is no charge to tax if the employer writes it off.

Exemption for commercial loans

There is an exemption for loans made to employees on commercial terms by employers who lend to the general public e.g. banks. The exemption will apply where:

- the loans are made by an employer whose business includes the lending of money
- loans are made to employees on the same terms and conditions as are available to members of the public
- a substantial number of loans on these terms are made to public customers.

4 COMPUTATION OF EMPLOYMENT INCOME

Once you have calculated the benefits taxable on the employee, the total employment income can be calculated. The computation should appear as follows:

	£
Income from employment (salaries, bonuses, commissions, fees, tips, etc.)	X
Taxable benefits	X
Less: Allowable expenses	(X)
Taxable employment income	X

5 IDENTIFY THE INFORMATION REQUIRED ON THE P11D

The form P11D must be completed for employees who received any taxable benefits during the tax year.

Form P11D requires the various benefits provided and taxable expenses paid to be listed on the form, under the appropriate heading. The employer must enter the value of the benefit and the amount of expense paid.

KEY TERMS

Form P11D – a return showing the taxable benefits and expenses provided to an employee during the tax year.

Director – a director is any person appointed as a director or who acts as a director.

Material interest – an individual has a material interest in a company if he or she holds 5% or more of its ordinary share capital.

Vouchers – documents that an individual can use to obtain goods and services.

Annual value – the rent the premises would command in the open market assuming that the tenant pays occupier's taxes and the owner pays for insurance, maintenance and repairs.

Job-related accommodation – accommodation is job-related if it is necessary for the performance of the employee's duties, or provided for the better performance of the employee's duties and, for that type of employment, it is customary for employers to provide living accommodation, or provided due to a special threat to the employee's security.

Pool car – a pool car is one which is used by more than one employee, not normally kept overnight at the residence of the employees using it and any private use is merely incidental to business use.

List price – the list price of a car is the inclusive price (i.e. including taxes) appropriate for the car on the assumption that it is sold in the UK as an individual sale in the retail market.

CO_2 emissions – carbon dioxide emissions.

Beneficial loan – a loan made to an employee on which the interest charged is less than the official rate.

Security asset – the term security asset includes intruder alarms, bullet-resistant glass and floodlighting.

Security services – these include bodyguards and specially trained chauffeurs.

Approved mileage allowances – sums that an employer can pay tax free to an employee who uses his or her own transport for business travel.

SELF TEST QUESTIONS

		Paragraph
1	What is the general rule used to value benefits?	1
2	Give five examples of exempt benefits.	2
4	What are the conditions that must be satisfied for accommodation to be treated as job-related?	3.3
5	How is the additional benefit for expensive living accommodation calculated?	3.3
6	What are the conditions that must be satisfied for a car to qualify as a pool car?	3.6
7	What percentage is the surcharge for diesel cars (assuming the RDE2 standard is not met)?	3.6
8	How is the car fuel benefit calculated?	3.7
9	What are the two methods used to calculate the benefit in respect of a beneficial loan?	3.9
10	What form is used to report taxable benefits for employees?	5

MULTIPLE CHOICE QUESTIONS

1 Blanca was provided by his employer with the use of a computer for private purposes on 1 October 2021. The market value of the computer when first provided was £4,300 and at 5 April 2022 the market value was £3,000.

What is the value of the benefit in respect of this computer for the tax year 2021/22?

A £600

B £860

C £430

D £300

2 Budget Ltd is an estate agency and provided the following benefits to a number of its employees during the tax year 2021/22. Which of the following is NOT taxable as employment income for the tax year 2021/22?

A Medical insurance provided to a key member of staff

B Free membership to the gym situated next door to the company headquarters

C A second mobile phone provided to the chief executive of the company

D A free place at the employer's on-site childcare facilities, for the sales director's child, which costs the employer £150 per week to provide.

3 Carla was provided with a company car by her employer on 1 April 2021. The diesel car has a list price of £35,000 and CO_2 emissions of 123g/km, and did not meet the RDE2 standard. Carla paid a contribution of £1,000 to her employer towards the initial purchase price of the car. Carla is not provided with fuel for private purposes.

What is the taxable benefit for Carla for the tax year 2021/22 in respect of the car?

A £9,520

B £10,880

C £10,200

D £11,220

4 Leo was provided with a house to live in by his employer. The employer rented the house from a local resident and paid rent of £32,000 p.a. Leo paid rent of £12,000 p.a. to his employer. The property has an annual value of £12,750 p.a.

What is the taxable value of this benefit, assuming the accommodation is not job-related?

A £12,750

B £12,000

C £20,000

D £750

For suggested answers, see the 'Answers' section at the end of the book.

PRACTICE QUESTION

ADRIANNE

Adrianne is employed by ABC Ltd at a salary of £50,000 per annum.

She was paid a bonus of £10,000 on 10 April 2021 based on the company's results for the year to 31 December 2020.

The following information relates to the tax year 2021/22.

1 Adrianne was provided with a car with a list price of £25,000 when first registered on 1 November 2020. The CO_2 emission figure is 109g/km.

Adrianne's mileage during the year was as follows:

Home to work	12,000
Visiting clients from work	7,000
Private	5,000
	24,000

The company paid the following running expenses:

	£
Replacement tyres	950
Insurance	600
Servicing	300
	1,850

The company paid for all petrol.

Adrianne was required to make a contribution of £50 per month as a condition of the car being available for private use.

2 Adrianne was provided with one mobile phone, which she used for business and private calls. The company paid £680 in rent and call charges of which 30% was in respect of private usage.

3 ABC Ltd paid for private medical insurance. The cost to the company was £250. Had Adrianne provided the insurance herself it would have cost her £280.

4 The company provided Adrianne with a credit card, and paid the following amounts:

	£
Cost of personal goods and services	2,500
Annual fee	35
Interest	100
	2,635

5 The company provided Adrianne with an interest free loan of £16,000, which, she used to pay for a holiday in Mauritius. The loan was provided in March 2021 and by 5 April 2022 Adrianne had made no repayments.

6 The company provided a suit for Adrianne's use. It cost £800 when first made available in January 2020. Its market value at 5 April 2021 is £75.

7 Adrianne paid professional subscriptions of £400.

Required:

Calculate Adrianne's employment income for the tax year 2021/22. **(15 marks)**

For a suggested answer, see the 'Answers' section at the end of the book.

Chapter 11

NATIONAL INSURANCE CONTRIBUTIONS

INTRODUCTION

This chapter considers the basic rules of national insurance. National insurance contributions (NICs) are payable by employees and the self-employed. Employers are also required to pay NICs on the salary and some of the benefits they pay to their employees.

This chapter covers syllabus areas B6 and C2 (h) to (i).

CONTENTS	LEARNING OUTCOMES
1 Class 1 NICs **2** Class 1A NICs **3** National insurance and the self-employed	At the end of this chapter, you should be able to: • compute basic class 1 national insurance contributions • understand the annual employment allowance • calculate national insurance contributions for the self-employed and contrast with employees.

1 CLASS 1 NICS

1.1 WHO IS LIABLE?

A liability for class 1 contributions arises where an individual:

- is employed, and
- is aged 16 or over, and
- has earnings in excess of the earnings threshold.

1.2 EMPLOYEE CONTRIBUTIONS

- Employee contributions, also known as primary contributions are the class 1 contributions payable by employees. They are payable on earnings above £9,568 (the earnings threshold). Contributions of 12% are payable on earnings in the range £9,569 to £50,270 a year. Contributions of 2% are payable on earnings above £50,270 a year.
- The contributions are **not** allowable deductions for income tax purposes.
- No employee contributions are payable by an employee who is of state pension age. The state pension age depends on an individual's date of birth and is gradually increasing. In a question, you will be told if a taxpayer is over state pension age.

1.3 EARNINGS FOR CLASS 1 PURPOSES

The earnings on which class 1 contributions are calculated comprise any remuneration derived from employment and paid in money or vouchers. The calculation is on gross earnings, before deductions that are allowable for income tax purposes, e.g. subscriptions to professional bodies, and before the deduction of the personal allowance. Gross earnings include:

- wages, salary, overtime pay, commission or bonus
- sick pay, including statutory sick pay
- tips and gratuities paid or allocated by the employer
- vouchers (cash and non-cash)
- mileage allowances in excess of 45p per mile (45p limit applies even if mileage exceeds 10,000 per year).

The following are disregarded in calculating gross earnings for employee contributions:

- benefits (other than those listed above)
- reimbursement of expenses actually incurred in carrying out the employment
- all pension contributions.

1.4 EMPLOYER'S CONTRIBUTIONS

Employers are liable to pay employer's class 1 contributions, also known as secondary contributions, on all earnings exceeding £8,840 a year. There is no upper earnings threshold, or upper age limit.

For 2021/22 employer's contributions are payable at the rate of 13.8%.

Example

Saif is employed by Mans Ltd and is paid £52,000 a year.

What NICs are payable in respect of Saif for the tax year 2021/22?

Solution

		£
Class 1 employee contributions:	(£50,270 – £9,568) × 12%	4,884
	(£52,000 – £50,270) × 2%	35
		4,919

This must be deducted from his wages under PAYE.

Class 1 employer's contributions:	(£52,000 – £8,840) × 13.8%	5,956

The employer pays the class 1 employer's and employee's NIC to HMRC.

1.5 EARNINGS PERIODS

Class 1 is normally calculated on either a weekly or monthly basis, according to how frequently the employee is paid. This is known as the earnings period.

- Calculations should be done on a weekly or monthly basis, as appropriate, in the examination, unless the earnings period is not given in which case they should be calculated using the annual thresholds, as in the previous example.

- For weekly or monthly calculations, the annual thresholds given in the rates and allowances table should be divided by 52 (weekly) or 12 (monthly).

Example

Julie is paid a wage of £250 a week. She was also paid a bonus of £10,000 in the last week of March 2022.

Calculate the total amount of NICs payable by Julie for the tax year 2021/22.

Solution

Julie will pay NICs on earnings of £250 a week for 51 weeks and earnings of £10,250 for the week in which the bonus was paid.

The lower and upper weekly thresholds for class 1 employee NICs are:

£9,568 ÷ 52 = £184

£50,270 ÷ 52 = £967

		£
(£250 – £184)	× 12% × 51 weeks	404
(£967 – £184)	× 12% × 1 week	94
(£10,250 – £967)	× 2% × 1 week	186
		684

Therefore, in the week in which her bonus is paid, £9,283 (£10,250 – £967) is charged at the rate of 2% as it exceeds the upper threshold for the week of payment.

As this example shows, an employee may pay less national insurance by being paid a low weekly wage and a large bonus.

Note: This question only asked for the NICs payable by Julie and therefore it was not necessary to calculate the class 1 employer's NICs, which are payable by her employer. Be careful to only answer the question asked.

1.6 ANNUAL EMPLOYMENT ALLOWANCE

The employment allowance is £4,000 per tax year and is deducted from an employer's class 1 NICs liability.

Note that the allowance:

- cannot be used against any other classes of NICs (e.g. class 1A)
- is only available to employers with total class 1 employer's contributions <£100,000 in the previous tax year
- is claimed as part of the normal payroll process through RTI (see Chapter 9)
- will be provided in the examination in the tax rates and allowances.

Information regarding the prior year's class 1 employer's NICs will be provided in the examination question where required.

1.7 DEDUCTION AND PAYMENT BY THE EMPLOYER

The employer calculates the employee and employer's contributions at each weekly or monthly pay date.

At the end of each PAYE month (5th) the total employee and employer's contributions become payable, along with income tax deducted under PAYE, not later than 14 days thereafter (i.e. by 19th or 22nd if paid electronically).

2 CLASS 1A NICS

Employers are required to pay class 1A contributions on the taxable value of most benefits provided to their employees. Class 1A does not include:

- items already subject to class 1 NICs, such as non-cash vouchers, or
- exempt benefits.

Class 1A NICs are computed using the value of the benefit calculated for income tax purposes. No contributions will be levied if there is no income tax benefit, e.g. if a car is not available for private use, or if the employee makes full reimbursement for private fuel used.

Contributions are at the rate of 13.8% for 2021/22. They must be paid by 19 July following the end of the tax year.

Only employers pay class 1A NIC. No charge falls on the employee.

ACTIVITY 1

Tingting is provided with private medical insurance costing £720, the private use of a car costing £26,000 with a benefit charge calculated at 35%, and private use petrol.

Calculate the class 1A contributions payable for the tax year 2021/22.

For a suggested answer, see the 'Answers' section at the end of the book.

3 NATIONAL INSURANCE AND THE SELF-EMPLOYED

3.1 LIABILITY

All self-employed persons over the age of 16 and under state pension age must pay both class 2 and class 4 contributions, if their trading profits exceed certain thresholds.

3.2 CLASS 4 CONTRIBUTIONS

- Class 4 contributions are payable on trading profits above £9,568. Contributions of 9% are payable on 'profits' in the range £9,569 to £50,270. The rate is 2% on 'profits' above £50,270.
- 'Profits' for class 4 purposes are the tax adjusted trading profits of the individual that are assessable to income tax after deducting trading losses (if any).
- Class 4 NICs are paid together with income tax and are due by 31 January following the end of the tax year; that is 31 January 2023 for 2021/22. However, unless the amounts are small, most taxpayers have to make two payments on account before 31 January 2023 (see Chapter 16 for details).
- An individual will continue to pay class 4 contributions until the **end** of the tax year in which he or she reaches state pension age.
- Class 4 contributions are payable on the total of all profits from self-employment, irrespective of the number of self-employed occupations. Therefore, if a taxpayer has more than one business, the profits should be added together before calculating class 4 NICs.

3.3 CLASS 2 CONTRIBUTIONS

- Class 2 contributions are payable at a weekly flat rate of £3.05 for 2021/22. The maximum payable for 2021/22 is therefore £159 (£3.05 $\times$ 52 weeks).
- Contributions are paid on 31 January following the end of the tax year; that is, 31 January 2023 for the 2021/22 tax year. There are no payments on account for class 2.

- Individuals with profits below the small profits threshold do not pay class 2 contributions. Profits are defined in the same way as for class 4. The small profits threshold for 2021/22 is £6,515.

- Class 2 contributions are payable at the same weekly flat rate regardless of the number of self-employed occupations. However, the earnings from all such occupations are aggregated to decide whether the small profits threshold is exceeded.

- A taxpayer does not have to pay class 2 NICs in respect of any week in which he or she is:

  – aged under 16; or

  – of state pension age or over.

ACTIVITY 2

Bill is a self-employed builder who has been in business for many years and prepares accounts to 31 March each year.

His taxable trading profit for the year ended 31 March 2022 is £51,850.

Calculate Bill's class 2 and class 4 NIC liabilities for the tax year 2021/22.

For a suggested answer, see the 'Answers' section at the end of the book.

3.4 CONTRAST NICS FOR THE SELF-EMPLOYED WITH NICS FOR EMPLOYEES

To summarise, the NICs payable by the self-employed and employees are as follows:

Self-employed		**Employed**	
		Employee:	
Class 4 on profits		Class 1 on earnings	
£1 – £9,568	0%	£1 – £9,568	0%
£9,569 – £50,270	9%	£9,569 – £50,270	12%
£50,271 and above	2%	£50,271 and above	2%
Class 2 at £3.05 a week		**Employer's:**	
		Class 1 at 13.8% on earnings above £8,840 a year	

All these rates are given in the tax tables supplied with your examination.

- NICs for the self-employed are less than for an employee.

- Class 1 and class 1A contributions payable by the **employer** are deductible in calculating the employer's taxable profits. This reduces their cost to the employer.

> **Example**
>
> If an employer pays corporation tax at the rate of 19%, the payment of £100 of employer's class 1 contributions will only cost the company £81 (£100 – £19 tax saving).

- Class 1 employee contributions paid by the employee and class 2 and 4 contributions paid by a trader are not an allowable tax deduction.

KEY TERMS

Employee contributions – class 1 contributions payable by employees.

Employer's contributions – class 1 contributions payable by employers.

Class 1 NICs – NICs payable by employees and employers.

Class 1A NICs – NICs payable by employers on benefits provided to employees.

Class 2 NICs – a weekly amount of NICs payable by the self-employed.

Class 4 NICs – a profits-related amount of NICs payable by the self-employed.

NIC employment allowance – an annual allowance that reduces the employer's class 1 employer's NICs liability.

SELF TEST QUESTIONS

		Paragraph
1	Give three examples of items included as earnings for class 1 purposes.	1.3
2	When must an employer account to HMRC for NICs?	1.7
3	Who is liable to pay class 1A NICs?	2
4	On what are class 1A NICs calculated?	2
5	When are class 4 contributions paid?	3.2
6	At what age can an individual stop paying class 4 contributions?	3.2
7	When are class 2 contributions paid?	3.3

MULTIPLE CHOICE QUESTIONS

1 Keith is an employee of K Ltd. Keith receives cash earnings of £31,608 and a car benefit valued at £5,800 in the tax year 2021/22.

How much class 1 employee national insurance contributions (NIC) does Keith suffer in respect of the tax year 2021/22?

A £3,042

B £2,645

C £3,341

D £3,793

2 Anastasia is self-employed and runs her own business as a caterer. She employs Patrice who is paid £15,000 p.a.

What classes of national insurance contributions is Anastasia liable to pay?

A Class 2 only

B Class 4 only

C Class 2 and class 4 only

D Class 2, class 4 and class 1 employer's contributions

3 Daanish is employed and had the following employment package from his employer for the tax year 2021/22.

	£
Salary	35,000
Employer pension contributions	3,250
A company car – taxable benefit	3,570

In addition, Daanish incurred business travel expenses of £400, which were not reimbursed by his employer.

Daanish's earnings for the purpose of calculating his class 1 national insurance contributions are:

A £35,000

B £38,250

C £34,600

D £38,570

For suggested answers, see the 'Answers' section at the end of the book.

PRACTICE QUESTIONS

CLARE (1)

Clare has been a self-employed computer consultant for many years. Her tax adjusted trading profits for the tax year 2021/22 are £54,000.

Required:

Calculate the NICs that Clare must pay in respect of her business for the tax year 2021/22.
(6 marks)

CLARE (2)

Clare employs two full time assistants at a salary of £15,000 p.a. each. This salary is paid monthly, and in December 2021 she also paid each assistant a bonus of £5,000.

Required:

Calculate the total NICs that Clare must pay to HMRC for the tax year 2021/22 in respect of her employees. **(6 marks)**

CLARE (3)

Clare provides one assistant with a diesel-engine company car, which does not meet the RDE2 standard and has a list price of £13,500 and CO_2 emissions of 100g/km. Clare pays for the assistant's private and business fuel.

Required:

Calculate the total NICs that Clare must account for to HMRC in the tax year 2021/22 in respect of the car. **(6 marks)**

For a suggested answer, see the 'Answers' section at the end of the book.

Chapter 12

PROPERTY INCOME

All UK income from land and buildings is taxed as income from a property business. This chapter looks at how property income is calculated and assessed. It also considers the special rules that apply to furnished holiday lettings.

This chapter looks at how the rules are applied to income received by individuals. The differences in the way the rules apply to companies are dealt with in the corporation tax chapters.

This chapter covers syllabus areas C3 (a) to (e).

CONTENTS	LEARNING OUTCOMES
1 Property income **2** Premiums received on the grant of a short lease **3** Furnished holiday lettings **4** Rent-a-room relief	At the end of this chapter, you should be able to: • identify property income assessable in respect of furnished and unfurnished property and premiums from short leases • outline the deductions allowable for revenue expenses, capital allowances, replacement furniture relief, repairs and renewals and the restriction for private use • describe rent-a-room relief • explain the treatment of furnished holiday lettings • understand how relief for a property business loss is given.

1 PROPERTY INCOME

1.1 INCOME LIABLE

The following income is taxable as property income:

- rents under any lease or tenancy agreement
- the premium received on the grant of a short lease (this is covered in the next section).

1.2 BASIS OF ASSESSMENT

Income from land and buildings is computed as if the letting of the property were a business.

- The amount taxable as property income is the rental business profit of the tax year.
- If the landlord lets more than one property, the different lettings all form one single business, so that the taxable amount is the aggregate of the profits and losses from each separate property.

Note that although the taxable income is computed as if the letting were a business, the profit is still normally taxable as property income, and the letting is not treated as an actual trade. An exception to this is furnished holiday lettings (see later). Occasionally the letting may constitute an actual trade, for example where bed and breakfast is provided, in which case the net income will be taxable as trading income.

Note also that normally the accounts for a property business of an individual are drawn up on the **cash** basis (not the accruals basis as for trading income). Thus, the taxable income for 2021/22 is the **rental income actually received** in the period 6 April 2021 to 5 April 2022, **less the expenses actually paid** for the same period.

It is possible for an election to be made to use the accruals basis and the accruals basis must be used if property income receipts exceed £150,000. The calculation of profits on the accruals basis can be seen in Chapter 21, as this is the only method of calculation for a company.

In examination questions involving **individuals and partnerships** you should always **use the cash basis** unless the question specifically states that the accruals basis should be applied.

Example

Eames owns a property that has been let throughout the tax year 2021/22. The rent is £1,000 per month and is due in arrears at the end of each month. The rent due on 31 March 2022 was not received by Eames until 15 April 2022.

What is the assessable rent for the tax year 2021/22?

The assessable rent is £11,000 (£1,000 × 11), i.e. the rent actually received in the tax year 2021/22.

ACTIVITY 1

Hembery owns a property that was let for the first time on 1 July 2021 at an annual rent of £5,000. The rent is paid quarterly in advance, starting on 1 July 2021.

Hembery paid allowable redecoration expenses of £200 in December 2021 and £400 in May 2022 for repairs completed in March 2022.

Compute the taxable property income for the tax year 2021/22.

For a suggested answer, see the 'Answers' section at the end of the book.

1.3 ALLOWABLE DEDUCTIONS

The general rule

The expenses allowable against the rental income are generally the same as for a trading business. These were discussed fully in the chapter on trading profits, but the main rules are given below.

To be allowable, the expenses must be incurred wholly and exclusively in connection with the property business. This covers items such as:

- insurance
- agent's fees
- other management expenses
- repairs.

Interest expense

Taxpayers with a property business may have taken out a loan to purchase or improve the property and therefore may pay interest on a loan.

Interest related to a non-residential property, such as a leased office or warehouse is fully deductible from rental income.

However, tax relief for the interest expense on residential property is restricted. This restriction is not examined in FTX.

Capital expenditure

Under the cash basis there is generally no distinction between capital and revenue expenditure in respect of plant and machinery and equipment for tax purposes, therefore:

- purchases are allowable deductions when paid for, and
- proceeds are treated as taxable receipts when an asset is sold.

However, this general rule is modified as follows for a property business. No deduction is allowed for:

- assets provided for use in a residential property, e.g. furniture, TV, etc.; unless they are used in a furnished holiday letting (see section 3). However, in an ordinary residential property business replacement furniture relief is available (see below).
- cars
- land and buildings.

Expenditure on plant and machinery (except cars) used in a property business, such as tools used for maintenance of the property or office equipment used for running is an allowable deduction from income when paid.

Cars

Capital allowances are available on cars (see Chapter 4). Alternatively, a flat rate expense deduction for car expenses can be claimed instead using the Approved Mileage Allowances of 45p and 25p per mile (see Chapter 10).

Replacement furniture relief

For **furnished residential** lettings **replacement furniture relief** is available.

- The relief allows a deduction for the replacement (i.e. not the original acquisition) of domestic items provided by the landlord.
- The allowable deduction is:
  replacement cost less any proceeds from the disposal of the original item
- The replacement cost allowed is limited to the cost of a similar item, excluding any improvement, but allowing for the modern equivalent.
- Domestic items are those acquired for domestic use for example, furniture, furnishings, household appliances (including white goods), carpets, curtains and kitchenware. However, 'fixtures' i.e. any plant and machinery that is fixed to a dwelling, including boilers and radiators are specifically excluded.
- This relief is not available to furnished holiday lettings (see section 3) and accommodation for which rent-a-room relief has been claimed (see section 4).

Example

Rin let a furnished flat throughout the tax year 2021/22. She paid for the following furniture during the tax year 2021/22:

		£
May 2021	Replacement kitchen table	1,750
June 2021	New conservatory furniture	3,500

The previous kitchen table was disposed of for £100. There was no conservatory furniture prior to the purchase in June 2021.

Calculate the allowable deduction (if any) from her property income in respect of the above expenditure.

Solution

Replacement furniture relief (£1,750 – £100)	£1,650

Note: No relief is available for the new conservatory furniture, as only replacement furniture is eligible for relief.

Private use

If the landlord occupies the property, the allowable expenditure must be restricted. For example, the landlord may have a cottage that he or she uses for one month each year. If the property is **available** for letting for the remaining 11 months, then 11/12 of the allowable expenditure will be deductible. Note that it is not necessary for the property to actually be let during the full 11 months. It is the availability for letting which determines the amount deductible.

Any expenditure that relates solely to the letting will be deductible in full; for example, advertising for tenants.

Example

Miles owns a furnished cottage that he lets out for 11 months each year, spending one month there himself every March. The monthly rent is £1,500 and is due on the 1st of the month. During the tax year 2021/22 the property was fully let except for Miles' stay in March 2022 and all rent receipts were received on the due date.

Expenses paid during the tax year 2021/22 were as follows:

		£
7 April 2021	Council tax	1,500
20 April 2021	Insurance for year to 31 March 2022	360
3 December 2021	Repairs to windows damaged by tenants	570
15 February 2022	Advertising for new tenants	250

Calculate the property income assessment for the tax year 2021/22.

Solution

Property income assessment 2021/22	£	£
Rent received (£1,500 × 11)		16,500
Less: Expenses relating solely to letting		
Repairs	570	
Advertising	250	
		(820)
Less: Expenses relating to whole year, less private use		
Council tax (£1,500 × 11/12)	1,375	
Insurance (£360 × 11/12)	330	
		(1,705)
Property income assessment		13,975

ACTIVITY 2

Salma owns a cottage that she lets out furnished at an annual rent of £3,600, payable on the first day of each month, in advance.

The tenant had vacated the property during June 2021 without having paid the rent due for June. Salma was unable to trace the defaulting tenant, but managed to let the property to new tenants from 1 July 2021. The new tenants paid each month's rent on time.

Salma paid the following expenses in respect of the letting of the property in 2021/22:

Date paid		
May 2021	Replaced an old washing machine with a new washer/dryer.	£2,000
June 2021	Insurance for year from 5 July 2021 (previous year – £420)	£480
November 2021	Drain clearance	£380
May 2022	Redecoration (work completed in March 2022)	£750

The old washing machine was scrapped for nil proceeds. An equivalent washing machine would cost only £1,200.

During the tax year 2021/22 Salma drove 100 miles in her car in respect of her property business. She uses the HMRC approved mileage allowances to calculate the expense deduction.

Calculate the property income assessable for the tax year 2021/22.

For a suggested answer, see the 'Answers' section at the end of the book.

1.4 LOSSES IN RESPECT OF PROPERTY INCOME

If the landlord owns more than one property, the profits and losses on all the properties, except furnished holiday lettings (see section 3), are aggregated to calculate the property income assessable for the tax year.

- This allows the loss arising on one property to be set against the profits arising on other properties.
- If there is an overall loss, the taxable property income for the tax year is £0.
- The loss is carried forward, and set against the taxable property income for the following year.
- If the income in the following year is insufficient to relieve the loss, the unrelieved balance is carried forward against future property income.
- Note that losses in respect of property income can never be carried back against income of previous years.

ACTIVITY 3

Sheila owns three properties that were rented out. Her taxable income and allowable expenses for the two tax years to 5 April 2022 were:

	Property		
	1	**2**	**3**
	£	£	£
Income			
2020/21	1,200	450	3,150
2021/22	800	1,750	2,550
Expenses			
2020/21	1,850	600	2,800
2021/22	900	950	2,700

What are Sheila's property income assessments for the tax years 2020/21 and 2021/22?

For a suggested answer, see the 'Answers' section at the end of the book.

2 PREMIUMS RECEIVED ON THE GRANT OF A SHORT LEASE

A premium is a lump sum payment made by the tenant to the landlord in consideration of the granting of a lease. Premiums paid by traders were dealt with in Chapter 3. Since the payment is in the nature of rent (a higher annual rent would be charged if no premium were paid) the landlord has a property income assessment on the premium received, **unless the premium is for a long lease (exceeding 50 years).** (Premiums on long leases are treated as capital receipts and are dealt with only under the capital gains legislation.)

A premium received on the grant of a short lease (for 50 years or less) is treated partly as rent assessed as property income in the tax year in which the lease is granted.

The amount taxable is calculated as follows:

	£
Premium	X
Less: 2% × (n – 1) × premium	(X)
Taxable as property income	X

where n is the duration of the lease in years.

This formula is **not** given in the examination, so **must be learned**.

If the tenant uses the property for business purposes he or she is entitled to a deduction for the amount of the lease premium taxable as property income, spread over the life of the lease (see Chapter 3).

ACTIVITY 4

A lease for 21 years is granted for a premium of £10,000 in the tax year 2021/22.

What is the amount of property income assessable for the tax year 2021/22?

For a suggested answer, see the 'Answers' section at the end of the book.

3 FURNISHED HOLIDAY LETTINGS

3.1 INTRODUCTION

Profits arising from the commercial letting of furnished holiday accommodation are treated as **earned** income arising from the operation of a single and separate trade, even though they are still taxable as property income.

The default basis of calculating profits is the cash basis as for an ordinary property business.

Any losses incurred are carried forward and set off against future profits from furnished holiday lettings ('FHL') only.

3.2 THE CONDITIONS

The letting will only be treated as a FHL if it is furnished, let on a commercial basis with a view to the realisation of profits, and satisfies the following conditions:

- it is available for letting for not less than 210 days a year
- it is actually let for at least 105 days in that 210 day period (excluding periods of 'longer term occupation' – see below).
- no more than 155 days in total are periods of 'longer term occupation'. A period of 'longer term occupation' is a continuous period of more than 31 days in which the property is occupied by the same person.

These conditions should be stated in days in the examination, and not in weeks or months.

3.3 TAX TREATMENT OF FURNISHED HOLIDAY LETTINGS

Unlike an ordinary property business, the profits from FHL's, while still taxed as property income, are treated as earned income. This results in the following tax advantages:

- The profits are relevant earnings for the purpose of pension scheme contributions (see Chapter 15).
- Capital gains tax rollover relief and business asset disposal relief are available where appropriate (see Chapter 20).

Also, unlike an ordinary residential property business, tax relief is available for capital expenditure on plant and machinery used in the FHL business e.g. furniture.

4 RENT-A-ROOM RELIEF

4.1 INTRODUCTION

If an individual lets furnished accommodation in his or her main residence, a special exemption applies.

If the gross annual receipts (before expenses or capital allowances) are £7,500 or below, they are exempt from tax.

This amount is not given in the examination.

4.2 THE RENT-A-ROOM SCHEME

The limit of £7,500 is reduced by half to £3,750 if, during a particular tax year, any other person also received income from letting accommodation in the property.

This rule allows a married couple or civil partners taking in lodgers to either have all the rent paid to one spouse/partner (who will then have the full limit of £7,500) or to have the rent divided between the spouses/partners (and each spouse/partner will then have a limit of £3,750).

An individual may elect to ignore the exemption for a particular tax year. This would be beneficial if, for example, a loss was incurred after taking account of expenses.

If the gross annual receipts are more than £7,500, individuals may choose between:

- paying tax on the excess of their gross rent over £7,500 (**without** relief for expenses), or
- being taxed in the ordinary way on their profit from letting (i.e. rent less expenses).

KEY TERMS

Replacement furniture relief – a deduction for the cost of replacing furniture, furnishings, appliances and kitchenware (but not the initial purchase).

Premium – a lump sum payment made by the tenant to the landlord in consideration of the granting of the lease.

Furnished holiday lettings – a type of short-term furnished letting which is treated as earned income and which therefore benefits from certain tax advantages.

Longer term occupation – a period of more than 31 days in which a property is occupied by the same person.

Rent-a-room relief – a relief that exempts income of up to £7,500 a year from the letting of accommodation within an individual's main residence.

SELF TEST QUESTIONS

		Paragraph
1	What is the basis of assessment for property income?	1.2
2	Give three examples of expenditure that is deductible from property income.	1.3
3	How is replacement furniture relief calculated?	1.3
4	How are losses in respect of property income relieved?	1.4
5	What is the formula used to calculate the taxable amount of a premium?	2
6	What are the conditions for a letting to be treated as a furnished holiday letting?	3.2
7	What are the tax advantages of a letting being treated as a furnished holiday letting?	3.3
8	How much is the rent-a-room exemption?	4.1
9	If gross rents exceed the rent-a-room limit, how will the income be taxed?	4.2

MULTIPLE CHOICE QUESTIONS

1 Zeinab bought a house in January 2021 that she rented out furnished to students from 1 June 2021. She charged rent of £600 per month, payable in advance on the first of each month. All rent was received on time during the tax year 2021/22. In August 2021, she paid £800 for the windows in the house to be repainted and £700 to replace broken kitchenware.

Calculate the property business profit for Zeinab for the tax year 2021/22.

A £5,100

B £5,800

C £5,900

D £4,500

2 Ganaraj granted a 45 year lease on a warehouse on 5 July 2021, charging a premium of £50,000. On 5 July 2021 he also received annual rent of £10,000. What is his assessable property income for the tax year 2021/22?

A £6,000

B £10,000

C £13,500

D £16,000

3 Percy rents out a home fully furnished. The house qualifies as a furnished holiday letting. For the tax year 2021/22 he paid expenses for repairs and furnishings as follows:

New wardrobe	£1,800
Replacement television	£1,600

Percy also has a brought forward property loss of £1,300 in respect of letting a room in his own home during the tax year 2020/21.

How much can Percy claim as a deduction from his furnished holiday letting income in respect of the above in the tax year 2021/22?

A £4,700

B £3,400

C £1,800

D £1,600

For suggested answers, see the 'Answers' section at the end of the book.

PRACTICE QUESTION

GITA

For many years Gita has owned six houses in Upland Avenue that are available for letting furnished.

The following details have been provided by the client.

			Property number			
	21	**23**	**25**	**38**	**40**	**67**
For y/e 5 April 2022	£	£	£	£	£	£
Annual rent due	1,600	2,040	2,060	1,820	4,200	2,400
Insurance paid	280	220	340	150	150	140

1 For each property the full annual rent was received during the tax year 2021/22 apart from in respect of Number 40.

2 Number 40 had new tenants in the year. The old tenant paid rent on the 25th of each month, but left on 30 September 2021 and defaulted on the rent due for the final month of £350. The cost of advertising for tenants was £450. The new tenants moved in on 1 December 2021 and paid 6 months' rent of £2,100 up front.

3 During the year Gita paid £1,800 for a dishwasher in number 40. The property had previously not had a dishwasher. During the year she also paid £700 to replace the carpets at number 21, paid £10,000 for a new roof for number 25 and paid £500 for a new computer, which she uses solely to manage her property business affairs. She had previously used a manual system to manage her property business affairs.

4 On 1 May 2021 Gita paid £12,000 for a car with CO_2 emissions of 40g/km. During the tax year 2021/22 she drove 2,000 business miles and 8,000 private miles in the car. Gita uses the HMRC approved mileage deduction in respect of the car.

Required:

Compute the assessable property income/allowable loss for the tax year 2021/22.

(10 marks)

For a suggested answer, see the 'Answers' section at the end of the book.

Chapter 13

INVESTMENT INCOME

INTRODUCTION

In Chapter 2 a pro forma income tax computation was given. This showed the allocation of income into non-savings income, savings income and dividends. This is necessary as different income tax rates apply to different sources of income. This chapter covers savings income and dividends.

An individual may choose to invest any surplus funds in banks, building societies or stocks and shares. The income from such investments may be taxable or tax free. It is important to know how the various types of income are dealt with. This chapter covers syllabus areas C3 (f) and (g).

CONTENTS	LEARNING OUTCOMES
1 Savings income **2** Dividends **3** Identify tax free investments **4** Identify the source documents used to complete the tax return	At the end of this chapter, you should be able to: • identify tax free investments • identify the source documents used to complete the tax return

1 SAVINGS INCOME

The main source of savings income is interest income.

1.1 INTEREST INCOME

The main examples of interest income are interest receipts from:

- Bank and building society accounts
- NS&I accounts
- UK government stocks (gilts)
- Loans between individuals
- NS&I Income Bonds
- Interest on quoted company loan notes.

The amount of interest income received in the tax year is taxed as savings income in the income tax computation.

Some other sources of interest, not listed above, are received net of income tax by individuals. However, savings income paid net of tax is **not examinable.**

1.2 BASIS OF ASSESSMENT

The actual basis of assessment applies. This means that the income taxable is the interest arising (i.e. **received** or **credited** to the account) during the tax year.

No account is taken of accrued interest, i.e. for income tax purposes interest arises when it is received.

Example

Vladimir received the following amounts of interest from his building society account:

31 December 2020	£275
31 December 2021	£235

In the tax year 2021/22 he is taxed on the December 2021 receipt as this is received during 2021/22.

The amount taxable is £235.

ACTIVITY 1

Patrick received the following interest:

		£
NS&I Investment account	31 December 2020	750
	31 December 2021	812
Gilts	1 December 2020	200
	1 June 2021	200
	1 December 2021	200
Bank interest	30 September 2020	175
	30 September 2021	400

Calculate Patrick's taxable interest for the tax year 2021/22.

For a suggested answer, see the 'Answers' section at the end of the book.

2 DIVIDENDS

Dividends received from a company resident in the UK are charged to income tax.

- The actual basis applies. For example, dividends accompanied by dividend vouchers dated between 6 April 2021 and 5 April 2022 inclusive are taxable in 2021/22.

Example

Chloe received dividends of £180 on 1 August 2021 and £200 on 1 May 2022.

The amount taxable in the tax year 2021/22 is £180 (the amount received during the 2021/22 tax year).

3 IDENTIFY TAX FREE INVESTMENTS

3.1 INTRODUCTION

The following investment income is exempt from tax:

- Proceeds of NS&I savings certificates
- Premium bond winnings
- Income and gains from an ISA (individual savings account).

3.2 NS&I SAVINGS CERTIFICATES

It is important to distinguish between income from NS&I **certificates**, which is exempt from tax, and income from NS&I **savings accounts**, which is taxable.

3.3 INDIVIDUAL SAVINGS ACCOUNTS (ISAs)

Individuals aged 16 or over, who are resident in the UK, are eligible to subscribe to an individual savings account (ISA) offered by financial institutions such as banks and building societies.

The income (interest or dividends) and gains on investments held in an ISA are exempt from income tax and capital gains tax.

4 IDENTIFY THE SOURCE DOCUMENTS USED TO COMPLETE THE TAX RETURN

Interest received will be shown on a taxpayer's bank statements. Dividends received will be shown on a dividend voucher.

These documents should be used to collate the information on investment income required to complete the tax return.

KEY TERMS

Actual basis of assessment – the income taxable is the interest arising (i.e. **received** or **credited** to the account) during the tax year.

Individual savings account – an investment that is exempt from income tax and capital gains tax.

SELF TEST QUESTIONS

	Paragraph
Give three examples of interest that is taxable.	1.1
What is the basis of assessment for interest income?	1.2
What is the basis of assessment for dividend income?	2
State three types of investment income that are exempt from income tax.	3.1

MULTIPLE CHOICE QUESTIONS

1 Reghan received the following during the tax year 2021/22. Which are subject to income tax?

1 Interest on an NS&I investment account

2 Bank interest

3 Proceeds from NS&I savings certificates

4 Profit on the sale of shares

A 1, 2 and 3

B 1 and 4

C 1 and 2 only

D 2 and 4

2 During the tax year 2021/22 Glennys had the following interest credited to her accounts:

Building society interest	£900
ISA interest	£600

In addition, interest accrued on her building society account as at 5 April 2022 was £200. This was credited to her account at the end of May 2022.

How much interest income is taxable in the tax year 2021/22?

A £1,500

B £1,700

C £900

D £1,100

For suggested answers, see the 'Answers' section at the end of the book.

PRACTICE QUESTION

Novak received the following income during the tax year 2021/22:

	£
Trading income	25,000
Building society interest	495
NS&I account interest	250
UK dividends received	6,090
Interest from NS&I savings certificates	155
Bank deposit interest	280
Dividends from an ISA	110

On 1 May 2022 Novak received a final dividend of £300 from a company in respect of its financial accounting period to 31 March 2022.

Required:

Prepare a schedule of taxable non-savings, savings and dividend income using the following format.

Income	Non-savings income	Savings income	Dividends
	£	£	£

(6 marks)

For a suggested answer, see the 'Answers' section at the end of the book.

Chapter 14

PERSONAL INCOME TAX COMPUTATIONS

INTRODUCTION

This chapter considers how the income tax liability is calculated. This is a key area of the syllabus. The examining team have stated that one of the 15 mark questions in section B will always be on income tax. The question will usually include a standard personal tax computation requiring the correct use of tax rates for non-savings, savings and dividend income.

This chapter also deals with relief for interest paid and for charitable giving as well as the calculation of an individual's personal allowance.

This chapter covers syllabus areas C1 (e) and C4.

CONTENTS

LEARNING OUTCOMES

By the end of this chapter, you should be able to:

- outline the key elements of a personal income tax computation
- explain the entitlement to and the amount of the personal allowance
- identify and explain the use of eligible interest
- illustrate the allocation of tax bands and tax rates against taxable income
- explain and illustrate the difference between tax liability and tax payable for the deduction of PAYE
- explain and illustrate charitable payments
- prepare examples of income tax computations.

1 OUTLINE THE KEY ELEMENTS OF A PERSONAL INCOME TAX COMPUTATION

1.1 LAYOUT OF A PERSONAL INCOME TAX COMPUTATION

An individual's income tax computation includes the gross amount of income from all chargeable sources. From this total income figure reliefs (qualifying interest payments and losses) are deducted to compute net income. The personal allowance is then deducted to arrive at a figure of taxable income.

An example of a personal income tax computation follows.

Taxpayer's name:

Income tax computation – 2021/22

	Non-savings income	**Savings income**	**Dividend income**	**Total income**
	£	£	£	£
Employment income	X			X
Trading income	X			X
Property income	X			X
Savings income		X		X
UK dividends			X	X
Total income	X	X	X	X
Less: Reliefs	(X)			(X)
Net income	X	X	X	X
Less: Personal allowance (Note)	(X)			(X)
Taxable income	X	X	X	X

Income tax:

	£
On non-savings income:	
At basic rate (20%)	X
At higher rate (40%)	X
At additional rate (45%)	X
On savings income:	
At starting rate (0%) – section 1.4	0
Savings income nil rate band – see section 1.4	0
At basic rate (20%)	X
At higher rate (40%)	X
At additional rate (45%)	X
On dividend income:	
Dividend nil rate band – see section 1.5	0
At basic rate (7.5%)	X
At higher rate (32.5%)	X
At additional rate (38.1%)	X
Income tax liability	X
Less: PAYE	(X)
Income tax payable	X

Reliefs comprise qualifying interest payments (see section 2 below) and trade losses (see Chapter 6).

Note: Entitlement to the personal allowance is reduced once net income exceeds £100,000 (see section 4).

In the FTX examination, the personal allowance and reliefs (i.e. qualifying interest payments and losses) **should always** be deducted from the taxpayer's income in the following order:

1 Non-savings income

2 Savings income

3 Dividend income.

1.2 THE RATES OF INCOME TAX

The rate of tax payable depends on the type of income (non-savings, savings or dividends) and the tax band into which it falls.

The normal tax rates, which apply to non-savings and savings income are as follows:

- The first £37,700 of taxable income falls within the basic rate band and is taxed at 20%.
- A higher rate of 40% is charged on income exceeding £37,700 but no more than £150,000 (the higher rate band).
- An additional rate of 45% is charged on income exceeding £150,000.

Special dividend rates of tax apply to dividend income falling in the different tax bands. These are covered in detail in section 1.5.

In addition:

- There is a savings income nil rate band, the amount of which depends on whether the individual is a basic or higher rate taxpayer and a starting rate of tax for savings income of 0%, which applies in certain circumstances. These are explained in section 1.4 below.
- There is a dividend nil rate band of £2,000, which is explained in section 1.5 below.

These rates and tax bands can be found in the tax tables at the front of this text. They will also be available to you in the examination.

1.3 NON-SAVINGS INCOME

Non-savings income is the first type of income to be taxed. It is taxed first at 20%, then 40% and finally 45%, depending on whether it falls in the basic rate, higher rate or additional rate band.

As covered in Chapter 2, the main sources of non-savings income are trading income (Chapter 3), employment income (Chapters 9 and 10) and property income (Chapter 12).

Examples: Income tax computations

1 Tony has net income of £50,955 in the tax year 2021/22 (none of which is savings or dividend income). He is entitled to a personal allowance of £12,570.

What is Tony's income tax liability for the tax year 2021/22?

Solution

Step 1 Calculate Tony's taxable income:

	£
Net income (all non-savings income)	50,955
Less: Personal allowance	(12,570)
Taxable income	38,385

Step 2 Calculate Tony's income tax liability:

£		£
37,700	at 20%	7,540
685	at 40%	274
38,385		7,814

2 Hassan has net income of £162,000 in the tax year 2021/22 (all of which is non-savings income). He is not entitled to any personal allowance.

What is Hassan's income tax liability for the tax year 2021/22?

Solution

Step 1 Calculate Hassan's taxable income:

	£
Net income	162,000
Less: Personal allowance	(0)
Taxable income	162,000

Step 2 Calculate Hassan's income tax liability:

£		£
37,700	at 20%	7,540
112,300	at 40%	44,920
12,000	at 45%	5,400
162,000		57,860

ACTIVITY 1

Teresa has net income of £60,290 in the tax year 2021/22. She is entitled to a personal allowance of £12,570.

What is Teresa's income tax liability for the tax year 2021/22 assuming none of the income is savings or dividends?

For a suggested answer, see the 'Answers' section at the end of the book.

1.4 SAVINGS INCOME

After non-savings income has been taxed, any remaining basic rate band is then allocated to savings income, followed by dividend income.

- Savings income is normally taxed in the same way as non-savings income, at the basic, higher and additional rates of tax as set out above.
- However, a **starting rate** of tax of 0% applies to the first £5,000 of savings income where it falls into the first £5,000 of **taxable** income. This will therefore only apply in limited circumstances.
- In addition basic rate and higher rate taxpayers are entitled to a **savings income nil rate band** (also known as the 'savings allowance' or 'personal savings allowance', although these terms will not be used in the examination). This means that there is no tax liability on part of their savings income.
- The **savings income nil rate band** is:
  - Basic rate taxpayer £1,000
  - Higher rate taxpayer £500
  - Additional rate taxpayer £Nil
- In summary the rates of tax on savings income are:

	Normal rates
Basic rate (First £37,700) (Note)	20%
Higher rate (£37,701 – £150,000)	40%
Additional rate (£150,000 and over)	45%
Savings income nil rate band:	
– Basic rate taxpayers	£1,000
– Higher rate taxpayers	£500

Note: A starting rate of 0% applies to savings income where it falls within the first £5,000 of taxable income.

- The rates of tax on savings income are shown in the tax rates and allowances provided in the examination.

Applying the appropriate rates of tax to savings income

Savings income is taxed as the next slice of income after non-savings income therefore the rates of tax applicable to savings income depend on the level of taxable non-savings income. The procedure to follow is:

1 Calculate income tax on non-savings income.

2 Apply the different rates of tax on savings income in the following order:

   (i) Starting rate

   (ii) Savings income nil rate band

   (iii) Normal rates (i.e. basic, higher and additional rates).

3 Consider the starting rate. This only applies in limited situations, i.e. where taxable non-savings income is less than £5,000. If:

   (i) No taxable non-savings income – the first £5,000 of taxable savings income is taxed at 0%, (i.e. it is tax free).

   (ii) Taxable non-savings income below £5,000 – savings income falling into the rest of the first £5,000 is taxed at 0%.

   (iii) Taxable non-savings income in excess of £5,000 – the 0% starting rate is not applicable.

4 If there is further savings income to tax, consider the savings income nil rate band. The amount of taxable income determines the highest rate of tax payable by the taxpayer and therefore the amount of the savings nil rate band. If the taxpayer:

   (i) pays only basic rate tax (i.e. taxable income £37,700 or less) – the next £1,000 falls in the savings income nil rate band and is taxed at 0%.

   (ii) pays any tax at the higher rate (i.e. taxable income £37,701 to £150,000) – the next £500 falls in the savings income nil rate band and is taxed at 0%.

   (iii) pays any additional rate tax (i.e. taxable income exceeds £150,000) – not applicable.

5 If there is further savings income to tax, apply the normal savings rates as follows:

   (i) The basic rate of 20% applies to savings income falling within the basic rate band, i.e. the first £37,700 of taxable income.

   (ii) The higher rate of 40% applies to savings income falling within the higher rate band, i.e. income in the range £37,701 to £150,000 of taxable income.

   (ii) The additional rate of 45% applies to savings income where taxable income exceeds £150,000.

Note that the basic and higher rate bands are first reduced by non-savings income and savings income that has been taxed at the starting rate and/or falls in the savings income nil rate band.

The above procedure may seem complicated but if you use the columnar layout of the income tax computation (see below) it is relatively easy to determine which rates to apply.

Example: Savings income

Eisha had property income of £12,600 and received bank interest of £6,625 in the tax year 2021/22. She is entitled to a personal allowance of £12,570.

Eisha's income tax liability for the tax year 2021/22 is calculated as follows:

Eisha

Income tax computation for the tax year 2021/22

	Non-savings income		Savings income	Dividend income	Total
	£		£	£	£
Property income	12,600				12,600
Interest received			6,625		6,625
Total income	12,600		6,625	0	19,225
Less: Personal allowance	(12,570)				(12,570)
Taxable income	30		6,625		6,655
Income tax:					
	£				£
On non-savings income – basic rate	30	× 20%			6
On savings income – starting rate	4,970	× 0%			0
	5,000				
On savings income – nil rate	1,000	× 0%			0
On savings income – basic rate	655	× 20%			131
	6,655				
Income tax liability					137

Note that the 0% starting rate band for savings income is firstly reduced by non-savings income before being applied to the savings income, i.e. only £4,970 of the savings starting rate band is available as there is £30 of taxable non-savings income.

Joseph is entitled to a savings income nil rate band of £1,000 as he is a basic rate taxpayer, i.e. taxable income does not exceed £37,700.

1.5 DIVIDEND INCOME

- All taxpayers, regardless of their level of income, are entitled to a £2,000 dividend nil rate band and this income is therefore tax free.
- Dividend income is then taxed at 7.5% if it falls in the basic rate band, at 32.5% if it falls in the higher rate band and 38.1% if taxable income exceeds £150,000.
- The dividend income taxed at the dividend nil rate reduces the available basic rate and higher rate bands when determining the rate of tax on the remaining dividend income.

- Dividend income is treated as the top slice of income.
- Due to the savings income and dividend nil rate bands, many taxpayers will not have any tax to pay in respect of their investment income.

The layout above shows separate columns for non-savings income, savings income and dividends. However, provided you can identify the amount of savings income and the amount of dividends remaining in taxable income, you can combine the three different types of income in one column.

Example: Dividend income

Bruno has a salary of £114,000, building society interest of £6,000 and dividends of £80,000. He is not entitled to any personal allowance.

Bruno's income tax liability for the tax year 2021/22 is calculated as follows:

Bruno – Income tax computation for the tax year 2021/22

	Non-savings income £	Savings income £	Dividend income £	Total £
Employment income	114,000			114,000
Interest received		6,000		6,000
Dividends			80,000	80,000
Total income	114,000	6,000	80,000	200,000
Less Personal allowance	0			0
Taxable income	114,000	6,000	80,000	200,000

Income tax:

	£		£
On non-savings income – basic rate	37,700	× 20%	7,540
On non-savings income – higher rate	76,300	× 40%	30,520
	114,000		
On savings income – higher rate	6,000	× 40%	2,400
On dividend income – nil rate	2,000	× 0%	0
On dividend income – higher rate	28,000	× 32.5%	9,100
	150,000		
On dividend income – additional rate	50,000	× 38.1%	19,050
	200,000		
Income tax liability			68,610

As Bruno is an additional rate taxpayer (i.e. taxable income exceeds £150,000), he is not entitled to a savings income nil rate band.

The dividends are treated as the top slice of Bruno's income. The first £2,000 is covered by the dividend nil rate band, the next £28,000 falls in the higher rate band and is taxed at 32.5% and £50,000 falls above the additional rate threshold and is taxed at 38.1%.

ACTIVITY 2

Dave has income from employment of £40,035, building society interest of £1,000 and dividend income of £10,000 in the tax year 2021/22. He is entitled to a personal allowance of £12,570.

What is Dave's income tax liability for the tax year 2021/22?

For a suggested answer, see the 'Answers' section at the end of the book.

1.6 INCOME TAX PAYABLE

Income tax liability is the total amount of tax that must be accounted for.

- Employment income will have had tax already deducted from it under PAYE.
- The PAYE already paid is deducted from the income tax liability to arrive at the figure of income tax payable.

The salary figure given in the question will be the gross figure, before the deduction of PAYE.

If the tax already paid by the taxpayer exceeds the income tax liability, the excess is normally repayable. Note, however, that this is unlikely to be the case as the PAYE code should ensure that the correct amount of tax is deducted.

Example

During the tax year 2021/22 Hanif received dividends of £18,300, bank interest of £3,000 and a salary of £30,150 from which PAYE of £3,500 had been deducted. He is entitled to a personal allowance of £12,570. His income tax payable is as follows:

	Non-savings income	**Savings income**	**Dividend income**	**Total**
	£	£	£	£
Employment income	30,150			30,150
Interest received		3,000		3,000
Dividends			18,300	18,300
Total income	30,150	3,000	18,300	51,450
Less: Personal allowance	(12,570)			(12,570)
Taxable income	17,580	3,000	18,300	38,880

Income tax:

	£		£
On non-savings income – basic rate	17,580	× 20%	3,516
On savings income – nil rate	500	× 0%	0
On savings income – basic rate	2,500	× 20%	500
On dividend income – nil rate	2,000	× 0%	0
On dividend income – basic rate	15,120	× 7.5%	1,134
	37,700		
On dividend income – higher rate	1,180	× 32.5%	384
	38,880		
Income tax liability			5,534
Less: PAYE			(3,500)
Income tax payable			2,034

Note: Hanif is a higher rate taxpayer (i.e. taxable income exceeds £37,700 but is less than £150,000) and is therefore entitled to a savings income nil rate band of £500.

Hanif is also entitled to a dividend nil rate band of £2,000.

The tax suffered via PAYE is deductible in calculating income tax payable.

ACTIVITY 3

Bernard received the following income in the tax year 2021/22:

	£
Salary (PAYE deducted £7,800)	50,690
Dividends	12,000
Building society interest	1,200

He is entitled to a personal allowance of £12,570.

Calculate the amount of income tax payable for the tax year 2021/22.

For a suggested answer, see the 'Answers' section at the end of the book.

2 INTEREST PAYMENTS

2.1 LOANS FOR QUALIFYING PURPOSES

Interest paid on a loan taken out for a qualifying purpose is deductible from total income in the taxpayer's personal income tax computation.

Relief may be claimed for any payment of interest, other than interest paid on bank overdrafts or credit cards.

The **qualifying purposes** to which the loan must be applied are as follows:

- The purchase of a share in a partnership, or the contribution of capital or loans by a partner for the purchase of plant or machinery for use in the partnership.
- The purchase of ordinary shares in, or loans to, a close trading company. A close company is one controlled by a limited number of persons, generally five or fewer.
- The purchase of ordinary shares in an employee controlled UK resident, unquoted trading company by a full time employee.
- The purchase of plant or machinery by an employee for use in his or her employment.
- The payment of inheritance tax by the personal representative of a deceased's estate.

2.2 INTEREST NOT ALLOWED AS A DEDUCTION FROM TOTAL INCOME

The following payments of interest are not deducted from total income:

- Interest wholly and exclusively for trade purposes which is deductible as a trading expense in arriving at the amount of taxable trading income.
- Interest incurred on borrowings to acquire or improve commercial letting property. The deduction is dealt with under the property income rules (see Chapter 12).

2.3 RELIEF FOR INTEREST PAYMENTS

Interest on loans for qualifying purposes is relieved by deducting the amount paid from the taxpayer's total income for the year of payment.

Example

Esperanza earns £46,565 and pays interest of £2,500 on a loan taken out to purchase a share in a partnership. She is entitled to a personal allowance of £12,570. Her taxable income for the tax year 2021/22 is as follows:

	£
Income (= total income)	46,565
Less: Interest	(2,500)
Net income	44,065
Less: Personal allowance	(12,570)
Taxable income	31,495

3 CHARITABLE GIVING

3.1 GIFT AID

Individuals who want to give money to charity in a tax efficient way can do so using the gift aid scheme.

- The donor has to declare that the payment is a gift aid payment. This can be done in writing to the charity or orally by phone, or electronically over the internet.
- Under the gift aid scheme, the payment to the charity is treated as if basic rate income tax had been deducted at source. The payment is grossed up by 100/80.
- If the individual is a basic rate taxpayer, the payment is ignored when calculating the income tax liability. This is because tax relief at the basic rate has been given by making the payment net. Note that the payment is **not** deducted in calculating taxable income.
- If the individual is a higher or additional rate taxpayer, further tax relief is given by increasing both the higher rate and additional rate thresholds by the gross amount of the contribution.
- There is no lower or upper limit on the amount gifted that can qualify for tax relief.
- The charity is able to reclaim the basic rate tax deducted.

Example

Noemi earns £53,650 and makes gift aid payments totalling £1,960. She is entitled to a personal allowance of £12,570. Her tax liability for the tax year 2021/22 is as follows:

	£
Net income	53,650
Less: Personal allowance	(12,570)
Taxable income	41,080

Her basic rate band is extended by the gross gift aid payment.

£37,700 + (£1,960 × $^{100}/_{80}$) = £40,150

Income tax:

	£		£
Non-savings income – basic rate	40,150	× 20%	8,030
Non-savings income – higher rate	930	× 40%	372
	41,080		
Income tax liability			8,402

The amount actually paid to the charity is £1,960 (i.e. net of basic rate tax). In order to achieve relief at the higher rate, the gross amount of £2,450 (£1,960 × 100/80) is used to extend the basic rate band. Relief actually obtained is as follows:

	£
£2,450 × 20% (at time of payment)	490
£2,450 × 20% (40% – 20%) (under the self-assessment procedure)	490
	980

Example

Saito earns £184,000 and makes gift aid payments totalling £6,000. He is not entitled to any personal allowance. His tax liability for the tax year 2021/22 is as follows:

	£
Net income	184,000
Less: Personal allowance	(0)
Taxable income	184,000

The thresholds of £37,700 and £150,000 are increased by the gross gift aid payment.

£37,700 + (£6,000 × $^{100}/_{80}$) = £45,200

£150,000 + (£6,000 × $^{100}/_{80}$) = £157,500

Income tax:

	£	£
Non-savings income – basic rate	45,200 × 20%	9,040
Non-savings income – higher rate	112,300 × 40%	44,920
Non-savings income – additional rate	26,500 × 45%	11,925
	184,000	
Income tax liability		65,885

In this case Saito has obtained a total of 45% relief.

	£
£7,500 × 20% (at time of payment)	1,500
£7,500 × 25% (45 – 20) (under the self-assessment procedure)	1,875
	3,375

- In order to qualify for relief under the gift aid scheme, the donor must have paid tax equivalent to the basic rate tax deducted at source from the gift aid payment.
- The tax must have been paid in the same tax year as the gift aid payment. It can be either income tax or capital gains tax.
- If the donor has not paid sufficient tax, it may be necessary to restrict his or her personal allowance to ensure the tax claimed by the charity has been paid. This is outside the scope of this examination syllabus.

Gift aid payments normally qualify for relief in the tax year of payment.

- However, a taxpayer can make a claim to treat the donation as if it had been made in the previous tax year.
- This would be beneficial if the taxpayer was a higher rate taxpayer in the previous tax year, but only a basic rate taxpayer in the year of payment.
- The claim must be made by 31 January in the tax year in which the payment was made.

3.2 PAYROLL GIVING

Payments to charity made under an approved payroll deduction scheme operated by an employer are allowable as employment income expenses (see Chapter 9).

- The employer deducts the donations from wages or salary before calculating the PAYE deductions, and pays them to an approved agent.
- The agent then distributes the funds to charities selected by the employee. The scheme is referred to as a 'Give As you Earn' (GAYE) Scheme, or Payroll Giving Scheme.
- There are no minimum or maximum payments.

Example

Tanni has a salary of £40,000 per year and pays £100 to Oxfam (a charity) each month through the payroll giving scheme. She has no other income and is entitled to a personal allowance of £12,570.

Tanni's taxable income is:

	£
Salary	40,000
Less: Payroll giving (£100 × 12)	(1,200)
	38,800
Less: PA	(12,570)
Taxable income	26,230

4 PERSONAL ALLOWANCE

4.1 INTRODUCTION

Every individual who is resident in the UK is entitled to a personal allowance.

- The amount for 2021/22 is £12,570. The personal allowance is deducted from the individual's net income in order to arrive at the figure of taxable income.
- Surplus personal allowance cannot be carried forward or back for relief in any other tax year.

4.2 REDUCTION OF PERSONAL ALLOWANCE

The personal allowance is gradually reduced for individuals with income in excess of £100,000.

The reduction of personal allowance is based on the taxpayer's adjusted net income (ANI) which is calculated as follows.

	£
Net income	X
Less: Gross gift aid donations	(X)
Gross personal pension contributions	(X)
Adjusted net income (ANI)	X

The calculation of gross personal pension contributions is covered in Chapter 15.

Where the taxpayer's adjusted net income exceeds £100,000 the personal allowance is reduced by:

50% × (ANI – £100,000)

If the resulting personal allowance is not a whole number, it must be rounded up to the nearest pound.

A taxpayer with ANI in excess of £125,140 will therefore be entitled to no personal allowance at all, as the excess above £100,000 is twice the personal allowance.

Example

Ethan had trading income of £112,000 in the tax year 2021/22. He also made gross gift aid donations of £4,000.

Required:

Compute Ethan's taxable income for the tax year 2021/22.

Solution

Income tax computation – 2021/22

	£
Trading income = Total income	112,000
Less: Adjusted PA (W)	(8,570)
Taxable income	103,430

Working	£	£
Basic personal allowance		12,570
Net income (note)	112,000	
Less: Gross gift aid donation	(4,000)	
Adjusted net income	108,000	
Less: Income limit	(100,000)	
	8,000	
Reduction of PA (50% × £8,000)		(4,000)
Adjusted PA		8,570

Note: In this example there is only one source of income and no reliefs, hence:
Trading income = Total income = Net income

ACTIVITY 4

Ariadne had employment income of £130,000 in the tax year 2021/22. She also made gross gift aid donations of £16,000.

Compute Ariadne's taxable income for the tax year 2021/22.

For a suggested answer, see the 'Answers' section at the end of the book.

ACTIVITY 5

Marwa received the following income in the tax year 2021/22:

	£
Salary (PAYE deducted £69,670)	175,000
Dividends	36,000
Bank interest	2,240

Calculate the amount of income tax payable for the tax year 2021/22.

For a suggested answer, see the 'Answers' section at the end of the book.

5 MARRIED COUPLES/CIVIL PARTNERS

5.1 INTRODUCTION

All taxpayers are taxed separately on their own income, have their own personal allowance, and must make their own annual income tax return. However, there are some tax implications that specifically affect married couples (and couples in a civil partnership).

5.2 PERSONAL ALLOWANCE

In some circumstances, an unused personal allowance up to £1,260 is transferable between spouses and civil partners. However, this is not examinable in FTX.

5.3 JOINT PROPERTY

Although the income of married couples or civil partners is calculated separately, special rules exist for dealing with income arising from jointly held assets.

- Income from assets held in joint names by a married couple or civil partners who live together will normally be split equally between them for tax purposes (the 50:50 rule).

- If the couple want a different split, they must jointly make a declaration of their actual beneficial interests in the asset and their income from it. In other words, if the ownership of the asset is 75:25, the income arising from the asset will be split in the same proportion if the couple make the declaration.

5.4 QUALIFYING INTEREST AND GIFT AID PAYMENTS

Relief for qualifying interest and gift aid payments is given to the spouse/civil partner who makes the qualifying payment.

If the couple make a payment jointly, the amount actually paid by each person is the amount allowed in their personal income tax computation. If the amount paid by each spouse or civil partner is unclear, for example because the payment is made from a joint bank account, the 50:50 rule will apply.

6 PREPARING INCOME TAX COMPUTATIONS

When preparing an income tax computation, you should proceed as follows.

- Identify sources of taxable income, remembering to:
  - separate out non-savings, savings and dividends income
  - exclude exempt income but make a note in your answer that it is exempt.
- Identify any qualifying interest payments, remembering to deduct from non-savings income before savings income and dividends.
- Calculate net income (and adjusted net income if relevant).
- Calculate the personal allowance and deduct it to arrive at taxable income. If no personal allowance is available, state why.
- Calculate the tax payable, remembering to:
  - tax non-savings income first, before savings income, and then dividend income as the top slice
  - increase the higher and additional rate thresholds for the grossed up value of any gift aid payments (or personal pension contributions – see Chapter 15) if taxable income exceeds £37,700
  - tax non-savings income at 20% in the basic rate band, at 40% where it falls above the higher rate threshold and at 45% where it falls above the additional rate threshold
  - apply the correct savings income nil rate band according to whether the individual is a basic or higher rate taxpayer and then tax the remainder of savings income at the same rates as non-savings income (remember that where non-savings income falls below £5,000 up to £5,000 of savings income is taxed at 0%).
  - tax dividends at 0% to the extent that they fall in the dividend nil rate band, 7.5% to the extent they fall into the basic rate band, at 32.5% where they fall above the higher rate threshold and at 38.1% where they fall above the additional rate threshold
  - to calculate tax payable deduct PAYE from the tax liability.

The examining team show a preference for the following layout:

	Non-savings income	Savings income	Dividend income	Total
	£	£	£	£
Total income	X	X	X	X
Less: Reliefs	(X)			(X)
Net income	X			X
Less: PA	(X)			(X)
Taxable income	X	X	X	X

This makes the next step less prone to error as the taxable income is then taxed in the order in which it appears in the final line, i.e. non-savings income first.

Remember, that non-savings income includes employment income, trading income and property income.

It is recommended that you use this layout in the examination. However, it is unlikely that you would be penalised for a slightly different layout that generated the correct key figures.

ACTIVITY 6

Sekou is employed by a bank. For the tax year 2021/22 he received the following remuneration package:

	£
Salary	41,000
Benefits	6,410

PAYE of £6,932 was deducted.

He received the following amounts from his investments in the tax year 2021/22:

	£
Building society interest	1,960
Interest on holding of £26,000 5% Treasury Stock 2021	1,300
NS&I investment account	82
Interest from individual savings account (ISA)	320

Sekou cashed in some NS&I savings certificates, which he had purchased for £1,200 in 2008, from which he received £2,490.

Sekou pays £55 each year to the National Trust (a charity) under gift aid.

Required:

Calculate Sekou's income tax payable for the tax year 2021/22.

For a suggested answer, see the 'Answers' section at the end of the book.

KEY TERMS

Earned income – income such as trading profits and employment income.

Savings income – interest from bank and building society accounts.

Total income – income from all sources.

Net income – income from all sources, less loss relief and qualifying interest payments.

Taxable income – net income less personal allowance.

Close company – a company controlled by a limited number of persons.

Gift aid payment – a payment to charity made under the gift aid scheme.

Income tax liability – the total income tax due for the year.

Income tax payable – the amount of income tax still owing after deducting PAYE.

SELF TEST QUESTIONS

		Paragraph
1	What are the rates of tax for savings income?	1.4
2	State the amount of savings income nil rate band available to a higher rate taxpayer.	1.4
3	State the amount of the dividend nil rate band.	1.5
4	What is the difference between income tax liability and income tax payable?	1.6
5	Give three examples of loans for qualifying purposes.	2.1
6	What relief is available for interest paid wholly and exclusively in the course of a trade?	2.2
7	How is higher rate tax relief for gift aid payments given?	3.1
8	How is the personal allowance reduced for those with high income?	4.2
9	How is the income from assets held in the joint names of a married couple normally taxed?	5.3

MULTIPLE CHOICE QUESTIONS

1 Sally has net income from employment and self-employment for the tax year 2021/22 of £51,615. She suffered PAYE on her employment income of £4,500.

What is Sally's income tax liability for the tax year 2021/22?

A £3,578

B £8,078

C £7,809

D £13,106

2 The only income Jane received during the tax year 2021/22 was dividends of £18,550.

What is Jane's income tax liability for the tax year 2021/22?

A £449

B £1,241

C £299

D £796

3 Annalisa has net income of £38,000 for the tax year 2021/22, which includes £3,000 of bank interest. Her bank interest will be taxed at 0% on the first £500 and 40% on £2,500.

A True

B False

4 Sasha has a salary of £135,000 and receives dividends of £25,000. She is not entitled to a personal allowance.

How will her dividends be taxed?

A £2,000 at 0% then £23,000 at 38.1%

B £2,000 at 0%, £15,000 at 32.5% and £8,000 at 38.1%

C £2,000 at 0%, £13,000 at 32.5% and £10,000 at 38.1%

D £2,000 at 0% then £23,000 at 32.5%

5 Which of the following interest payments is deductible from total income to arrive at net income?

A Interest on a loan to buy an interest in a partnership

B Interest on a loan to invest in further plant for a sole trader's business

C Interest on a loan to purchase shares in a UK company that is quoted on the London Stock Exchange.

D Interest on a loan to purchase a foreign holiday home

6 Harry made gift aid donations to the NSPCC of £500 in the tax year 2021/22. This is the cash amount paid. His only income is employment income of £51,650.

What is his income tax liability for the tax year 2021/22?

A £12,995

B £8,092

C £7,992

D £7,967

7 Yusuf had net income of £110,700 and made a gift aid donation of £2,400 in the tax year 2021/22.

What is his personal allowance for the tax year 2021/22?

A £7,220

B £8,420

C £8,720

D £12,570

8 Lucy and Ricardo have been married for 10 years. Lucy owns 75% of a rental home and Ricardo owns the other 25%. Rental income (net of expenses) received from the property is £15,000 p.a. They have not made any elections in relation to the property. How is this income taxed on the couple?

A Lucy is taxed on the full £15,000 and Ricardo is not taxable

B Lucy is taxed on £7,500 and Ricardo is taxed on £7,500

C Lucy is taxed on £11,250 and Ricardo is taxed on £3,750

D The income is not taxable

For suggested answers, see the 'Answers' section at the end of the book.

PRACTICE QUESTION

JOHN AND FIONA

John and Fiona Smeech were married in 2016. In the tax year 2021/22 they had the following income.

	John	Fiona
	£	£
Salary	51,514	10,340
Tax under PAYE	(7,100)	0
Building society interest received	2,500	7,500
Bank interest received	400	0

John made a gift aid payment of £339 net to the Church of St James.

Required:

Compute the income tax payable by John and Fiona in respect of the tax year 2021/22.

(10 marks)

For a suggested answer, see the 'Answers' section at the end of the book.

Chapter 15

PENSION CONTRIBUTIONS

INTRODUCTION

The Government is keen to encourage individuals to save for their retirement. Therefore, tax relief is available to encourage people to invest in a pension scheme.

Employees may have the option of joining a company pension scheme (known as an occupational pension scheme). Everyone may contribute to a personal (private) pension plan.

This chapter covers syllabus areas C5.

CONTENTS	LEARNING OUTCOMES
1 Relief for contributions **2** Occupational pension schemes **3** Personal pension schemes **4** Limits on relief	At the end of this chapter, you should be able to: • identify the schemes available • define net relevant earnings • explain the maximum contributions allowed for tax relief • show how the relief is given • show the tax effects of employer contributions on both the employer and the employee.

1 RELIEF FOR CONTRIBUTIONS

1.1 THE RELIEF AVAILABLE

Tax relief is available on contributions into a pension scheme up to the higher of:

(i) £3,600 (the basic amount) and

(ii) the individual's net relevant earnings in the tax year.

Relevant earnings include:

- employment income,
- trading income, and
- income from furnished holiday lettings.

An individual with no earnings can therefore make a maximum gross contribution of £3,600.

Contributions can only get relief in the tax year in which they are **paid**.

The way in which the tax relief is given depends on whether the individual is contributing to an **occupational pension scheme** or a **personal pension scheme**.

2 OCCUPATIONAL PENSION SCHEMES

2.1 HOW IS RELIEF GIVEN?

Contributions made by an employee are deducted from earnings. Tax relief is given at source by deducting the payment from employment income before calculating income tax payable under PAYE. This ensures that relief is automatically given at the taxpayer's highest marginal rate of tax. However, the payment is not deductible from earnings when calculating national insurance contributions.

2.2 EMPLOYER CONTRIBUTIONS

An occupational pension scheme is one set up by an employer for the benefit of their employees. Contributions may be made by the employer and the employee.

Contributions paid by the employer are deductible in calculating the employer's taxable profits. They are **not classed as taxable benefits** for the employee, so they are not subject to income tax or national insurance.

There is no restriction on the amount that can be contributed by employers. However, both employee and employer contributions count towards the annual limit of £40,000 (see section 4.1 below).

ACTIVITY 1

Shaun is employed earning an annual salary of £43,000. His employer operates an occupational pension scheme; Shaun contributes 8% of his salary into the scheme and his employer contributes a further 9%.

In the tax year 2021/22 Shaun also has property income of £15,000 (not furnished holiday lettings).

Calculate Shaun's income tax liability for the tax year 2021/22.

For a suggested answer, see the 'Answers' section at the end of the book.

3 PERSONAL PENSION SCHEMES

3.1 INTRODUCTION

Any individual (including employees) may pay contributions into a personal pension scheme to provide funds for his or her retirement.

Contributions into personal pension schemes may be made by:

- the individual, and
- any third party on behalf of the individual (for example the employer, a spouse, parent or grandparent).

One type of personal pension scheme is a stakeholder pension. Stakeholder pensions have to meet certain standards to ensure they offer value for money, are flexible, secure and have a limit on annual management charges.

3.2 HOW IS RELIEF GIVEN?

Personal pension plan contributions are paid net of basic rate tax. If the individual is a higher or additional rate taxpayer, the additional relief due is given by increasing the higher rate and additional rate thresholds by the gross amount of the contribution. The gross amount of the contribution is the amount paid multiplied by 100/80.

The gross contribution is also deducted, (with any gross gift aid payments), from net income to give adjusted net income for the purpose of calculating the level of personal allowance.

Example

Djeneba is a self-employed plumber. Her taxable trading income for the tax year 2021/22 was £122,000. She paid a personal pension contribution of £12,000 (net amount).

Her income tax liability for the tax year 2021/22 is calculated as follows:

			£
Trade profits			122,000
Less: PA (W1)			(9,070)
Taxable income			112,930
Income tax	£		
On non-savings income (W2)	52,700	× 20%	10,540
	60,230	× 40%	24,092
	112,930		
Tax liability			34,632

Workings

(1) **Personal allowance**

	£	£
Basic personal allowance		12,570
Net income	122,000	
Less: Gross PPC (£12,000 × 100/80)	(15,000)	
Adjusted net income	107,000	
Limit	(100,000)	
	7,000	
Withdrawal of PA – 50% of the excess		(3,500)
Adjusted PA		9,070

(2) **Higher rate threshold**

	£
Standard	37,700
Add: Gross PPC	15,000
	52,700

ACTIVITY 2

Daphne, aged 40, is a self-employed dressmaker. Her taxable trading income for the tax year 2021/22 is £60,650. She also receives savings income of £1,500 per year.

Calculate:

(a) The maximum pension payment she can make that will be eligible for tax relief in the tax year 2021/22.

(b) Daphne's income tax liability for the tax year 2021/22 assuming that she pays a personal pension contribution of £10,000 (gross).

For a suggested answer, see the 'Answers' section at the end of the book.

Example

Jessica runs her own fitness business. Her taxable trading income for the tax year 2021/22 is £172,000. She paid a personal pension contribution of £8,000 (net amount).

Her income tax liability for the tax year 2021/22 is calculated as follows:

				£
Trade profits				172,000
Less: PA (Income too high for PA)				(0)
Taxable income				172,000
Income tax	£			
On non-savings income	47,700	(W)	× 20%	9,540
	112,300		× 40%	44,920
	160,000	(W)		
	12,000		× 45%	5,400
	172,000			
Tax liability				59,860

Working	**Higher rate threshold**	**Additional rate threshold**
	£	£
Standard	37,700	150,000
Add: Gross personal pension contribution (£8,000 × 100/80)	10,000	10,000
	47,700	160,000

Note that even though the occupational and personal pension schemes have different ways of giving tax relief, the total relief is the same for both types of scheme. It is however, important to be clear about which type of contribution the question is dealing with and to treat it accordingly.

4 LIMITS ON RELIEF

4.1 THE ANNUAL ALLOWANCE

Although an individual can receive tax relief on contributions of up to 100% of his or her relevant earnings, contributions in excess of the annual allowance of £40,000 have tax relief clawed back.

The annual allowance charge therefore cancels out the tax relief that will have been given. There is no charge where contributions have not qualified for tax relief. The calculation of this tax charge is **not examinable**.

4.2 THE LIFETIME ALLOWANCE

There is an overall lifetime allowance of £1,073,100 that applies to the total funds that can be built up within a person's pension schemes. Where this limit is exceeded there is an additional tax charge when that person subsequently withdraws the funds in the form of a pension. Calculation of this tax charge is **not examinable**.

KEY TERMS

Annual allowance – the maximum amount of contributions that can receive tax relief in a particular tax year.

Lifetime allowance – the total funds that can be built up within a person's pension schemes without suffering an additional tax charge when the pension funds are withdrawn.

Occupational pension scheme – a scheme set up by an employer for its employees.

Personal pension scheme – a type of pension scheme available to the self-employed, employees, and individuals without earnings.

Relevant earnings – earnings that entitle an individual to make payments in excess of £3,600 into a pension scheme. They comprise trading income, employment income and profits from furnished holiday lettings.

SELF TEST QUESTIONS

		Paragraph
1	What is the maximum contribution an individual can make into a pension scheme and obtain tax relief?	1.1
2	How is relief for employee contributions into an occupational pension scheme given?	2.1
3	What are the tax implications of an employer's contributions into an occupational pension scheme?	2.2
4	How is relief for personal pension scheme contributions given?	3.2
5	What are the tax implications of making a contribution in excess of the annual allowance?	4.1

MULTIPLE CHOICE QUESTIONS

1 Isaiah is self-employed. For the tax year 2021/22 Isaiah's taxable profits were £70,000 and he paid personal pension contributions of £22,000.

By how much will Isaiah's basic rate band be extended?

A £3,600

B £22,000

C £27,500

D £40,000

2 In respect of employer's contributions into a registered pension scheme, which of the following statements is incorrect?

A Employer's contributions are tax deductible in calculating the employer's taxable trading profits

B Employer's contributions are an exempt benefit for the employee

C The employer's contributions are included in the annual allowance available to the employee

D Contributions to the pension scheme by the employer can be deducted from the employee's earnings when calculating the tax to deduct under PAYE

3 Yasmin has net income of £119,500. In the tax year 2021/22 she made a gift aid payment of £2,400 (gross amount) and a personal pension contribution of £10,000 (gross).

What is her personal allowance for the tax year 2021/22?

A £5,470

B £9,020

C £7,820

D £12,570

For suggested answers, see the 'Answers' section at the end of the book.

PRACTICE QUESTIONS

1 STEVE

Steve, aged 30, is self-employed and has the following income for the tax year 2021/22:

	£
Trading income	50,650
Savings income	10,000

In addition, Steve made a contribution of £8,400 (gross) into his personal pension scheme.

Calculate Steve's income tax liability for the tax year 2021/22. **(6 marks)**

2 Omar

Omar has been trading for many years as a barrel manufacturer. His taxable trading income for the tax year 2021/22 was £39,690.

During the tax year 2021/22 he received building society interest of £2,480. His only other income taxable in that year was £12,300 interest, which arose on his holding of gilt-edged stock.

He paid personal pension plan contributions totalling £4,000 (gross) in 2021/22.

Calculate Omar's income tax liability for the tax year 2021/22. **(7 marks)**

For suggested answers, see the 'Answers' section at the end of the book.

Chapter 16

SELF-ASSESSMENT

INTRODUCTION

Earlier chapters have dealt with the income tax computation, looked at how various sources of income are taxed and at the deductions available.

This chapter explains how the tax is paid under the rules of self-assessment. It covers syllabus areas: C6 (a) to (e), (g) and (h).

CONTENTS	LEARNING OUTCOMES
1 Filing a tax return **2** Calculating the tax liability **3** Errors **4** Notification of chargeability **5** Penalties for failure to submit a return **6** Standard penalties **7** Records **8** Payment of tax **9** Interest and penalties for late payment **10** Duties and responsibilities of a tax practitioner	At the end of this chapter, you should be able to: • explain and apply the features of the self-assessment system as it applies to individuals • detail the responsibilities that individuals have for disclosure of income and payment of tax to the relevant authorities • describe the duties and responsibilities of a tax practitioner • compute payments on account and balancing payments/repayments • list the information and records that taxpayers need to retain for tax purposes • explain the tax authority's filing and payment process in relation to all personal income • explain the system of penalties and interest as it applies to income tax and capital gains.

1 FILING A TAX RETURN

Each year, where HM Revenue and Customs (HMRC) consider it necessary, the taxpayer will be sent a notice to file a self-assessment tax return.

The date by which the return must be submitted depends on whether the taxpayer files a traditional paper return or files his or her return online.

Type of return	**Filing date**
Paper	31 October following the end of the tax year, i.e. 31 October 2022 for 2021/22
Online	31 January following the end of the tax year, i.e. 31 January 2023 for 2021/22

In each case, the deadline is extended to three months after the issue of the notice to file a tax return, if later.

It is important in the examination to state the precise date, including the year, for return submission dates.

The return consists of a summary form with supplementary pages, which vary according to an individual's income and gains position. Some of the supplementary pages are covered in other chapters.

2 CALCULATING THE TAX LIABILITY

The tax return includes a section for the taxpayer to calculate his or her own tax liability (hence the term 'self-assessment'). This self-assessment is required even if the tax due is nil or if a repayment is due.

HMRC will calculate the tax liability on behalf of the taxpayer if a paper return is submitted by the 31 October deadline. The calculation by HMRC is treated as a self-assessment on behalf of the taxpayer. HMRC will not make any judgement on the accuracy of the figures included in the return, but will merely calculate the tax liability based on the information submitted.

Where a return is filed online, a calculation of the tax liability is provided automatically.

HMRC periodically issues statements of account. These show the amount of self-assessed tax payable and any interest or penalties. Any payments made by the taxpayer are deducted in calculating the amount payable.

3 ERRORS

HMRC may correct any obvious errors and anything else that they believe to be incorrect by reference to the information they hold within nine months of the date that they receive the return. For example, they will correct arithmetical errors or errors of principle. This process of repair does not mean that HMRC has necessarily accepted the return as accurate.

The taxpayer can amend his or her return within 12 months of the 'filing date'. The 'filing date' is 31 January following the tax year. For 2021/22, amendments must therefore be made by 31 January 2024 (irrespective of whether the return is online or paper based).

If an error is discovered at a later date, the taxpayer can make an overpayment relief claim to recover any tax overpaid within four years of the end of the tax year (5 April 2026 for 2021/22).

A penalty under the 'standard' penalty regime can be charged for the submission of an incorrect tax return (see section 6 below).

4 NOTIFICATION OF CHARGEABILITY

Taxpayers **who do not receive a notice to file a return** are required to notify HMRC if they have income or chargeable gains on which tax is due.

The time limit for notifying HMRC of chargeability is six months from the end of the tax year in which the liability arises i.e. 5 October 2022 for new income received in 2021/22. A penalty can be charged if a taxpayer does not notify HMRC.

Notification is **not necessary** if there is no actual tax liability. For example, if the income or chargeable gain is covered by allowances or exemptions.

Penalties under the 'standard' penalty regime (see section 6 below) may be levied by HMRC if the taxpayer fails to notify chargeability but note that the minimum penalty is 30%. There is no zero penalty for a genuine mistake, however if a person makes a full and unprompted disclosure within 12 months of the due date for the tax which becomes due as a result of the failure to notify, the penalty can be reduced to zero.

There is no penalty until tax is unpaid as a result of failing to notify.

The amount of penalty depends upon the taxpayer's behaviour, or the reasons for failing to notify.

5 PENALTIES FOR FAILURE TO SUBMIT A RETURN

Failure to submit a tax return by the due date will result in a penalty as follows:

Immediate penalty	£100
Delays of more than 3 months	£10 per day for up to 90 days
Delays of more than 6 months	5% of tax due
Delays of more than 12 months (non-deliberate withholding of information)	5% of tax due
Delays of more than 12 months late (deliberately withholding information):	
– Without concealment (maximum penalty)	70% tax due
– With concealment (maximum penalty)	100% tax due

The penalties are cumulative.

The tax based penalties are each subject to a minimum amount of £300.

The penalties for submitting a return more than 12 months late can be reduced for disclosure with higher reductions if the disclosure is unprompted.

Example

Taika does not submit his return online for the tax year 2021/22 until 10 October 2023. The tax due is £175. What are the maximum penalties due?

Solution

A fixed penalty of £100 is due as the return is submitted after the filing date of 31 January 2023.

Daily penalties of £10 per day could be imposed for 90 days as the return is more than 3 months late.

A further penalty of 5% of the tax due is charged as the return is more than six months late. As 5% of the tax due is less than the minimum of £300, the tax-based penalty charged will be £300.

6 STANDARD PENALTIES

The penalties for certain tax offences have been standardised. For your examination, a standard penalty can apply to late notification of chargeability and for the submission of incorrect tax returns.

In your examination, these standard penalties also apply to corporation tax and VAT.

The level of penalty is a percentage of the revenue lost as a result of the inaccuracy or under assessment and depends on the behaviour of the taxpayer as follows:

Taxpayer's behaviour	Maximum penalty (% of lost revenue)	Minimum penalty – unprompted disclosure	Minimum penalty – prompted disclosure
Genuine mistake	No penalty	No penalty	No penalty
Failure to take reasonable care	30%	0%	15%
Deliberate understatement	70%	20%	35%
Deliberate understatement with concealment	100%	30%	50%

Penalties can be reduced where the taxpayer makes full disclosure and cooperates with HMRC to establish the amount of tax unpaid.

These penalties (excluding a genuine mistake) are included in the tax tables.

7 RECORDS

Taxpayers are required to keep all records necessary to make a correct and complete return. For a business (including the letting of property), the records that must be kept include records of:

- all receipts and expenses
- all goods purchased and sold
- all supporting documents relating to the transactions of the business, such as accounts, books, contracts, vouchers and receipts.

Other taxpayers should keep evidence of income received such as dividend vouchers, P60s, copies of P11Ds and bank statements.

For taxpayers with a business, all their records (not just those relating to the business) must be retained until five years after the filing date. For 2021/22 records must therefore be retained until 31 January 2028.

For other taxpayers, records must be retained until 12 months after the filing date (31 January 2024 for 2021/22).

A penalty of up to £3,000 may be charged for failure to retain adequate records. The maximum penalty is only likely to be imposed in the most serious cases, such as where a taxpayer deliberately destroys his or her records in order to obstruct an HMRC enquiry.

8 PAYMENT OF TAX

8.1 PAYMENTS ON ACCOUNT

Payments on account may be required if the taxpayer's income tax liability in the previous year exceeded any PAYE paid.

The first payment is due on 31 January **in** the tax year. The second payment is due six months later, that is on 31 July following the end of the tax year. The due dates for payments on account for 2021/22 are therefore:

- first payment on account – 31 January 2022
- second payment on account – 31 July 2022.

Payments on account are based on the **previous year's** income tax and class 4 NIC liability. No payments on account are made for capital gains tax (CGT) or class 2 NICs.

The payments on account are based on the figure of tax remaining after giving credit for any tax paid via PAYE. The tax liability for the previous year, net of PAYE, is known as the 'relevant amount'.

Each payment on account is 50% of the relevant amount of income tax and class 4 NICs, if appropriate.

Class 2 NICs are payable under self-assessment on 31 January following the end of the tax year, i.e. by 31 January 2023 for the 2021/22 tax year.

Example

Leeta runs a small business but also has a part time job. Her tax liability for the tax year 2020/21 was £14,846. This is made up as follows:

	£
Income tax liability	20,200
Less: PAYE	(8,500)
Income tax payable	11,700
Class 2 NICs	159
Class 4 NICs	1,100
Capital gains tax	1,893
Total payable	14,852

Her payments on account for 2021/22 are found by taking the income tax payable and class 4 NICs due for 2020/21 and halving this total to give the amount of each payment.

	£
Income tax payable	11,700
Class 4 NICs	1,100
	12,800
Payment on account (£12,800 ÷ 2) due on 31 January 2022 and 31 July 2022	6,400

ACTIVITY 1

Chloe's tax liability for the tax year 2020/21 was as follows:

	£
Income tax liability	9,400
Less: PAYE	(2,100)
Income tax payable	7,300
Class 2 NICs	159
Class 4 NICs	700
CGT	3,493
Total payable	11,652

State the amounts of payments on account due for the tax year 2021/22 and the dates on which payments are due.

For a suggested answer, see the 'Answers' section at the end of the book.

8.2 PAYMENTS ON ACCOUNT NOT REQUIRED

Payments on account are not required if:

- the relevant amount for the previous tax year is less than £1,000, or
- more than 80% of the income tax liability for the previous tax year was met by deduction of tax at source. This will mean that most employed people will not have to make payments on account, since more than 80% of their tax liability is likely to be paid through PAYE, or
- there is no relevant amount in the previous tax year. For example, if a taxpayer, whose only income was from employment in 2020/21, commences self-employment on 1 May 2021 he or she will not have to make payments on account for 2021/22, since he or she is very unlikely to have a relevant amount for 2020/21.

8.3 BALANCING PAYMENTS

The balancing payment is due on 31 January following the end of the tax year. For 2021/22 this is 31 January 2023.

The balancing payment is the total tax liability for the year (income tax, class 2 and 4 NICs and CGT), less PAYE and less payments made on account.

It is possible that a balancing repayment will be due, in which case HMRC will repay the amount of tax overpaid.

Where the amount of tax due changes as a result of an amendment to the self-assessment (by either the taxpayer or HMRC), any additional tax due must be paid within 30 days of the notice of amendment if this is later than the normal due date.

ACTIVITY 2

Continuing with Activity 1, suppose that Chloe's tax liability for the tax year 2021/22 is as follows:

	£
Income tax liability	10,800
Less: PAYE	(2,500)
Income tax payable	8,300
Class 2 NICs	159
Class 4 NICs	800
CGT	4,590
Total tax payable	13,849

State the amount of balancing payment and the date on which it is due. Also, state the payments on account due for the tax year 2022/23 and the dates on which they are due.

For a suggested answer, see the 'Answers' section at the end of the book.

9 INTEREST AND PENALTIES FOR LATE PAYMENT

9.1 INTEREST

Interest is automatically charged if tax is paid late, whether it is income tax, class 2 or 4 NICs or CGT.

Interest is paid by HMRC on any overpayment of tax. Interest runs from the date of actual payment to the date of repayment.

The calculation of this interest is outside the examination syllabus.

9.2 PENALTY FOR UNPAID TAX

Interest on tax paid late is not a penalty, since it merely compensates for the advantage of paying late. Therefore, to further encourage compliance, penalties can also be imposed where income tax, class 2 or 4 NIC or CGT is paid late. Penalties do not apply to payments on account.

Where a balancing payment is not paid until more than 30 days after the due date (31 January following the tax year), a penalty equal to 5% of the tax unpaid is imposed. A further 5% penalty arises if the tax is still unpaid six months after the due date and again after 12 months.

Where additional tax becomes due as a result of an amendment to a self-assessment, a penalty is only imposed if the additional tax is not paid within 30 days of the due date. The due date in this situation is 30 days after the amendment. (This differs from interest, which runs from the 31 January following the tax year.)

Penalties may be mitigated by HMRC, for example if there is a reasonable excuse for the non-payment of the tax. Insufficiency of funds is not a reasonable excuse.

Example

Lily's balancing payment due for 2021/22 is £5,000. Only £1,200 of this was paid on 31 January 2023.

Explain whether Lily will be liable to a penalty.

Solution

A penalty of £190 (£3,800 at 5%) will be due if the tax of £3,800 is not paid by 2 March 2023.

A further penalty of £190 will be due if the tax is not paid by 31 July 2023 and again if the tax is not paid by 31 January 2024.

10 DUTIES AND RESPONSIBILITIES OF A TAX PRACTITIONER

10.1 INTRODUCTION

An ACCA tax adviser has duties and responsibilities to:

- the client
- HM Revenue and Customs
- ACCA.

An adviser owes the greatest duty to his or her client.

10.2 ACCA GUIDELINES ON PROFESSIONAL ETHICS

The ACCA's ethical rules are set out in the Professional Code of Ethics and Conduct. This code sets out the standards expected of members and students and gives a framework of principles that should be applied.

Fundamental principles	
Objectivity	Members should not allow bias, conflicts of interest or undue influence of others to override professional or business judgements.
Professional behaviour	Members must comply with relevant laws and regulations and avoid any action that discredits the profession.
Professional competence and due care	It is important to ensure members maintain their professional knowledge and skill and they should be diligent and act in accordance with applicable technical and professional standards.
Integrity	Members should be straightforward and honest in all their professional and business relationships.
Confidentiality	Members should not disclose information to other parties (including HMRC) without the client's permission, unless there is a legal or professional right or duty to disclose, nor use the information for personal advantage.

10.3 CONFIDENTIALITY

A tax adviser has an overriding duty of confidentiality towards his or her client. Under normal circumstances, a client's tax affairs should not be discussed with third parties (even after the client has ceased to be a client).

The exceptions to this rule are where:

- authority has been given by the client, or
- there is a legal, regulatory or professional right or duty to disclose e.g. in the case of suspected money laundering.

The duty of confidentiality also relates to dealings with HMRC.

However, the tax adviser must ensure that, whilst acting in the client's best interest, he or she must consult with HMRC staff in an open and constructive manner.

ACTIVITY 3

Which of the following statements is NOT correct?

A Accountants need to follow the rules of confidentiality even in a social environment.

B If money laundering is suspected, accountants are allowed to break the rules of confidentiality.

C Rules of confidentiality towards a client must be followed even after the business relationship has ended.

D Accountants must follow the rules of confidentiality irrespective of the situation.

For a suggested answer, see the 'Answers' section at the end of the book.

10.4 DEALINGS WITH HM REVENUE AND CUSTOMS

It is important to ensure that information provided to HMRC is accurate and complete.

An adviser must not assist a client to plan or commit any offence.

If a member becomes aware that the client has committed a tax irregularity, he or she must discuss it with the client and ensure that proper disclosure is made.

Examples would include:

- not declaring income that is taxable
- claiming reliefs to which the client is not entitled
- not notifying HMRC where they have made a mistake giving rise to an underpayment of tax, or an increased repayment.

Where a client has made an error:

- it is necessary to decide whether it is a genuine error or a deliberate or fraudulent act.

Once an error has been discovered the member must discuss the matter with his or her client and explain the consequences of non-disclosure (e.g. interest, penalties and in extreme cases criminal prosecution). If the client refuses to disclose, even after written advice from the adviser, then the adviser should:

- Cease to act for the client.
- Write to HMRC stating that they have ceased to act for the client but without explaining the reason.
- Consider whether a report should be made under the Money Laundering Regulations.

KEY TERMS

Self-assessment – the system whereby an individual calculates and pays his or her income tax, class 2 and 4 NICs and capital gains tax liability.

Statement of account – a statement issued by HMRC showing the amount of tax owing together with any interest or penalties due.

Payments on account – payments made by the taxpayer prior to the finalisation of his or her liability for the year. They are made on 31 January in the tax year and 31 July in the following tax year.

Balancing payment – additional tax payable on 31 January following the end of the tax year.

Late payment penalty – a penalty imposed if a balancing payment remains outstanding 30 days after the due date. The sum due is 5% of the outstanding liability. Further 5% penalties can be imposed if tax is still unpaid at 6 months and 12 months after the due date.

SELF TEST QUESTIONS

		Paragraph
1	By what date should a paper self-assessment tax return for 2021/22 be submitted?	1
2	By what date should an online tax return for 2021/22 be submitted?	1
3	How long does HMRC have in which to correct any obvious errors or mistakes?	3
4	Amendments by the taxpayer to the 2021/22 return should be made by what date?	3
5	What is the time limit for notifying HMRC of chargeability to tax?	4
6	What is the initial penalty for failing to submit a return?	5
7	For how long must a self-employed person retain his or her business records?	7
8	What is the penalty for failure to retain records?	7
9	What are the due dates of payment under self-assessment?	8.1
10	How are payments on account calculated?	8.1
11	When are payments on account not required?	8.2
12	When is a late payment penalty imposed?	9.2
13	What should a tax adviser do if his or her client refuses to correct a material tax error?	10.4

MULTIPLE CHOICE QUESTIONS

1 Jonas has been a sole trader for a number of years. His tax payable for the tax year 2021/22 amounts to £12,000.

On which dates were/are Mr Jones' payments on account due for this amount?

A 31 January 2022 and 31 July 2022

B 31 January 2023 and 31 July 2023

C 31 July 2022 and 31 January 2023

D 31 October 2022 and 31 January 2023

2 Claudia received a notice to file a tax return for the tax year 2021/22 on 20 June 2022 and submitted the return online on 24 August 2023. The tax due on the return was £470. Assuming **NO** daily penalties are imposed, what is the maximum penalty that can be levied?

A £100

B £123

C £400

D £470

3 Kaleel is required to make payments on account of his tax liability. For the tax year 2020/21, his income tax liability was £22,440, of which £2,400 was collected under PAYE. He estimates that his income tax payable for the tax year 2021/22 will be £26,400.

What is the amount of the first payment on account that Kaleel should make on 31 January 2022 in respect of his income tax liability for the tax year 2021/22?

Ignore national insurance.

A £10,020

B £11,220

C £12,000

D £13,200

For suggested answers, see the 'Answers' section at the end of the book.

PRACTICE QUESTIONS

1 PAYMENT SCHEDULE

Sorrel has total income tax and class 4 liabilities (net of PAYE) for the tax year 2020/21 of £3,000 and £4,632 for the tax year 2021/22.

Using the above information, prepare a schedule showing the amounts of tax due and the due dates in respect of the tax years 2021/22 and 2022/23. **(6 marks)**

2 TAX RETURNS

Assuming HMRC issues a notice to file a tax return for the tax year 2021/22 to Hanif on 10 April 2022, state the dates by which:

(i) the return must be submitted if Hanif wants to submit a paper return

(ii) the return must be submitted if Hanif wants to submit an online return

(iii) Hanif can correct any errors in the return. **(6 marks)**

For a suggested answer, see the 'Answers' section at the end of the book

Chapter 17

OVERVIEW OF CAPITAL GAINS TAX

INTRODUCTION

This is the first of four chapters on capital gains tax. This chapter deals with the capital gains tax calculation. It covers disposal proceeds, acquisition costs and the indexation allowance available to companies. It is essential to fully master this chapter, which covers the basic calculation, before moving on to other areas.

Most of this chapter considers the application of capital gains tax to disposals made by individuals. Although companies are chargeable to tax on their gains, there are some important differences in the way their gains are calculated. These differences are considered in detail in the later parts of the chapter.

This chapter covers syllabus areas D1, D2 (a) (b) (d) (e), D5, E4 (a) (b) (c) (e).

CONTENTS	LEARNING OUTCOMES
	At the end of this chapter, you should be able to: • define chargeable persons, chargeable disposals and chargeable assets • outline the basic calculation including the deduction of expenses of purchase and sale • explain the circumstances when market value may be used for the transfer value • calculate disposals of post 31 March 1982 assets including enhancement expenditure • compute chargeable gains for individuals and companies • explain the use of capital losses for individuals and companies

	• explain the entitlement to the annual exempt amount • compute the amount of capital gains tax payable • outline the administrative framework for capital gains tax • record relevant details of gains and the capital gains tax payable legibly and accurately in the tax return • calculate indexation allowance up to the date of sale using a given indexation factor for companies.

1 THE SCOPE OF CAPITAL GAINS TAX

1.1 INTRODUCTION

Capital gains tax is charged on gains arising on chargeable disposals of chargeable assets by chargeable persons. The tax is charged on individuals on gains arising in a tax year.

1.2 CHARGEABLE PERSONS

The term chargeable person covers companies as well as individuals. Although remember that companies pay corporation tax on their chargeable gains, not capital gains tax (see section 8).

A chargeable person is liable on all disposals of assets whether in the UK or abroad.

The following persons are exempt from capital gains tax:

- registered pension funds
- charities (to the extent that they use the gains for charitable purposes).

1.3 CHARGEABLE DISPOSAL

The term chargeable disposal includes the following:

- the sale of the whole or part of an asset
- the gift of an asset
- the receipt of a capital sum derived from an asset
- the loss or total destruction of an asset (irrespective of whether or not the owner is compensated by a capital sum for the loss).

The following disposals are exempt from capital gains tax:

- disposals on an individual's death
- disposals to charities.

1.4 CHARGEABLE ASSETS

All assets are chargeable to capital gains tax unless specifically exempt. The main exempt assets are:

- foreign currency for personal expenditure
- motor cars including veteran and vintage cars (except those unsuitable for private use)
- an individual's main residence if it is covered by private residence relief (see Chapter 20)
- medals for bravery (unless acquired by purchase)
- some chattels (dealt with in Chapter 18)
- gilt edged securities and qualifying corporate bonds
- debts
- individual savings account (ISA) investments
- pension and annuity rights
- NS&I savings certificates and premium bonds
- prizes and betting winnings
- damages for personal injury.

Exempt assets are outside the scope of capital gains tax. Consequently, whilst gains are not taxable, losses are not allowable either.

2 THE CALCULATION OF CHARGEABLE GAINS

2.1 OVERVIEW OF THE CALCULATION

A chargeable gain represents the increase in value of an asset during the time it has been owned by the taxpayer. It is therefore calculated by comparing the price paid for it and the price at which it is now being sold.

An illustration of how to set out the computation is shown overleaf.

2.2 ILLUSTRATION OF CHARGEABLE GAIN CALCULATION

	£
Disposal proceeds	80,000
Less: Incidental disposal costs	(500)
	79,500
Less: Allowable expenditure	(30,000)
Chargeable gain	49,500

When the chargeable gains or allowable losses on each asset have been calculated, they are combined. The computation for an individual continues as follows:

Pro forma CGT computation: Mona – 2021/22

	£
Total 2021/22 chargeable gains (say)	25,000
Less: Total 2021/22 allowable losses (say)	(3,000)
Net chargeable gains for the year	22,000
Less: Annual exempt amount for 2021/22	(12,300)
	9,700
Less: Allowable losses brought forward at 6 April 2021 (say)	(1,700)
Taxable gains for 2021/22	8,000

2.3 ANNUAL EXEMPT AMOUNT

Every **individual** receives an annual exempt amount (AEA). For 2021/22 it is £12,300. If the net chargeable gains for the year do not exceed that amount, no tax is chargeable.

If the AEA is not utilised in any particular tax year, then it is wasted. It cannot be carried forward or backward to another tax year.

The following standardised terms will be used in the requirements of examination questions on capital gains tax:

Net chargeable gains for the year – the total chargeable gains less allowable losses arising on assets disposed of in the tax year, before deducting the annual exempt amount.

Taxable gains – the net chargeable gains after deducting the annual exempt amount and capital losses brought forward.

3 DISPOSAL PROCEEDS

The date of disposal is the date the contract is made (rather than the date of transfer of the asset, which may be different).

As a general rule, the disposal proceeds taken into account in the computation is the amount of consideration received for the asset. So, if Juan sells some shares to Sally for £20,000, it is £20,000 that Juan takes into his chargeable gains computation.

Market value is substituted for actual proceeds if the bargain was not made at arm's length, for example, if the asset was gifted rather than sold. The market value is the price that the asset might reasonably be expected to fetch on a sale on the open market.

If the asset is a building on which structures and buildings allowances (SBAs) have been claimed, on disposal the SBAs claimed to date should be added to the sales proceeds, thereby increasing the chargeable gain. See Chapter 4.

4 ALLOWABLE EXPENDITURE

4.1 INTRODUCTION

The following types of expenditure are allowable deductions in calculating a chargeable gain:

- the acquisition cost of the asset
- expenditure on enhancing the value of the asset (improvement expenditure)
- expenditure incurred to establish, preserve or defend the taxpayer's title to the asset (e.g. legal fees for a boundary dispute)
- incidental costs arising both on the acquisition of the asset and its disposal.

No deduction is permitted for:

- money paid out of public funds (e.g. costs covered by grants or subsidies)
- payments under insurance policies against damage, injury, loss or depreciation of the asset
- payments of interest
- payments that are deductible in computing income tax
- any amount representing the cost of the taxpayer's own labour.

4.2 INCIDENTAL COSTS

The following types of expenditure are deductible as incidental costs of acquisition or disposal:

- fees and commissions for professional services (surveyors, valuers, auctioneers, accountants, legal advisors, stockbrokers, or other agents)
- advertising costs to find a buyer or seller
- the costs of a legal conveyance or transfer (including stamp duties)
- reasonable costs incurred in making valuations necessary for computing the gain, particularly where market value is required.

It is necessary to distinguish between the incidental costs of acquisition and those of disposal, because they are treated differently for the purposes of the indexation allowance available to companies (see later in this chapter).

4.3 ACQUISITION COST

The acquisition cost is usually the price paid when the asset was purchased. However, if the owner was given the asset, the market value of the asset at the date of the gift is used as the cost of acquisition. If the asset was inherited, the market value at the date of death (referred to as probate value) is used.

Example

Winnie received two assets on 1 June 2021.

The first was inherited from her grandfather. Her grandfather had bought the asset for £20,000 in 1986; it was worth £42,000 at the date of her grandfather's death and is worth £45,000 on 1 June 2021.

The cost of this asset to Winnie is £42,000, the market value at the date of death.

The second asset was received as a gift from a friend. This asset had cost £37,500 and is worth £67,900 on 1 June 2021.

The cost of this asset for Winnie is £67,900, the market value at the date of the gift.

4.4 IMPROVEMENT EXPENDITURE

To be deductible, improvement expenditure must meet two tests:

- it must be spent with the purpose of **permanently** enhancing the value of the asset
- it must be reflected in the state or nature of the asset at the time of disposal.

Revenue costs like repairs and maintenance and insurance are not improvement expenditure.

ACTIVITY 1

Cedric purchased an asset in August 2005 for £10,000. He spent £2,100 in June 2007 on improving the asset and £60 every year on insuring the asset. He sold it in December 2021 for £20,000.

Calculate the chargeable gain.

For a suggested answer, see the 'Answers' section at the end of the book.

5 LOSSES

5.1 INTRODUCTION

The treatment of losses depends on whether the loss is incurred in the same tax year as the gain or in an earlier year.

5.2 GAINS AND LOSSES INCURRED IN THE SAME TAX YEAR

Where allowable losses arise, they are set off against chargeable gains arising in the same tax year.

The set off cannot be restricted to avoid wasting all or part of the annual exempt amount. For example, if in 2021/22, Bill has chargeable gains of £14,000 and allowable losses of £9,000, his net chargeable gains are £5,000. This is covered entirely by his annual exempt amount of £12,300. Bill does not have the option of deducting only £1,700 of losses so that his net gains are £12,300 (which would be covered exactly by the annual exempt amount).

Any losses that cannot be set off against gains of the same tax year (because the gains are insufficient) are carried forward and set off against future gains.

5.3 LOSSES BROUGHT FORWARD FROM AN EARLIER TAX YEAR

Losses brought forward from an earlier year are treated differently to losses incurred in the same tax year as gains.

Any losses brought forward from earlier years are offset **after** the annual exempt amount has been deducted from the net chargeable gains for the year (i.e. current year gains less current year losses). Capital losses brought forward are therefore not wasted against current year net chargeable gains that are covered by the annual exempt amount.

Any unused losses brought forward are carried forward again to the next year. They can be carried forward indefinitely.

Example

Wilson has the following chargeable gains and allowable losses for the tax years 2020/21 and 2021/22. Show how the losses will be used.

	2020/21	**2021/22**
	£	£
Chargeable gains	8,000	16,000
Allowable losses	(15,000)	(2,000)

Solution

His losses will be dealt with as follows:

	2020/21	**2021/22**
	£	£
Chargeable gains	8,000	16,000
Allowable losses	(15,000)	(2,000)
Net allowable loss c/f	(7,000)	
Net chargeable gains for the year		14,000
Less: Annual exempt amount		(12,300)
		1,700
Less: Allowable loss b/f		(1,700)
Taxable gains		0

The allowable loss brought forward of £7,000 is offset against the net chargeable gains of 2021/22 after offset of the annual exempt amount. Therefore, only £1,700 of the loss brought forward is used and £5,300 (£7,000 – £1,700) is available to carry forward to 2022/23.

ACTIVITY 2

Tomoharu, Lior and Harry made chargeable gains and allowable losses for the tax years 2021/22 and 2022/23 as set out below.

		Tomoharu	Lior	Harry
		£	£	£
2021/22				
	Chargeable gains	12,000	4,000	5,000
	Allowable losses	8,000	7,000	6,000
2022/23				
	Chargeable gains	14,900	13,800	7,000
	Allowable losses	2,000	1,000	2,000

Calculate the taxable gains for Tomoharu, Lior and Harry for both the tax years 2021/22 and 2022/23 and the amount of any losses carried forward at the end of 2022/23.

Assume the annual exempt amount is the same in the tax year 2022/23 as for 2021/22.

For a suggested answer, see the 'Answers' section at the end of the book.

6 COMPUTATION OF CAPITAL GAINS TAX LIABILITY

6.1 NORMAL RATES OF CGT

Generally, capital gains tax is charged at the lower rate of 10% and the higher rate of 20% on taxable gains.

The rate of capital gains tax is dependent upon the amount of a taxpayer's taxable income. Taxable gains are taxed **after** taxable income (i.e. as the top slice).

Where taxable gains fall into the remaining basic rate band, following the taxation of the individual's income, CGT is at the lower rate.

To the extent that any gains (or any part of gains) exceed the basic rate band, they are taxed at the higher rate.

Any unused income tax personal allowance cannot be used to reduce taxable gains.

Example

Kamila has taxable income of £33,200 for the tax year 2021/22. She has taxable gains on the sale of shares of £19,900.

What is her capital gains tax liability for the tax year 2021/22?

Solution

Capital gains tax liability for 2021/22

	£		£
Lower rate: remaining BRB (£37,700 – £33,200)	4,500	× 10%	450
Higher rate	15,400	× 20%	3,080
Taxable gains	19,900		
Capital gains tax liability			3,530

ACTIVITY 3

Peter has chargeable gains on the sale of shares of £18,000 and allowable losses of £2,500 in the tax year 2021/22. He has taxable income of £36,090.

What is his capital gains tax liability for the tax year 2021/22?

For a suggested answer, see the 'Answers' section at the end of the book.

6.2 RESIDENTIAL PROPERTY RATES OF CGT

There are higher rates of CGT in relation to the disposal of residential property. The lower rate for taxable gains falling in the basic rate band is 18% and the higher rate is 28%.

In practice, a taxpayer's main residential property (i.e. his or her home) will usually be exempt from CGT under the private residence relief rules (PRR) (see Chapter 20). However, where the gain on the disposal of a residential property is not fully exempt (e.g. on a residential investment property which is let out or a main residence that is not fully exempt by PRR) it is taxed at the higher rates.

The taxpayer can offset the AEA and capital losses against whichever gains he or she chooses. In order to maximise the reliefs they should be offset firstly against residential property gains, as they are taxable at higher rates than other gains.

The unused basic rate band may also be offset in the most beneficial way, however the tax saving will be the same regardless of the gains against which it is used (as the difference between the lower and higher rates is 10% in both cases). This is illustrated in the example below.

In the examination you may use either calculation method. In this study text we have chosen to allocate the unused basic rate band against other gains before residential gains.

Example

In the tax year 2021/22 Janet realised the following chargeable gains:

	£
Residential property	50,300
Commercial property	30,000

Janet's taxable income for the tax year 2021/22 is £16,200.

What is her capital gains tax liability for the tax year 2021/22?

Solution

Capital gains tax liability for 2021/22

	Total	Other gains	Residential property
	£	£	£
Residential property	50,300		50,300
Commercial property	30,000	30,000	
Total gains	80,300	30,000	50,300
Less: AEA	(12,300)	–	(12,300)
Taxable gains	68,000	30,000	38,000

	£		£
Lower rate (other)	21,500	× 10%	2,150
Higher rate (other)	8,500	× 20%	1,700
	30,000		
Higher rate (residential)	38,000	× 28%	10,640
Taxable gains	68,000		
Capital gains tax liability			14,490

Alternative calculation:

	£		£
Lower rate (residential)	21,500	× 18%	3,870
Higher rate (residential)	16,500	× 28%	4,620
	38,000		
Higher rate (other)	30,000	× 20%	6,000
Taxable gains	68,000		
Capital gains tax liability			14,490

Working: Janet's unused basic rate is £21,500 (£37,700 – £16,200).

ACTIVITY 4

In the tax year 2021/22 Lisa realised the following chargeable gains:

	£
Residential property	15,000
Antique table	18,000

Lisa's taxable income for 2021/22 is £27,200.

What is her capital gains tax liability for 2021/22?

For a suggested answer, see the 'Answers' section at the end of the book.

7 ADMINISTRATION AND PAYMENT OF TAX

7.1 INTRODUCTION

Capital gains tax is charged for tax years. Chargeable gains and allowable losses arising on disposals between 6 April 2021 and 5 April 2022 are therefore subject to tax for the tax year 2021/22.

A payment on account in respect of the CGT on residential property gains is due within 30 days of disposal, along with a return.

For all other gains, CGT is due on 31 January following the tax year, i.e. by 31 January 2023 for 2021/22. With the exception of residential property, there are no payments on account of CGT.

Candidates will be expected to state the due dates for the disposal of residential property and the balance of tax for all of the disposals in the tax year. However, questions will not be set requiring the calculation of the payment on account on residential property disposals. Only the total capital gains tax due for the year will be required.

7.2 RETURNS OF INFORMATION

A taxpayer is obliged to give written notice of his or her chargeable gains to HMRC within six months of the end of the tax year, unless he or she has already been issued with a notice to complete a tax return.

If the taxpayer fails to notify HMRC of his or her gains, he or she may be liable to a penalty. (See Chapter 16 for penalties for late notification.)

There are a few exceptions to the requirement to provide information. The most commonly used concerns gains of small amounts. Where in a tax year an individual realises chargeable gains (before deduction of allowable losses) of not more than the annual exempt amount and the disposal proceeds are not more than four times the annual exempt amount, a simple statement to this effect constitutes the required notice. It is then up to HMRC to decide whether to request further details.

Accordingly, for 2021/22 information does not need to be provided if gains are less than £12,300 and proceeds less than £49,200.

No notice is required on the disposal of certain exempt assets, notably:

- cars
- foreign currency for personal expenditure and
- prizes and betting winnings.

7.3 CONTENTS OF THE TAX RETURN

Most taxpayers will report their taxable gains on the annual tax return. The capital gains supplementary pages (Form SA108) of the tax return cover four pages. Page 4 allows taxpayers to provide additional information and explanations to support their tax return and is not examinable.

- Page 1 summarises the total gains and losses on residential property and other property and assets.

- Page 2 summarises the gains and losses on quoted and unquoted shares and securities.
- Page 3 summarises the use and carry forward of losses and business asset disposal relief (see Chapter 20).

7.4 COMPLETION OF THE FORM

In the examination, you may be required to state the figures that should be entered in the relevant boxes on the supplementary pages for capital gains.

- In the examination, figures must be entered in the correct boxes.
- You will normally be asked to complete the boxes for just one page of any form.
- You do not need to fill in every box, only relevant ones.
- The narrative on the return is fairly self-explanatory and should be used to assist in deciding which figures to include in which boxes.

7.5 PAGE CG1

The page is used to record gains and losses on residential property, other property and assets in the year.

Summary of gains information:

- Box 1 enter taxpayer's name (if given).

Summary of information about residential property disposals:

- Box 3 enter the number of disposals of residential property.
- Box 4 enter the sale proceeds received on the disposals.
- Box 5 enter the total allowable costs on the disposals.
- Box 6 enter the chargeable gains made on the disposals before deducting losses.
- Box 7 enter the losses made on the disposals.

Ignore other boxes.

Summary of information about other property and asset disposals:

- Box 14 enter the number of disposals of other property and assets.
- Box 15 enter the sale proceeds received on the disposals.
- Box 16 enter the total allowable costs on the disposals.
- Box 17 enter the chargeable gains on the disposals before deducting losses.
- Box 19 enter the losses made on the disposals.

Ignore other boxes.

7.6 PAGE CG2

The page asks for information about the disposal of listed (quoted) and unlisted (unquoted) shares and securities. Calculations of gains on shares are dealt with in Chapter 19.

Summary of information about quoted shares and securities:

- Box 23 enter the number of disposals of quoted shares and securities in the year. For these purposes, count the disposal of the same class of shares in the same company on the same day as a single disposal.
- Box 24 enter the sale proceeds received on the disposals.
- Box 25 enter the total allowable costs on the disposals.
- Box 26 enter the chargeable gain on the disposals before deducting losses.
- Box 27 enter any losses made on the disposals.

Ignore other boxes.

Summary of information about unquoted shares and securities:

- Box 31 enter the number of disposals of unquoted shares and securities in the year. For these purposes, count the disposal of the same class of shares in the same company on the same day as a single disposal.
- Box 32 enter the sale proceeds received on the disposals.
- Box 33 enter the total allowable costs on the disposals.
- Box 34 enter the chargeable gain on the disposals before deducting losses.
- Box 35 enter any losses made on the disposals.

Ignore other boxes.

7.7 PAGE CG3

The page is used to record losses in the year, losses brought forward that are used in the year and losses carried forward.

Summary of gains information:

- Box 45 enter any losses brought forward and used in the year (remember that brought forward losses are deducted from net chargeable gains for the year after the annual exempt amount of £12,300).
- Box 47 if all losses are not offset in the year, enter the amount of losses remaining to be carried forward to set against future net chargeable gains.
- Box 50 enter gains qualifying for business asset disposal relief (Chapter 20).

Ignore other boxes.

HM Revenue & Customs

Capital Gains Tax summary

Tax year 6 April 2021 to 5 April 2022 (2021-22)

1 Your name

2 Your Unique Taxpayer Reference (UTR)

You must enclose your computations, including details of each gain or loss, as well as filling in the boxes.

Residential property (and carried interest) Please read the notes before filling in this section.

3 Number of disposals

4 Disposal proceeds
£ · 0 0

5 Allowable costs (including purchase price)
£ · 0 0

6 Gains in the year, before losses – any gains included in boxes 9, 11 and 13 amounts must be included in this total
£ · 0 0

7 Losses in the year – any losses included in boxes 9 and 11 amounts must be included in this total
£ · 0 0

8 If you're making any claim or election, put the relevant code in the box

9 Total gains or losses on UK residential property reported on Capital Gains Tax UK Property Disposal returns
£ · 0 0

10 Tax on gains in box 9 already charged
£ · 0 0

11 Total gains or losses on non-UK residential property or carried interest reported on Real Time Transaction returns
£ · 0 0

12 Tax on gains in box 11 already paid
£ · 0 0

13 Carried interest
£ · 0 0

Other property, assets and gains Please read the notes before filling in this section.

14 Number of disposals

15 Disposal proceeds
£ · 0 0

16 Allowable costs (including purchase price)
£ · 0 0

17 Gains in the year, before losses – do not include attributed gains included in box 18. Any gains included in box 21 amounts must be included in this total
£ · 0 0

18 Attributed gains where personal losses cannot be set off
£ · 0 0

19 Losses in the year – any losses included in box 21 amounts must be included in this total
£ · 0 0

20 If you're making any claim or election, put the relevant code in the box

21 Total gains or losses on the disposal of an asset of this type reported on Real Time Transaction returns
£ · 0 0

22 Tax on gains in box 21 already paid
£ · 0 0

SA108 2021 Page CG 1 HMRC 12/20

Listed shares and securities Please read the notes before filling in this section.

23 **Number of disposals**

24 **Disposal proceeds**

£ · 0 0

25 **Allowable costs (including purchase price)**

£ · 0 0

26 **Gains in the year, before losses** – any gains included in box 29 amounts must be included in this total

£ · 0 0

27 **Losses in the year** – any losses included in box 29 amounts must be included in this total

£ · 0 0

28 **If you're making any claim or election, put the relevant code in the box**

29 **Total gains or losses on the disposal of an asset of this type reported on Real Time Transaction returns**

£ · 0 0

30 **Tax on gains in box 29 already paid**

£ · 0 0

Unlisted shares and securities Please read the notes before filling in this section.

31 **Number of disposals**

32 **Disposal proceeds**

£ · 0 0

33 **Allowable costs (including purchase price)**

£ · 0 0

34 **Gains in the year, before losses** – any gains included in box 37 amounts must be included in this total

£ · 0 0

35 **Losses in the year** – any losses included in box 37 amounts must be included in this total

£ · 0 0

36 **If you're making any claim or election, put the relevant code in the box**

37 **Total gains or losses on the disposal of an asset of this type reported on Real Time Transaction returns**

£ · 0 0

38 **Tax on gains in box 37 already paid**

£ · 0 0

39 **Gains exceeding the lifetime limit for employee shareholder status shares**

£ · 0 0

40 **Gains invested under Seed Enterprise Investment Scheme and qualifying for relief**

£ · 0 0

41 **Losses used against income** – amount claimed against 2021-22 income

£ · 0 0

42 **Amount in box 41 relating to share loss relief in 2021-22 to which Enterprise Investment Scheme or Seed Enterprise Investment Scheme Relief is attributable**

£ · 0 0

43 **Losses used against income** – amount claimed against 2020-21 income

£ · 0 0

44 **Amount in box 43 relating to share loss relief in 2020-21 to which Enterprise Investment Scheme or Seed Enterprise Investment Scheme Relief is attributable**

£ · 0 0

SA108 2021 Page CG 2

Losses and adjustments Please read the notes before filling in this section.

Losses set against 2021-22 capital gains

45 Losses brought forward and used in-year

£ · 0 0

46 Income losses of 2020-21 set against gains

£ · 0 0

2021-22 capital losses – other information

47 Losses available to be carried forward

£ · 0 0

48 Losses used against an earlier year's gain

£ · 0 0

Investors' Relief and Business Asset Disposal Relief (previously 'Entrepreneurs' Relief')

49 Gains qualifying for Investors' Relief

£ · 0 0

50 Gains qualifying for Business Asset Disposal Relief

£ · 0 0

50.1 Lifetime allowance of Business Asset Disposal Relief and Entrepreneurs' Relief claimed – the total amount claimed to date

£ · 0 0

Tax adjustments to 2021-22 capital gains

51 Adjustments to Capital Gains Tax

£ – · 0 0

52 Additional liability for non-resident or dual resident trusts

£ · 0 0

Non-resident Capital Gains Tax (NRCGT) on UK property or land and indirect disposals

Please read the notes before filling in this section.

52.1 For direct disposals of UK residential property or properties, put the total gains chargeable to NRCGT in the box

£ · 0 0

52.2 For direct disposals of non-residential UK properties or land, or indirect disposals of any UK properties or land, put the total gains chargeable to NRCGT in the box

£ · 0 0

52.3 If any of the gains in box 52.2 are from indirect disposals, put 'X' in the box

52.4 Tax on gains in boxes 52.1 and 52.2 already charged

£ · 0 0

52.5 Total losses available against NRCGT gains for the year

£ · 0 0

SA108 2021 Page CG 3

Example

From the following information show the entries to be completed on pages CG1, CG2 and CG3 for Zineb Alami.

Capital transactions carried out during the tax year 2021/22 were:

12 May 2021	Antique necklace sold for £150,000. Purchased 21 April 2009. Chargeable gain £40,000.
1 November 2021	ABC plc shares sold for £20,000. Purchased 10 February 2002. Chargeable gain £15,000.
23 February 2022	XYZ Ltd shares sold for £5,000. Purchased 16 January 2010. Allowable loss £8,000.

Zineb Alami had capital losses brought forward from 2020/21 of £3,000.

Note that shares in a 'plc' are likely to be quoted shares. Shares in a 'Ltd' are always unquoted. None of the disposals qualify for business asset disposal relief.

Zineb Alami's capital gains supplementary pages tax return entries

Box 1	Zineb Alami
Box 14	1
Box 15	£150,000
Box 16	£110,000
Box 17	£40,000
Box 23	1
Box 24	£20,000
Box 25	£5,000
Box 26	£15,000
Box 31	1
Box 32	£5,000
Box 33	£13,000
Box 35	£8,000
Box 45	£3,000

ACTIVITY 5

Carlos Silva made the following disposals in the tax year 2021/22.

1 A house, which he bought on 11 April 1990 (an investment property), was sold on 10 September 2021 for £275,000. The chargeable gain was £20,000.

2 A painting, which he bought on 19 May 2011, was sold on 26 June 2021 for £18,500. The chargeable gain was £3,500.

3 Shares in LMN plc, which he bought on 3 August 2010, were sold on 30 September 2021 for £10,000 at an allowable loss of £8,000.

Capital losses brought forward were £14,000. None of the disposals qualify for business asset disposal relief.

You are required to show the entries to be completed on pages CG1, CG2 and CG3 of his tax return set out below.

For a suggested answer, see the 'Answers' section at the end of the book.

HM Revenue & Customs

Capital Gains Tax summary

Tax year 6 April 2021 to 5 April 2022 (2021-22)

1 Your name

2 Your Unique Taxpayer Reference (UTR)

You must enclose your computations, including details of each gain or loss, as well as filling in the boxes.

Residential property (and carried interest) Please read the notes before filling in this section.

3 Number of disposals

4 Disposal proceeds £ ·00

5 Allowable costs (including purchase price) £ ·00

6 Gains in the year, before losses – any gains included in boxes 9, 11 and 13 amounts must be included in this total £ ·00

7 Losses in the year – any losses included in boxes 9 and 11 amounts must be included in this total £ ·00

8 If you're making any claim or election, put the relevant code in the box

9 Total gains or losses on UK residential property reported on Capital Gains Tax UK Property Disposal returns £ ·00

10 Tax on gains in box 9 already charged £ ·00

11 Total gains or losses on non-UK residential property or carried interest reported on Real Time Transaction returns £ ·00

12 Tax on gains in box 11 already paid £ ·00

13 Carried interest £ ·00

Other property, assets and gains Please read the notes before filling in this section.

14 Number of disposals

15 Disposal proceeds £ ·00

16 Allowable costs (including purchase price) £ ·00

17 Gains in the year, before losses – do not include attributed gains included in box 18. Any gains included in box 21 amounts must be included in this total £ ·00

18 Attributed gains where personal losses cannot be set off £ ·00

19 Losses in the year – any losses included in box 21 amounts must be included in this total £ ·00

20 If you're making any claim or election, put the relevant code in the box

21 Total gains or losses on the disposal of an asset of this type reported on Real Time Transaction returns £ ·00

22 Tax on gains in box 21 already paid £ ·00

SA108 2021 Page CG 1 HMRC 12/20

Listed shares and securities Please read the notes before filling in this section.

23 **Number of disposals**

24 **Disposal proceeds**
£ .00

25 **Allowable costs (including purchase price)**
£ .00

26 **Gains in the year, before losses** – any gains included in box 29 amounts must be included in this total
£ .00

27 **Losses in the year** – any losses included in box 29 amounts must be included in this total
£ .00

28 **If you're making any claim or election, put the relevant code in the box**

29 **Total gains or losses on the disposal of an asset of this type reported on Real Time Transaction returns**
£ − .00

30 **Tax on gains in box 29 already paid**
£ .00

Unlisted shares and securities Please read the notes before filling in this section.

31 **Number of disposals**

32 **Disposal proceeds**
£ .00

33 **Allowable costs (including purchase price)**
£ .00

34 **Gains in the year, before losses** – any gains included in box 37 amounts must be included in this total
£ .00

35 **Losses in the year** – any losses included in box 37 amounts must be included in this total
£ .00

36 **If you're making any claim or election, put the relevant code in the box**

37 **Total gains or losses on the disposal of an asset of this type reported on Real Time Transaction returns**
£ − .00

38 **Tax on gains in box 37 already paid**
£ .00

39 **Gains exceeding the lifetime limit for employee shareholder status shares**
£ .00

40 **Gains invested under Seed Enterprise Investment Scheme and qualifying for relief**
£ .00

41 **Losses used against income** – amount claimed against 2021-22 income
£ .00

42 **Amount in box 41 relating to share loss relief in 2021-22 to which Enterprise Investment Scheme or Seed Enterprise Investment Scheme Relief is attributable**
£ .00

43 **Losses used against income** – amount claimed against 2020-21 income
£ .00

44 **Amount in box 43 relating to share loss relief in 2020-21 to which Enterprise Investment Scheme or Seed Enterprise Investment Scheme Relief is attributable**
£ .00

SA108 2021 Page CG 2

Losses and adjustments

Please read the notes before filling in this section.

Losses set against 2021-22 capital gains

45 Losses brought forward and used in-year

£ · 0 0

46 Income losses of 2020-21 set against gains

£ · 0 0

2021-22 capital losses – other information

47 Losses available to be carried forward

£ · 0 0

48 Losses used against an earlier year's gain

£ · 0 0

Investors' Relief and Business Asset Disposal Relief (previously 'Entrepreneurs' Relief')

49 Gains qualifying for Investors' Relief

£ · 0 0

50 Gains qualifying for Business Asset Disposal Relief

£ · 0 0

50.1 Lifetime allowance of Business Asset Disposal Relief and Entrepreneurs' Relief claimed – the total amount claimed to date

£ · 0 0

Tax adjustments to 2021-22 capital gains

51 Adjustments to Capital Gains Tax

£ − · 0 0

52 Additional liability for non-resident or dual resident trusts

£ · 0 0

Non-resident Capital Gains Tax (NRCGT) on UK property or land and indirect disposals

Please read the notes before filling in this section.

52.1 For direct disposals of UK residential property or properties, put the total gains chargeable to NRCGT in the box

£ · 0 0

52.2 For direct disposals of non-residential UK properties or land, or indirect disposals of any UK properties or land, put the total gains chargeable to NRCGT in the box

£ · 0 0

52.3 If any of the gains in box 52.2 are from indirect disposals, put 'X' in the box

52.4 Tax on gains in boxes 52.1 and 52.2 already charged

£ · 0 0

52.5 Total losses available against NRCGT gains for the year

£ · 0 0

SA108 2021 Page CG 3

8 CHARGEABLE GAINS FOR COMPANIES

8.1 INTRODUCTION

Although companies are classed as chargeable persons, they are not subject to capital gains tax itself but rather suffer corporation tax on their chargeable gains. The tax year is not the basis period for companies. Their gains form part of their taxable total profits for the accounting period in which they arise.

8.2 INDEXATION ALLOWANCE

The calculation of chargeable gains for companies differs from that for individuals, as companies are entitled to receive an indexation allowance.

The indexation allowance is an attempt to ensure that chargeable gains are subject to tax only to the extent that they represent an increase in real terms in an asset's value. The part of the gain that is due to inflation is excluded from the tax. However, the indexation allowance was frozen as at December 2017.

The indexation factor is calculated by reference to the increase in the retail prices index (RPI) from the date the asset was purchased to the earlier of the date it was sold and December 2017.

An asset that is purchased after December 2017 is not entitled to any indexation allowance. An asset that is purchased before December 2017 and sold after this date is entitled to the indexation allowance up until December 2017.

The indexation factor is applied to the **allowable expenditure** (original cost, incidental costs of purchase and enhancements). Each element of allowable expenditure must be indexed separately, from the month the expenditure was incurred. However, incidental costs of disposal do not qualify for indexation allowance even if incurred before the month of disposal.

The indexation is calculated based on the retail price index (RPI) in the month of acquisition and disposal (or December 2017 if earlier). In the examination you will always be supplied with the indexation factor to use in the question and will **not** have to calculate the indexation factor from the underlying RPI figures.

Example

Eye Ltd bought an investment property for £25,000 on 1 April 1998. On 15 July 2002 the company spent £7,000 on a loft extension. The property was sold on 31 August 2021 for £100,000.

Calculate the chargeable gain arising on Eye Ltd's disposal of the property.

Use the following indexation factors in your answer:

April 1998 to December 2017	0.710
July 2002 to December 2017	0.581

Solution

		£
Sale proceeds		100,000
Less: Cost		(25,000)
Enhancement expenditure		(7,000)
Unindexed gain		68,000
Less: Indexation allowance:		
On acquisition expenditure:	(£25,000 × 0.710)	(17,750)
On enhancement expenditure:	(£7,000 × 0.581)	(4,067)
Chargeable gain		46,183

8.3 RESTRICTIONS ON THE INDEXATION ALLOWANCE

The indexation allowance can be used to reduce or eliminate a gain, but it cannot create or increase an allowable loss.

ACTIVITY 6

On 1 May 2021 Stanislav Ltd sold an antique vase for £12,000 and a painting for £20,000. It incurred auctioneer's fees of 1% of the proceeds. The company acquired both assets on 1 July 2010 for £13,000 and £17,000, respectively.

Indexation allowances of £3,172 and £4,148 relate to the period of ownership (up to December 2017) of the vase and the painting respectively.

Calculate the chargeable gain or allowable loss arising on the sale of the vase and the painting.

For a suggested answer, see the 'Answers' section at the end of the book.

8.4 ANNUAL EXEMPT AMOUNT AND CAPITAL LOSSES

Finally, note that companies are **NOT** entitled to the annual exempt amount. They are taxable on all their chargeable gains less allowable losses.

Allowable losses are therefore set off in full against chargeable gains, regardless of whether they arise in the current year or are brought forward.

8.5 KEY DIFFERENCES BETWEEN INDIVIDUALS AND COMPANIES

	Individuals	**Companies**
Gains subject to	Capital gains tax – tax separately from income	Corporation tax – include in TTP – tax with income
Taxable period	Tax year	Accounting period
Annual exempt amount (AEA)	✓	×
Indexation allowance	×	Yes, but only to December 2017
Matching rules **(See Chapter 19)**	Shares purchased: 1 on the same day 2 in the **following 30 days** (FIFO) 3 in the share pool	Shares purchased: 1 on the same day 2 in the **previous 9 days** (FIFO) 3 in the share pool
Treatment of capital losses	• Offset against current year gains without restriction • Carry forward against net gains for current year after offset of AEA	• Offset against current year gains without restriction • Carry forward against future net gains without restriction
Business asset disposal relief, gift holdover relief and PRR **(See Chapter 20)**	✓	×
Rollover relief **(See Chapter 20)**	✓	✓ (but not on goodwill)

KEY TERMS

Annual exempt amount – an allowance given to **individuals only** to reduce their chargeable gains and calculate their taxable gains.

Chargeable person – an individual or a company.

Chargeable disposal – includes the sale of the whole or part of an asset and a gift of an asset.

Chargeable asset – any asset other than an exempt asset.

Net chargeable gains for the year – the chargeable gains after deducting allowable losses, in the current year, but before deducting the annual exempt amount (individuals only).

Taxable gains – the chargeable gains after deducting the annual exempt amount and allowable losses brought forward.

Disposal proceeds – is usually the consideration received for the asset. However, it may be replaced with market value if the bargain is not at arm's length.

Incidental costs – the costs associated with buying or selling an asset. For example, legal fees and advertising costs.

Indexation allowance – an allowance given to **companies only**, to compensate for the effects of inflation up until December 2017. It is calculated using the retail prices index.

Chargeable gain (companies) – the chargeable gain after deducting indexation allowance.

SELF TEST QUESTIONS

		Paragraph
1	On what gains is CGT charged?	1.1
2	Who is a chargeable person for CGT purposes?	1.2
3	Give two examples of persons who are exempt from CGT.	1.2
4	Give four examples of exempt assets.	1.4
5	On what date does a disposal occur for capital gains tax?	3
6	When is market value substituted for the actual sale proceeds?	3
7	What are the four categories of allowable expenditure?	4.1
8	Why must incidental costs of acquisition and disposal be treated separately?	4.2
9	What tests must improvement expenditure meet to be deductible?	4.4
10	How does the set off of a current year capital loss differ from the set off of a loss brought forward?	5
11	At what rates does an individual pay capital gains tax on non-residential property?	6.1
12	At what rates does an individual pay capital gains tax on residential property?	6.2

13	On what date is CGT due?	7.1
14	How does the calculation of a chargeable gain for a company differ from the calculation for an individual?	8
15	When is the indexation allowance restricted?	8.3

MULTIPLE CHOICE QUESTIONS

1 On 23 April 2021, Peter sold his holiday home for £174,000, before agent's fees of 2%. He had purchased the property on 5 June 2010 for £129,600. The seller incurred fees in June 2010 of £2,400.

What is the value of the chargeable gain arising on this disposal?

A £38,520

B £40,920

C £42,000

D £44,400

2 Owen has the following chargeable gains and allowable losses for the tax years 2020/21 and 2021/22.

	2020/21	**2021/22**
	£	£
Chargeable gains	10,000	17,000
Allowable losses	(21,000)	(1,900)

What loss, if any, is available to carry forward to the tax year 2022/23?

A £18,200

B £8,200

C £2,800

D £0

3 X Ltd sold a building for proceeds of £330,000. The building cost £250,000. Surveyor and agents fees totalling £2,500 were also paid by X Ltd in relation to the purchase.

What is the chargeable gain or allowable loss arising on this disposal?

Use an indexation factor of 0.316.

A £1,000

B (£2,290)

C £0

D (£1,500)

For suggested answers, see the 'Answers' section at the end of the book.

PRACTICE QUESTIONS

1 Valentina

Valentina made the following disposals in the year ended 5 April 2022:

(a) A house, which she bought for £9,000 on 3 April 2001 and let to tenants thereafter. She added a garage at a cost of £5,000 in January 2020 and the house was sold on 1 July 2021. The net proceeds of sale were £68,350.

(b) Sold a vintage Alfa Romeo motor car for £76,500 on 19 December 2021. The car had cost £17,400 on 31 March 2009. During her period of ownership, Valentina had never actually used the car on the road.

Valentina had capital losses brought forward at 6 April 2021 of £2,191. Her taxable income for the tax year 2021/22 is £32,585.

Required:

Calculate Valentina's capital gains tax liability for the tax year 2021/22. **(10 marks)**

2 STEEL LTD

Facts as in Practice Question 1, except the disposals were made by Steel Ltd in its year ended 31 March 2022.

Required:

Calculate the figure to be included as net chargeable gains in computing the taxable total profits for the year ended 31 March 2022.

Indexation factors are:

April 2001 to December 2017	0.607
March 2009 to December 2017	0.316

(10 marks)

For suggested answers, see the 'Answers' section at the end of the book.

Chapter 18

CHATTELS, PART DISPOSALS, COMPENSATION AND INSURANCE

INTRODUCTION

This chapter covers the special rules that apply to the disposal of chattels. It also covers the rules that apply when only part of an asset is disposed of or when compensation is received following the loss or destruction of an asset.

This chapter covers syllabus areas D2 (f) and D4 (a) to (d).

CONTENTS	LEARNING OUTCOMES
1 Define chattels 2 The calculation of gains on non-wasting chattel disposals 3 Part disposals 4 Compensation and insurance receipts	At the end of this chapter, you should be able to: • define chattels • explain and demonstrate the calculation of gains on chattel disposals • compute the amount of allowable expenditure for a part disposal • calculate gains on part disposals • calculate gains where compensation or insurance proceeds are received for assets lost or destroyed.

1 DEFINE CHATTELS

Chattels are defined as tangible, movable property.

A wasting chattel is an asset with a predictable life not exceeding 50 years. 'Life' means the asset's useful life, having regard to the purpose for which it was originally acquired.

A non-wasting chattel is a chattel that is not a wasting chattel.

Examples

Non-wasting chattels	Wasting chattels	Assets which are not chattels
Paintings Jewellery Antique furniture	Racehorses Greyhounds Yachts Movable plant and machinery Computers	Freehold land Buildings Shares Fixed plant and machinery

Wasting chattels are exempt from capital gains tax, unless capital allowances could be claimed by the disposer. Therefore, plant and machinery used in a business is chargeable (unless bought and sold for < £6,000 – see below).

2 THE CALCULATION OF GAINS ON NON-WASTING CHATTEL DISPOSALS

2.1 THE EXEMPTION

A non-wasting chattel that is purchased for less than £6,000 and sold for less than £6,000 is exempt from capital gains tax.

2.2 MARGINAL RELIEF

Where a non-wasting chattel, which was bought for less than £6,000, is sold for more than £6,000 a marginal relief is available. In these circumstances the gain is the lower of:

- The gain calculated as normal
- 5/3 × (**gross** disposal consideration – £6,000)

Thus two calculations are needed, one using the marginal relief formula and the other computing the gain in the normal way.

Example

Jonas sells an antique table for £8,200 in March 2022 but has to pay selling costs of £250. The table cost £3,400 in May 2009.

The chargeable gain is the lower of:

1 The gain calculated as normal

	£
Proceeds	8,200
Less: Selling costs	(250)
Net sale proceeds	7,950
Less: Cost	(3,400)
Gain	4,550

2 5/3 (£8,200 – £6,000) = 3,667

The gain is £3,667.

Note that the 5/3 rule is applied to the gross sale proceeds before deducting selling expenses.

ACTIVITY 1

Andrew sold a picture on 1 February 2022 for £6,600 that he acquired on 1 March 1999 for £3,200.

Calculate the chargeable gain.

For a suggested answer, see the 'Answers' section at the end of the book.

2.3 LOSSES

Where a non-wasting chattel that cost over £6,000 is sold at a loss, the figure of £6,000 is substituted for the actual **gross** sale proceeds. This restricts the amount of loss available for relief.

ACTIVITY 2

Brian bought an antique table for £6,500 in September 1999 and sold it for £5,600 in December 2021. He incurred £250 to advertise it for sale.

Calculate the allowable loss.

For a suggested answer, see the 'Answers' section at the end of the book.

The rules in respect of non-wasting chattels can be summarised as follows:

Buy \ Sell	Proceeds ≤ £6,000	Proceeds > £6,000
Cost > £6,000	Allowable loss but actual **gross** proceeds are replaced by deemed proceeds of £6,000	Normal rules apply
Cost ≤ £6,000	Exempt	Chargeable but gain restricted to: (**gross** sale proceeds – £6,000) × $\frac{5}{3}$

2.4 CHATTELS WITH CAPITAL ALLOWANCES

Any capital allowances that have been claimed in respect of a chattel are ignored if the chattel is disposed of at a gain. This is because they are recovered by means of a balancing charge or reduced written down value carried forward under the capital allowances rules.

If the chattel is disposed of at a loss, relief for the loss will not be allowed for capital gains tax purposes because relief has already been given under the capital allowances system. The capital allowances are deducted from the asset's allowable expenditure for capital gains tax purposes.

Rule for chattels with capital allowances

- Sold for more than original cost – calculate gain as normal
- Sold for less than original cost – no gain or capital loss

3 PART DISPOSALS

A part disposal is normally regarded as a chargeable disposal for capital gains tax purposes.

The problem with part disposals is identifying how much of the allowable expenditure can be deducted from the sale proceeds. This is done by applying the fraction set out below to the whole cost of the asset. The fraction is:

$$\frac{A}{A+B}$$

A = Gross disposal proceeds for the part disposed of **before** deducting selling expenses

B = Market value of the remainder at the time of the disposal

The remaining cost represents the cost of the part retained.

Any incidental costs of acquisition should also be apportioned in the same way. This can be done as a separate calculation, or they can be added to the cost before it is apportioned.

Example

Inji purchased a commercial building for £250,000. She later sold part of it for £100,000 and at that time the part she retained was worth £200,000.

Calculate the allowable expenditure available to Inji on the part disposal.

Solution

The part disposal fraction is:

$$\frac{\text{Disposal consideration (£100,000)}}{\text{Disposal consideration (£100,000) + Market value of remainder (£200,000)}}$$

Thus the allowable expenditure is:

£250,000 × £100,000/£300,000 = £83,333.

(The gain is £100,000 – £83,333 = £16,667)

Example

Fergus bought a 10 hectare field in June 2011 for £150,000. He sold 2 hectares in October 2021 for £40,000 incurring £1,200 of legal costs. The value of the remaining 8 hectares was £200,000.

Calculate the chargeable gain on the part disposal of the field and the cost carried forward in respect of the part retained.

Solution

		£
Proceeds		40,000
Less: Selling costs		(1,200)
		38,800
Less: Cost	$\frac{40,000}{40,000 + 200,000}$ × £150,000	(25,000)
Chargeable gain		13,800
Cost of part retained (£150,000 – £25,000)		125,000

Note that questions involving hectares of land are quite popular with the examining team. It is important to remember to split the cost of the land between the parts sold and kept by using their respective values, not the number of hectares.

4 COMPENSATION AND INSURANCE RECEIPTS

4.1 INTRODUCTION

In most circumstances a capital transaction has two parties, a buyer and a seller.

- The seller takes the agreed price into his or her disposal calculation as proceeds.
- The buyer has normally incurred allowable expenditure that will be used to calculate any gain or loss when he or she eventually disposes of the asset.

However, when an asset is destroyed, and the asset's owner receives compensation (from either the perpetrator or an insurance company) the position is different.

- The owner has received a capital sum without disposing of the asset
- The payer has received nothing in return.

Consequently, a separate set of rules is required.

4.2 ASSETS LOST OR DESTROYED

If an asset is lost or wholly destroyed, there is a deemed disposal of the asset.

- If **no compensation** is received, the disposal proceeds are nil (unless the owner receives consideration for scrapping the asset). The deduction of the allowable expenditure may give rise to a **loss**.
- Where the **owner receives compensation**, a capital gains tax computation is performed using the compensation as the **disposal proceeds**. The taxpayer can claim that the destruction/loss of the asset is treated as a no gain/no loss disposal if the compensation is used to buy a replacement asset.

4.3 REPLACING AN ASSET – FULL REINVESTMENT

Where all of the compensation is used to buy a replacement asset **within 12 months**, and the taxpayer makes the necessary claim, the deemed disposal proceeds for the old asset are treated as being equal to the cost of that asset, so that the gain is nil (no gain/no loss). If the insurance proceeds are greater than the deemed disposal proceeds under the no gain/no loss computation, the excess is deducted from the cost of the replacement asset carried forward.

This means no gain is taxed immediately and a higher gain is taxed in the future on the disposal of the replacement asset.

Example

Nika purchased an asset for £31,200 on 1 October 1997, which was destroyed by fire on 30 September 2021. Nika received compensation of £36,000 from her insurance company on 1 January 2022. She purchased a replacement asset for £40,000 on 1 February 2022.

Assuming that Nika makes the necessary no gain/no loss claim, calculate the allowable expenditure (base cost) for the replacement asset.

Solution

In the absence of a no gain/no loss election a gain would arise as follows:

	£
Proceeds	36,000
Less: Cost	(31,200)
Gain	4,800

However, as Nika has made a no gain/no loss election, the proceeds are deemed to be £31,200 (i.e. the cost of the asset), therefore no gain arises in January 2022.

As the actual proceeds received exceed the cost of the asset, the excess (i.e. the actual gain of £4,800) is deducted from the cost of the replacement asset.

Replacement asset base cost (£40,000 – £4,800)	£35,200

Effectively, the gain of £4,800 has been deferred (i.e. it is not charged now) and will instead be charged when the replacement asset is sold.

4.4 REPLACING AN ASSET – SOME PROCEEDS NOT SPENT

If the taxpayer does not spend all the compensation on replacing the asset, then he or she can still make the claim described above. However, the gain must be split into two parts:

- Gain charged now = proceeds not spent
- Gain deferred by electing for no gain/no loss treatment = balance.

Example

What is the position if Nika, in the previous example, spent the following on a replacement asset?

(i) £34,800

(ii) £30,000

Solution

(i) Gain charged now (January 2022) = £1,200 (Proceeds £36,000 – spent £34,800)

Balance of gain £3,600 (£4,800 – £1,200) is deducted from cost of new asset.

Base cost of new asset is £31,200 (£34,800 – £3,600)

(ii) No gain/no loss election is not possible as proceeds not spent of £6,000 exceed the gain of £4,800. Therefore, the gain of £4,800 arises in January 2022. The base cost of the replacement asset is the full cost of £30,000.

KEY TERMS

Chattels – tangible, movable property such as paintings, furniture and jewellery.

Wasting chattel – a chattel with a predictable life not exceeding 50 years.

No gain/no loss election –deemed disposal proceeds are equal to the cost of the asset.

SELF TEST QUESTIONS

		Paragraph
1	What are chattels?	1
2	How are gains on non-wasting chattels sold for more than £6,000 restricted?	2.2
3	How are losses restricted where non-wasting chattels are disposed of for less than £6,000?	2.3
4	What fraction is used to apportion the cost of an asset when a part disposal is made?	3
5	Within what period must a taxpayer purchase a replacement asset if he or she is to avoid being taxed on any compensation received?	4.3

MULTIPLE CHOICE QUESTIONS

1 Walton Ltd bought 20 hectares of land on 13 November 2016 for £30,000. On 22 November 2021, the company sold 10 hectares for £60,000 and the market value of the remaining land at that time was £15,000.

Assume indexation factor of:

November 2016 to December 2017 0.047

What is the chargeable gain arising on the disposal of the land in November 2021?

A £44,295

B £42,885

C £34,872

D £34,308

2 Laticia makes the following capital disposals in the tax year 2021/22:

1. A machine, which she used for business purposes, that was purchased for £8,000 and sold for £10,000.
2. A greyhound that was purchased for £7,000 and sold for £15,000.
3. A painting that was purchased for £4,000 and sold for £7,500.
4. Land that was purchased for £1,000 and sold for £5,200.

Which of these capital disposals are chargeable to capital gains tax?

A 1, 2 and 3

B 1 and 4 only

C 3 and 4 only

D 1, 3 and 4

3 Nikhil purchased a valuable painting, which was destroyed in a fire. He received compensation from his insurance company but did not purchase a replacement.

The transaction is treated as follows:

A No gain arises, as there is no disposal

B The transaction is treated as a disposal at no gain/no loss

C The value of the insurance proceeds received are treated as a chargeable gain

D A gain/loss is computed using the normal chargeable gains rules

---

For suggested answers, see the 'Answers' section at the end of the book.

PRACTICE QUESTIONS

1 MILANA

Milana had the following transactions in assets in the year ended 5 April 2022:

(a) Sold a piece of sculpture for £6,500 on 30 August 2021, which she had bought for £3,900.

(b) Sold a one-tenth interest in a racehorse on 31 August 2021 for £6,200. The interest had cost £1,340 in November 2007.

(c) Received insurance of £35,000 on 6 February 2022 following the destruction of a painting in a fire. The painting had cost £11,000. None of the insurance proceeds were used to replace the painting.

(d) Sold a piece of Chinese jade for £29,000 on 1 September 2021. This was purchased at auction in April 1992 for £12,200.

Required:

Calculate Milana's capital gains tax liability for the tax year 2021/22, if any, assuming her taxable income is £52,000. **(10 marks)**

2 MAISIE

Maisie had the following transactions in assets in the year ended 5 April 2022:

(a) Sold a rare Russian icon on 24 May 2021 for £5,600, which had cost £6,300.

(b) Sold three hectares out of a 12 hectare plot of land on 14 December 2021 for £8,000. The whole plot had cost £2,000 in June 2007. On 14 December 2021 the unsold hectares had an agreed market value of £20,000.

Required:

Calculate Maisie's capital gains tax liability for the tax year 2021/22, if any, assuming her taxable income is £27,000. **(6 marks)**

For suggested answers, see the 'Answers' section at the end of the book.

Chapter 19

SHARES AND SECURITIES

INTRODUCTION

Shares and securities are chargeable assets. Any gain made on the disposal of chargeable shares and securities is taxable and any loss is allowable. It is important to thoroughly understand this chapter and to master the matching rules.

This chapter covers syllabus area D2 (c), D3 and E4 (d) (e).

CONTENTS	LEARNING OUTCOMES
1 Introduction **2** Valuation rules **3** The matching rules **4** The share pool for companies **5** Changes in share capital **6** Qualifying corporate bonds and listed government securities	At the end of this chapter, you should be able to: • demonstrate the calculation of market value for quoted shares and securities • outline the matching rules for individuals • compute gains and losses on disposals by individuals • outline the matching rules for companies • compute gains and losses on disposals by companies • illustrate the impact of bonus and rights issues on shareholdings • identify exempt disposals (gilts and qualifying corporate bonds).

1 INTRODUCTION

Shares and securities present a particular problem for capital gains tax computations, because any two shares in a company (of a particular class) are indistinguishable. If shares have been acquired on more than one occasion, it is difficult to identify which have been disposed of when only part of the shareholding is sold.

For instance, Marko buys ordinary shares in Smith plc as follows.

	Shares	Cost
		£
16 December 1991	1,000	2,500
17 June 2004	1,500	4,500

If, in January 2022 Marko sells 600 shares, has he sold some from the first purchase, some from the second purchase or a mixture of the two?

In order to calculate Marko's chargeable gain or allowable loss, we must be able to identify his expenditure.

This chapter sets out the capital gains tax rules as they apply to shares and securities. The essential principles of capital gains tax remain, but they are supplemented by a system of **matching rules** to identify which shares or securities are being sold.

2 VALUATION RULES

The capital gains tax computation usually starts with the figure of sale proceeds. However, if the shares are gifted rather than sold, the market value is used instead.

The market value of quoted shares or securities is determined by taking the mid-price (i.e. average) of the closing prices quoted in the Stock Exchange Daily Official List on the disposal date.

Example

The closing prices of shares in Bresnan plc are 460p – 468p.

The capital gains tax value of a share in Bresnan plc is 464p (½ × (460 + 468))

Therefore, the value of 1,000 shares is £4,640.

ACTIVITY 1

The closing prices of shares in XYZ plc quoted in the Stock Exchange Daily Official List are 230p – 250p.

If a disposal of XYZ plc shares were made on that day, other than on an arm's length bargain, what would be their value for capital gains tax?

For a suggested answer, see the 'Answers' section at the end of the book.

3 THE MATCHING RULES

3.1 INTRODUCTION

The matching rules apply when a person has made more than one purchase of shares or securities of the same class in the same company. In this situation, the matching rules should always be applied before calculating any gains. Where more than one share acquisition is matched with the disposal, separate gains should be calculated for each.

The matching rules are not needed where, for example, someone buys both preference shares and ordinary shares in a company, as they are distinguishable.

Shares and securities are subject to the same rules and so, for the rest of the chapter, the term 'shares' covers both.

There are different matching rules for companies and for individuals. This is because companies received the indexation allowance until December 2017.

3.2 THE MATCHING ORDER FOR INDIVIDUALS

Shares sold by an individual are matched against acquisitions in the following order:

- shares acquired on the same day as the sale
- shares acquired within the **following** 30 days
- shares in the share pool. The share pool comprises all shares acquired prior to the date of disposal.

Example

On 18 February 2022 Frances sold 5,000 shares in Fosdyke Ltd for £26,000.

Her acquisitions have been as follows:

8 April 2000	7,000 shares for £6,300
26 March 2012	2,000 shares for £4,000
10 August 2012	1,000 shares for £3,600
15 March 2022	500 shares for £3,000

Calculate Frances' taxable gains for the tax year 2021/22.

Solution

5,000 shares sold are matched with:

		No. of shares	Cost £
(a)	Shares purchased within the following 30 days 15 March 2022	500	3,000
(b)	Shares in the share pool		
	8 April 2000	7,000	6,300
	26 March 2012	2,000	4,000
	10 August 2012	1,000	3,600
		10,000	13,900

The balance of 4,500 shares (5,000 – 500) is taken from the share pool.

For capital gains tax purposes, Frances is treated as making two separate disposals of shares in Fosdyke Ltd (but only one for the purpose of completing the tax return – see Chapter 17). The sale proceeds are apportioned between these two separate disposals according to the number of shares in each category.

		£
15 March 2022	Sale proceeds (500/5,000 × £26,000)	2,600
	Less: Cost	(3,000)
	Allowable loss	(400)
Share pool	Sale proceeds (4,500/5,000 × £26,000)	23,400
	Less: Cost (4,500/10,000 × £13,900)	(6,255)
	Chargeable gain	17,145

Summary

Chargeable gain	17,145
Less: Allowable loss	(400)
Net chargeable gains	16,745
Less: Annual exempt amount	(12,300)
Taxable gains	4,445

3.3 THE MATCHING ORDER FOR COMPANIES

Where shares are sold by a company, they are matched against acquisitions in the following order:

- shares acquired on the same day (as the sale)
- shares acquired during the nine days before the sale (taking earlier acquisitions first if there are more than one)
- shares in the share pool.

4 THE SHARE POOL FOR COMPANIES

4.1 INTRODUCTION

A pool held by a company contains the following:

- shares held on 1 April 1985 that were acquired after 31 March 1982
- shares acquired on or after 1 April 1985.

The pool only ever contains shares of the same class of the same company, so any company may have several 'pools', each one concerned with a different class of share or shares in different companies.

The examining team may require you to calculate a basic pool for shares held by a company.

4.2 SETTING UP THE POOL

The pool records the number of shares held, their unindexed cost and their indexed cost (that is original cost plus indexation to date).

Where a company acquired shares before 1 April 1985, the examination question will always give the value of the pool at 1 April 1985.

Alternatively, questions will only include purchases after 1 April 1985.

4.3 PURCHASES AFTER 1 APRIL 1985

Shares are added to the pool when a purchase is made and removed from it on a sale.

- On a purchase the allowable cost is added to the totals in the unindexed pool and indexed pool.
- An indexation allowance is added to the pool of indexed cost immediately before each 'operative event'.
- An 'operative event' is a purchase, a sale or any other event that changes the total indexed cost (such as rights issues, which are dealt with later in the chapter).

The indexation allowance included in the pool is known as an indexed rise.

- The indexation factor is multiplied by the indexed cost total immediately after the previous operative event.
- The indexation allowance is added every time the indexed cost total alters, rather than only when the shares are sold.
- Where the operative event is the first after April 1985, the indexed rise is calculated from April 1985 to the operative event.
- As the indexation allowance is not available after December 2017, where the operative event is after 31 December 2017 the indexed rise is calculated using the indexation factor for December 2017, rather than the date of the operative event.

Example

Daisy Ltd had pool balances as follows at 1 April 1985:

No of shares	3,200
Cost of shares	£8,750
Indexed cost	£9,277

Daisy Ltd bought a further 500 shares for £1,300 on 6 July 1985 and another 1,300 shares for £3,300 on 10 October 1988.

What is the indexed cost of the pool on 10 October 1988?

Use the following indexation factors in your answer:

April 1985 to July 1985	0.005
July 1985 to October 1988	0.150

Solution

	No of shares	Unindexed cost	Indexed cost
		£	£
Brought forward at 1 April 1985	3,200	8,750	9,277
6 July 1985 – purchase			
Indexed rise (£9,277 × 0.005)			46
			9,323
Additional shares	500	1,300	1,300
	3,700	10,050	10,623
10 October 1988 – purchase			
Indexed rise (£10,623 × 0.150)			1,593
			12,216
Additional shares	1,300	3,300	3,300
Total holding at 10 October 1988	5,000	13,350	15,516

4.4 MAKING DISPOSALS FROM THE POOL

When there is a disposal of shares held in the pool, firstly the pool is indexed up to the earlier of the date of the 'operative event' or December 2017 and then the number of shares sold is deducted from the share column. The unindexed cost and indexed cost are apportioned equally between all the shares in the pool and the relevant proportion is deducted.

The gain or loss on disposal is calculated as follows:

	£
Proceeds	X
Less: Unindexed cost	(X)
Less: Indexation allowance (Indexed cost – unindexed cost)	(X)
Chargeable gain	X

Example

Following on from the previous example, let us suppose that Daisy Ltd sold 3,000 shares for £44,000 on 1 February 2022.

Calculate the chargeable gain arising on the disposal.

The indexation factor from October 1988 to December 2017 is 1.540.

	No of shares	Unindexed cost	Indexed cost
		£	£
B/f at 10 October 1988	5,000	13,350	15,516
February 2022 – sale			
Indexed rise to December 2017 (£15,516 × 1.540)			23,895
			39,411
Sale of shares	(3,000)		
Reduction of unindexed and indexed cost			
$\frac{3,000}{5,000}$ × £13,350/£39,411		(8,010)	(23,647)
Balance c/f	2,000	5,340	15,764

	£
Sale proceeds	44,000
Less: Unindexed cost (above)	(8,010)
Unindexed gain	35,990
Less: Indexation allowance (£23,647 – £8,010)	(15,637)
Chargeable gain	20,353

Note: The indexation allowance is not available after December 2017

ACTIVITY 2

Japer Ltd sold all of its 25p ordinary shares in Carrot plc on 19 November 2021 for net sale proceeds of £8,379.

Its previous dealings in these shares were as follows

Purchases	No of shares	Cost £
10 October 1990	300	600
11 August 2006	585	2,160

Required:

Calculate the chargeable gains arising in respect of this disposal.

Assume the following indexation factors:

October 1990 – August 2006	0.529
August 2006 – December 2017	0.396

For a suggested answer, see the 'Answers' section at the end of the book.

5 CHANGES IN SHARE CAPITAL

5.1 BONUS ISSUES

A bonus issue (also known as a scrip or capitalisation issue) occurs when additional shares are issued, but at no extra cost to the shareholder.

For the purpose of the matching rules, every purchase of shares made before the bonus issue takes place has the appropriate number of bonus shares added to it.

For individuals the bonus shares will just be added in to the pool.

For companies, as there is no cost associated with the acquisition of the bonus shares, there is no need to index the cost in the pool before adding the bonus shares to it.

Example

Rayner acquired shares in Pollock plc as follows:

5 May 2003 purchased	4,000 shares
7 August 2006 purchased	1,000 shares
9 November 2006 1 for 5 bonus issue	
3 February 2022 purchased	1,500 shares

He sold 4,000 Pollock plc shares on 18 January 2022.

Show how the shares sold are matched.

Solution

Order of matching		**Number of shares**
(a) Shares acquired in the following 30 days		
3 February 2022 purchase		1,500
(b) Shares in the pool (as increased by bonus issue)		
5 May 2003 purchase	4,000	
7 August 2006 purchase	1,000	
	5,000	
Add 1 for 5 bonus	1,000	
	6,000	
Number to complete sale	(2,500)	2,500
Balance remaining in pool	3,500	
Shares sold		4,000

5.2 RIGHTS ISSUES

Rights issues are similar to bonus issues in that new shares are acquired as a result of an existing holding and the number of new shares acquired is in proportion to the existing holding. Therefore, for the purpose of the matching rules, the new shares are deemed to have been acquired at the same time as the original shares.

However, in contrast to bonus issues, the shareholder has to subscribe new money to acquire rights issue shares. Subscribing new money increases the cost of the total shareholding.

For individuals, the rights shares, and their cost, are just added to the pool.

For companies, as there is a cost associated with the acquisition of rights shares, the share pool is indexed before adding the rights shares to it (in the same way as for a purchase).

Example

Carlota had the following transactions in the shares of Rudderham plc.

April 2007	purchased 1,200 shares for £3,200
January 2010	purchased 900 shares for £1,500
February 2014	took up 1 for 3 rights issues at £2.30 per share
August 2021	sold 2,000 shares for £15,750

Calculate the chargeable gains or allowable losses on the disposal in August 2021.

Solution

Order of matching

Shares in the pool (as increased by rights issue)

	Shares no.	**Cost £**
April 2007 purchase	1,200	3,200
January 2010 purchase	900	1,500
	2,100	4,700
Add 1 for 3 rights (700 × £2.30)	700	1,610
	2,800	6,310
Number sold (2,000/2,800 × £6,310)	(2,000)	(4,507)
Balance remaining in pool	800	1,803

Calculation of chargeable gain

Shares matched against the pool

	£
Proceeds	15,750
Less: Cost	(4,507)
Chargeable gain	11,243

6 QUALIFYING CORPORATE BONDS AND LISTED GOVERNMENT SECURITIES

Listed UK government securities (also known as gilt edged securities or gilts) are not subject to capital gains tax or to corporation tax on gains. Therefore, no chargeable gains or allowable losses arise on their disposal.

Qualifying corporate bonds are also exempt disposals for individuals, and are therefore not subject to capital gains tax.

A qualifying corporate bond is one which:

- represents a normal commercial loan
- is expressed in sterling and has no provision for either conversion into, or redemption in, any other currency
- was issued after 13 March 1984 or was acquired by the disposer after that date (whenever it was issued).

The term 'corporate bond' includes permanent interest-bearing shares in building societies.

KEY TERMS

Matching rules – the rules used to determine the order in which shares have been disposed of.

The share pool for individuals – the computation showing the number of shares of the same class in the same company, owned by an **individual**, together with their cost.

The share pool for companies – the computation showing the number of shares of the same class in the same company, owned by a **company**, together with their cost and indexed cost.

Operative event – a purchase, a sale or any other event (such as a rights issue) that changes the total cost of the share pool for companies.

Indexed rise – the indexation allowance included in the share pool for companies.

Bonus issues – additional shares are issued, but at no extra cost to the shareholder. They are also known as scrip or capitalisation issues.

Rights issue – additional shares are sold to existing shareholders in proportion to their shareholdings.

Gilts (gilt-edged securities) – listed UK Government securities.

Corporate bonds – a normal commercial loan, such as a debenture.

Qualifying corporate bond – a corporate bond that is expressed in sterling and has no provision for either conversion into, or redemption in, any other currency. It must also have been issued after 13 March 1984 or have been acquired by the holder after that date.

SELF TEST QUESTIONS

		Paragraph
1	Why are the matching rules necessary?	1
2	How are quoted shares valued?	2
3	What is the matching order for individuals?	3.2
4	What is the matching order for companies?	3.3
5	How are purchases after 1 April 1985 dealt with in the share pool for companies?	4.3
6	How do the matching rules apply to bonus issues?	5.1
7	What is a qualifying corporate bond?	6

MULTIPLE CHOICE QUESTIONS

1 Peta sold 400 shares in Blue plc on 13 December 2021. She had acquired her shares in the company as follows:

	Number of shares
6 April 2007	200
14 February 2011	500
5 January 2022	100

Applying the share matching/identification rules, for tax purposes the 400 shares sold by Peta are correctly identified as follows:

A 400 of the 500 shares acquired on 14 February 2011

B The 100 shares acquired on 5 January 2022 and then 300 of the shares in the share pool, which consists of the shares acquired on 6 April 2007 and 14 February 2011

C The 200 shares acquired on 6 April 2007 then 200 of the shares acquired on 14 February 2011

D The 100 shares acquired on 5 January 2022, then the 200 shares acquired on 6 April 2007 and then 100 of the shares acquired on 14 February 2011

2 Bobby made a gift of Fiddler plc shares to his son on 1 May 2021.

On that day, the closing prices of shares in Fiddler plc were quoted in the Stock Exchange Daily Official List at 260p and 276p.

What is the value of the Fiddler plc shares for capital gains tax purposes?

A 276p

B 268p

C 260p

D 264p

For suggested answers, see the 'Answers' section at the end of the book.

PRACTICE QUESTION

GORE AND BLOOD

The details of Gore's holdings of £1 ordinary shares of Blood plc are as follows:

		No of shares	**Cost £**
8 March 2008	Purchased	1,000	5,000
7 May 2011	Purchased	500	3,050
20 December 2021	Purchased	280	2,060

On 11 December 2021 Gore sold 1,500 shares for £10,484.

Required:

Calculate the chargeable gain or allowable loss on the disposal in the tax year 2021/22.

(10 marks)

For a suggested answer, see the 'Answers' section at the end of the book.

Chapter 20

CAPITAL GAINS TAX RELIEFS

INTRODUCTION

This chapter covers capital gains tax reliefs. There are different types of relief:

- private residence relief, which **exempts** part or all of the gain
- business asset disposal relief, which **reduces the tax rate**
- rollover relief and gift holdover relief, which merely **defer** the gain to a later year.

Private residence relief applies when an individual disposes of their main residence.

Business asset disposal relief reduces the capital gains tax payable on certain qualifying business disposals.

Gift holdover relief is available when an individual gifts a business asset. The gain is deferred by reducing the base cost for the person receiving the asset.

Rollover relief is available to defer a gain when an individual or a company disposes of a qualifying business asset and reinvests in another qualifying business asset.

This chapter covers syllabus areas D6 and E4 (f).

CONTENTS	LEARNING OUTCOMES
	At the end of this chapter, you should be able to: • outline the rules governing private residence relief, and explain and calculate the amount of relief • explain and apply business asset disposal relief as it applies to individuals • outline availability, and explain and calculate gift holdover relief • calculate the restriction of gift holdover relief as a result of a sale at undervalue

	• outline availability, and explain and calculate rollover relief • calculate the relief available on the partial reinvestment of sale proceeds • explain the consequences of reinvestment in depreciating or non-depreciating assets.

1 PRIVATE RESIDENCE RELIEF (PRR)

1.1 INTRODUCTION

If a property has been occupied as an individual's private residence throughout his or her period of ownership, any gain on its disposal is exempt from capital gains tax. Similarly, any losses sustained by the taxpayer on the disposal of such a property are not allowable for CGT.

1.2 PERIODS OF NON-OCCUPATION

A charge to capital gains tax can arise if the owner does not occupy his or her property for a period. In such a situation, the gain on the property is calculated and then time apportioned according to the periods of occupation and non-occupation.

The gain relating to periods of occupation (and deemed occupation) is exempt and is calculated using the formula:

$$\text{Total gain} \times \frac{\text{Period of occupation}}{\text{Total period of ownership}}$$

Example

Johan bought a house on 1 January 1996 for £19,000. He sold the house on 31 December 2021 for £250,000.

He occupied the house for 20 out of the 26 years of his ownership.

The chargeable gain on disposal is:	£
Proceeds	250,000
Less: Cost	(19,000)
Gain before relief	231,000
Less: Private residence relief (20/26 × £231,000)	(177,692)
Chargeable gain after relief	53,308

Note that any gain remaining after deducting private residence relief and any available annual exempt amount is taxed at the residential rates of 18% and 28%.

Deemed occupation

The following periods are treated as periods of occupation and are therefore **exempt**:

(a) periods totalling up to three years in which the individual was absent for any reason

(b) periods in which the individual was employed abroad

(c) periods totalling up to four years in which the individual was prevented from living in his or her property because:

- his or her place of work was too far from his or her property
- his or her employer required him or her to live elsewhere.

These periods of deemed occupation can only apply if:

- no other property qualified for relief during the absence, and
- the property was actually occupied as the individual's main residence at some point both before and after the period of non-occupation.

However, there is no need for actual occupation after (b) and (c) above, if the individual was unable to resume residence in his or her previous home because the terms of his or her employment required him or her to work elsewhere.

Note also that the periods of deemed occupation may be combined and so, in exceptional circumstances, a taxpayer could find himself benefiting from all of them at different times. Where an individual is absent for longer than the periods permitted, only any gain relating to the excess period is taxable.

If a taxpayer buys a new home, he or she may not be able to move in immediately due to works on the house, or a delay in selling the previous home. However, if he or she moves in within two years of purchase, the delay can be treated as a period of residence.

The final nine months of ownership

Provided a property has been occupied as the taxpayer's main private residence at some point during the taxpayer's ownership, the gain relating to the final 9 months of ownership is exempt from CGT.

Unlike the rules for the other periods of deemed occupation, there is no need for the owner to reoccupy the property at the end of the 9 month period. He or she may even let his or her property or elect for another property to be treated as his or her private residence without losing the benefit of the exemption. It should be noted, however, that the exemption does not apply to any part of the property used exclusively for business purposes throughout the period of ownership.

Example

Arthur bought a house on 1 January 2002 and sold it on 30 September 2021 making a gain of £189,000.

He occupied the house as follows:

1 January 2002 – 31 December 2003	Lived in house
1 January 2004 – 30 June 2010	Employed overseas
1 July 2010 – 31 December 2014	Travels the world
1 January 2015– 30 September 2021	Lived in the house

Arthur's chargeable gain is:	£
Gain	189,000
Less: PRR relief	
219/237 (W) × £189,000	(174,646)
Chargeable gain after relief	14,354

Working

Dates		**Exempt (months)**	**Chargeable (months)**
1 Jan 2002 – 31 Dec 2003	Occupation	24	
1 Jan 2004 – 30 Jun 2010	Working overseas	78	
1 Jul 2010 – 31 Dec 2014	Travelling (3 years exempt)	36	18
1 Jan 2015 – 30 Sep 2021	Occupied	81	
		219	18

ACTIVITY 1

On 1 April 1998 Polina purchased a house in Southampton, which she lived in until she moved to a rented flat on 1 July 1998. She remained in the flat until 1 October 2000 when she accepted a year's secondment to her firm's New York office. On coming back on 1 October 2001, she moved into a relative's house, where she stayed until she returned to her own home on 1 February 2002. On 1 July 2002 she moved in with her girlfriend in Newcastle. Here she remained until she sold her Southampton house on 1 February 2022 making a gain of £200,000.

State, giving reasons in each case, the deemed and actual periods of occupation and the periods of non-occupation of the property and calculate the chargeable gain after private residence relief.

For a suggested answer, see the 'Answers' section at the end of the book.

1.3 BUSINESS USE

Where a house, or part of it, is used wholly and exclusively for business purposes, it clearly cannot be used as residential accommodation at the same time. Therefore, the business element of the gain is chargeable to CGT.

In the FTX examination, you will not be expected to calculate a capital gains tax liability for a private residence that has also been used for business purposes.

1.4 NOMINATION OF MAIN RESIDENCE

Where an individual has more than one residence, he or she can choose which of them is to be treated as his or her private residence for capital gains purposes by notifying HMRC in writing. The election must be made within two years of acquiring an additional residence, otherwise HMRC can decide as a question of fact which residence is the main residence.

2 BUSINESS ASSET DISPOSAL RELIEF (BADR)

2.1 INTRODUCTION

Business asset disposal relief is available to **individuals** making qualifying **business** disposals.

2.2 THE RELIEF

The relief operates as follows:

- The first £1 million of gains on 'qualifying business disposals' is taxed at 10%.
- The £1 million limit is a lifetime limit, which is diminished each time a claim for the relief is made.
- Any gains above the £1 million limit are taxed in full at the usual rate, depending on the individual's taxable income.
- Gains qualifying for business asset disposal relief and taxed at the 10% rate are deemed to utilise any remaining basic rate band before any non-qualifying gains are taxed.

Taxpayers can choose to deduct:

- allowable losses (other than any losses on assets that are part of the disposal of the business), and
- the annual exempt amount

from gains not qualifying for business asset disposal relief – remember that these should be deducted from gains taxed at the residential property rates first.

2.3 QUALIFYING BUSINESS DISPOSALS

The relief applies to the disposal of:

- the **whole or part** of a business carried on by the individual either alone or in partnership.
- assets of the individual's or partnership's trading business that has **now ceased**
- shares **provided**:
  - the shares are in the individual's 'personal trading company', and
  - the individual is an employee of the company (part time or full time).

Note that the disposal of an individual business asset used for the purposes of a continuing trade **does not qualify**. There must be a disposal of the whole or part of the trading business. The sale of an asset in isolation will not qualify.

In the FTX examination, an individual's 'personal trading company' is one in which the individual owns at least 5% of the ordinary shares.

2.4 QUALIFYING OWNERSHIP PERIOD

The business or shares being disposed of must have been owned by the individual making the disposal for two years prior to the disposal and in the case of shares the company must have been the individual's personal trading company and the individual must have been employed by the company for at least two years prior to the disposal.

Where the disposal is an asset of the individual's or partnership's trading business that has now ceased the business must have been owned for at least two years prior to the date of cessation and the disposal must also take place within three years of the cessation of trade.

2.5 TIME LIMIT FOR CLAIM

The relief must be claimed within 12 months of the 31 January following the end of the tax year in which the disposal is made.

For 2021/22 disposals, the relief must be claimed by 31 January 2024.

Example

In the tax year 2021/22, Katherine sold her trading business which she set up in 2003 and realised the following gains/ (losses).

	£
Factory	275,000
Goodwill	330,000
Warehouse	(100,000)

Katherine also sold her shares in a quoted trading company and realised a gain of £600,000. The disposal of these shares does not qualify for business asset disposal relief.

Calculate Katherine's capital gains tax liability for the tax year 2021/22 assuming she has taxable income of £30,000 and claims business asset disposal relief on the disposal of the business.

Solution

Assuming these are the only capital disposals Katherine has made, her capital gains tax liability is calculated as follows:

	Gains not qualifying for business asset disposal relief	Gains qualifying for business asset disposal relief
2021/22	£	£
Sale of trading business		
Factory		275,000
Goodwill		330,000
Warehouse		(100,000)
		505,000
Sale of trading company shares		
Gain on shares	600,000	
	600,000	505,000
Less: Annual exempt amount (Note 1)	(12,300)	0
Taxable gains	587,700	505,000
	£	£
Capital gains tax:		
Gains qualifying for business asset disposal relief £505,000 × 10%		50,500
Gains not qualifying for business asset disposal relief £587,700 × 20% (Note 2)	117,540	
Total tax (£117,540 + £50,500)	£168,040	

Notes:

1 The annual exempt amount is set against gains not qualifying for business asset disposal relief as these are taxed at a higher rate.

2 Gains qualifying for business asset disposal relief are deemed to use up the balance of Katherine's basic rate band so her non-qualifying gains are taxed at 20%.

3 RELIEF FOR GIFTS OF BUSINESS ASSETS (GIFT HOLDOVER RELIEF)

3.1 INTRODUCTION

A gift is a chargeable disposal for CGT purposes (unless it occurs on death) and so tax may be payable. The donor, however, has received no funds with which to meet this tax bill. For gifts of certain **business** assets by an **individual**, a relief may be claimed which allows the donor to effectively defer the capital gain until the gift is disposed of by the recipient.

To calculate the chargeable gain for a gift, the **market value** of the asset is used instead of the sale proceeds. When gift holdover relief is claimed, the market value of the asset, less the donor's chargeable gain, is used as the acquisition cost of the asset for the donee.

For a straightforward gift:

Donor (Giver)		**Donee (recipient)**	
Proceeds = MV	X	Base cost of asset gifted – use as cost for future disposals of the asset	
Less: Cost	(X)		
Gain before relief	X	MV	X
Less: Gift holdover relief	(X)	Less: Gift holdover relief	(X)
Gain after gift holdover relief	0	Base cost	X

ACTIVITY 2

Jonas bought an asset for £35,000 in September 2002. In June 2021 he gifted it to Sandra, when its market value was £40,000. The asset qualified for relief for gifts of business assets.

Show Jonas's capital gains tax position on the gift to Sandra and calculate Sandra's allowable expenditure to be used in a future disposal.

For a suggested answer, see the 'Answers' section at the end of the book.

3.2 WHO MAY CLAIM THE RELIEF?

The relief is available to individuals, not companies. Both the donor and donee must claim within four years from the end of the tax year in which the gift was made.

For a gift in the tax year 2021/22, the claim must be made by 5 April 2026.

3.3 QUALIFYING ASSETS

An individual may only claim the relief where the gift is of a qualifying asset. The following are the principal categories of qualifying asset.

Assets used in the trade of:

- the donor (i.e. where he or she is a sole trader)
- the donor's personal company

Shares and securities of trading companies provided that:

- the shares or securities are not quoted on either a recognised stock exchange or the unlisted securities market, or
- the shares or securities are those of the individual's personal company

An individual's **personal company** is one in which he or she holds at least 5% of the voting rights.

3.4 SALES AT AN UNDERVALUE

Gift holdover relief is also available where qualifying assets are sold for less than their market value. However, if the sale proceeds exceed the original cost, the excess proceeds over cost are chargeable to tax immediately. The balance of the gain can be deferred via gift holdover relief.

Example

Webster purchased shares in an unquoted trading company in November 2004 for £50,000. In January 2022 he sold them to his grandson, Albert, for £70,000 when their value was £165,000. Webster and Albert claimed relief for a gift of business assets.

Calculate:

(a) the chargeable gain, if any, incurred by Webster.

(b) the allowable expenditure to be used in a future disposal by Albert.

Solution

(a) Webster – gain on shares sold at an undervalue in January 2022

	£
Market value of shares in January 2022	165,000
Less: Cost	(50,000)
Chargeable gain before reliefs	115,000
Less: Gift holdover relief (balancing figure)	(95,000)
Chargeable gain (Sale proceeds £70,000 – Cost £50,000)	20,000

(b) Albert – allowable expenditure

	£
Market value of shares, January 2022	165,000
Less: Gift holdover relief	(95,000)
Allowable expenditure	70,000

3.5 COMPANY ASSETS NOT WHOLLY USED FOR TRADING PURPOSES

Where the subject of the gift is shares in the donor's personal company, the gain eligible for gift holdover relief is restricted to the business proportion of the chargeable assets of the company. The gift holdover relief is therefore calculated using the following fraction:

$$\frac{\text{Market value of company's chargeable business assets}}{\text{Market value of company's chargeable assets}}$$

A chargeable asset is an asset the disposal of which is chargeable to capital gains tax. This definition therefore excludes assets such as inventory, receivables and bank balances.

A chargeable business asset is a chargeable asset, which is used for trading purposes rather than investment purposes.

Note that it is not necessary to calculate gains on the individual assets, but only on the value of the shares. The asset values are only relevant for calculating the gift holdover relief restriction.

Example

Jin has been a full-time working director of Porcelain Products Ltd since 1 December 2009 and has owned 10% of the company's ordinary shares since 1 December 2010.

He resigned from the company in 2015 but kept the shares until 1 December 2021 when he gifted his 10% shareholding, valued at £950,000, to his daughter Jun.

The agreed capital gain on the disposal of the shares was £700,000. Jin and Jun signed an election to hold over the gain on the gift.

The market values of the assets held by the company at 1 December 2021 were:

	£
Land and buildings	550,000
Motor cars	80,000
Cash	45,000
Receivables	35,000
Inventory	50,000
Shares held as investments	60,000

Calculate Jin's chargeable gain in the tax year 2021/22; and the base cost of the shares acquired by Jun.

Solution

Jin – Capital gains computation – 2021/22

	£
Total gain on disposal of shares	700,000
Less: Gift holdover relief (W) £700,000 × (£550,000/£610,000)	(631,148)
Chargeable gain	68,852

Notes:

1 Motor cars, cash, receivables and inventory are not chargeable assets, as they are not liable to capital gains tax.

2 Shares are chargeable assets, but are not business assets as they are held for investment purposes.

3 The gain is taxed at 10% or 20% depending on the level of Jin's taxable income in 2021/22. It does **not** qualify for business asset disposal relief because Jin did not work for the company in the two years before the disposal.

Base cost for Jun	£
MV at date of gift	950,000
Less: Gift holdover relief (held over gain)	(631,148)
Base cost	318,852

In the FTX examination, questions will not test both business asset disposal relief and other reliefs.

4 ROLLOVER RELIEF

4.1 INTRODUCTION

This relief allows the gain on the disposal of qualifying **business** assets to be deferred when the proceeds are reinvested in qualifying business assets. It therefore allows taxpayers to replace assets used in their trade without incurring an immediate liability to capital gains tax.

The relief is available to **both** individuals and companies.

The relief generally works by deducting the gain made on the old asset from the cost of the new one.

However, the relief is modified when the replacement assets are depreciating assets, such as fixed plant and machinery, when the gain on the old asset is simply deferred and not deducted from the base cost of the new asset (see Section 6).

4.2 INDEXATION ALLOWANCE FOR COMPANIES

The old asset qualifies for indexation allowance up to the earlier of the date of sale and December 2017.

If the replacement asset is acquired before December 2017 it qualifies for indexation allowance from the date of purchase to December 2017. However, the indexation allowance is calculated on the cost as reduced by the rolled over gain.

A replacement asset acquired after December 2017 will not qualify for indexation allowance.

Example

Smythe Ltd purchased an asset qualifying for rollover relief in January 2005 for £80,000. In May 2007 the company sold the asset for £180,000 and spent £200,000 in August 2007 on a new qualifying asset.

The new asset is sold without replacement in December 2021 for £360,000.

Calculate the chargeable gain arising when the new asset is sold in December 2021.

Assume the following indexation factors:

January 2005 – May 2007	0.092
August 2007 – December 2017	0.342

Solution

	£
Cost of new asset	200,000
Less: Gain on old asset rolled over (W)	(92,640)
Deductible cost of new asset	107,360
Sale proceeds of new asset (Dec 2021)	360,000
Less: Cost (Aug 2007)	(107,360)
Unindexed gain	252,640
Less: Indexation allowance to December 2017 (£107,360 × 0.342)	(36,717)
Chargeable gain	215,923

Working – gain on old asset

	£
Disposal proceeds	180,000
Less: Cost	(80,000)
Unindexed gain	100,000
Less: Indexation allowance (£80,000 × 0.092)	(7,360)
Chargeable gain	92,640

4.3 QUALIFYING ASSETS

The following are the main categories of qualifying assets:

- land and buildings that are both occupied and used for trading purposes
- fixed (i.e. not movable) plant and machinery
- goodwill (for individuals only).

To benefit from rollover relief the taxpayer's old and new assets must fall within one of the categories set out above, but not necessarily the same one. Thus a taxpayer could sell a factory and reinvest in fixed plant. It is not necessary that the assets should be used in the **same** trade, because rollover relief treats all trades carried on by a taxpayer as one.

Note that where the replacement assets are fixed plant and machinery the treatment of the deferred gain is modified, i.e. it is simply deferred rather than deducted from the cost of the fixed plant and machinery. This is covered in more detail in Section 6.

For companies (not individuals) goodwill is not a qualifying asset, as the profit arising on the disposal of goodwill by a company is not treated as a chargeable gain.

4.4 TIME PERIOD FOR REINVESTMENT

The acquisition of the replacement asset must occur during a period that begins one year **before** the sale of the old asset and ends three years after the sale.

4.5 TIME LIMIT FOR CLAIM

The taxpayer must make a claim within four years from the later of:

- the end of the tax year (accounting period for companies) in which the disposal occurred, or
- the tax year (accounting period for companies) in which the replacement asset was acquired.

5 PARTIAL REINVESTMENT OF PROCEEDS

Where only part of the sale proceeds are used to purchase a new asset, only part of the gain can be rolled over. The amount that **cannot** be rolled over (and is therefore chargeable) is the lower of:

- the proceeds that have not been reinvested
- the chargeable gain.

The balance of the gain is the amount of rollover relief that can be claimed.

Example

Nia bought a factory in September 2010 for £661,600. In December 2021, wishing to move to a more convenient location, she sold the factory for £750,000. She moved into a rented factory until March 2022 when she purchased and moved into a new factory.

What is the base cost of the new factory if it was purchased for:

(a) £700,000

(b) £650,000?

Solution

	£
Disposal proceeds (old factory)	750,000
Less: Cost	(661,600)
Chargeable gain	88,400

(a) New factory purchased for £700,000

As not all of the proceeds have been reinvested, the rollover relief is restricted as follows:

		£
Purchase cost of new factory		700,000
Less: Gain on old factory	88,400	
Less: Restriction on rollover – proceeds not reinvested (£750,000 – £700,000)	(50,000)	
Gain rolled over		(38,400)
Base cost of new factory		661,600

(b) New factory purchased for £650,000

In this case, the amount of proceeds not reinvested of £100,000 (£750,000 – £650,000) exceeds the gain made on the old factory. Thus none of the gain is eligible to be rolled over and so there is no adjustment to the base cost of the new factory. It remains at the purchase price of £650,000.

6 REINVESTMENT IN DEPRECIATING ASSETS

6.1 INTRODUCTION

Rollover relief is modified where the replacement asset is a 'depreciating asset'. A depreciating asset is one that is either:

- a wasting asset (i.e. having a predictable life of not more than 50 years), or
- an asset that will become a wasting asset within 10 years.

Thus any asset with a predictable life of not more than 60 years is a depreciating asset.

The main examples of depreciating assets are fixed plant and machinery or leasehold property (where there are not more than 60 years left to run on the lease.).

6.2 TREATMENT OF GAIN ON REINVESTMENT IN A DEPRECIATING ASSET

The gain on the old asset is normally rolled over against the cost of the new asset. This does not happen when the new asset is a depreciating one. In these circumstances, it is simply deferred (held over) until the **earliest** of three events. These are:

- the **disposal** of the depreciating asset
- the depreciating asset **ceasing to be used** for trading purposes
- **10 years** after the depreciating asset was **acquired**.

At this time the gain on the old asset simply becomes taxable. It is not deducted from the cost of the depreciating asset, even where the event that triggers the charge is its sale.

As seen above, if only part of the proceeds is reinvested, an element of the gain becomes taxable immediately.

Example

Cooper Ltd purchased a freehold factory in July 2002 for £250,000. In May 2008 the company sold it for £420,000 and in June 2010 bought fixed plant and machinery. In December 2021 the fixed plant and machinery was sold for £650,000.

Calculate the chargeable gains or allowable losses arising in December 2021 if Cooper Ltd bought the fixed plant and machinery for:

(a) £450,000

(b) £400,000.

Assume the following indexation factors:

July 2002 to May 2008	0.223
June 2010 to December 2017	0.241

Solution

(a) Purchase for £450,000

	£
Disposal proceeds of fixed plant	650,000
Less: Cost	(450,000)
Unindexed gain	200,000
Less: Indexation allowance to December 2017	
0.241 × £450,000	(108,450)
Chargeable gain	91,550

The held over gain of £114,250 (W) on the sale of the factory in May 2008 also becomes chargeable, because the depreciating asset has been sold.

Working – gain on sale of factory in May 2008

	£
Disposal proceeds	420,000
Less: Cost	(250,000)
Unindexed gain	170,000
Less: Indexation allowance	
0.223 × £250,000	(55,750)
Chargeable gain held over	114,250

(b) Purchase for £400,000

In this case not all the disposal proceeds of the factory (£420,000) have been reinvested in the depreciating asset. The amount not reinvested, £20,000 (£420,000 – £400,000), was chargeable to tax in May 2008. The remainder of the gain on the factory, £94,250 (£114,250 – £20,000) is held over until the disposal of the fixed plant and machinery in December 2021, when it becomes chargeable.

The gain on the disposal of the plant and machinery is calculated as follows:

	£
Disposal proceeds	650,000
Less: Cost	(400,000)
Unindexed gain	250,000
Less: Indexation allowance to December 2017	
0.241 × £400,000	(96,400)
Chargeable gain	153,600

Note that the held over gain is not deducted from the cost of the plant and machinery.

KEY TERMS

Private residence – the individual's only or main home.

Deemed occupation – a period in which the individual is treated for tax purposes as if he or she were living in the property (an exempt period).

Personal company – broadly a company in which the individual holds at least 5% of the voting rights.

Chargeable asset – an asset the disposal of which is chargeable to capital gains tax. This definition therefore excludes assets such as inventory, receivables and bank balances.

Chargeable business assets – a chargeable asset that is used for trading purposes rather than investment purposes.

Depreciating asset – an asset, which is either a wasting asset (i.e. having a predictable life of not more than 50 years) or which will become a wasting asset within 10 years.

SELF TEST QUESTIONS

		Paragraph
1	List the periods in which an individual is deemed to occupy his or her private residence.	1.2
2	What constitutes a qualifying business disposal for business asset disposal relief?	2.3
3	What is the time limit for a claim for business asset disposal relief?	2.5
4	On what assets may gift holdover relief be claimed?	3.3
5	What are the classes of assets qualifying for rollover relief?	4.3
6	What is the period during which the replacement asset must be acquired?	4.4
7	What is a depreciating asset?	6.1
8	What are the three circumstances that bring a held over gain on a depreciating asset into charge?	6.2

MULTIPLE CHOICE QUESTIONS

1 Kalid purchased a freehold warehouse that is used in his business in September 2003 and sold it for £550,000 in May 2021, generating a capital gain of £290,000. He purchased a new warehouse in February 2022 for £515,000.

Assuming a claim for rollover relief is made, what is the chargeable gain on the sale of the warehouse?

A £290,000

B £255,000

C £35,000

D £0

2 Martha had owned her house since 1 January 2010. She moved in as soon as she bought it and occupied it until 1 January 2012 when she left to travel the world. Whilst travelling, she got married and moved to Bermuda and did not reoccupy the property. She sold the house on 1 January 2022.

In calculating the amount of the private residence relief available to Martha, what is the period of her occupation? Include periods of both actual and deemed occupation.

A 12 years

B 5 years 9 months

C 2 years 9 months

D 2 years

3 Leo is a sole trader. He sold a factory in December 2021, which he had used in his business since 2003. Leon can claim to rollover the gain on the factory against which of the following?

A The purchase of a new factory in May 2021 which will be used in Leo's trade

B The purchase of a commercial property in January 2022, which will be let to, tenants for 7 years

C The purchase of a shop in December 2021 which will be rented by his sister

D The purchase of a new forklift truck in December 2021 for use in Leon's trade

For suggested answers, see the 'Answers' section at the end of the book.

PRACTICE QUESTIONS

1 Hina

On 6 April 1999 Hina purchased a freehold house. She occupied the house until 6 October 2009 when her employment required that she live some distance from her home. On 6 October 2020, having been told she was going to work permanently in the distant location, Hina returned to her house for a month's holiday during which she redecorated the house and put it on the market. It was sold on 6 July 2021.

Required:

State, giving reasons in each case, the deemed and actual periods of occupation and the periods of non-occupation of the property. **(6 marks)**

2 Hope

Hope is the sole proprietor of a small garage business. In June 2021 she sold a hydraulic vehicle lift (an item of fixed plant and machinery) for £35,000, net of expenses. The lift had cost £27,450 in June 2008. In May 2021 she bought some freehold land, to extend forecourt parking, for £60,000. Hope claims rollover relief.

Required:

(a) Calculate the chargeable gain, if any, on the disposal of the hydraulic lift **(4 marks)**

(b) Calculate the cost of the new land for future capital gains tax purposes **(2 marks)**

(c) Explain the position if the proceeds had instead been used for purchase of a new hydraulic lift. **(4 marks)**

(Total: 10 marks)

For suggested answers, see the 'Answers' section at the end of the book.

Chapter 21

OUTLINE OF CORPORATION TAX

INTRODUCTION

This chapter explains how a company's income, gains and expenses are dealt with in arriving at the taxable total profits.

A thorough understanding of this chapter is essential as:

- these matters may be examined as a long computational question, and
- this chapter is a building block towards an understanding of the more advanced aspects of corporation tax.

The examining team have stated that one of the 15 mark questions in section B will always be on corporation tax. It will usually contain a standard corporation tax computation. It may also include trading income adjustments, administration and loss relief claims. The question may include computations for long and short periods of account and the calculation of capital allowances.

This chapter covers areas E1, E2 and E7.

CONTENTS	LEARNING OUTCOMES
1 The charge to tax **2** Taxable total profits **3** Calculation of tax adjusted trading profit **4** Capital allowances **5** Interest income **6** Property business profits **7** Chargeable gains **8** Qualifying charitable donations **9** Dividends	At the end of this chapter, you should be able to: • identify the scope of corporation tax; chargeable entities, chargeable income and chargeable gains • identify accounting periods including periods longer and shorter than 12 months • identify the basis of assessment for all sources of income • recognise the expenditure that is allowable in calculating the tax adjusted trading profit • explain how relief can be obtained for pre-trading expenditure

10 Long periods of account **11** Corporation tax return (Part 1)	• compute capital allowances as for income tax, and the main pool super deduction of 130% and special rate pool first year allowance of 50% for expenditure incurred from 1 April 2021 to 31 March 2023 • compute property business profits • explain the treatment of interest paid and received under the loan relationship rules • explain the treatment of qualifying charitable donations • compute taxable total profits • complete corporation tax returns correctly and submit them within statutory time limits.

1 THE CHARGE TO TAX

1.1 INTRODUCTION

Corporation tax is charged on the **profits** of **companies resident** in the UK by reference to the **taxable total profits** arising in each **accounting period**.

A company is any body corporate, limited or unlimited, or unincorporated association. This does not include a partnership, a local authority or a local authority association.

1.2 RESIDENCE

A company is regarded as resident in the UK if it satisfies one of two tests:

- it is incorporated in the UK, or
- its central management and control is in the UK. A company's central management and control is usually considered to be where the directors' board meetings are held.

1.3 ACCOUNTING PERIOD

It is essential to differentiate between an 'accounting period' and a 'period of account':

- A period of account is any period for which a company prepares accounts. It is usually 12 months in length, but may be shorter or longer than this.
- An accounting period is the period for which a charge to corporation tax is made. It can never be longer than 12 months.

An accounting period begins when:

- a company starts to trade
- the profits of a company first become liable to corporation tax
- the previous accounting period ends, providing that the company is still liable to corporation tax.

An accounting period ends on the earliest of:

- 12 months after the beginning of the accounting period
- the end of the company's period of account
- the company beginning or ceasing to trade
- the company beginning or ceasing to be resident in the UK
- the company ceasing to be liable to corporation tax
- the appointment of an administrator or a liquidator.

As an accounting period must not exceed 12 months, if a company has a period of account longer than 12 months, this must be split into two accounting periods, the first of 12 months and the second of the remainder of the period of account. Note that the period of account **must** be split in this way, no other split is possible. So for example, if H plc has a 17 month period of account to 31 December 2021, it must be split into two periods – 12 months to 31 July 2021 and 5 months to 31 December 2021. The rules for splitting income and gains into the two periods are dealt with in section 10.

ACTIVITY 1

A Ltd prepares accounts for the 15-month period from 1 October 2020 to 31 December 2021. What are the accounting periods of A Ltd?

For a suggested answer, see the 'Answers' section at the end of the book.

1.4 COMPANIES AND INDIVIDUALS COMPARED

There are a number of differences between the way a company is assessed to corporation tax and the way an individual is assessed to income tax and capital gains tax:

COMPANY	INDIVIDUAL
• Companies are assessed on profits arising in an accounting period.	• Individuals are assessed on income and gains arising in tax years.
• There is no personal allowance.	• Personal allowance is available to set against income.
• Chargeable gains are assessed to corporation tax.	• Chargeable gains are assessed to capital gains tax.
• Indexation allowance may be available on disposals of chargeable assets up to December 2017.	• Indexation allowance is never available in computing chargeable gains.
• There is no annual exempt amount for chargeable gains.	• An annual exempt amount is available for chargeable gains.
• The corporation tax computation only requires one column for all income and gains.	• The income tax computation must be split into three columns to breakdown the different types of income.

2 TAXABLE TOTAL PROFITS

A corporation tax computation is necessary to calculate the amount of profits that are charged to corporation tax for an accounting period. The computation includes the worldwide income of a company, plus any chargeable gains. Note that dividends received from other companies are **not** taxable income for a company and are not included in taxable profits.

The computation of taxable total profits should be laid out as follows:

X Ltd corporation tax computation for the 12 months ended 31 March 2022

	£
Tax adjusted trading profit	X
Interest income	X
Property business profits	X
Chargeable gains (e.g. sale of shares at a profit)	X
Total profits	X
Less: Qualifying charitable donations (QCD) relief	(X)
Taxable total profits	X

The use of this layout is essential in any corporation tax examination question. The company and the accounting period ('AP') should be identified. Each separate source of income should also be identified.

3 CALCULATION OF TAX ADJUSTED TRADING PROFIT

3.1 INTRODUCTION

As for the trading profits of an individual, the net profit disclosed by a company's statement of profit or loss needs adjusting to arrive at the net trading profit for tax purposes. The adjustments necessary can be classified, **in a similar way to income tax**, under the following headings:

		£	£
Net profit before tax per accounts			X
Add:	Expenditure not allowable for taxation purposes	X	
	Expenditure allowable for taxation purposes	0	
			X
			X
Less:	Income credited in the accounts but not taxable as trading income	X	
	Expenditure not charged in the accounts but allowable for the purposes of taxation	X	
	Income included in the accounts that is taxable as trading income (e.g. trade related patent royalties)	0	
	Capital allowances	X	
			(X)
Tax adjusted trading profit			X

Note that the figure provided in the examination may be after some or all of the above adjustments have already been made. If the figure is described as 'trading income' or 'adjusted trading profits', then all the adjustments have been made. If the figure provided is described as the 'adjusted trading profit before interest and capital allowances' then only the trading interest payable and capital allowances available need to be deducted.

If the requirement specifies that unadjusted items should be included in your answer, it is important that, in addition to the adjustments required, you also remember to include any items that **do not** require adjustment, indicating with the use of a 0 that no adjustment is required.

3.2 EXPENDITURE

The rules regarding disallowable expenditure are basically the same as those for income tax, covered in Chapter 3. However, the following points should be noted:

- When adjusting profits for corporation tax purposes, no adjustment is necessary for private expenses. Thus, where a car is provided for an employee and the company pays all the expenses, for both business and private use, the full amount is deductible. The employee then has taxable employment income for any benefit he or she has received.

- Appropriations of profit are not allowable expenditure. The sorts of appropriations a company may make are the payment of dividends and transfers to reserves.

- Any costs incurred directly by a company in obtaining long term finance are allowable, for example fees, commission, legal expenses. The costs are allowed as a trading expense if the loan is such that the interest is a trading expense, e.g. a 20 year loan to buy a new factory.

- Interest payable on borrowings for a trading purpose is allowed as a trading expense (on an accruals basis).

- Any revenue expenditure incurred in the seven years before a company commences to trade is treated as an expense on the day that the company starts trading. For example, if a company that started to trade on 1 April 2021 had spent £6,000 in the previous six months on advertising, this expenditure would be treated as if it had been incurred on 1 April 2021.

- Patent royalties paid are treated as a trading expense deductible on an accruals basis. There should be no need to adjust for them if they have been correctly charged through the accounts.

3.3 INCOME

Certain items of income may be included in the accounts, but are not taxable as trading income. The main items are as follows:

- income taxed under another category, such as property income

- all interest received is assessed as interest income

- capital receipts are taxed as chargeable gains

- items that are exempt, such as dividends received.

Note that for the purposes of the FTX examination all patent royalties are held for a trading purpose. They are chargeable on an accruals basis and included in trading income. There should be no need to adjust for them if they have been correctly charged through the accounts.

4 CAPITAL ALLOWANCES

Capital allowances are treated as a trading expense for corporation tax purposes, just as they are for individual traders. The rules for most capital allowances have been dealt with in detail earlier in the study text. Capital allowances must be deducted from trading profits and not from any other income.

4.1 CAPITAL ALLOWANCES FOR COMPANIES

Capital allowances are computed as follows for companies:

- Allowances are given for accounting periods by reference to acquisitions and disposals in that accounting period.

- If the accounting period is less than 12 months, the annual investment allowance and writing down allowances are proportionately reduced. First year allowances (FYA) are not reduced.

- As stated in section 1.3, an accounting period can never exceed 12 months; therefore the allowances will never be increased.

- The private use of an asset, by an employee or director, has no impact on the calculation of allowances.

- New plant and machinery (excluding cars) purchased from 1 April 2021 to 31 March 2023 by companies (but not by individuals) qualifies for a 130% super deduction (main pool assets) or 50% FYA (special rate pool assets) – see below.

The structures and buildings allowance is also available for companies. This is calculated as for individual traders.

Example

(a) Conifer Ltd prepared accounts for the year ended 31 March 2022. On 1 November 2021 a car costing £10,000 was bought for the managing director, who used the car 80% for business purposes. The car has CO_2 emissions of 46g/km.

(b) Mr Bramble prepares accounts to 31 March annually. On 1 November 2021 he bought a car for £10,000, which he used 80% for business purposes. The car has CO_2 emissions of 46g/km.

(c) Birch Ltd prepares accounts for the nine months ended 31 December 2021. On 1 June 2021 the company bought a car for £20,000, which has CO_2 emissions of 105g/km.

You are required to calculate the capital allowances in each of the above situations.

Solution

(a) Conifer Ltd

Capital allowances for the year to 31 March 2022

WDA: £10,000 × 18% =	£1,800

(b) Mr Bramble

Capital allowances for year ended 31 March 2022

WDA: £10,000 × 18% =	£1,800
Allowances available £1,800 × 80% =	£1,440
TWDV c/f (£10,000 – £1,800)	£8,200

Note that the TWDV c/f for Mr Bramble is £8,200 (£10,000 – £1,800), as the business use reduction only applies to the allowances that can be claimed, not the actual writing down allowance, which reduces the TWDV.

(c) Birch Ltd

Capital allowances for the nine month period ended 31 December 2021

WDA: £20,000 × 6% × $\frac{9}{12}$ =	£900

4.2 ENHANCED CAPITAL ALLOWANCES FOR COMPANIES

Companies purchasing qualifying new plant and machinery between 1 April 2021 and 31 March 2023 inclusive are eligible to claim:

- 130% super deduction for assets that would ordinarily go into the main pool, and

- 50% first year allowance for special rate pool assets.

The reliefs will only be available on new assets and are not available on:

- cars (but is available for expenditure on other vehicles e.g. vans)
- second-hand assets
- assets purchased in the final accounting period of trading.

These enhanced capital allowances are only available for companies, not individuals.

For qualifying main pool additions, the 130% super deduction should be claimed where possible instead of the AIA. However, for special rate pool expenditure AIA should be claimed in preference to the 50% FYA. This is covered in further detail below.

Additions qualifying for the super deduction should be included in an 'FYA' column at 130% × cost, showing this working in the label. The super deduction will then equal the amount added. Once the super deduction has been given to an asset, there is no balance left to transfer to the main pool.

Additions purchased prior to 1 April 2021 will not qualify for enhanced capital allowances and should be allocated the AIA and WDA as shown in Chapter 4.

A question will not be set in the exam involving the disposal of an asset on which enhanced capital allowances were claimed.

Accounting periods straddling 31 March 2023 will also not be examinable.

A detailed capital allowances pro forma computation for companies, covering all the possible additions is shown overleaf.

Pro forma capital allowances computation for companies

	AIA	FYA	Main pool	Special rate pool	Short life asset	Allowances
	£	£	£	£	£	£
TWDV b/f			X	X	X	
Additions:						
Not qualifying for AIA/FYA:						
Cars (1 – 50g/km)			X			
Cars (over 50g/km)				X		
Qualifying for super deduction						
Plant and machinery acquired on/after 1.4.21 (X × 130%)		X				
Super deduction at 130%		(X)				X
		0				
Qualifying for AIA:						
Special rate pool expenditure (pre 1.4.21)	X					
AIA (Max £1,000,000 in total)	(X)					X
				X		
Main pool expenditure (second-hand/pre 1.4.21)	X					
AIA (Max £1,000,000 in total)	(X)					X
			X			
Special rate pool expenditure (on/after 1.4.21)	X					
AIA (Max £1,000,000 in total)	(X)					X
Balance of special rate pool expenditure for FYA		X				
Disposals (lower of original cost and sale proceeds)			(X)	(X)	(X)	
			X	X	X	
BA/(BC)					X/(X)	X/(X)
Small pools WDA (if applicable)						
WDA at 18%			(X)			X
WDA at 6%				(X)		X
WDA at 6%/18% (depending on emissions)						X
Additions qualifying for FYAs:						
Enhanced FYA at 50% on balance of special rate pool expenditure		(X)				X
				X		
Zero emissions cars		X				
FYA at 100%		(X)				X
			0			
TWDV c/f		0	X	X		
Total allowances						X

Example

Toe Ltd prepares accounts to 31 March each year. In the year ended 31 March 2022 the company purchased the following assets for use in its trade:

1 second-hand printing machine for £50,000

2 new packaging plant for £80,000.

The tax written down value brought forward on the main pool was £25,000.

Calculate the capital allowances for the year ended 31 March 2022.

Solution

Capital allowances computation

		Main pool	**Allowances**
y/e 31 March 2022	£	£	£
TWDV		25,000	
Additions:			
Qualifying for super deduction			
Packaging plant (130% × £80,000)	104,000		
Super deduction	(104,000)		104,000
	0		
Qualifying for AIA:			
Second-hand printing machine	50,000		
AIA	(50,000)		50,000
		0	
WDA (18% × £25,000)		(4,500)	4,500
TWDV c/f		20,500	
Total allowances			158,500

For qualifying special rate pool expenditure in the examination:

- first claim the AIA (max £1,000,000)
- then claim FYA on 50% of the remaining cost
- then transfer the balance to the special rate pool, **after** the WDA.

Additions qualifying for the 50% FYA do not also qualify for WDA in the same period. The balance after AIA and FYA is brought into the special rate pool at the end of the computation, after WDA on the pool balance. This means it is included in the TWDV carried forward on which WDA is given in subsequent periods.

Example

Foot Ltd prepares accounts to 31 March each year. In the year ended 31 March 2022 the company purchased integral features for its factory, for £1,300,000. The company also purchased a car with CO_2 emissions of 140g/km for £40,000.

The tax written down value brought forward on the special rate pool was £160,000.

Calculate the capital allowances for the year ended 31 March 2022.

Solution

Capital allowances computation

		Special rate pool	**Allowances**
y/e 31 March 2022	£	£	£
TWDV		160,000	
Addition not qualifying for AIA/FYA:			
Car with emissions > 50g/km		40,000	
		200,000	
WDA (6% × £200,000)		(12,000)	12,000
Additions qualifying for AIA & FYA:			
Integral features	1,300,000		
AIA	(1,000,000)		1,000,000
	300,000		
FYA (50% × £300,000)	(150,000)		150,000
		150,000	
TWDV c/f		338,000	
Total allowances			1,162,000

5 INTEREST INCOME

The figure included in taxable total profits for interest income is interest received less interest payable on non-trade related loans.

Interest received is usually credited in the company's accounts on an 'accruals' basis. It is always treated as non-trading and is taxable as interest income.

The treatment of interest payable depends on the purpose of the loan:

- If it is for a trading purpose (e.g. to provide working capital or buy plant) it is a trading expense.
- If it is for a non-trading purpose (e.g. on a loan to buy commercially let property) it is deducted from interest received. The net figure will then be included in the corporation tax computation.

The examination question will either state whether the interest is trade or non-trade or will give sufficient information to determine how it should be treated.

Interest, whether paid or received, is always dealt with on an accruals basis for corporation tax purposes.

Example

Birdie Ltd opened a bank deposit account on 1 April 2021. Interest of £1,500 was credited to the account on 30 June 2021 and £4,300 on 31 December 2021.

At 31 March 2022, the company estimated that £1,700 of bank interest had been earned but not yet received between 1 January and 31 March 2022.

During the year ended 31 March 2022, the company had interest payable of £2,000 on a loan taken out so that the company could invest in the shares of a supplier company.

In the corporation tax computation:

	£
Interest receivable (£1,500 + £4,300 + £1,700)	7,500
Less: interest on non-trade loan	(2,000)
Interest income	5,500

In the examination, one net figure of £5,500 for interest income must be shown in the corporation tax computation. Failure to net off non-trade related interest expenses from interest income, and thus show two separate figures will result in a loss of marks.

6 PROPERTY BUSINESS PROFITS

The main difference for computing taxable property business profits for companies compared to individuals (see Chapter 12) is that the taxable property business profit **must** be calculated using the **accruals basis** for the company's accounting period. This means that rental income and property expenses are taxable/deductible based on when they are due rather than when they are paid. This is the same basis that is used for calculating trading profits.

Other rules concerning the computation of the taxable property business profits that apply to individuals generally also apply to companies apart from in respect of the following.

- Capital expenditure is not an allowable deduction for companies.
  - Capital allowances (see Chapter 4) may be claimed for expenditure on plant and machinery (including cars) used for running the property business.
  - Replacement furniture relief is available for the replacement of domestic items in a residential property.
  - A company cannot choose to use the HMRC approved mileage allowances instead of capital allowances in respect of motoring expenses.
- Interest paid by companies is not an expense of the property letting business. Instead, it is deducted from any interest received, and the net figure is taxable as interest income (as shown in section 5).

- Specific impaired debts are allowable, whilst a general allowance for impaired debts is not allowable. If a tenant leaves without paying the outstanding rent, the amount owed can be deducted as an expense. However, the landlord could **not** have a tax deduction for a general allowance of (say) 5% of rent due in case a tenant should default.
- Property business losses are deducted from the company's total profits before qualifying charitable donations of the same accounting period. Any excess is carried forward and offset against total profits in future accounting periods.

As for individuals, premiums on short leases are also taxed as property income.

Example

ABC Ltd owns two properties, K and L. K is let at an annual rent of £5,000. L was let at an annual rent of £3,000 until 1 October 2021 when the rent was increased to £4,000 p.a. Rents are payable quarterly in advance on 31 March, 30 June, 30 September and 31 December.

Expenses payable for the year to 31 March 2022 are:

	K	**L**
	£	£
Insurance	800	750
Agent's fees	500	375
Repairs	1,000	2,900

The agent's fees for L related to the period to 31 March 2022 but were not actually paid until May 2022. The repairs on property K related to a redecoration of the building. Those on property L related to re-felting the roof and replacing broken tiles.

Compute the property business profits taxable for the year to 31 March 2022.

Solution

Accounting period to 31 March 2022

	K	**L**
	£	£
Rent accrued for year	5,000	
(£3,000 × $^6/_{12}$) + (£4,000 × $^6/_{12}$)		3,500
Expenses		
Insurance	(800)	(750)
Agent's fees (accruals basis)	(500)	(375)
Repairs	(1,000)	(2,900)
Profit/ (loss)	2,700	(525)
Taxable as property business profits (£2,700 – £525)		2,175

Note: The timing of the receipt of the rent and payment of the agent's fees is not relevant under the accruals basis.

7 CHARGEABLE GAINS

When a company disposes of a capital asset, the chargeable gain is basically calculated in the same way as for individuals (generally disposal proceeds less allowable deductions). The rules for companies were covered in Chapter 17. The differences can be summarised as follows.

- Companies are entitled to an indexation allowance until December 2017, which can reduce or eliminate a gain.
- Companies do not have an annual exempt amount.
- Companies do not pay capital gains tax, instead their chargeable gains are included in their taxable total profits for an accounting period, on which corporation tax is payable.
- There is no difference between the treatment of current and brought forward losses. They are both deducted from gains as soon as possible and net gains are then included in the corporation tax computation. Capital losses cannot be deducted from any other income of the company.

8 QUALIFYING CHARITABLE DONATIONS

Qualifying charitable donations are deducted from the total of profits from all sources, after any loss reliefs, to arrive at the figure of taxable total profits.

All amounts paid to charity, which are not already allowed as trading expenses (that is small donations to local charities), are treated as qualifying charitable donations.

Note that charitable donations made by a company are paid **gross** so no grossing up is required. They are deducted on a cash paid basis in the accounting period when paid.

9 DIVIDENDS

Dividends paid are appropriations of profit, and are not tax allowable.

Dividends received are not taxable and must not be included in taxable total profits.

It may be necessary to show that the dividends are tax free income, depending on the requirements of the question.

Example

The following is a summary of the statement of profit or loss of Ash Ltd for the year ended 31 March 2022.

	£	£
Gross trading profit		319,760
Loan interest receivable		61,000
Patent royalties receivable		18,480
Building society interest receivable		2,800
Dividends received		8,400
Profit on sale of capital asset		5,000
		415,440
Less: Trade expenses (all allowable)	94,000	
Loan note interest payable	6,800	
Payment to charity	3,192	
		(103,992)
Net profit per accounts		311,448

Capital allowances for the year have been calculated as £7,920. All amounts shown for interest (paid or received) have been calculated on an accruals basis.

The capital asset was disposed of in January 2022, giving rise to a chargeable gain of £3,920.

The loan note interest was payable in respect of loan notes issued to fund the purchase of plant and machinery for use in the trade.

The payment to charity qualifies as a qualifying charitable donation.

Calculate the taxable total profits for the year ended 31 March 2022.

Solution

Step 1 The net profit per accounts must be adjusted for tax purposes. Any income that is not taxed as trading income or is exempt must be deducted, and any expenses that are not allowable deductions from trading income must be added back. The capital allowances must then be deducted to arrive at the tax adjusted trading profit figure.

		£	£
Net profit per accounts			311,448
Less:	Loan interest receivable	61,000	
	Patent royalties receivable	0	
	Building society interest receivable	2,800	
	Dividends received	8,400	
	Profit on sale of capital asset	5,000	
			(77,200)
			234,248
Add:	Loan note interest payable		0
	Payment to charity		3,192
			237,440
Less:	Capital allowances		(7,920)
Tax adjusted trading profit			229,520

Since the patents will be held for trading purposes, there is no need to adjust for the royalties received. The loan note interest was paid for trading purposes, so again no adjustment is required.

Step 2 The taxable total profits can now be computed using the layout given earlier in this chapter.

Ash Ltd: Taxable total profits for the year ended 31 March 2022

	£
Tax adjusted trading profit	229,520
Interest income (£2,800 + £61,000)	63,800
Chargeable gain	3,920
Total profits	297,240
Less: QCD relief	(3,192)
Taxable total profits	294,048

ACTIVITY 2

The following information relates to Holl Ltd for the year ended 31 March 2022.

	£
Trading profit (adjusted for taxation purposes, but before the deduction of capital allowances)	1,433,000
Capital allowances	60,000
Bank interest receivable	25,000
Rents receivable	15,000
Dividend received	20,000
Donation to national charity	4,000

Calculate the taxable total profits for the year ended 31 March 2022.

For a suggested answer, see the 'Answers' section at the end of the book.

10 LONG PERIODS OF ACCOUNT

Where a company prepares accounts for a period of more than 12 months, this must be split into two accounting periods of the first 12 months and the remainder of the period of account, as explained earlier in this chapter.

Profits and qualifying charitable donations are allocated between the two accounting periods (APs) as follows:

	Method of allocation
• Trading profits before capital allowances	Adjust profit for full period of account for tax purposes and then apportion on a time basis
• Capital allowances and balancing charges	Separate calculation for each accounting period. (AIA and WDAs are proportionately reduced in the second accounting period which is less than 12 months)
• Property business profits (e.g. rent)	Allocated on accruals basis unless insufficient information available in which case use a time apportionment basis
• Interest income	Interest receivable and payable on non-trade loans allocated on an accruals basis
• Chargeable gains	Include in the accounting period in which the disposal takes place
• Qualifying charitable donations	Deducted from the profits of the accounting period in which they are paid

Example

Printer Ltd has prepared accounts for the 16 months to 31 August 2022, with the following information.

	£
Adjusted trading profit before capital allowances	365,000
Building society interest receivable:	
Accrues at rate of £211 per month	3,376
Rents from property	26,015
Chargeable gains	
Disposal on 31 March 2022	25,700
Disposal on 1 May 2022	49,760
Dividend received from UK company on 1 February 2022	10,000
Donation to national charity	
Paid 31 July 2021	6,000
Paid 31 January 2022	6,000

Capital allowances for the two APs derived from the 16 month period of account are £20,000 for the first AP and £6,250 for the second AP.

Show how the company's period of account will be divided into accounting periods (APs) and compute the taxable total profits for each AP assuming, where relevant, that all income is deemed to accrue evenly.

Solution

The procedure to be followed is exactly the same as for a 12 month period, but incorporating the allocation rules. The two periods should be set out in columns side by side, including the income in the relevant period.

	12 months to 30 April 2022	4 months to 31 August 2022
	£	£
Trading profit (W1)	253,750	85,000
Non-trade interest income (W2)	2,532	844
Property income (W3)	19,511	6,504
Chargeable gains	25,700	49,760
Total profits	301,493	142,108
Less: QCD relief (W4)	(12,000)	0
Taxable total profits	289,493	142,108

Notes:

The dividend received is exempt from corporation tax.

The chargeable gains are allocated according to the date of the transaction.

Workings

(W1) Trading profit

	Total	12m	4m
	£	£	£
Adjusted profit (see note)	365,000	273,750	91,250
Less: Capital allowances		(20,000)	(6,250)
Trading profit		253,750	85,000

Note: The adjusted trading profit before capital allowances is time apportioned, i.e. 12/16 × £365,000 in the first period and 4/16 × £365,000 in the second period.

(W2) Non-trade interest – Building society interest

The question tells us that the interest accrues at £211 per month.

	Total	12m	4m
	£	£	£
Interest income	3,376	2,532	844

(W3) Property income

Rental income is taxable as property income, which is assessed on an accruals basis for the 16 months and then time apportioned into the two APs:

	Total	12m	4m
	£	£	£
Property income	26,015	19,511	6,504

(W4) Qualifying charitable donations

	£	
Donation to national charity:		
31 July 2021	6,000	
31 January 2022	6,000	
	12,000	In y/e 30 April 2022

£Nil in 4 months to 31 August 2022 as none paid.

ACTIVITY 3

Oak Ltd prepared accounts for the 15 month period to 30 June 2022, with results as follows:

	£
Trading profit (adjusted for tax purposes, but before the deduction of capital allowances, loan note interest and patent royalties)	1,383,880
Bank interest (receivable 31 March 2022)	20,900
Bank interest (receivable 31 March 2023)	22,720
Property income (received 1 April 2022)	10,000
Chargeable gain (asset disposed of 1 June 2022)	16,000
Loan note interest (amount actually paid, interest due annually on 1 May 2021 and 1 May 2022)	48,000
Patent royalties (amount paid 30 June 2022)	30,000
Donation to national charity paid 1 December 2021	3,000

The company bought used plant costing £350,000, and a new computer costing £1,000, on 1 June 2022. It had made no previous acquisitions qualifying for capital allowances.

The bank interest receivable on 31 March is for the 12 months ended on that date.

The loan notes were issued to raise funds to purchase premises used for the trade.

The patent royalties were paid on 30 June 2022 for the 15 months to date.

The rent was paid in advance in respect of the year from 1 April 2022.

Calculate the taxable total profits for each accounting period in the 15 month period to 30 June 2022.

For a suggested answer, see the 'Answers' section at the end of the book.

11 CORPORATION TAX RETURN (PART 1)

11.1 THE RETURN – FORM CT600

The corporation tax return, CT600, must be completed for the accounting period. The return is 11 pages long; however, in an examination you would only be required to show the boxes that should be completed on various parts of the return.

- The first page includes details of the company and the accounting period. You may be required to complete these parts in the examination.
- The remainder of page one includes check boxes regarding various aspects of the return. The top of page 2 shows whether any supplementary pages are required. These parts are outside the scope of your studies.
- The computation of taxable total profits is covered on the second half of page 2, page 3 and the top of page 4. The details that you may be required to complete on these pages are covered below.
- The corporation tax payable calculation appears on the bottom half of page 4. This is covered in the next chapter.
- Page 8 and the top of page 9 require details of capital allowances and are covered below.
- Page 9 includes details of losses arising in the year and is covered below.
- Pages 5 to 7 and 10 to 11 cover various aspects of corporation tax that are beyond the FTX syllabus, as well as details of the company's bank account if a repayment is due, and a declaration that the return is complete and correct. You should not be required to complete these pages in the examination.

11.2 COMPANY INFORMATION

At the top of the first page of the return, a company must enter the following details:

- Company name
- Company registration number and tax reference (these will not require completion in the examination unless they are provided in the question)
- Return period (i.e. accounting period).
- The section on Northern Ireland will not require completion in the examination.

HM Revenue & Customs

Company Tax Return

CT600 (2021) Version 3

for accounting periods starting on or after 1 April 2015

Your Company Tax Return

If we send the company a 'Notice' to deliver a Company Tax Return it has to comply by the filing date or we charge a penalty, even if there is no tax to pay.

A return includes a Company Tax Return form, any supplementary pages, accounts, computations and any relevant information. The CT600 Guide tells you how the return must be formatted and delivered. It contains general information you may need to deliver your return, links to more detailed advice and box-by-box guidance for this form and the supplementary pages.

The forms in the CT600 series set out the information we need and provide a standard format for calculations.

Company information

1 Company name

2 Company registration number

3 Tax reference

4 Type of company

Northern Ireland

Put an 'X' in the appropriate box(es) below

5 NI trading activity

6 SME

7 NI employer

8 Special circumstances

About this return

This is the above company's return for the period

30 from DD MM YYYY

35 to DD MM YYYY

Put an 'X' in the appropriate box(es) below

40 A repayment is due for this return period

45 Claim or relief affecting an earlier period

50 Making more than one return for this company now

55 This return contains estimated figures

60 Company part of a group that is not small

65 Notice of disclosable avoidance schemes

Transfer Pricing

70 Compensating adjustment claimed

75 Company qualifies for SME exemption

CT600(2021) Version 3 Page 1 HMRC 04/21

11.3 CALCULATION OF TAXABLE TOTAL PROFITS

The bottom of page 2 to the top of page 4 covers the calculation of taxable total profits. You should note that the corporation tax return still uses old terminology such that it refers to this figure as profits chargeable to corporation tax.

Many of the boxes are beyond the FTX syllabus. However, the boxes that you may need to complete in the examination are:

	Boxes
Turnover	145
Tax adjusted trading profit	155
Non-trade interest	170
Property business profits	190
Chargeable gains	210
Capital losses (current year and brought forward)	215
Property losses (current year and brought forward)	250
Trading losses (current year and carried back)	275
Check box if losses in box 275 include carried back losses	280
Trading losses brought forward and claimed against total profits	285
Qualifying charitable donations	305

Note that trading losses brought forward are offset against total profits and should be entered in Box 285. Box 160, which also deals with trading losses brought forward, is not examinable.

You will also need to complete any relevant sub-total boxes, which include 165, 220, 235, 295, 300 and 315. The detail of what should be included in these sub-total boxes is clearly described on the return and these instructions should be followed.

Note that trading, capital and property losses are covered in Chapter 23.

The remainder of page 4 dealing with the calculation of the tax is covered in Chapter 22.

Tax calculation

Turnover

145 **Total turnover from trade** £ .00

150 **Banks, building societies, insurance companies and other financial concerns** – put an 'X' in this box if you do not have a recognised turnover and have not made an entry in box 145

Income

155 **Trading profits** £ .00

160 **Trading losses brought forward set against trading profits** £ .00

165 **Net trading profits** – box 155 minus box 160 £ .00

170 **Bank, building society or other interest, and profits from non-trading loan relationships** £ .00

172 **Put an 'X' in box 172 if the figure in box 170 is net of carrying back a deficit from a later accounting period**

CT600(2020) Version 3 Page 2 HMRC 04/20

Income - continued

175	Annual payments not otherwise charged to Corporation Tax and from which Income Tax has not been deducted	£ . 0 0
180	Non-exempt dividends or distributions from non-UK resident companies	£ . 0 0
185	Income from which Income Tax has been deducted	£ . 0 0
190	Income from a property business	£ . 0 0
195	Non-trading gains on intangible fixed assets	£ . 0 0
200	Tonnage Tax profits	£ . 0 0
205	Income not falling under any other heading	£ . 0 0

Chargeable gains

210	Gross chargeable gains	£ . 0 0
215	Allowable losses including losses brought forward	£ . 0 0
220	Net chargeable gains - box 210 minus box 215	£ . 0 0

Profits before deductions and reliefs

225	Losses brought forward against certain investment income	£ . 0 0
230	Non-trade deficits on loan relationships (including interest) and derivative contracts (financial instruments) brought forward set against non-trading profits	£ . 0 0
235	Profits before other deductions and reliefs - net sum of boxes 165 to 205 and 220 minus sum of boxes 225 and 230	£ . 0 0

Deductions and reliefs

240	Losses on unquoted shares	£ . 0 0
245	Management expenses	£ . 0 0
250	UK property business losses for this or previous accounting period	£ . 0 0
255	Capital allowances for the purposes of management of the business	£ . 0 0
260	Non-trade deficits for this accounting period from loan relationships and derivative contracts (financial instruments)	£ . 0 0

CT600(2021) Version 3 Page 3 HMRC 04/21

Deductions and Reliefs - continued

Box	Description	Amount
263	Carried forward non-trade deficits from loan relationships and derivative contracts (financial instruments)	£ . 0 0
265	Non-trading losses on intangible fixed assets	£ . 0 0
275	Total trading losses of this or a later accounting period	£ . 0 0
280	Put an 'X' in box 280 if amounts carried back from later accounting periods are included in box 275	
285	Trading losses carried forward and claimed against total profits	£ . 0 0
290	Non-trade capital allowances	£ . 0 0
295	Total of deductions and reliefs - total of boxes 240 to 275, 285 and 290	£ . 0 0
300	Profits before qualifying donations and group relief - box 235 minus box 295	£ . 0 0
305	Qualifying donations	£ . 0 0
310	Group relief	£ . 0 0
312	Group relief for carried forward losses	£ . 0 0
315	Profits chargeable to Corporation Tax - box 300 minus boxes 305, 310 and 312	£ . 0 0
320	Ring fence profits included	£ . 0 0
325	Northern Ireland profits included	£ . 0 0

11.4 CAPITAL ALLOWANCES SECTION

Information about capital allowances and balancing charges must be entered on page 8 and the top of page 9 of the return.

	Boxes
Total annual investment allowance	690
AIA and WDA in special rate pool	695
Balancing charge (if any) in special rate pool	700
AIA and WDA in the main pool	705
Balancing charge (if any) in the main pool	710
Structures and buildings allowance	711
WDA on short life assets	725
Balancing charges (if any) on short life assets	730
FYA on zero emission cars	726
Disposal value (if any) of zero emission cars	727
Additions on which FYA claimed	760
Additions of integral features to the special rate pool	770
Additions to the main pool and short life assets	775

Boxes 713 to 724 and 735 to 752 will not be used as these are beyond the FTX syllabus.

Information about capital allowances and balancing charges

Allowances and charges in calculation of trading profits and losses

	Capital allowances	Balancing charges
Annual investment allowance	690 £	
Machinery and plant - special rate pool	695 £	700 £
Machinery and plant - main pool	705 £	710 £
Structures and buildings	711 £	
Business premises renovation	715 £	720 £
Other allowances and charges	725 £	730 £
	Capital allowances	**Disposal value**
Electric charge-points	713 £	714 £
Enterprise zones	721 £	722 £
Zero emissions goods vehicles	723 £	724 £
Zero emissions cars	726 £	727 £

Allowances and charges not included in calculation of trading profits and losses

	Capital allowances	Balancing charges
Annual investment allowance	735 £	
Structures and buildings	736 £	
Business premises renovation	740 £	745 £
Other allowances and charges	750 £	755 £
	Capital allowances	**Disposal value**
Electric charge-points	737 £	738 £
Enterprise zones	746 £	747 £
Zero emissions goods vehicles	748 £	749 £
Zero emissions cars	751 £	752 £

CT600(2021) Version 3 Page 8 HMRC 04/21

Qualifying expenditure

Box		
760	Machinery and plant on which first year allowance is claimed	£ .00
765	Designated environmentally friendly machinery and plant	£ .00
770	Machinery and plant on long-life assets and integral features	£ .00
771	Structures and buildings	£ .00
775	Other machinery and plant	£ .00

Note that the above return is not updated for the new enhanced capital allowances, as that return is not yet available.

11.5 LOSSES SECTION

A limited amount of information about losses may be required on the bottom part of page 9 of the return.

	Boxes
Trade losses arising in the current year	780
Property business losses arising in the current year	805
Capital losses arising in the current year	825

The remainder of the boxes on this page are beyond the FTX syllabus.

Losses, deficits and excess amounts

Amount arising

	Amount	Maximum available for surrender as group relief
Losses of trades carried on wholly or partly in the UK	780 £	785 £
Losses of trades carried on wholly outside the UK	790 £	
Non-trade deficits on loan relationships and derivative contracts	795 £	800 £
UK property business losses	805 £	810 £
Overseas property business losses	815 £	
Losses from miscellaneous transactions	820 £	
Capital losses	825 £	
Non-trading losses on intangible fixed assets	830 £	835 £

11.6 COMPLETING THE RETURN

When stating the figures that should be completed on the tax return form in an examination it is important to note that:

- The return is expected to be completed with accuracy.
- Figures should be entered in the correct boxes.

Example

Victor Ltd has the following results for its year ended 31 March 2022.

Show the entries to be completed for the computation of taxable total profits on the form CT600.

	£	£	**CT600 box**
Tax adjusted trading profit		100,000	155
Non-trade interest		20,000	170
Property business profits		5,000	190
Chargeable gains	8,000		210
Less: Capital losses	(3,000)		215
		5,000	220
Total profits		130,000	300
Less: QCD relief		(8,000)	305
Taxable total profits		122,000	315

Do not forget to include sub-totals and totals (i.e. boxes 165, 235, 300 and 315).

Victor Ltd's corporation tax return entries

Box 155	£100,000
Box 165	£100,000
Box 170	£20,000
Box 190	£5,000
Box 210	£8,000
Box 215	£3,000
Box 220	£5,000
Box 235	£130,000
Box 300	£130,000
Box 305	£8,000
Box 315	£122,000

Example

Capital allowances computation for X Ltd for the year ended 31 March 2022

		Main pool	Special rate pool	Short life asset	Allowances
	£	£	£	£	£
TWDV b/f		14,000	8,000	5,000	
Additions:					
Not qualifying for AIA:					
– Car (CO_2 emissions 40g/km)		10,000			
Qualifying for AIA:					
– used plant and machinery	23,000				
Less AIA					
(Max £1,000,000 in total)	(23,000)				23,000
		0			
Disposals (lower of original cost and sale proceeds)		(3,500)	(8,400)		
		20,500	(400)	5,000	
BC			400		(400)
WDA at 18%		(3,690)		(900)	4,590
TWDV c/f		16,810		4,100	
Total allowances					27,190

Show how this information would be included in the CT600 form.

X Ltd's corporation tax return entries

Box 690	£23,000
Box 700	£400
Box 705	£26,690
Box 725	£900
Box 775	£33,000

KEY TERMS

Company – any body corporate, limited or unlimited, or unincorporated association.

Period of account – any period for which a company prepares accounts. It is usually 12 months in length, but may be shorter or longer than this.

Accounting period – the period for which a charge to corporation tax is made. It can never be longer than 12 months.

Long period of account – for corporation tax purposes, a period that exceeds 12 months.

SELF TEST QUESTIONS

		Paragraph
1	What are the two tests used to determine whether a company is UK resident?	1.2
2	What is the definition of an accounting period?	1.3
3	Give three examples of when an accounting period ends.	1.3
4	What are the differences between how capital allowances are computed for companies and for individuals?	4.1
5	Which assets qualify for enhanced capital allowances and at what rates?	4.2
6	How is interest relieved if it is paid on borrowings taken out to buy commercially let property?	5, 6
7	When a company prepares accounts for a period that exceeds 12 months, what will be the company's accounting periods?	10
8	How are trading profits allocated when the period of account exceeds 12 months?	10

MULTIPLE CHOICE QUESTIONS

1 Harvey Ltd started trading on 1 April 2021 and prepared its first set of accounts to 31 May 2022.

What is Harvey Ltd's first accounting period?

A 2 months ended 31 May 2021

B 12 months ended 31 March 2022

C 13 months ended 30 April 2022

D 14 months ended 31 May 2022

2 Bailey Ltd prepared accounts for the three month period ended 31 March 2022. On 1 February 2022 a car costing £18,000 was purchased for the sales director and used by him 60% for business purposes. The car has CO_2 emissions over 50g/km.

What are the capital allowances available on this car for the three months ended 31 March 2022?

A £1,080

B £810

C £270

D £162

3 Bennett Ltd prepares accounts for the year ended 31 March 2022. The following information is available:

	£
Adjusted trading profits before capital allowances	56,000
Bank interest receivable	3,000
Dividends received	8,000

The tax written down value of the main pool was £26,667 on 1 April 2021 and on 1 January 2022 the company purchased a second-hand lorry for £14,000.

What are Bennett Ltd's taxable total profits for the year ended 31 March 2022?

A £40,200

B £48,200

C £51,680

D £37,200

For suggested answers, see the 'Answers' section at the end of the book.

PRACTICE QUESTIONS

1 SPRINGVALE LTD

Springvale Ltd has been carrying on a manufacturing business since 2005 and the following is a summary of the statement of profit or loss for the year to 31 March 2022.

		£	£
Trading profit			162,372
Loan note interest (Note 1)			1,200
Bank deposit interest			359
Dividend received			400
			164,331
Less:	Expenses		
	Director's remuneration	37,840	
	Depreciation	44,400	
	Loan note interest payable (Note 2)	480	
	Entertaining expenses (all customers)	420	
	Donation paid to national charity	3,800	
	Patent royalty payable	350	
	Salaries and wages	16,460	
	Rent and business rates	1,650	
	Audit fee	350	
	Trade expenses (Note 3)	15,418	(121,168)
Net profit before taxation			43,163

Notes:

1 Loan note interest is receivable annually on 31 March.

2 Of the loan note interest payable of £480, £80 was accrued at 31 March 2022. The loan note was issued to raise funds to finance trading activities.

3 The trade expenses include the following items:

	£
Christmas gifts	
Wines and spirits for UK customers	320
5,000 ballpoint pens with company's name	250
Legal costs	
Re issue of loan note (see Note 2)	500
Re staff service agreements	90

4 The tax written down value on 1 April 2021 of the main pool was £15,544.

On 10 July 2021 the company purchased a new lathe for £1,200 and new plant for £2,000. On 1 December 2021 plant that had cost £11,000 in March 2020 was sold for £1,500. On 1 February 2022 new plant costing £3,520 and a motor car costing £16,250 were purchased (the private use of this car by the sales director was calculated at one third). The car has CO_2 emissions of 95g/km.

5 During the year the company made a chargeable gain after indexation of £51,160.

Required:

Compute the taxable total profits for the year ended 31 March 2022. **(15 marks)**

2 SUPERSCOFF PLC

Superscoff plc is a trading company operating a fast food retailing business. The statement of profit or loss for the 12 months to 31 March 2022 shows the following.

		£	£
Gross profit			1,489,055
Bank deposit interest			1,200
Dividends received			6,000
Rent (net of expenses) (Note 1)			1,460
Gain on investments (Note 2)			798
			1,498,513
Less:	Expenses		
	Salaries and wages	146,323	
	Rates, light and heat	11,650	
	Travelling expenses	13,200	
	Entertaining (Note 3)	6,000	
	Advertising (Note 4)	18,600	
	Depreciation	27,800	
	Director's remuneration	40,000	
	General expenses (Note 5)	3,150	
	Loan note interest paid (Note 6)	8,800	
	Dividend paid	31,950	(307,473)
Net profit			1,191,040

Notes:

1 The rent received is in respect of the adjacent shop premises let at £4,000 per annum, payable quarterly in arrears. The rent due on 31 March 2022 had not been received by the due date. The company incurred expenses of £250 on administration, £40 on agents' fees, and £1,250 being part of the cost shared with the tenant of installing a new shop front.

2 The gain on the investments arises on the sale of 5,000 shares in Finefish Ltd, purchased and sold in May 2021, and is equal to the chargeable gain.

3 The entertaining expenses comprise £4,750 cost of entertaining customers, and £1,250 for the staff Christmas party.

4 Advertising includes the cost of 500 calendars, bearing the company's name, at a cost of £2 each.

5 General expenses comprise:

	£
Subscriptions to BHRCA, the trade association	40
Donation to Oxfam	500
Fine for breach of hygiene regulations	250
Allowable expenses	2,360
	3,150

6 The loan notes were issued to other companies to fund trading operations. The interest is payable half-yearly on 30 September and 31 March.

7 The company is entitled to capital allowances of £5,000.

Required:

Calculate the taxable total profits for the 12 months ended 31 March 2022.

(15 marks)

3 AMOS LTD

Amos Ltd has supplied the following information about its capital allowances position:

The tax written down value of the plant and machinery, for capital allowances purposes, on 1 April 2021 was as follows:

	£
Main pool	11,400
Special rate pool (car costing £18,750 with CO_2 emissions of 150g/km used 60% privately by managing director)	6,750

During the year ended 31 March 2022 the following transactions took place:

1 August 2021	Sold the MD's car for £6,350 and purchased a replacement for £22,500. Private use remains at 60%. This car has CO_2 emissions of 100g/km.
1 March 2022	Sold a cold food display cabinet for £1,200 (cost £2,500 in July 2019).
31 March 2022	Purchased thermal insulation, an integral feature, for £1,800,000.

Required:

Compute the capital allowances for the 12 months ended 31 March 2022. **(10 marks)**

For suggested answers, see the 'Answers' section at the end of the book.

Chapter 22

CALCULATION AND PAYMENT OF CORPORATION TAX

INTRODUCTION

This chapter covers the computation of the corporation tax liability of a company. A thorough understanding of this chapter is necessary to deal with basic corporation tax questions.

This chapter covers syllabus areas E 3, 7 and 8.

CONTENTS	LEARNING OUTCOMES
1 The corporation tax liability **2** Payment of corporation tax **3** Corporation tax return (Part 2) **4** Self-assessment for companies	At the end of this chapter, you should be able to: • identify the financial year(s) relevant to an accounting period • calculate the corporation tax liability • complete corporation tax returns correctly and submit them within statutory time limits • explain and apply the features of the self-assessment system as it applies to companies, including the use of iXBRL • explain the system of penalties and interest as it applies to corporation tax • recognise the time limits that apply to the filing of returns and the making of claims

	• recognise the due dates for the payment of corporation tax under the self-assessment system • explain how large companies are required to account for corporation tax on a quarterly basis • list the information and records that taxpayers need to retain for tax purposes.

1 THE CORPORATION TAX LIABILITY

1.1 INTRODUCTION

In the previous chapter, you learned how to calculate the figure of taxable total profits. This chapter looks at the calculation of the corporation tax liability and its payment.

The rate of corporation tax is fixed by reference to financial years. A financial year runs from 1 April to the following 31 March and is identified by the calendar year in which it begins.

The year commencing 1 April 2021 is the Financial Year 2021 (FY2021). Financial years should not be confused with tax years for income tax, which run from 6 April to the following 5 April.

1.2 CORPORATION TAX RATE FY2021

All companies pay tax at 19% for FY2021.

> **Example**
>
> For the year ended 31 March 2022, Gamma Ltd has taxable total profits of £70,000.
>
> Delta plc has taxable total profits of £3,000,000 for the 9 months to 31 December 2021.
>
> Calculate the corporation tax liability of each of the companies.

	£
Gamma Ltd	
Taxable total profits	70,000
Corporation tax liability	
£70,000 × 19%	13,300
Delta plc	
Taxable total profits	3,000,000
Corporation tax liability	
£3,000,000 × 19%	570,000

1.3 CORPORATION TAX RATE FY2020

The rate of corporation tax for FY2020 (and FY2019 and FY2018) was also 19%.

Where a company's accounting period falls into two financial years then the corporation tax liability must be calculated for each financial year if the corporation tax rates have changed. However, the rates (as seen above) have not changed in recent years. If accounting periods did span two financial years where there had been a change in tax rate, this is **not examinable** for FTX.

When the corporation tax rate has not changed, the corporation tax liability does not need to be calculated separately.

Example

Flute Ltd had taxable total profits of £400,000 in the year ended 31 December 2021.

Calculate Flute Ltd's corporation tax liability for the year ended 31 December 2021.

Solution

The company's AP falls into FY2020 and FY2021. The rate of corporation tax was 19% in both financial years.

	£
Taxable total profits	400,000
FY2020/FY2021	
Corporation tax liability (£400,000 × 19%)	76,000

ACTIVITY 1

Oboe Ltd had taxable total profits of £2,100,000 for the year ended 30 June 2021.

Calculate the corporation tax liability for the year ended 30 June 2021.

For a suggested answer, see the 'Answers' section at the end of the book.

2 PAYMENT OF CORPORATION TAX

2.1 THE DUE DATE OF PAYMENT

All payments of corporation tax must be made electronically.

Companies must normally pay corporation tax within nine months and one day of the end of the accounting period (AP). A company with a year ended 31 January 2022 must pay corporation tax by 1 November 2022. The precise due date (including the year) must be given in order to earn a mark in the examination.

A company with a long period of account, such as the 15 months ended 31 March 2022, has two payment dates.

AP 1 = 12 months ended 31 December 2021, payment date 1 October 2022.

AP 2 = 3 months ended 31 March 2022, payment date 1 January 2023.

This normal payment date rule does not however apply to large companies (see below).

2.2 PAYMENT BY INSTALMENTS

'Large' companies are required to make quarterly payments on account of their corporation tax liability. A 'large' company is one with 'profits' of more than £1,500,000 but no more than £20 million.

A 'very large' company is one with 'profits' of more than £20 million. These companies are **not examinable**.

For FTX purposes 'profits' are the same as taxable total profits.

Note that the £1,500,000 limit is time apportioned for short accounting periods.

Example

H plc has profits of £1,200,000 for the nine month accounting period ended 31 December 2021.

H plc has profits in excess of £1,125,000 (£1,500,000 × 9/12) and therefore must pay corporation tax by instalments.

Exceptions to the rule

A company is not required to make quarterly instalment payments if it was not 'large' in the previous period, unless its profits exceed £10 million.

This £10 million limit is also time apportioned for short APs.

Due dates

The first two instalments fall in months 7 and 10 **during** the accounting period. The second two instalments fall in months 1 and 4 of the next accounting period. Instalments are due on the 14th day of the month. Thus, the corporation tax for the year ended 31 December 2021 is due in four equal instalments on 14 July 2021, 14 October 2021, 14 January 2022 and 14 April 2022.

Each instalment should be 25% of the total corporation tax liability. As the first two instalments are due before the accounting period has ended and the final tax liability for the year is known, companies have to estimate their liability. The estimates should be reviewed regularly and payments revised as necessary.

Interest is charged on underpayments, but such interest is tax deductible from interest income as a payment of non-trade related interest. Similarly, overpayments attract interest payable by HMRC, but this is taxable as interest income.

Example

Froome Ltd has taxable total profits of £450,000 for the year ended 31 March 2022.

Compute the corporation tax liability and state the due date of payment.

Solution

	£
Taxable total profits	450,000
Corporation tax liability:	
£450,000 × 19%	85,500

The due date is 1 January 2023. No instalments are due as profits are less than £1,500,000.

ACTIVITY 2

Ash Ltd has the following results for the year ended 31 March 2022.

	£
Tax adjusted trading profit	1,480,000
Chargeable gain	80,000

Calculate the corporation tax liability and state the due dates of payment.

For a suggested answer, see the 'Answers' section at the end of the book.

2.3 LONG PERIODS OF ACCOUNT

Since a long period of account is made up of two separate accounting periods there are two separate due dates. It is possible that one of these will be due in a single payment and one via instalments, but you will never be required to calculate instalments for a short accounting period.

The two amounts of tax due for the separate periods should not be totalled together as they are due on separate dates.

3 CORPORATION TAX RETURN (PART 2)

3.1 CALCULATION OF CORPORATION TAX LIABILITY

In the previous chapter, we started looking at the form CT600.

We can now complete the tax calculation sections on the bottom of page 4. The narrative for the boxes should assist in determining what should be entered in which box.

The boxes likely to be completed are as follows:

Box	**Detail**
330	Shows the financial year. Care should be taken to ensure that the financial year is identified by the year in which it **starts**.
335	Taxable total profits
340	Rate of tax
345	Tax calculated at the appropriate rate. On the real return tax is entered in £ and pence. However, in the FTX examination all calculations and workings should be done to the nearest pound.
430 & 440	Shows the total corporation tax liability.

Boxes 380 – 395 will only be used if a period straddles two financial years, and therefore these will not be required in the FTX examination, since this scenario is not examinable where there has been a change in the rate of tax.

Tax calculation

Enter how much profit has to be charged and at what rate

	Financial year (yyyy)		Amount of profit		Rate of tax %		Tax
330		335	£	340		345	£ p
		350	£	355		360	£ p
		365	£	370		375	£ p
380		385	£	390		395	£ p
		400	£	405		410	£ p
		415	£	420		425	£ p

Corporation Tax - total of boxes 345, 360, 375, 395, 410 and 425	430	£ .
Marginal relief for ring fence trades	435	£ .
Corporation Tax chargeable box 430 minus box 435	440	£ .

CT600(2021) Version 3 Page 4 HMRC 04/21

Example

Small Ltd has the following results:

	£
Year ended 31 March 2022	
Taxable total profits	290,000
Corporation tax liability:	
£290,000 × 19%	55,100

Solution

Small Ltd's corporation tax return entries

Box 330	2021
Box 335	£290,000
Box 340	19%
Box 345	£55,100
Box 430	£55,100
Box 440	£55,100

ACTIVITY 3

Clent Ltd has the following corporation tax liability for the year ended 31 March 2022.

Corporation tax liability

	£
Taxable total profits	370,160
Corporation tax liability :	
FY2021	
£370,160 × 19%	70,330

Show the entries to be completed on the relevant sections of the corporation tax return.

For a suggested answer, see the 'Answers' section at the end of the book.

4 SELF-ASSESSMENT FOR COMPANIES

4.1 PAYMENT OF TAX

A company is required to pay its corporation tax liability by the due date whether or not a return has been filed and a self-assessment completed. All payments must be made electronically.

Interest will automatically be charged on underpaid tax, and paid on overpaid tax. Interest charged and paid must be taken into account for corporation tax purposes, by inclusion in the interest income computation.

4.2 NOTIFICATION OF CHARGEABILITY

A company coming within the scope of corporation tax for the first time must notify HMRC within three months of the start of its first accounting period. A company that has not received a notice to file a tax return must notify HMRC of its chargeability to corporation tax within 12 months of the end of the accounting period. Penalties may be charged for failure to notify.

4.3 FILING THE RETURN AND SELF-ASSESSMENT

HMRC issues a formal notice requiring a company to make a corporation tax return. The return incorporates a self-assessment, which is the company's computation of the corporation tax due.

All limited companies must file their self-assessment tax returns online. Unlike self-assessment for individuals, there are no provisions under which the company can require HMRC to calculate the tax liability from information provided in the tax return on its behalf.

The return must be accompanied by accounts and computations of any figures that are not immediately recognisable from the accounts. Estimated figures may only be used if there are special reasons why the company has been unable to supply the correct figure.

The accounts must be filed online using eXtensible Business Reporting Language (iXBRL). This is an electronic format for business information which 'tags' each item of information electronically making it easier for computer analysis. iXBRL is widely used for financial reporting worldwide.

Small companies can use software provided by HMRC, which will automatically produce accounts and tax computations in the correct format. Companies with more complex accounts have a number of options they could use:

- Other software that automatically produces iXBRL accounts and computations.
- A tagging service, which will apply the appropriate tags to accounts and computations.
- Software that enables the appropriate tags to be added to accounts and computations.

The tags used are contained in dictionaries known as taxonomies. There are different taxonomies for different purposes. The tagging of tax computations uses the corporation tax computational taxonomy, which includes over 1,200 relevant tags.

The corporation tax return must be filed within 12 months of the end of the accounting period or, if later, within three months of the issue of the notice to file the return. Automatic penalties are imposed for late filing. Remember that all due dates in the examination should be stated in full, including the year, it is not sufficient to simply state the rule to be applied.

4.4 AMENDING AND CORRECTING THE RETURN

HMRC may correct any obvious errors and anything else that they believe to be incorrect by reference to the information they hold within nine months of the date that they receive the return. For example, they will correct arithmetical errors or errors of principle. This process of repair does not mean that HMRC has necessarily accepted the return as accurate.

The company has 12 months from the due filing date within which it may amend its return. Amendments may be made not only to correct errors and mistakes but also, for example, if the company wishes to amend its claim for capital allowances.

If a company discovers a mistake in its tax return after this period, it may make a claim for repayment relief within four years of the end of the accounting period.

4.5 RECORDS

The company must keep records for at least six years from the end of its accounting period. This period is extended to the last date enquiries could be raised, or to the date enquiries are closed, if this is later. There is a maximum penalty of £3,000 for failing to keep proper records.

An example of the business records that will be useful to keep includes the following:

- annual accounts, including the statement of profit or loss and statement of financial position
- bank statements and paying-in slips
- a cash book and any other account books
- purchases and sales books or ledgers
- invoices and any record of daily takings such as till rolls
- order records and delivery notes
- a petty cash book
- other relevant business correspondence.

4.6 PENALTIES

Failure to notify chargeability

- Failure to notify chargeability may lead to a standard penalty based on a percentage of the tax unpaid 12 months after the end of the accounting period.
- The percentages are as for individuals – see Chapter 16.

Penalty for submission of incorrect returns

- A company that submits an incorrect return may be subject to a standard penalty based on a percentage of the lost tax revenue and their behaviour.
- The percentages are as for individuals – see Chapter 16.

Late filing of returns

Return overdue by	Penalty	
	First and second consecutive offences	**Third (or more) consecutive offence**
Up to 3 months	£100	£500
3 to 6 months	£200	£1,000
Over 6 months	£200 plus 10% of the unpaid tax	£1,000 plus 10% of the unpaid tax
Over 12 months	£200 plus 20% of the unpaid tax	£1,000 plus 20% of the unpaid tax

Unpaid tax is the tax due but not paid as at 18 months after the end of the return period (i.e. six months after the date when the return was due).

KEY TERMS

Financial year – runs from 1 April to the following 31 March and is identified by the calendar year in which it begins.

Large company – a company is regarded as large for corporation tax payment purposes if its profits exceed £1,500,000 (but are no more than £20 million), as adjusted for short accounting periods.

iXBRL (eXtensible Business Reporting Language) – an electronic format for business information which 'tags' each item of information electronically making it easier for computer analysis.

SELF TEST QUESTIONS

		Paragraph
1	When is the due date of payment of corporation tax?	2.1
2	When must a company pay its liability in quarterly instalments?	2.2
3	When must a company file its return?	4.3
4	For how long must records be retained?	4.5
5	What is the penalty for filing a return two months late?	4.6

MULTIPLE CHOICE QUESTIONS

1 Roberts plc prepares accounts to 31 March each year and its taxable total profits for the year ended 31 March 2022 are £1,800,000. Roberts plc had taxable total profits for the year ended 31 March 2021 of £920,000.

Which of the following statements is correct with respect to Roberts plc's corporation tax liability for the year ended 31 March 2022?

A The liability is payable on 1 January 2023

B The liability is payable on 31 March 2023

C The liability is payable in 4 equal instalments beginning on 14 October 2021

D The liability is payable in 4 equal instalments beginning on 14 October 2022

2 Smith and Jones Ltd had the following results for the year ended 31 March 2022:

	£
Adjusted trading profits before capital allowances	330,000
Bank interest receivable	9,000
UK dividends received	27,000

The tax written down value on the main pool as at 1 April 2021 was £57,778. There were no additions or disposals of plant and machinery during the year.

What is the corporation tax liability for the year ended 31 March 2022?

A £60,724

B £64,410

C £67,564

D £62,434

For suggested answers, see the 'Answers' section at the end of the book.

PRACTICE QUESTION

DREW PLC

Drew plc prepares accounts to 31 March annually. During the year ended 31 March 2022, the company's tax adjusted trading profit before interest payable was £531,250. Also during the year the company realised a chargeable gain of £1,000 and paid a charitable donation to a national charity of £500.

Bank deposit interest of £2,000 was received during the year, with an opening accrual of £640 and a closing accrual of £890.

Interest payable during the year was as follows:

	£
On a 5 year bank loan to fund purchase machinery	1,000
On an overdraft facility to fund working capital	300
On late paid corporation tax	150

Interest payable on the loan to purchase machinery includes an accrual of £200 for interest payable as at 31 March 2022.

Required:

Calculate the corporation tax liability for the year ended 31 March 2022. **(15 marks)**

For a suggested answer, see the 'Answers' section at the end of the book.

Chapter 23

CORPORATION TAX LOSSES

INTRODUCTION

This chapter deals with the different ways that companies that incur losses can obtain relief. It covers the syllabus area E5.

CONTENTS	LEARNING OUTCOMES
	At the end of this chapter, you should be able to: • explain the loss reliefs available for both trade and non-trade losses • illustrate the use of the loss reliefs in a basic calculation – trade losses – non-trade losses • explain the impact of cessation of trade on trade and non-trade losses • compute corporation tax repayable following a loss relief claim.

1 INTRODUCTION

1.1 LOSS RELIEFS AVAILABLE

This chapter deals primarily with trading losses incurred by a company. However, trading losses are not the only losses that a company can incur.

The rules for property business losses and trading losses arising prior to 1 April 2017 are different from those set out in this chapter and are not examinable.

1.2 CAPITAL LOSSES

Where a company disposes of a capital asset and incurs a loss, this capital loss can only be set off against current chargeable gains or, where none are available, future chargeable gains. A capital loss can never be carried back and relieved against chargeable gains for earlier periods.

Capital losses cannot be set against income.

An examination question may give a company's results in columnar form, and include a capital loss. When transferring these figures across into a computation of total profits, never include the capital loss, unless there are chargeable gains to set it against.

Marks will not be awarded in the examination if capital losses are deducted anywhere other than from chargeable gains.

When a business ceases, any unused capital losses are lost.

1.3 PROPERTY BUSINESS LOSSES

Property business losses are automatically offset (i.e. mandatory, no claim required) against total profits before qualifying charitable donations (QCDs) of the current period.

Any unrelieved property business loss is carried forward and a claim can be made to offset it against future total profits (before QCDs). The claim can specify the amount of the loss to offset; therefore qualifying charitable donations need not be wasted. The claim must be made within two years of the end of the accounting period in which the loss is relieved.

The examining team have stated that if the loss is deducted in the wrong place – for example from property income – then full marks will not be given.

A property business loss can never be carried back to a previous accounting period and when a business ceases, any unused property business losses are lost.

2 CARRY FORWARD OF TRADING LOSSES

2.1 DETAILS OF THE RELIEF

Where a company incurs a trading loss, it may carry the loss forward and set it off against total profits (before QCDs).

A claim must be made to offset the loss in a future accounting period within two years of the end of the accounting period in which the loss is relieved. The claim can be for all or part of the loss carried forward, therefore QCDs need not be wasted.

The loss can be carried forward indefinitely.

Again, no marks will be awarded if brought forward trading losses are deducted from any figure other than total profits.

2.2 COMPUTATION OF THE LOSS

A company's trading loss is computed in the same way as a company's tax adjusted trading profit, i.e. after adding back items such as depreciation and entertaining and after deducting capital allowances.

Example

Rose Ltd has the following results for its first two years to 31 August 2022.

	Year ended	
	31 August 2021	31 August 2022
	£	£
Tax adjusted trading profit/(loss)	(20,000)	18,000
Interest income	6,000	9,000
Capital loss	(2,000)	
Chargeable gains		7,000
Donations to national charity	(1,000)	(1,000)

Calculate the taxable total profits for the two periods, assuming that the trading loss is carried forward and offset in the year ended 31 August 2022.

Show any losses carried forward at 1 September 2022.

Solution

Trading losses carried forward are relieved against total profits (before QCDs) of subsequent accounting periods.

Capital losses can only be set against current or future chargeable gains.

Rose Ltd

Total profits for the two years ended 31 August 2022

	Year ended 31 August 2021	Year ended 31 August 2022
	£	£
Tax adjusted trading profit	0	18,000
Interest income	6,000	9,000
Chargeable gains (£7,000 – £2,000)		5,000
Total profits	6,000	32,000
Less: Loss relief b/f		(20,000)
Less: QCD relief	(1,000)	(1,000)
Taxable total profits	5,000	11,000
Loss carried forward (£20,000 – £20,000)		0

3 CURRENT YEAR AND CARRY BACK RELIEF

3.1 INTRODUCTION

Where a company incurs a trading loss it may claim to set the loss against total profits (before QCDs) of the loss making accounting period. The loss relief is an all or nothing claim, i.e. the amount of the loss relief cannot be specified but the full loss must be utilised or reduce total profits to £Nil. If the loss exceeds the total profits and the company claims current year loss relief, any QCDs paid will be wasted.

Any remaining trading loss may then be carried back and set against total profits (before QCDs) of the 12 months preceding the loss making accounting period.

There is a temporary extension to the period for which losses can be carried back, but this is not covered in this chapter as it is not examinable.

Note that it is not necessary for a company to make a carry back claim. However, if it wishes to do so, it must first relieve the loss against total profits of the current period. The loss carried back cannot be restricted and the loss offset is therefore the lower of the unrelieved loss and the amount of the total profits. Again, if the loss exceeds the profits in the period, any QCDs made will be wasted.

Any loss remaining unrelieved after a claim against total profits has been made is carried forward and relieved against future total profits.

Losses must be dealt with in the order that they arise. Thus, a loss in the year to 31 December 2020 must be relieved before a loss arising in the year to 31 December 2021 can be carried back.

A claim for loss relief against total profits must be made within two years of the end of the loss making accounting period.

3.2 LAYOUT OF COMPUTATION

When dealing with loss relief questions, you should set out your answer using the layout shown in the following pro forma. This pro forma shows the order in which losses should be relieved assuming relief is to be claimed **as soon as possible**.

The loss arises in the y/e 31 March 2021

		y/e 31 March	
	2020	2021	2022
	£	£	£
Tax adjusted trading profit	X	0	X
Other income	X	X	X
Chargeable gains less capital losses	X	X	X
Total profits	X	X	X
Less: Loss relief – CY & PY	(X)[2]	(X)[1]	–
Less: Loss relief b/f	–	–	(X)[3]
	0	0	X
QCD relief	0	0	(X)
Taxable total profits	0	0	X

Corporation tax questions involving losses may seem daunting at first. The key to answering them successfully is to adopt a systematic approach as follows.

1. Prepare the taxable total profits pro forma for the relevant accounting periods. This will enable you to enter headings for loss relief in the appropriate place.
2. The various amounts of income are then entered into the pro forma.
3. Identify the losses. Where there is more than one loss, deal with the earliest loss first, claiming relief in the appropriate place in the pro forma.
4. Remember that normally losses may only be carried back for 12 months, but terminal losses (see later) may be carried back for three years.
5. As the losses are relieved, complete a loss memorandum, detailing how the loss has been relieved.

Example

Clover Ltd has the following results for the accounting periods ended 31 August 2022 and 31 August 2023:

	Year to 31 August 2022	Year to 31 August 2023
	£	£
Tax adjusted trading profit/(loss)	60,000	(49,000)
Property business profits	2,000	1,500
Donations to national charity	1,500	500

Calculate the taxable total profits for both periods, assuming that the loss is offset as soon as possible. Show any losses available to carry forward at 1 September 2023.

Solution

First prepare a taxable total profits computation for both periods. The loss must be set against total profits for the period ended 31 August 2023 before it can be carried back against the total profits of the 12 months to 31 August 2022.

Underneath the taxable total profits computation prepare a loss memorandum, to show how the loss is relieved and any amounts carried forward at 1 September 2023.

Clover Ltd

Taxable total profits computation for the two years ending 31 August 2023

	Year to 31 August 2022	Year to 31 August 2023
	£	£
Tax adjusted trading profit	60,000	0
Property business profits	2,000	1,500
Total profits	62,000	1,500
Less: Loss relief		
Current AP		(1,500)
Carry back 12 months	(47,500)	
	14,500	0
Less: QCD relief	(1,500)	0
Taxable total profits	13,000	0
Unrelieved QCD relief		500

Loss memorandum

	£
Loss for year ended 31 August 2023	49,000
Less: Loss relief: y/e 31 August 2023	(1,500)
y/e 31 August 2022	(47,500)
	0

Note: Current year and carry back loss claims are deducted from total profits before the deduction of qualifying charitable donations and cannot be restricted to preserve relief for the donations. The donations are unrelieved and cannot be carried forward or back.

ACTIVITY 1

Lily Ltd has the following results for the periods to 31 December 2022:

	Year to 31 Dec 2020	Year to 31 Dec 2021	Year to 31 Dec 2022
	£	£	£
Tax adjusted trading profit/ (loss)	18,000	20,000	(100,000)
Donations to national charity	2,000	1,000	2,000

Calculate the taxable total profits for all three periods, assuming that all possible loss relief claims are made.

Show any losses available to carry forward at 1 January 2023.

ACTIVITY 2

Languish Ltd has the following results for the periods to 31 March 2023:

	Year to 31 March 2021	Year to 31 March 2022	Year to 31 March 2023
	£	£	£
Tax adjusted trading profit/ (loss)	50,000	(85,000)	22,500
Interest income	5,000	4,000	500
Donations to national charity	2,000	1,000	3,000

Calculate the taxable total profits for all three periods, assuming that current year and carry back claims are made and that loss carried forward is offset to the extent it is beneficial.

Show any losses available to carry forward at 1 April 2023.

For a suggested answer, see the 'Answers' section at the end of the book.

4 TERMINAL LOSSES

A trading loss arising in the last 12 months of trading may be carried back for three years against total profits on a last in first out basis. A loss arising on the cessation of trade is usually referred to as a 'terminal loss'.

Note that it is only trading losses that can be carried back three years on cessation. The treatment of other types of losses is as outlined in section 1.

As for a normal 12 month carry back claim it is not possible to specify the amount of loss to offset, i.e. it is an all or nothing claim against total profits. This may result in wasted QCDs.

Any losses remaining after the three-year carry back are unrelieved.

Example

Daisy Ltd made up accounts to 31 March each year and ceased to trade on 31 March 2022.

Results have been as follows:

	Year ended			
	31 Mar 2019	31 Mar 2020	31 Mar 2021	31 Mar 2022
	£	£	£	£
Tax adjusted trading profit/(loss)	36,200	25,700	4,200	(80,000)
Property business profits	1,000	800	900	500
Interest income	750	900	840	400
Chargeable gains	3,000	0	2,000	0
Donations to national charity	300	300	300	300

Show the taxable total profits for all years, assuming that the loss is relieved as soon as possible.

Solution

	Year ended			
	31 Mar 2019	31 Mar 2020	31 Mar 2021	31 Mar 2022
	£	£	£	£
Tax adjusted trading profit	36,200	25,700	4,200	0
Property business profits	1,000	800	900	500
Interest income	750	900	840	400
Chargeable gains	3,000	0	2,000	0
Total profits	40,950	27,400	7,940	900
Less: Loss relief	(40,950)	(27,400)	(7,940)	(900)
	0	0	0	0
Less: QCD relief	wasted	wasted	wasted	wasted
Taxable total profits	0	0	0	0
Unrelieved QCD relief	£300	£300	£300	£300

Loss memorandum		£
Loss incurred in y/e 31 March 2022		80,000
Less: Loss relief	y/e 31 March 2022	(900)
	y/e 31 March 2021	(7,940)
	y/e 31 March 2020	(27,400)
	y/e 31 March 2019	(40,950)
Loss remaining unrelieved		2,810

No relief is available for the £300 qualifying charitable donations paid in each of the last four accounting periods, nor is relief available for the remaining loss of £2,810.

ACTIVITY 3

Tulip Ltd has the following results for the four accounting periods ended 31 March 2022:

	Year ended			
	31 Mar 2019	31 Mar 2020	31 Mar 2021	31 Mar 2022
	£	£	£	£
Tax adjusted trading profit/ (loss)	8,000	5,000	19,000	(44,000)
Property business profits	6,000	6,000	6,000	6,000
Interest income	1,500	1,000	1,200	1,400
Chargeable gains	0	2,000	0	1,900
Donations to national charity	500	500	500	500

Tulip Ltd ceased trading on 31 March 2022.

Calculate the taxable total profits for all four years, assuming that losses are relieved as soon as possible.

For a suggested answer, see the 'Answers' section at the end of the book.

5 CORPORATION TAX REPAYABLE FOLLOWING A LOSS RELIEF CLAIM

Where a trading loss is relieved against total profits of the loss making accounting period, or against future total profits, the loss relief will be included at the time of the original corporation tax computation.

Where a trading loss is carried back against total profits of the preceding 12 (or 36) months, the corporation tax liability of the earlier period(s) will usually have been paid. The carry back claim will therefore generate a repayment of corporation tax. In addition, relief for QCDs may have been given in the original corporation tax computation, but may become unrelieved after a loss carry back claim.

The best way to deal with such questions is to:

First – calculate the tax for the previous year without the loss, then

Second – deduct the loss and recalculate the tax due.

The difference between the first and second calculations is the tax repayment due.

ACTIVITY 4

Cosmos Ltd had the following results for the two years ended 31 March 2022:

	Year ended	
	31 Mar 2021	**31 Mar 2022**
	£	£
Trading profit/loss	200,000	(250,000)
Interest income	20,000	20,000
Qualifying charitable donation	(1,000)	(1,000)

Show the original (before loss relief) and revised calculations of the corporation tax payable for the year to 31 March 2021 assuming the loss is relieved as soon as possible. Show the amount of any losses carried forward as at 1 April 2022.

For a suggested answer, see the 'Answers' section at the end of the book.

KEY TERMS

Terminal loss – a loss arising on the cessation of trade.

SELF TEST QUESTIONS

		Paragraph
1	How are capital losses relieved?	1.2
2	How are property business losses relieved?	1.3
3	When a company carries a trading loss forward, what is it set against?	2.1
4	When a company relieves a trading loss in the loss making accounting period, what is the loss relieved against?	3.1
5	Can a company claim to carry back a trading loss if it has not claimed to relieve the loss in the period in which it was incurred?	3.1
6	If a company claims to relieve a trading loss against the current year's profits, must any remaining loss be carried back and relieved against earlier profits?	3.1
7	How far can a terminal loss be carried back?	4

MULTIPLE CHOICE QUESTIONS

1 Bath Ltd has the following results for its first two years of trading:

	Year ended 31 March 2021	Year ended 31 March 2022
	£	£
Adjusted trading profit/(loss)	100,000	(240,000)
Bank interest receivable	4,000	6,000
Donations to national charity	2,000	1,000

Assuming Bath Ltd uses its loss as early as possible, what is the trading loss carried forward to the year ended 31 March 2022?

A £234,000

B £136,000

C £133,000

D £130,000

2 Dartmouth Ltd realises a trading loss of £140,000 in the year ended 31 March 2022. The loss is carried back against total profits for the year ended 31 March 2021.

By what date must a claim in respect of these losses be made?

A 31 March 2022

B 31 March 2023

C 31 March 2024

D 31 March 2025

For suggested answers, see the 'Answers' section at the end of the book.

PRACTICE QUESTIONS

1 SWANEE LTD

Swanee Ltd has the following results for the year ended 31 March 2022:

	£
Trading loss per accounts (Notes (a) – (c))	(96,000)
Interest income – bank deposit interest	3,500
Chargeable gain	14,500
Net loss	(78,000)

Notes:

(a) The trading loss is after charging

	£
Depreciation	10,800
Entertaining customers	1,200

(b) All other expenses are allowable for corporation tax.

(c) The balance on the capital allowances main pool of plant and machinery on 1 April 2021 was £22,222. There were no purchases or sales during the year ended 31 March 2022.

(d) Swanee Ltd has the following results for the year ending 31 March 2021:

	£
Tax adjusted trading profits	40,000
Bank deposit interest	2,000
Chargeable gain	0
	42,000

Required:

(a) Compute the trading loss for the year ended 31 March 2022 **(4 marks)**

(b) Show how the trading loss is relieved assuming it is relieved as soon as possible. **(6 marks)**

(Total: 10 marks)

2 FLOUNDER LTD

Flounder Ltd has the following results up to its date of ceasing to trade.

	Trading profit/(loss) before CAs	Capital allowances	Interest received
	£	£	£
12 m/e 31 December 2017	20,000	3,800	900
12 m/e 31 December 2018	27,000	7,200	1,000
12 m/e 31 December 2019	30,000	5,400	1,200
12 m/e 31 December 2020	13,500	4,050	1,300
12 m/e 31 December 2021	(75,000)	6,600	1,400

Assume that the amount of interest received is also the amount accruing for the period.

Required:

Show how the trading loss is relieved. **(10 marks)**

For suggested answers, see the 'Answers' section at the end of the book.

Chapter 24

VALUE ADDED TAX

INTRODUCTION

VAT can be examined as either a MCQ or as part of a question involving a business, or as a distinct and separate scenario.

This chapter covers syllabus areas F1 – 8.

CONTENTS	LEARNING OUTCOMES
1 The scope of VAT 2 Registration 3 Types of supply 4 Computing VAT liability 5 Accounting for VAT 6 Invoices 7 Records 8 Special accounting schemes 9 Errors 10 Communicating VAT information	By the end of this chapter, you should be able to: • describe the scope of VAT and identify sources of information on VAT • explain the relationship between the organisation and the relevant government agency • recognise the circumstances in which a person must register for VAT • explain the advantages of voluntary VAT registration • explain the circumstances in which a person may request exemption from registration • explain how and when a person can deregister for VAT • explain and contrast the types of supply • explain the detail required on VAT invoices • detail the basic VAT administration requirements

	• describe the annual accounting, cash accounting and flat rate schemes • compute VAT liabilities • make adjustments and declarations for any errors or omissions identified in previous VAT returns • account for VAT • communicate VAT information.

1 THE SCOPE OF VAT

1.1 INTRODUCTION

Value added tax (VAT) is a tax on goods and services consumed in the UK. The basic principle of VAT is that it is a tax borne by the final consumer.

VAT is charged on the supply of goods and services in the UK where the supply is a **taxable supply** by a **taxable person** in the course or furtherance of a business carried on by him. The meaning of these terms is discussed below.

1.2 RATE OF VAT

The standard rate of VAT is 20%.

There are also zero-rated supplies, which are taxable but at a rate of 0% (see section 3.3) and reduced-rated supplies, which are taxable at 5% (see section 3.1).

1.3 TAXABLE PERSON

A taxable person is someone who is, or is required to be, registered for VAT.
A taxable person may be a company, a partnership or an individual.

A taxable person is required to charge and collect VAT from their customers (the **output VAT**). Against this they are allowed to reclaim the tax they have paid to suppliers (the **input VAT**). The end consumer (i.e. the general public) bears the VAT cost, as they are unable to reclaim the VAT.

Example

Transaction	**Net price**	**VAT**	**Trader's VAT account**	**Paid to HMRC**
	£	£	£	£
Producer sells raw materials to wholesaler	100	20	20	20
Wholesaler sells to a manufacturer	200	40	40 – 20	20
Manufacturer sells to retailer	300	60	60 – 40	20
Retailer sells to consumer	500	100	100 – 60	40
				100

The total VAT payable of £100 is ultimately borne by the end consumer, who pays a total of £600 for the finished product (net price £500 plus VAT £100).

Since taxable persons collect output VAT from their customers and recover their input VAT from HMRC, VAT has (in theory) a neutral effect on business costs.

1.4 TAXABLE SUPPLIES

The term supply means 'the passing of possession of goods pursuant to an agreement' and anything else done for consideration.

A supply must meet four conditions before it is within the scope of VAT.

It must be made:

- by a taxable person
- for a consideration
- in the UK
- in the course or furtherance of business.

Consideration generally involves the payment of money for the goods or services received. However, there are two exceptions to the rule requiring consideration:

- business gifts are taxable supplies unless it is either a sample or the gift is valued at £50 or less and does not form part of a series of gifts to the same person, and
- the use of business goods or assets for non-business purposes by the proprietor is classed as a taxable supply.

1.5 SOURCES OF INFORMATION ABOUT VAT

Legislation

The main source of law on VAT is the VAT Act 1994 as amended by annual Finance Acts and other regulations issued by Parliament.

GOV.UK website

HMRC expect taxpayers to be able to answer many of their queries by searching the GOV.UK website at https://www.gov.uk/government/organisations/hm-revenue-customs. Many of the HMRC publications are available here.

VAT guide

HMRC issue guidance called the VAT Guide (VAT Notice 700). This is the main guide to VAT rules and procedures. There are regular amendments to the Guide to keep it up-to-date.

The VAT Guide is available online on the HMRC website. As it is a large document (over 200 pages long), it is broken into sections on the website. It can be searched online.

If you are dealing with accounting for VAT and VAT returns in practice, then you should become familiar with the contents of the VAT Guide in order to be able to refer to it when necessary.

VAT helpline and general enquiries

If a taxpayer cannot find the answer to their queries on the GOV.UK website then the website allows online VAT enquiries or webchats. A telephone helpline is available for urgent enquiries. When you ring, you should have a note of your VAT registration number and postcode.

Taxpayers can also email or write to HMRC with VAT queries.

1.6 HMRC

As mentioned above, HM Revenue and Customs (HMRC) is the government body that is responsible for administering VAT.

VAT offices across the country are responsible for different aspects of VAT administration including registration, collection of outstanding tax and general enquiries. HMRC also carry out visits to taxpayers to check that they are complying with VAT rules.

HMRC powers

HMRC have certain powers that help it administer the tax. These include:

- Inspecting premises
- Examining records
- Making assessments for underpaid tax
- Charging penalties for breaches of VAT rules
- Determining whether certain supplies are liable for VAT.

Visits by VAT officers

VAT officers can visit premises to inspect records and make checks.

HMRC clearance

HMRC will, in limited circumstances, issue its view (a 'clearance') on how it will deal with particular transactions, where there is uncertainty about how the law applies. This clearance is binding on HMRC provided the taxpayer has given all the necessary facts. However, it is not binding on the taxpayer who may choose to ignore it when completing a return, but should draw HMRC's attention to the particular entry in the return. This may lead to a dispute with HMRC that will need to be resolved by the Tax Tribunal.

The advice given in VAT Notice 700 for obtaining guidance from HMRC on VAT matters is:

"To help HMRC to give you the best service, please always give the full facts.

Most enquiries can be dealt with by calling the VAT general enquiries helpline. For detailed questions or case specific transactions you should write to or email HMRC.

The VAT Written Enquiries Team does not provide rulings or opinions. To get HMRC's view of a transaction, apply for a non-statutory clearance. There are a number of conditions to meet before HMRC will issue its view of a transaction."

Communicating with HMRC

If you write to HMRC, the letter should give the contact details and VAT registration number of the business and should set out the nature of the query or information required.

2 REGISTRATION

2.1 COMPULSORY REGISTRATION

Unregistered traders are required to keep a continual eye on their taxable turnover. At the end of every month, they must calculate their taxable turnover for the previous 12 months. A trader is required to register if their taxable turnover (standard and zero-rated) for the previous 12 months exceeds £85,000. Taxable turnover for a period does not include supplies of capital assets (e.g. sale of machine).

A trader liable to registration must notify HMRC not later than **30 days** after the end of the month in which taxable turnover in the previous 12 months exceeds the statutory threshold. In an examination you must be exact – it is 30 days **not** one month.

The date of registration is the first day of the second month after the trader's taxable supplies rose above the threshold, or an earlier agreed date.

Example

Hill Ltd commenced trading on 1 January 2020. Its monthly taxable supplies are:

	2020	**2021**
	£	£
January	4,800	8,400
February	4,900	10,200
March	5,000	10,930
April	5,100	11,000
May	5,140	11,170
June	5,210	11,140
July	5,280	11,260
August	5,350	11,530
September	5,420	11,790
October	5,790	12,860
November	6,050	12,930
December	6,530	13,000

In addition, in October 2020 the company sold a machine for £1,100.

From what date is Hill Ltd liable to register for VAT?

Solution

At the end of April 2021 Hill Ltd's taxable turnover for the past year is:

	£
Value of supplies for registration purposes:	
Supplies to customers	85,300
Supply of machine (disregarded)	–
	85,300

Hill Ltd is thus liable to register, and must notify HMRC by 30 May 2021.

The date of registration is the first day of the second month after the trader's taxable supplies exceeded the threshold, or an earlier agreed date.

The date from which Hill Ltd will be registered for VAT is the first day of the second month after the month in which the threshold is exceeded, i.e. 1 June 2021.

A trader can claim exemption from registration if HMRC is satisfied that his or her taxable turnover in the following year will not exceed £83,000.

Future registration test

The historical turnover test described above is subject to an overriding provision. If at any time a trader who makes taxable supplies has reason to believe that their taxable turnover for a future 30 day period is likely to exceed £85,000, they must notify HMRC no later than the end of that 30 day period and will normally be registered with effect from the **start** of that period. (Note that the supplies in this 30 day period are viewed **in isolation**.)

Thus, if a trader starts a new business with reasonable expectations of high turnover, or an established trader expands his or her business, this provision could well require him to register immediately.

ACTIVITY 1

Cat Ltd signs a lease for new business premises on 1 January 2022 and opens for business on 1 April 2022. The company estimates, from 1 April 2022, that taxable supplies will be in the region of £87,000 per month.

When is Cat Ltd liable to register?

For a suggested answer, see the 'Answers' section at the end of the book.

If a trader makes wholly zero-rated supplies VAT registration is not compulsory, even if they exceed the registration threshold.

2.2 PENALTIES FOR LATE REGISTRATION

If a trader is liable to register but fails to do so, then a standard penalty system applies as for individuals and companies (failure to notify penalty) – See Chapter 16.

There is no penalty applied until tax is unpaid as a result of the failure to notify.

The penalty can range from 0% to 100% of the tax unpaid. HMRC have stated that they will not normally levy a penalty where the trader is less than 12 months late with registration and pays any tax due within the 12 month period.

2.3 VOLUNTARY REGISTRATION

A trader that makes taxable supplies, but is not currently liable to register under the historical or future registration tests, is permitted to voluntarily register for VAT. HMRC will register the trader from the date of the request for voluntary registration, or a mutually agreed earlier date.

Input VAT can be recovered if a person is registered. It is therefore beneficial to voluntarily register where:

- The person makes mainly zero-rated supplies. Input VAT is recovered on purchases and no VAT is charged on zero-rated sales.
- The person makes standard-rated supplies mainly to VAT registered customers. Input VAT is recovered on purchases and although output VAT must be charged on sales, this is recoverable by the customers. It should therefore be possible to charge output VAT on top of the pre-registration selling price, as the actual cost to the customer, after the recovery of VAT, will not change.
- In addition, registration may give the impression of a more substantial business than is otherwise the case.

2.4 DEREGISTRATION

Compulsory

A registered trader ceases to be liable to registration when they cease to make taxable supplies. The trader must notify HMRC of this event within 30 days. They are then deregistered from the date of cessation.

For example, if Jig Ltd closes down its business on 10 January 2021, the company must notify HMRC on or before 9 February 2021 and is then deregistered from 10 January 2021.

Voluntary

A trader may deregister voluntarily at any time if they anticipate that their taxable supplies in the next 12 months will not exceed the deregistration threshold of £83,000.

2.5 EXEMPTION FROM REGISTRATION

A trader making only zero-rated supplies can apply for exemption from registration. However, this means they cannot recover their input tax, and so is only likely if the trader does not want the administrative burden of complying with VAT regulations or they do not have much input tax to recover.

3 TYPES OF SUPPLY

3.1 INTRODUCTION

VAT is charged on taxable supplies.

A taxable supply is a supply of goods or a supply of services, as defined above, which is not an exempt supply.

From this definition, it can be seen that it is necessary to divide supplies of goods and services between exempt supplies on the one hand and taxable supplies on the other in order to determine whether VAT should be charged.

Taxable supplies are mainly charged to tax at one or other of two rates. These are the zero-rate and the standard-rate of 20%.

There is also a reduced-rate of 5%, which applies to items such as domestic heat and power. For your examination you need to be aware of this rate but do not need to know any details.

3.2 STANDARD-RATED SUPPLIES

Any taxable supply that is not charged to tax at the zero-rate is charged to tax at the standard-rate.

The standard-rate of VAT is 20% of the VAT-**exclusive** value of the goods and services supplied. This is equivalent to 1/6 (20/120) of the VAT-**inclusive** value (i.e. consideration) of the goods or services supplied.

The fraction 1/6 is known as the 'VAT fraction'.

Care should be taken in the examination to use the correct calculation to determine the VAT – 20% of a VAT-exclusive figure or 1/6 of a VAT-inclusive figure.

There are some exceptions. A VAT rate of 5% applies to the supply of fuel and power (e.g. electricity) for domestic use, and to the installation of energy saving materials in homes (e.g. solar panels).

3.3 ZERO-RATED SUPPLIES

The zero-rate is a tax rate of nil.

Thus, although no tax is charged on a supply taxed at the zero-rate, it is in all other respects treated as a taxable supply. It is therefore taken into account in determining whether a trader is a taxable person, and input VAT attributable to it is recoverable. In these two respects, it has the opposite effect to an exempt supply.

The zero-rate applies to goods and services generally regarded as necessities. You do not need to have detailed knowledge of those items that are zero-rated. However, it is useful to know the main items.

The most important zero-rated items are briefly described below.

Food: Food used for human consumption unless it is either a supply in the course of catering (e.g. in a restaurant) or is classed as a luxury item, such as alcohol or confectionery.

Books and other printed matter: (e.g. newspapers, books, maps and sheet music). Electronic publications, but not audiobooks.

Construction of dwellings, etc.: This includes new buildings for residential or charitable use, but not the reconstruction of an existing building.

Transport: Transporting passengers by road, rail, sea or air, but excluding smaller vehicles designed to carry less than ten passengers (e.g. not taxis).

Drugs, medicines and appliances: Drugs supplied on prescription and certain appliances and equipment supplied to the disabled.

Charities: Gifts to charities are zero-rated.

Clothing and footwear: Young children's clothing and footwear.

3.4 EXEMPT SUPPLIES

The position of an exempt supply in the scheme of VAT is as follows:

- **no** VAT is charged on it
- it is **not** taken into account in determining whether a trader is a taxable person
- input VAT attributable to the supply cannot normally be recovered.

As for zero rating, you do not need to have detailed knowledge of those items that are exempt. However, it is useful to know the main items. The most important exempted items are briefly described below.

Land: Transfers of land and rights over land, but not all buildings.

Insurance: Insurance premiums.

Finance: Financial services including making loans, hire purchase, share dealing and banking services.

Education: If provided by schools and universities.

Health: The services of registered doctors, dentists, opticians, chemists and hospitals (but not health farms).

Sports: Entry fees to sports competitions used to provide prizes or charged by non-profit making sporting bodies.

You must be careful to distinguish between traders making zero-rated supplies and those making exempt supplies.

	Exempt	**Zero-rated**
Can register for VAT?	No	Yes
Charge output VAT to customers?	No	Yes at 0%
Can recover input tax?	No	Yes

4 COMPUTING VAT LIABILITY

4.1 OUTPUT VAT

Output VAT is the tax charged on supplies made by a taxable person.

Where the consideration for a supply is paid in money, the value of the supply is the trader's VAT-exclusive selling price less the amount of any discount received, i.e. VAT is calculated on the amount that the customer actually pays.

Trade discounts may be offered to a loyal customer or for buying in large quantities. Thus if Ant Ltd's VAT-exclusive selling price is £1,000, and it offers a trade discount of 3.7% to a customer, VAT is charged on £963 (i.e. £1,000 less 3.7% thereof = £37).

Prompt payment discounts may be offered for paying within an agreed timescale. In this case, output VAT is charged on the actual amount received. The supplier may not know, when the invoice is raised, whether the customer will qualify for the discount by paying promptly. The supplier must therefore charge VAT on the invoice on the full price and either:

- issue a credit note if the discount is taken or
- show full details of the terms of the prompt payment discount and include a statement that the customer can only recover input tax based on the amount paid to the supplier. If the discount is taken, the supplier must then adjust their records to account for output tax on the amount received.

4.2 INPUT VAT

Input VAT is the VAT paid by taxable persons on goods and services supplied to them. Input VAT is recoverable from HMRC provided the following conditions are met:

- The claimant was a taxable person when the VAT was incurred. However, there is an exception for pre-registration input VAT (see below).
- The supply was made to the taxable person making the claim.
- The supply is supported by evidence. This will normally be the VAT invoice.
- The claimant uses the goods or services for business purposes. Thus, personal expenses are not eligible for input VAT credit. An apportionment is made where goods and services are acquired partly for business purposes and partly for private purposes.

  However, if fuel for private motoring is provided to the owner or an employee, the input tax is not apportioned. See section 4.4 below.

Although VAT can only normally be recovered where the claimant is a taxable person at the time that the VAT was incurred, **pre-registration input VAT** can be recovered where:

- **goods** were acquired in the **four years** before the date of registration, and are still held at the time of registration
- **services** were acquired in the **six months** before the date of registration.

Capital vs revenue expenditure

Unlike other taxes, there is no distinction between capital and revenue expenditure for VAT.

Provided the assets are used for the purposes of the trade, the related input VAT is recoverable on both capital assets (i.e. purchase of plant and machinery, delivery vans, equipment, etc.) and revenue expenditure.

If capital assets are subsequently sold, output VAT must be charged as a taxable supply of goods.

However, the exception to this rule is the purchase of motor cars (see below).

4.3 IRRECOVERABLE VAT

Input VAT on the following goods and services cannot be recovered:

- **Business entertainment**. This means hospitality of any kind e.g. food, drink, accommodation or recreational facilities. The irrecoverable input VAT cannot be deducted when calculating the trading profit. Note that input VAT on entertaining employees and **overseas** customers is recoverable.

- **Motor cars**. Input VAT is generally not recoverable on motor cars unless they are used 100% for business purposes. In practice, this means that most businesses will be unable to reclaim VAT on cars unless for example, they are a taxi firm, self-drive hire firm, driving school or car leasing company.

Input VAT remains irrecoverable on the purchase of all other business cars where there is any private use. When these cars are subsequently sold output VAT will not be charged.

On the sale of the car where input VAT has been reclaimed, output VAT must be accounted for on the full selling price.

Where a business **leases a motor car** that is used partly for private motoring, then only 50% of the input VAT on the leasing charge is recoverable.

ACTIVITY 2

You are given the following information about business costs for the quarter to 31 December 2021. Complete the table to show the amount of input tax that can be recovered on each of these standard-rated items.

	Item	VAT-inclusive cost £	Input tax recoverable £
1	Car to be used by the managing director 60% for business and 40% privately.	16,600	
2	Delivery van	17,500	
3	Staff party – staff were each allowed to bring a guest. Half the cost is estimated to be for these guests.	630	
4	Entertaining UK customers and suppliers	526	
5	Entertaining overseas customers	150	
6	Car to be used as a pool car (i.e. available for all employees and kept at the business premises)	11,475	
7	Lease costs for the quarter for a car that will be used 80% for business use and 20% privately by the Sales Director	960	

For a suggested answer, see the 'Answers' section at the end of the book.

4.4 FUEL FOR PRIVATE USE

All the input tax suffered on the cost of fuel is recoverable, even where there is some private use by an employee or the business owner.

However, output tax must be charged as follows:

- Where the full cost of the private fuel is reimbursed by the employee/owner, output VAT is payable on the cost of fuel reimbursed.
- If the employee does not reimburse the employer, output VAT is due based on a prescribed fuel scale charge. These rates depend on the CO_2 emissions of the car and will be given in an examination question, if required.

4.5 IMPAIRMENT LOSS RELIEF

When a customer fails to pay, provided there is a good commercial reason (e.g. goods are damaged in transit) the supplier may issue a credit note. Where the failure to pay is due to bankruptcy, insolvency or other reasons, then the supplier may claim impairment loss relief.

The relief is claimed by including the VAT on the impairment loss in the total of input VAT on the VAT return.

Relief is given where:

- a supply of goods and services has been made for consideration in money or by barter
- output VAT has been accounted for and paid by the supplier
- the whole or part of the debt has been written off as irrecoverable in the supplier's books, and
- at least **six months** has elapsed since the time that payment was due.

On a claim by the supplier, impairment loss relief is given for the VAT chargeable on the outstanding amount less any amount subsequently received in respect of that impaired debt.

Claims for impairment loss relief are subject to a four-year time limit.

Customers who do not pay for goods or services within six months of the date that payment was due must repay the input tax that they have claimed.

5 ACCOUNTING FOR VAT

5.1 RETURN PERIODS

Taxable persons account for VAT by reference to VAT periods. Traders who pay VAT normally have VAT periods of three months. Traders who normally receive repayments of VAT can elect for VAT periods of one month (this has the advantage of receiving refunds at an earlier date).

To ensure that the flow of VAT returns is spread evenly over the year, the three-month VAT periods are staggered. HMRC do this by allocating VAT periods according to the class of trade being carried on. However, traders may apply for VAT periods that fit in with their own financial year.

The trader's first VAT period starts on the date of VAT registration and the final VAT period ends on the date that the registration is cancelled.

5.2 THE TIME OF SUPPLY (THE TAX POINT)

VAT is normally accounted for on a quarterly basis, so it is important to know the time of a supply to identify the quarter it falls in. Also, if the standard-rate of VAT were to change or if the classification of a supply altered (e.g. a zero-rated supply became standard-rated), it would be necessary to ascertain whether a supply had been made before or after the change.

The basic tax point is determined as follows:

- goods are treated as supplied when they are collected, delivered or made available to a customer
- services are treated as supplied when they are performed.

The basic tax point is amended in two situations:

1. **Where a tax invoice is issued or a payment is received before the basic tax point**. In these circumstances, the date of issue of the invoice or date of payment is the time when the supply is treated as taking place.

2 **Where a tax invoice is issued within 14 days after the basic tax point.** In these circumstances, provided a tax point has not already arisen under (1) above, the date of issue of the invoice is the time when the supply is treated as taking place. The 14 day period can be extended if HMRC so agree (for example, where the trader invoices on a monthly basis).

Example

Taran is in business selling computers. He delivers computers to a customer on 20 July, sends an invoice dated 31 July and receives payment on 29 August.

The tax point date would normally be 20 July, the delivery date, but as an invoice is raised within 14 days the '14 day rule' applies. The actual tax point will be 31 July.

There are special rules for certain supplies of goods that do not fit naturally into the above rules. In particular:

- **Goods on sale or return**. The time of supply is the earlier of the date when the sale is adopted by the customer or 12 months after the despatch of the goods.

- **Continuous supplies**. Supplies such as electricity (goods) and tax advice (services) do not have a basic tax point. The time of supply is the earlier of a tax invoice being issued and a payment received.

ACTIVITY 3

On 30 October 2021, Oak Ltd ordered a new felling machine, and on 16 November 2021, paid a deposit of £25,000. The machine was despatched to Oak Ltd on 30 November 2021. On 12 December 2021 an invoice was issued to Oak Ltd for the balance due of £75,000. This was paid on 20 December 2021.

What is the tax point for:

(a) the £25,000 deposit?

(b) the balance of £75,000?

For a suggested answer, see the 'Answers' section at the end of the book.

5.3 VAT RETURN

A VAT return shows the total output VAT and total input VAT and the net VAT that is either payable to or repayable from HMRC for the VAT period to which it relates.

All businesses must file their VAT returns and pay any VAT due electronically, within **one month and seven days** of the end of the relevant VAT period.

Under the Government's Making Tax Digital (MTD) project businesses with taxable turnover above the VAT threshold of £85,000 are required to keep VAT records digitally. These digital records of supplies, purchases, output VAT payable and input VAT recoverable are used, in conjunction with MTD compatible software, to automatically compile a digital VAT return. The business is then required to review the VAT return and confirm that it is correct and can be submitted to HMRC.

The information that is required to compile a VAT return, either through MTD or online is as follows:

Pro forma VAT return

Box 1	VAT due in this period on sales and other outputs	
Box 4	VAT reclaimed in the period on purchases and other inputs	
Box 5	Net VAT to be paid to HM Revenue and Customs or reclaimed by you	
Box 6	Total value of sales and all other outputs excluding any VAT	
Box 7	Total value of purchases and all other inputs excluding any VAT	

Notes:

- Box numbers must be stated in the examination in any VAT return questions.
- Previous errors that are being corrected on the current return (see section 9) are included with output VAT in box 1.
- Impairment loss relief is included with input VAT in box 4.
- Zero-rated supplies and purchases are included with standard-rated supplies and purchases in boxes 6 and 7.

Example

Janet is in business and has been registered for VAT for several years. She has been keeping her VAT records digitally since 1 April 2020 and the following information relates to her transactions for the quarter ended 31 March 2022. All items are standard-rated and are stated excluding VAT.

	£
Sales (Note 1)	146,525
Purchases of goods	67,902
Purchase returns	4,560
Purchase of a car (Note)	12,500
Entertaining UK customers	5,140

In addition, Janet has recorded an impairment loss relief claim in respect of a seven month old debt, which she has just written off. The debt is £2,550.

Note 1 – In the quarter Janet offered a prompt payment discount of 2% for payment within 14 days to two of her customers, who made credit purchases of £13,500 each. Only one of the customers paid within the discount period. These credit sales are reflected in the sales figure above, but the discount is not.

Note 2 – The car is to be used by an employee 60% privately.

Show how the above information will be shown in the VAT return that will be prepared and transmitted digitally to HMRC for the quarter ended 31 March 2022. Use the VAT return pro forma shown above.

Solution

Box 1	VAT due in this period on sales and other outputs	29,251
Box 4	VAT reclaimed in the period on purchases and other inputs	(13,178)
Box 5	Net VAT to be paid to HM Revenue and Customs or reclaimed by you	16,073
Box 6	Total value of sales and all other outputs excluding any VAT	146,255
Box 7	Total value of purchases and all other inputs excluding any VAT	80,982

Workings

1	Total value of sales	£
	Total sales per question	146,525
	Discount given: £13,500 × 2%	(270)
		146,255
2	Output VAT	
	£146,255 × 20%	29,251
3	Input VAT	
	Purchases (£67,902 × 20%)	13,580
	Purchase returns (£4,560 × 20%)	(912)
	Impairment loss relief (£2,550 × 20%)	510
		13,178
4	Purchases	
	Of goods	67,902
	Returns	(4,560)
	Car	12,500
	Entertaining	5,140
		80,982

Notes:

Impairment loss relief is added to input VAT recoverable.

No input VAT can be recovered on cars with private use or on UK customer entertaining, however these are still included in the total value of purchases in box 7.

6 INVOICES

VAT registered traders making supplies to other taxable persons are required to issue a document, known as a VAT invoice, not later than 30 days after the time when a taxable supply of goods or services is treated as being made.

The original VAT invoice is sent to the customer and forms their evidence for reclaiming input VAT. A digital copy must be kept by the supplier to support the calculation of output VAT.

A VAT invoice need not be issued if the supplies are exempt, zero-rated or if the customer is not a taxable person. A VAT invoice must contain the following particulars:

- an identifying number
- the date of supply
- the supplier's name, address and VAT registration number
- the customer's name and address
- the type of supply made
- a description that identifies the goods or services supplied
- the value and rate of VAT for each supply
- the total VAT-exclusive amount
- the rate of any cash discount offered
- the amount of VAT payable.

Invoices can be less detailed than normal if the consideration for the supply is £250 or less. This less detailed invoice must show the following information:

- the supplier's name, address and VAT registration number
- the date of supply
- a description of the goods or services supplied
- the consideration for the supply
- the rate of VAT in force at the time of supply.

In the examination, many of the details required on a VAT invoice could be guessed with a little common sense.

7 RECORDS

Records must be kept of all goods and services received and supplied in the course of a business.

Businesses with taxable turnover above the VAT threshold of £85,000 are required to keep their VAT records digitally. The records must be sufficient to allow the VAT return to be completed and to allow HMRC to check the return.

Records must be kept up-to-date and must be preserved for six years.

In practice, the main records that must be kept are as follows:

- Business name, address, VAT registration number and details of any VAT accounting schemes used (see section 8)
- Details of supplies made and received by the business
- Total amount of VAT due on sales and reclaimable on purchases

- For each supply made, the time of supply, value of supply and rate of output VAT charged (at each VAT rate)
- For each supply received, the time of supply, value of supply (including any VAT that will not be reclaimed) and the amount of input VAT that will be reclaimed.

8 SPECIAL ACCOUNTING SCHEMES

8.1 THE CASH ACCOUNTING SCHEME

The cash accounting scheme allows traders to account for VAT on the basis of when payment is received from customers or when payments are made to suppliers. Thus the tax point becomes the time of receipt or payment.

Traders are eligible to use the cash accounting scheme if their taxable turnover does not exceed £1,350,000 p.a. In addition, all VAT returns and VAT payments must be up-to-date.

A major advantage of the cash accounting scheme is that automatic impairment loss relief is available, as output VAT is only accounted for if and when payment is received from the customer.

A trader must leave the scheme if their taxable turnover exceeds £1,600,000 per year.

The cash accounting scheme cannot be used for goods that are invoiced more than six months in advance of the payment date, or where an invoice is issued prior to the supply actually taking place. These measures prevent the creation of an early input VAT claim for the customer, long before the supplier (using the cash accounting scheme) has to account for the output VAT.

8.2 THE ANNUAL ACCOUNTING SCHEME

The annual accounting scheme allows traders to submit a VAT return just once each year. This yearly VAT period will often coincide with the business's financial year.

Traders are eligible to use the annual accounting scheme if their taxable turnover does not exceed £1,350,000 p.a. In addition, the trader must be up-to-date with VAT returns. A trader must leave the scheme if their taxable turnover exceeds £1,600,000 per year.

The annual VAT return must be submitted within two months after the end of the annual VAT period. Nine payments on account are due at the end of months 4 – 12 of the annual VAT period. Any balancing payment is made at the time that the return is submitted. Each payment on account represents 10% of the net VAT liability for the previous year.

Businesses can join the annual accounting scheme as soon as they are registered for VAT. In this case, the payments on account in the first year of registration are based on an estimate of the VAT liability for the current year.

Example

Jump Ltd applied to use the annual accounting scheme from 1 February 2021. The company's net VAT liability for the year ended 31 January 2021 was £3,600. The actual net VAT liability for the year ended 31 January 2022 is £3,821.

What returns and payments must Jump Ltd make for the year ended 31 January 2022?

Solution

Jump Ltd's annual VAT return must be submitted by 31 March 2022. Payments of VAT will be made as follows:

	£
Monthly payments:	
31 May 2021 to 31 January 2022 – 9 at £360 (£3,600 × 10%)	3,240
Final payment due on 31 March 2022 (£3,821 – £3,240)	581
	3,821

8.3 THE FLAT RATE SCHEME

The optional flat rate scheme is aimed at simplifying the way in which small businesses calculate their VAT liability. The scheme can be used if the expected taxable turnover for the next 12 months does not exceed £150,000.

The scheme aims to reduce the administrative burden on small businesses by allowing them to apply a flat rate of VAT to their **total VAT-inclusive turnover** (inclusive of zero-rated and exempt supplies as well as the output VAT charged). The flat rate is a percentage appropriate to their trade sector. In the first year of VAT registration a 1% reduction on the flat rate percentage is given.

A higher flat rate of 16.5% applies to all types of business with limited, or no purchases of goods.

In the FTX examination, the relevant flat rate percentage will always be provided in the question.

Businesses using the scheme still have to issue tax invoices to their VAT registered customers, but they do not have to record the details of invoices issued or purchase invoices received to calculate their VAT.

A business has to leave the scheme if total turnover (including VAT) exceeds £230,000.

> **Example**
>
> Apple Ltd has annual sales of £75,000 all of which are standard-rated and are to the general public. The company incurs standard-rated expenses of £4,500 p.a. These figures are inclusive of VAT.
>
> Calculate Apple Ltd's VAT liability using:
>
> (a) the normal method, and
>
> (b) the flat rate scheme.
>
> Assume that the relevant flat rate percentage for Apple Ltd's trade is 12%, that this is not the first year they have been VAT registered and that the standard-rate of 20% applies throughout.

Solution

(a) Using the normal method Apple Ltd would have the following VAT liability:

		£
Output VAT	£75,000 × 1/6 =	12,500
Input VAT	£4,500 × 1/6 =	(750)
VAT payable		11,750

(b) Using the flat rate scheme, Apple Ltd would have the following VAT liability: £75,000 × 12% = £9,000.

By using the flat rate scheme there is a VAT saving of £2,750 (£11,750 – £9,000). Administration is also simplified. Apple Ltd will not have to issue VAT invoices, as none of its customers are VAT registered.

9 ERRORS

If a trader incurs an error on a VAT return whereby the error is at or less than a de minimis figure – the trader can correct the error on the next VAT return.

If a trader incurs an error that is greater than a de minimis figure, they must voluntarily disclose the error to HMRC.

De minimis figure – higher of:

- £10,000 or
- 1% × turnover (capped at £50,000).

> **Example**
>
> Dexter discovers that in his last VAT return he made an error, which means he has underpaid VAT by £12,400. His VAT-exclusive sales for the current quarter are £142,500.
>
> Can he include this error on his next VAT return or must it be separately disclosed?

Solution

The de minimis is the higher of £10,000 and 1% of turnover, £1,425 (since this is less than £50,000). The error therefore exceeds the de minimis of £10,000. Therefore, it must be separately disclosed.

10 COMMUNICATING VAT INFORMATION

10.1 CHANGES IN THE RATE OF VAT

A change in the rate of VAT has a major effect on the business accounting system including the following:

- Sales invoices need to be produced with the correct rate of VAT.
- Sales prices used in quotes or for pricing invoices must include the correct rate of VAT.
- Retail businesses need to make sure that prices displayed to the public are correct.
- Staff expense claims must reclaim the correct rate of VAT on (for example) mileage expenses.
- The correct input tax reclaim must be made for purchases and expenses. Input VAT claimed should be whatever figure is shown on the invoice for the purchase or expense. However, staff would need to know the details of any rate change so that they can query any actual errors with suppliers.

However, whether or not a change in VAT rate is passed on to the customer is a commercial decision for a business to make. The current prices can be maintained and the cost of a VAT increase (or profit from a VAT decrease) can be absorbed by the business.

The accounting software must be updated to produce sales invoices at the correct rate and to deal with differing rates of VAT on purchase invoices. If the VAT is calculated at the point of sale by the till system, the system must be adjusted to take account of the new rate.

It is important that the change takes place at the correct time. For example, new prices would need to be quoted to customers from the date of change. However, sales invoices must use the rate of VAT relevant to the tax point date and not necessarily the date the invoice is raised.

10.2 INFORMING STAFF

A number of different staff within a business would need to be told about a rate change and its effects.

- IT department staff – to ensure the relevant changes are made to the computerised accounting system.
- Sales ledger staff – to raise or check sales invoices correctly.
- Purchase ledger staff – so that they can check purchase invoices correctly.
- Sales staff – to ensure customers are given correct prices.

- Marketing department staff – so that any new brochures or publicity material is correct.
- Staff generally – to ensure their expense claims are made correctly.

10.3 ADVISING MANAGERS OF THE IMPACT OF VAT PAYMENTS

Once the return has been completed it must be submitted to HMRC and any VAT owing paid over to HMRC. Businesses must submit the return and pay the VAT electronically.

It will be important for the financial accountant, (or other person responsible for managing the business cash), to know when the payment will be made, so that they can make sure that the funds are available in the bank account at the correct time.

Example

To: Financial Accountant

From: Dawn Jones

Date: 17 April 2022

Subject: VAT return

I have completed the VAT return for the quarter ended 31 March 2022. The amount of VAT payable is £23,561.

This will be paid electronically on 7 May 2022.

If you need any further information, please contact me.

Dawn (Junior Accountant)

KEY TERMS

Taxable person – a person who is, or is required to be, registered for VAT.

Output VAT – the VAT charged to customers.

Input VAT – the VAT paid to suppliers.

Supply – the passing of the possession of goods pursuant to an agreement and anything else done for consideration.

Consideration – usually the payment of money for the goods or services received.

Taxable supply – a supply of goods or services that is not an exempt supply.

Standard-rated supply – a supply on which VAT is charged at the rate of 20%.

Zero-rated supply – a taxable supply that is charged at a nil rate of tax.

Exempt supply – a supply on which no VAT is charged. As it is not a taxable supply, it is not possible to recover any input VAT attributable to it.

Irrecoverable VAT – refers to input tax that cannot be reclaimed. It relates to items such as entertaining and motor cars.

Return period – a period for which a trader must account for VAT. It is usually three months in length.

Tax point – the time at which a supply is treated as taking place.

Basic tax point – the date on which services are performed or goods are made available to a customer.

VAT return – shows the total output VAT and total input VAT for the VAT period to which it relates.

Making Tax Digital (MTD) – a government system requiring businesses above the VAT threshold to keep VAT records digitally.

Cash accounting scheme – an optional scheme which allows small traders to account for VAT on the basis of when payments are made to suppliers and when payments are received from customers.

Annual accounting scheme – an optional scheme that allows small traders to complete one VAT return a year.

Flat rate scheme – an optional scheme that allows small traders to calculate VAT by applying a flat rate percentage to their total VAT-inclusive turnover.

Errors – subject to a de minimis level, may be corrected on the next VAT return or voluntarily disclosed.

SELF TEST QUESTIONS

		Paragraph
1	Who is a taxable person for VAT purposes?	1.3
2	What are the four conditions that a supply must meet in order to be within the scope of VAT?	1.4
3	Once a trader has exceeded the VAT registration threshold, within what period must they notify HMRC?	2.1
4	Give three examples of zero-rated supplies.	3.3
5	Give three examples of exempt supplies.	3.4
6	How should a prompt payment discount be dealt with by a suppler?	4.1
7	In what circumstances can pre-registration input VAT be recovered?	4.2
8	Give two examples of items on which the input tax is irrecoverable.	4.3
9	How much time must elapse before relief for an impairment loss can be claimed?	4.5
10	What is the basic tax point for a supply of goods?	5.2
11	In what circumstances is the basic tax point amended?	5.2
12	When must a VAT return be submitted to HMRC?	5.3
13	State four items that must be included on a VAT invoice.	6
14	For how long must records be retained?	7
15	What is the maximum figure of taxable turnover a trader can have if they wish to join the cash accounting scheme?	8.1
16	What is the maximum figure of taxable turnover a trader can have if they wish to join the annual accounting scheme?	8.2
17	How are the payments on account due under the annual accounting scheme calculated?	8.2
18	How are errors on VAT returns dealt with by traders?	9

MULTIPLE CHOICE QUESTIONS

1 Eastwood Ltd sold goods to a customer for £4,400. The goods were made available to the customer on 14 June although the customer paid in full on 10 June. An invoice was issued on 15 June.

The tax point for this supply is:

A 10 June

B 14 June

C 15 June

D 28 June

2 Yannick operates a business. He is registered for VAT and uses the flat rate scheme. In his quarter ended 31 December 2021 he had a VAT-inclusive turnover of £132,000. This is comprised of standard-rated sales of £96,000 and zero-rated sales of £36,000. Yannick's VAT-inclusive standard-rated expenses for the period were £25,000. The flat rate scheme percentage for his type of business is 9.5%.

What is the VAT payable by Yannick for the quarter ended 31 December 2021?

A £7,600

B £9,120

C £11,833

D £12,540

For suggested answers, see the 'Answers' section at the end of the book.

PRACTICE QUESTIONS

1 KITE LTD

Kite Ltd started trading on 1 April 2021, and its turnover is as follows:

	£
One month ended 30 April 2021	29,000
Quarter ended 31 July 2021	57,100
Quarter ended 30 October 2021	59,500
Quarter ended 31 January 2022	65,000

Assume that the amounts accrue evenly.

Required:

Advise Kite Ltd when it is liable to register for VAT, when HMRC should have been notified, and from when the registration is effective. **(6 marks)**

2 CART LTD

Cart Ltd is registered for VAT and its sales are mainly standard-rated but with some zero-rated supplies. The following information relates to the company's VAT return for the quarter ended 31 March 2022:

1 Standard-rated sales amounted to £228,000 and zero-rated sales to £12,000.

2 Standard-rated purchases and expenses amounted to £71,280. This figure includes £960 for entertaining customers.

3 On 15 January 2022 the company wrote off impairment losses of £4,000 and £1,680 in respect of invoices due for payment on 10 August and 5 November 2021 respectively. VAT at 20% was charged on these invoices.

4 On 30 March 2022 the company purchased a motor car at a cost of £32,900 for the use of a director, and machinery at a cost of £42,300. Both these figures are inclusive of VAT. The motor car is used for both business and private mileage.

Unless stated otherwise, all of the above figures are exclusive of VAT.

Required:

Calculate the amount of VAT payable by Cart Ltd for the quarter ended 31 March 2022. **(10 marks)**

For suggested answers, see the 'Answers' section at the end of the book

ANSWERS TO ACTIVITIES, MULTIPLE CHOICE QUESTIONS AND PRACTICE QUESTIONS

CHAPTER 1

MULTIPLE CHOICE QUESTIONS

1 The correct answer is D.

2 The correct answer is C.

3 The correct answer is D.

4 The correct answer is A.

CHAPTER 2

MULTIPLE CHOICE QUESTIONS

1 The correct answer is C. Income from an ISA is exempt.

2 The correct answer is C. All the others are received gross.

3 The correct answer is A. Profit on the sale of shares is a capital profit.

PRACTICE QUESTION

KATE

Income tax computation – 2021/22

	Non-savings income	Savings income	Total
	£	£	£
Employment income	41,970		41,970
Interest (£1,520 + £890)		2,410	2,410
Property income	1,890		1,890
Total income	43,860	2,410	46,270
Less: Interest payments	(2,160)		(2,160)
Net income	41,700	2,410	44,110
Less: PA	(12,570)		(12,570)
Taxable income	29,130	2,410	31,540

CHAPTER 3

ACTIVITY 1

Mariya: Tax adjusted trading profits – year ended 31 December 2021

		£	£
Net profit per accounts		6,868	
Add:	Advertising	0	
	Staff wages (Note 1)	0	
	Rates	0	
	Refurbishing second-hand press (Note 2)	522	
	Redecorating administration offices	0	
	Building extension (Note 2)	1,647	
	Car expenses (£555 × 25%)	139	
	Write off of trade debts	0	
	Increase in allowance for impairment losses	0	
	Recovery of impaired debt written off		0
	Telephone	0	
	Heating and lighting	0	
	Subscription to Printers' association	0	
	Subscription to Chamber of Commerce	0	
	Gifts to customers (calendars) (Note 3)	0	
	Gifts to customers (food hampers) (Note 3)	95	
	Depreciation (£1,428 + £218 + £735)	2,381	
Less:	Profit on sale of premises		1,073
	Interest received		677
	Capital allowances		1,700
		11,652	3,450
		(3,450)	
Adjusted trading profit		8,202	

Notes:

1 The expenditure on the staff Christmas lunch is an allowable deduction for the employer. On the assumption that it does not exceed £150 a head it will not be taxed on the employees as an employment benefit (See Chapter 10).

2 Refurbishment of the second-hand press is disallowed because the expenditure was necessary before the press was brought into use in the business. The extension of the paper store created a new asset and was not the repair of part of an existing one and is therefore disallowed capital expenditure.

3 Gifts to customers are disallowed unless they amount to £50 or less per customer during the year and display a conspicuous advert for the business. Gifts of food (or drink, tobacco or vouchers) are disallowed irrespective of their cost.

MULTIPLE CHOICE QUESTIONS

1 The correct answer is B.

Annual lease cost	£4,800
Disallowable amount (15% × £4,800)	£720

2 The correct answer is D.

D is the correct answer because fines incurred by the owner of the business are not deductible.

Parking fines incurred by employees are generally deductible.

The other costs are deductible.

3 The correct answer is B.

B is the correct answer because interest on late paid tax is a personal liability of the owner of the business rather than the business itself, and is disallowable.

The legal fees in respect of the new shop are capital expenditure and also disallowed.

The write off of trade debts and subscribing to a trade related magazine are both allowable for tax purposes.

4 The correct answer is C.

Repayment interest on a tax repayment received by an individual is not taxable.

All the other items are taxable as trading income.

PRACTICE QUESTION

HOLLY

Tax adjusted trading profits – year ended 30 November 2021

	£	£
Net profit per accounts	12,758	
Wages	0	
NI contributions – staff	0	
Rent ($\frac{1}{3}$ × £2,343)	781	
Business rates	0	
Insurance	0	
Light and heat ($\frac{1}{3}$ × £1,101)	367	
Motor car expenses (25% × £1,380)	345	
Advertising	0	
Holly – speeding fine	150	
Depreciation	2,066	
Impairment losses	0	
Stationery	0	
Printing	0	
Subscriptions – political party	200	
Subscriptions – trade association	0	
Entertaining customers	2,249	
Redecoration of offices	0	
Income tax	12,800	
Professional charges – accountancy	0	
Professional charges – debt collection	0	
Goods for own use (£1,350 × $\frac{140}{100}$)	1,890	
Proceeds for computer		240
Interest on Government securities		1,540
	33,606	1,780
	(1,780)	
Tax adjusted trading profit	31,826	

CHAPTER 4

ACTIVITY 1

GABRIELLE

Capital allowances computation

	£	Main pool £	Allowances £
Year ended 31 March 2022			
Additions:			
Not qualifying for AIA:			
Car		10,000	
Qualifying for AIA:			
Plant and machinery	27,000		
AIA	(27,000)		27,000
Balance to pool		0	
		10,000	
WDA (18% × £10,000)		(1,800)	1,800
TWDV c/f		8,200	
Total allowances			28,800
Year ended 31 March 2023			
WDA (18% × £8,200)		(1,476)	1,476
TWDV c/f		6,724	
Total allowances			1,476

Tax adjusted trading profit

Year ended	**Adjusted profit** £	**Capital allowances** £	**Tax adjusted trading profit** £
31 March 2022	60,500	(28,800)	31,700
31 March 2023	54,000	(1,476)	52,524

ACTIVITY 2

GAVIN

Capital allowances computation

	£	Main pool £	Allowances £
Period ended 31 July 2021			
Additions:			
Not qualifying for AIA:			
Car		11,500	
Qualifying for AIA:			
Plant and machinery	356,666		
AIA (Note)	(333,333)		333,333
Balance to pool		23,333	
		34,833	
WDA (18% × £34,833 × 4/12)		(2,090)	2,090
TWDV c/f		32,743	
Total allowances			335,423
Year ended 31 July 2022			
WDA (18% × £32,743)		(5,894)	5,894
TWDV c/f		26,849	
Total allowances			5,894

Note: For the period ended 31 July 2021 the maximum AIA is proportionately reduced to £333,333 (£1,000,000 × 4/12).

Both the AIA and the WDA are time apportioned to reflect the 4 month period.

Tax adjusted trading profits

	Adjusted trading profit £	Capital allowances £	Tax adjusted trading profit £
Period ended 31 July 2021	395,000	(335,423)	59,577
Year ended 31 July 2022	145,000	(5,894)	139,106

ACTIVITY 3

SANDY

		Main pool	Allowances
Year ended 31 March 2022	£	£	£
TWDV b/f at 1 April 2021		4,900	
Additions qualifying for AIA	20,000		
AIA	(20,000)		20,000
Balance to pool		0	
		4,900	
Less: Disposal (lower of cost and proceeds)		(800)	
		4,100	
WDA (18% × £4,100)		(738)	738
TWDV c/f at 31 March 2022		3,362	
Total allowances			20,738

ACTIVITY 4

GERALD

Capital allowances computation

		Main pool	Private use car 1	Private use car 2	Business use	Allowances
Y/e 31 March 2022	£	£	£	£	%	£
TWDV b/f		11,700	11,600			
Additions:						
No AIA:						
Cars (1 – 50g/km)		9,400				
Cars (> 50g/km)				16,000		
Qualifying for AIA:						
Plant	8,800					
Less: AIA	(8,800)					8,800
Balance to pool		0				
Disposal proceeds			(5,500)			
		21,100	6,100	16,000		
Balancing allowance			(6,100)		× 40%	2,440
WDA (18% × £21,100)		(3,798)				3,798
WDA (6% × £16,000)				(960)	× 55%	528
TWDV c/f		17,302		15,040		
Total allowances						15,566

Note: The full cost of car 2 is added to the private use asset column and the full WDA is deducted. The restriction for private use only happens when the allowance is added to the total allowances column.

Similarly, the disposal proceeds of car 1 are deducted in full from the private use asset column. The private use restriction is only applied to the balancing allowance when it is added to the total allowances column.

ACTIVITY 5

GEMMA

1 **Capital allowances computation – without making a short life asset election**

		Main pool	Allowances
	£	£	£
Year ended 31 March 2022			
TWDV b/f		25,000	
Addition qualifying for AIA			
(£1,005,000 + £15,000)	1,020,000		
Less: AIA (maximum)	(1,000,000)		1,000,000
Balance to pool		20,000	
		45,000	
Less: WDA (18% × £45,000)		(8,100)	8,100
TWDV c/f		36,900	
Total allowances			1,008,100
Year ended 31 March 2023			
WDA (18% × £36,900)		(6,642)	6,642
TWDV c/f		30,258	
Total allowances			6,642
Year ended 31 March 2024			
Disposal proceeds		(1,750)	
		28,508	
WDA (18% × £28,508)		(5,131)	5,131
TWDV c/f		23,377	
Total allowances			5,131

2 **Capital allowance computation – with a short life asset election**

		Main pool	Short life asset	Allowances
	£	£	£	£
Year ended 31 March 2022				
TWDV b/f		25,000		
Addition qualifying for AIA	1,005,000		15,000	
Less: AIA (maximum) (Note)	(1,000,000)			1,000,000
		5,000		
			–	
		30,000	15,000	
Less: WDA (18% × £30,000)		(5,400)		5,400
Less: WDA (18% × £15,000)			(2,700)	2,700
TWDV c/f		24,600	12,300	
Total allowances				1,008,100
Year ended 31 March 2023				
WDA 18% × £24,600/£12,300)		(4,428)	(2,214)	6,642
TWDV c/f		20,172	10,086	
Total allowances				6,642
Year ended 31 March 2024				
Disposal proceeds			(1,750)	
			8,336	
Balancing allowance			(8,336)	8,336
WDA (18% × £20,172)		(3,631)		3,631
TWDV c/f		16,541		
Total allowances				11,967

Note: The AIA is matched against the main pool expenditure first, leaving £5,000 (£1,005,000 – £1,000,000) of expenditure qualifying for WDA in the main pool.

There is no AIA matched against the short life asset, therefore the full £15,000 will qualify for the WDA at 18%, leaving £12,300 expenditure to be carried forward in the short life asset pool.

Advice for Gemma

The total allowances claimed without making the election are £1,019,873 (£1,008,100 + £6,642 + £5,131).

If the election is made, the allowances available for the three years are £1,026,709 (£1,008,100 + £6,642 + £11,967).

Note that the election just accelerates allowances available and only changes the timing of the allowances. However, if not covered by the AIA it is recommended that the short life treatment be taken if it is expected that a balancing allowance will arise on disposal.

ACTIVITY 6

GORDON

Capital allowances computation

		Main pool	Short life asset	Private use car	Business use	Allowances
P/e 31 December 2021	£	£	£	£	%	£
Additions:						
No AIA:						
Car (48g/km) (Note 1)		10,400				
Private use car (> 50g/km)				15,800		
Qualifying for AIA:						
Equipment	277,875		3,250			
Less: AIA (Max) (Note 2)	(250,000)		(0)			250,000
Balance to main pool		27,875				
		38,275	3,250	15,800		
WDA (18% × 3/12)		(1,722)	(146)			1,868
WDA (6% × 3/12)				(237)	× 60%	142
TWDV c/f		36,553	3,104	15,563		
Total allowances						252,010

Notes:

1 Private use by an employee is not relevant. A separate private use asset column is only required where there is private use by the owner of the business.

2 The AIA is applied pro rata for the three month period. The maximum allowance is therefore £250,000 (£1,000,000 × 3/12). The AIA is allocated to the main pool plant and machinery in priority to the short life asset.

MULTIPLE CHOICE QUESTIONS

1 The correct answer is D.

D is the correct answer because the car is not eligible for the AIA, but attracts a WDA at 18%, time apportioned for the short 9 month accounting period and adjusted for private use, as follows:

9 months ended 31 January 2022

	Private use asset	**Bus use (30%)**	**Allowances**
	£		£
Addition – no AIA or FYA	12,500		
WDA (18% × 9/12)	(1,688)	× 30%	506

2 The correct answer is A.

The capital allowances given are as follows:

	Special rate pool
Year ended 30 June 2022	£
TWDV b/f	0
Addition	18,000
WDA at 6%	(1,080)
	16,920
Year ended 30 June 2023	
Disposal proceeds	(17,200)
Balancing charge	(280)

3 The correct answer is C.

4 The correct answer is A.

Structure and buildings allowance = 500,000 × 3% × 9/12 = £11,250

PRACTICE QUESTIONS

1 BORIS

Capital allowances on plant and machinery

		Main pool	Car (B.U. 70%)	B.U. %	Allowances
	£	£	£		£
Year ended 31 March 2022					
TWDV b/f		7,000			
Additions:					
No AIA or FYA:					
Cars (1 – 50g/km)		6,600	6,600		
Qualifying for AIA:					
Lorries	10,500				
Plant	9,000				
	19,500				
AIA	(19,500)				19,500
Balance to pool		0			
Disposal proceeds		(5,500)			
		8,100	6,600		
WDA – 18%		(1,458)			1,458
WDA – 18%			(1,188)	× 70%	832
TWDV c/f		6,642	5,412		
Total allowances					21,790
Year ended 31 March 2023					
TWDV b/f		6,642	5,412		
Additions:					
No AIA or FYA:					
Car (1 – 50g/km)		5,200			
Qualifying for AIA:					
Plant	1,000				
AIA	(1,000)				1,000
Balance to pool		0			
Disposal proceeds		(2,000)	(2,000)		
		9,842	3,412		
Balancing allowance			(3,412)	× 70%	2,388
WDA – 18%		(1,772)			1,772
Additions FYA zero emissions	5,200				
FYA 100%	(5,200)				5,200
		0			
TWDV c/f		8,070	0		
Total allowances					10,360

2 CHARLIE CEASING

		Main pool	Private use car	B.U.	Allowances
	£	£	£	%	£
Year ended 5 August 2021					
TWDV		1,210			
Additions:					
No AIA or FYA:					
Car (1 – 50g/km)			16,100		
Qualifying for AIA:					
Equipment	450				
Van	2,550				
	3,000				
AIA	(3,000)				3,000
		–			
Disposal proceeds (£100 + £250)		(350)			
		860	16,100		
Small pool WDA		(860)			860
WDA (18% × £16,100)			(2,898)	× 80%	2,318
TWDV c/f		0	13,202		
Total allowances					6,178
Year ended 5 August 2022					
Additions:					
No AIA or WDA in year of cessation					
Equipment		1,200			
Disposal proceeds:					
Equipment		(100)			
Plant and equipment		(2,250)			
Van (lower of cost and proceeds)		(2,550)			
Car			(5,455)		
		(3,700)	7,747		
Balancing charge		3,700			(3,700)
Balancing allowance			(7,747)	× 80%	6,198
Total allowances					2,498

Note: Any assets retained by the owner (e.g. the car) must be brought into the computation as a disposal at the lower of cost and market value.

3 CORDELIA

Adjusted profit – year ended 30 June 2022

		£	£
Net profit per accounts		46,107	
Add:	Drawings	5,200	
	Light and heat	0	
	Telephone	0	
	Private motor expenses (£752 × 30%)	226	
	Depreciation	6,940	
	Stationery	0	
	Entertaining	1,670	
	Political donation	200	
	Chamber of Commerce subscription	0	
	Printing	0	
Less:	Sale proceeds of plant		2,000
	Bank interest received		750
	Capital allowances (W)		4,482
		60,343	7,232
		(7,232)	
Tax adjusted trading profit		53,111	

Working – Capital allowances

	Main pool	Private use car (70% B.U.)		Allowances
	£	£		£
TWDV b/f	15,000			
Addition (not qualifying for AIA or FYA)		17,000		
Disposal	(2,000)			
	13,000			
WDA (18%)	(2,340)			2,340
WDA (18%)		(3,060)	× 70%	2,142
TWDV c/f	10,660	13,940		
Total allowances				4,482

CHAPTER 5

ACTIVITY 1

The assessable amounts of trading income are as follows:

		£
2019/20		
(1 July 2019 – 5 April 2020)	(£42,000 × 9/21)	18,000
2020/21 (see note)		
(12 m/e 31 March 2021)	(£42,000 × 12/21)	24,000
2021/22		
(12 m/e 31 March 2022)		27,000

Note: There is an accounting period ending in the second tax year which is more than 12 months long, so the assessment is the 12 months ending on the accounting reference date in that year.

ACTIVITY 2

The assessable amounts of trading income are as follows:

		£
2019/20		
(1 September 2019 – 5 April 2020)	(£30,000 × 7/10)	21,000
2020/21 (see note)		
(1 September 2019 – 31 August 2020)	(£30,000 + (2/12 × £48,000))	38,000
2021/22		
(12 m/e 30 June 2021)		48,000

Note: Because the accounting period ending in the second tax year covers less than 12 months, the assessment is based on the profits of the first 12 months of trading.

ACTIVITY 3

The assessable amounts of trading profit are as follows:

		£
2019/20		
(1 July 2019 – 5 April 2020)	(£55,000 × 9/22)	22,500
2020/21 (see note)		
(6 April 2020 – 5 April 2021)	(£55,000 × 12/22)	30,000
2021/22		
(12 m/e 30 April 2021)	(£55,000 × 12/22)	30,000

Note: Because there is no accounting period ending in the second tax year, the assessment is based on the actual profits for the tax year, i.e. 6 April 2020 to 5 April 2021.

The profits for the year ended 30 April 2022 will not be assessed until tax year 2022/23 under the current year basis.

ACTIVITY 4

The overlap profits are those of the period 1 May 2020 – 5 April 2021, i.e. £55,000 × 11/22 = £27,500.

Note: You can check your answer by comparing the total of the trading income assessments with the figure(s) for adjusted profits:

(Trading income assessments £22,500 + £30,000 + £30,000) – £55,000 adjusted profits = £27,500 overlap profits.

ACTIVITY 5

(a) The assessable amounts of trading income are as follows:

	£
2020/21	
(Year ended 30 April 2020)	40,000
2021/22	
(23 months from 1 May 2020 to 31 March 2022)	
(£42,000 + £38,000)	80,000
Less: Overlap profits	(27,000)
Final assessable amount	53,000

This level of profit will be taxed partly at the higher rate of 40% (see Chapter 14).

(b) If the business ceased on 30 April 2022, the assessments would have been:

	£
2020/21	
(Year to 30 April 2020)	40,000
2021/22	
(Year to 30 April 2021)	42,000
2022/23	
(Period to 30 April 2022)	38,000
Less: Overlap profits	(27,000)
Final assessable amount	11,000

Note: In part (a) the assessment for 2021/22 covers 23 months because there are two accounting periods ending in the same tax year. In part (b) this situation has been avoided by delaying cessation until after 5 April 2022. This minimises the amount of tax payable at the higher rate of 40%. This kind of planning would not be required in the FTX examination but is useful to illustrate how the closing year rules apply.

ACTIVITY 6

(a) **Capital allowances computation**

		Main pool	Car (1) (B.U. 60%)	Car (2) (B.U. 60%)	Allowances
15 m/e 30 June 2022	£	£	£	£	£
Additions:					
No AIA – car			8,000		
Qualifying for AIA					
Equipment (£6,900 + £5,100 + £1,600)	13,600				
AIA (Note)	(13,600)				13,600
		0			
		0	8,000		
WDA (18% × 15/12)			(1,800) × 60%		1,080
TWDV c/f		0	6,200		
Total allowances					14,680
y/e 30 June 2023					
Additions no AIA – car				16,000	
Disposal proceeds			(4,000)		
			2,200		
Balancing allowance			(2,200) × 60%		1,320
WDA (18% × £16,000)				(2,880) × 60%	1,728
TWDV c/f		0		13,120	
Total allowances					3,048

Note: The AIA is proportionately increased for a period exceeding 12 months i.e. here is a maximum of £1,250,000 (£1,000,000 × 15/12).

(b) **Tax adjusted trading profit computation**

	15 m/e 30 June 2022	12 m/e 30 June 2023
	£	£
Adjusted profit (before CAs)	27,360	21,660
Less: CAs	(14,680)	(3,048)
Taxable trading profits	12,680	18,612

Assessments

			£
2021/22	6 April 2021 – 5 April 2022	12/15 × £12,680	10,144
2022/23	12 m/e 30 June 2022	12/15 × £12,680	10,144
2023/24	12 m/e 30 June 2023		18,612

(c) Overlap period = 1 July 2021 – 5 April 2022

9/15 × £12,680 £7,608

MULTIPLE CHOICE QUESTIONS

1 The correct answer is B.

B is the correct answer because the business has ceased in 2021/22 and therefore the basis period is from the end of the basis period taxed in the previous tax year until the date of cessation (i.e. the entire period not yet taxed).

The profits assessed in 2020/21 were the year ended 31 August 2020.

The profits assessable in the period to cessation are then reduced by overlap profits.

(£16,800 + £8,400) – £4,800 = £20,400

2 The correct answer is B.

The profit assessed in the first tax year 2021/22 is the profit arising from 1 June 2021 to 5 April 2022 i.e. 10/12 of £50,000.

3 The correct answer is C.

C is the correct answer because Xosé commenced trading in 2020/21, the assessment for which is calculated as profits between 1 February 2021 and 5 April 2021.

In the second year, 2021/22, there is no set of accounts ending at all, and therefore Xosé will be assessed on the actual profits arising in the tax year i.e. 6 April 2021 to 5 April 2022.

The first set of accounts ends on 30 June 2022, which falls in the tax year 2022/23.

PRACTICE QUESTIONS

1 GRACE (PART ONE)

Capital allowances computation

		Main pool	Car (B.U. 80%)		Allowances
10 months ended 31 October 2022	£	£	£		£
Additions with no AIA			16,000		
Additions with AIA	7,480				
	2,600				
	10,080				
AIA (max £833,333) (Note)	(10,080)				10,080
Balance to main pool		0			
WDA (18% × £16,000 × $^{10}/_{12}$)			(2,400)	× 80%	1,920
TWDV c/f		0	13,600		
Total allowances					12,000

Year ended 31 October 2023			
TWDV b/f	0	13,600	
Disposal – equipment	(560)		
	(560)	13,600	
Balancing charge	560		(560)
WDA at 18%	–	(2,448) × 80%	1,958
TWDV c/f	0	11,152	
Total allowances			1,398

Note: The AIA is proportionately reduced for a short period to £833,333 i.e. £1,000,000 × $\frac{10}{12}$.

2 GRACE (PART TWO)

Tax adjusted trading profit computation

	10 m/e 31 Oct 2022	12 m/e 31 Oct 2023
	£	£
Adjusted profit (pre CA)	31,786	45,954
Capital allowances (as above)	(12,000)	(1,398)
Tax adjusted trading profits	19,786	44,556

		£
2021/22 (1 Jan 2022 – 5 April 2022)	£19,786 × 3/10	5,936
2022/23 (1 Jan 2022 – 31 Dec 2022)	£19,786 + (£44,556 × 2/12)	27,212
2023/24 (1 Nov 2022 – 31 Oct 2023)		44,556

Overlap periods 1 Jan 2022 – 5 April 2022 and 1 Nov 2022 – 31 Dec 2022

Overlap profits	(£19,786 × 3/10) + (£44,556 × 2/12)	13,362

Overlap profits are deducted from the assessable amount for the tax year in which the business ceases.

CHAPTER 6

ACTIVITY 1

	2019/20	**2020/21**	**2021/22**
	£	£	£
Trading income (CYB)	0	3,000	10,000
Less: Loss relief b/f	0	(3,000)	(2,000)
Revised trading income	0	0	8,000

Working – Loss memorandum

	£
Trading loss y/e 31 December 2019 (2019/20)	5,000
Less: Relief in 2020/21	(3,000)
	2,000
Less: Relief in 2021/22	(2,000)
Loss carried forward to 2022/23	0

Note: The loss is set off against the first profits to arise, to the maximum extent possible. Thus £3,000 of the loss is set off in 2020/21 and the remainder carried forward to 2021/22, where it is set off against profits that are more substantial.

ACTIVITY 2

The loss is £6,000 for the tax year 2021/22 (in which Graham's loss making period of account ended). This can be deducted from the total income of 2021/22 and/or 2020/21.

ACTIVITY 3

The loss for the year ended 31 December 2021 arises in the tax year 2021/22, thus claims can be made against total income for 2021/22 and/or 2020/21.

	2020/21	**2021/22**
	£	£
Trading income (year ended 31 December 2020)	31,200	
Trading income (year ended 31 December 2021)		0
Other income	5,000	3,500
Total income	36,200	3,500
Less: Loss relief	(36,200)	0
Net income	0	3,500
Less: PA	0	(3,500)
Taxable income	0	0

Losses of £11,800 (W) remain unrelieved after a claim for 2020/21 has been made against total income. They are available for carry forward.

Working – Loss memorandum

	£
2021/22 – loss of y/e 31 December 2021	48,000
Less: Used in 2020/21	(36,200)
Available for carry forward against future trading profits	11,800

Note: By making a claim for only 2020/21 against total income Adrian obtained relief for his loss as rapidly as possible, without wasting his personal allowance for 2021/22 and will be able to claim a refund of the tax paid in 2020/21. In this way, he has maximised the amount of loss to carry forward to use against future trading profits.

The best course of action would depend on the personal circumstances of each case but, as a general principle, there is clearly no point in claiming relief against total income where the personal allowance already covers all or most of the net income (as here in 2021/22).

The highest tax saving, however, would be if the whole of the £48,000 loss was carried forward against trading profits of 2022/23 as Adrian is a higher rate taxpayer in that tax year. Although, this leads to a time delay in receiving relief for the loss.

MULTIPLE CHOICE QUESTIONS

1 The correct answer is C.

C is the correct answer because the trading loss can be:

- Carried forward and set against future trading profits, but the loss is incurred in 2021/22 and will therefore be available to carry forward to 2022/23.
- The loss can be set against total income (not taxable income) of 2021/22 and/or 2020/21. There is no need for the claim for 2020/21 to be made before that of 2021/22.

2 The correct answer is B.

B is the correct answer because Janice should make a claim to offset the loss in 2020/21, but not in 2021/22 when her income is covered by the personal allowance.

Janice cannot offset the loss against the year ended 30 June 2019, which is taxable in 2019/20.

The loss is utilised as shown below:

	2020/21	2021/22
	£	£
Trading profits	25,000	0
Bank interest	5,000	5,000
Total income	30,000	5,000
Less: Loss claim	(30,000)	–
	0	5,000
Less: PA	Wasted	(5,000)
Taxable income	0	0

	£
Loss arising in 2021/22	(45,000)
Utilised in 2020/21	30,000
Loss available to c/f to 2022/23	(15,000)

3 The correct answer is B.

A is false because there is no limit on time for carrying a loss forward.

C is false because a claim against total income can be made for the year of loss and/or the previous year in any order.

D is false because a loss claimed against total income is deducted before the personal allowance and the offset cannot be restricted to preserve the personal allowance.

PRACTICE QUESTION

THANAYI

Taxable income computations – Thanayi

	2020/21	2021/22
	£	£
Trading income	12,055	0
Employment income	6,600	6,825
Property income	3,520	4,000
Total income	22,175	10,825
Loss relief	(13,375)	0
Net income	8,800	10,825
Less: PA (max)	(8,800)	(10,825)
Taxable income	0	0

Note: Surplus PA is wasted

	£
Loss arising in 2021/22	(13,375)
Utilised in 2020/21	13,375
Loss available to c/f to 2022/23	0

CHAPTER 7

ACTIVITY 1

The partnership profits for the year ended 30 September 2021 are allocated as follows:

	Total	David	Peter
	£	£	£
1 October 2020 to 30 June 2021			
(profits £16,500 × $\frac{9}{12}$ = £12,375)			
Salaries ($\frac{9}{12}$)	3,750	2,250	1,500
Balance (3:2)	8,625	5,175	3,450
	12,375	7,425	4,950
1 July 2021 to 30 September 2021			
(profits £16,500 × $\frac{3}{12}$ = £4,125)			
Salaries ($\frac{3}{12}$)	2,500	1,500	1,000
Balance (2:1)	1,625	1,083	542
	4,125	2,583	1,542
Total allocation	16,500	10,008	6,492

The partners' trading income assessments for 2021/22 are:

David	£10,008
Peter	£6,492

ACTIVITY 2

Profits are allocated between the partners as follows:

	Total	Malika	Khadija	Dania
	£	£	£	£
y/e 30 June 2019	10,000	5,000	5,000	–
y/e 30 June 2020	13,500	6,750	6,750	–
y/e 30 June 2021	18,000	9,000	–	9,000

Malika is assessed as follows, based upon a commencement on 1 July 2018:

			£
2018/19	1 July 2018 to 5 April 2019	£5,000 × $^9/_{12}$	3,750
2019/20	Year ended 30 June 2019		5,000
2020/21	Year ended 30 June 2020		6,750
2021/22	Year ended 30 June 2021		9,000

She has overlap profits of £3,750, which she carries forward until she leaves the partnership.

Khadija is assessed as follows, based upon a commencement on 1 July 2018 and a cessation on 1 July 2020:

			£
2018/19	1 July 2018 to 5 April 2019	£5,000 × $^9/_{12}$	3,750
2019/20	Year ended 30 June 2019		5,000
2020/21	Year ended 30 June 2020	(£6,750 – £3,750)	3,000

Khadija's profits for 2020/21 are reduced by her overlap profits of £3,750.

Dania is treated as commencing on 1 July 2020, and is assessed on her share of the partnership profits as follows:

			£
2020/21	1 July 2020 to 5 April 2021	£9,000 × $^9/_{12}$	6,750
2021/22	Year ended 30 June 2021		9,000

She has overlap profits of £6,750, which she carries forward until she leaves the partnership.

MULTIPLE CHOICE QUESTIONS

1 The correct answer is D.

D is the correct answer because profits are allocated as follows:

	Total	Desmond	Elijah	Fatima
	£	£	£	£
6 April 2021 – 5 January 2022				
£72,000 × 9/12 – split evenly	54,000	27,000	27,000	
6 January 2022 – 5 April 2022				
£72,000 × 3/12 – split 3:2:1	18,000	9,000	6,000	3,000

Fatima's trading income assessment for 2021/22 (her first tax year of trade) is on the actual basis (i.e. 6 January 2022 – 5 April 2022) and is therefore £3,000.

2 The correct answer is D.

D is the correct answer because the partnership continues despite Aaqib's resignation. Only Aaqib has to consider the closing year rules to calculate his trading income assessment for 2021/22, i.e. his final year.

3 The correct answer is C.

	Total	Nick	David
	£	£	£
1 July 2021 to 31 December 2021			
(profits £92,000 × $\frac{6}{12}$ = £46,000)			
Salaries ($\frac{6}{12}$)	7,500	–	7,500
Balance (3:2)	38,500	23,100	15,400
	46,000	23,100	22,900
1 January 2022 to 30 June 2022			
(profits £92,000 × $\frac{6}{12}$ = £46,000)			
Balance (equal shares)	46,000	23,000	23,000
	92,000	46,100	45,900

PRACTICE QUESTION

LILY, MAUD AND NINA

Profits are allocated between the partners as follows:

	Total	Lily	Maud	Nina
	£	£	£	£
Year ended 31 December 2019	88,000	44,000	44,000	–
Year ended 31 December 2020	98,000	49,000	49,000	–
Year ended 31 December 2021	120,000	40,000	40,000	40,000

Lily and Maud are both taxed as follows, based upon a commencement on 1 January 2019:

			£
2018/19	1 January 2019 to 5 April 2019	£44,000 × $\frac{3}{12}$	11,000
2019/20	Y/e 31 December 2019		44,000
2020/21	Y/e 31 December 2020		49,000
2021/22	Y/e 31 December 2021		40,000

They both have overlap profits of £11,000.

Nina is treated as commencing on 1 January 2021 and is taxed on her share of the partnership profits as follows:

			£
2020/21	1 January 2021 to 5 April 2021	£40,000 × $\frac{3}{12}$	10,000
2021/22	Y/e 31 December 2021		40,000

She has overlap profits of £10,000.

CHAPTER 8

ACTIVITY 1

Petra's partnership supplementary pages entries

Your name	Petra Flannery	
Box 2	Books and comics	
Box 6	1 October 2020	
Box 7	30 September 2021	
Box 8	£74,514	(£130,400 × 4/7)
Box 14	£4,000	
Box 16	£74,514	
Box 17	£15,400	
Box 18	£59,114	(£74,514 – £15,400)
Box 20	£59,114	
Box 28	£9,263	(£16,210 × 4/7)

PRACTICE QUESTION

CAPONE

Capone's self-assessment tax return entries

Box 17	£227,452	
Box 19	£35,110	
Box 20	£740	
Box 21	£9,860	(£9,740 + £120)
Box 22	£2,620	
Box 25	£240	
Box 27	£6,030	
Box 28	£375	
Box 29	£4,190	(£3,400 + £750 + £40)
Box 30	£770	
Box 31	£287,387	
Box 34	£14,000	
Box 37	£1,460	
Box 42	£3,750	(£3,350 + £400)
Box 43	£130	
Box 44	£4,190	(£4,150 + £40)
Box 45	£570	(£250 + £20 + £300)
Box 46	£24,100	

CHAPTER 9

ACTIVITY 1

The bonus is treated as received on the earlier of:

(a) the actual payment – 10 April 2021, or

(b) the date Stephen became entitled to the payment – 31 March 2021.

The bonus is therefore treated as received on 31 March 2021 and is taxed in 2020/21.

ACTIVITY 2

As Shaun is a director, the bonus is treated as received on the earliest of:

(a) the actual payment – 10 April 2022

(b) the date Shaun became entitled to the payment – 20 February 2022

(c) the end of a period of account, where earnings are determined before the end of that period – 31 December 2021.

The bonus is therefore treated as received on 31 December 2021 and is taxed in 2021/22.

MULTIPLE CHOICE QUESTIONS

1 The correct answer is D.

2 The correct answer is A.

A is the correct answer because Shakera is taxed on her salary plus the bonus received during the tax year (i.e. the £8,000 bonus received in 2021/22), less the travel costs. The travel costs are deductible as they were incurred necessarily in the performance of the duties of her employment.

3 The correct answer is B.

B is the correct answer because none of the other costs are incurred wholly, exclusively and necessarily for the purpose of employment. However, relief is given for travel between two places of work for the same employer.

PRACTICE QUESTION

SAHAR

Computation of employment income – 2021/22

	£
Salary	103,000
Bonus (Note 1)	8,000
	111,000
Less:	
Payroll giving (5% × £103,000) (Note 2)	(5,150)
Computer skills courses (Note 3)	0
Employment income	105,850

Explanation of treatment

1 Under the receipts basis for directors the bonus is treated as received, and therefore taxed, when it is determined. Thus, the bonus determined in May 2021 is taxable in 2021/22.

2 Payroll giving is an allowable employment income expense.

3 The cost of computer skills courses is not incurred in the performance of her duties. The expense must be incurred in actually carrying out the duties of the job. It is not sufficient for the expense to be relevant to the job.

CHAPTER 10

ACTIVITY 1

			£	£
Basic charge				
Higher of	(i)	annual value	3,000	
	(ii)	rent paid by employer	0	
				3,000
Expensive accommodation charge				
(£200,000 – £75,000) × 2%				2,500
Taxable benefit				5,500

ACTIVITY 2

(a) (i) **Property acquired June 2016**

			£	£
Basic charge				
Higher of	(i)	annual value	1,700	
	(ii)	rent paid by employer	0	
				1,700
Expensive accommodation charge (W1)				
		(£105,000 – £75,000) × 2%		600
				2,300

		£
Restriction for part-year occupation		
	(June 2021 – March 2022) (10/12 × £2,300)	1,917
Less:	Contributions paid by employee (10 months)	(1,000)
Taxable benefit		917

(ii) **Property acquired June 2011**

		£	£
Basic charge			
Higher of (i) annual value		1,700	
(ii) rent paid by employer		0	
			1,700
Expensive accommodation charge (W2)			
	(£165,000 – £75,000) × 2%		1,800
			3,500
Restriction for part-year occupation			
	(10/12 × £3,500)		2,917
Less:	Contributions paid by employee (10 months)		(1,000)
Taxable benefit			1,917

(b) **Cost of providing accommodation**

	Scenario (a)(i)	**Scenario (a)(ii)**
	£	£
Original cost + improvements (W1)	105,000	
Market value (W2)		165,000
Garage extension (September 2021)	10,000	10,000
	115,000	175,000

Workings

(W1) **Cost of providing accommodation – 2021/22**

	£
Cost (June 2016)	90,000
Improvements:	
Conservatory (Feb 2017)	15,000
Redecoration (Aug 2018) **Note 1**	0
Extension (September 2021) **Note 2**	0
Cost of providing accommodation	105,000

Note 1: The redecoration does not represent capital expenditure and therefore is not included in the calculation.

Note 2: Only those improvements up to the start of the tax year are included. As this expenditure does not take place until September 2021, it will not be included in the calculation until 2022/23.

(W2) **Market value**

As Sacha has moved in more than 6 years after the employer acquired the property, the cost is the market value at the date the property was made available to Sacha, i.e. £165,000.

The improvement in February 2017 can be ignored, as this will already be incorporated in the market value in June 2021.

As in scenario (a)(i) the improvements that take place in 2021/22 do not come into the calculation until the following year.

ACTIVITY 3

Taxable benefit

	£
Market value when first made available	1,800
Benefit (20% × £1,800)	360
Less: Employee contributions (12 × £5)	(60)
Taxable benefit 2021/22	300

Note: Where the benefit is provided for only part of a tax year, it is reduced proportionately. This would have applied in 2020/21 since the computer was first made available on 1 January 2021.

ACTIVITY 4

(a) **Taxable benefit**

		£	£
Market value when given to Brian			150
Market value when first made available		600	
Less:	Benefit already assessed 2020/21 £600 × 20% × 10/12	(100)	
			500
Take higher value			500
Less:	Price paid		(100)
Taxable benefit in 2021/22			400

(b) If the asset provided had been a car, Brian would have been assessed on £50 (market value £150 less paid £100).

ACTIVITY 5

	£	£
Car benefit – £24,000 × 33% (W1) × 8/12 (W2)	5,280	
Less: Payment for use (W3)	(800)	
		4,480
Fuel – (£24,600 × 33% × 8/12) (W4)		5,412
Taxable benefit		9,892

Workings

(W1) Percentage based on CO_2 emissions 147g/km rounded down to 145

(145 – 55)/5 = 18%   Percentage = 15% + 18% = 33%.

(W2) Availability – car

Car first made available on 1 August 2021 – thus available for 8 months of 2021/22.

(W3) Payment for use

Payment made for 8 months at £100/month = £800.

(W4) Availability – car fuel

Same proportionate reduction applies as for car benefit (i.e. 8 months available).

Notes:

1 The amounts of Charles' private mileage and business mileage have no impact on the calculations.

2 The car benefit covers the costs of servicing, insurance and maintenance therefore no further benefit arises in respect of these.

3 Charles does not qualify for a reduction in the fuel charge because he does not pay for all fuel used for private motoring.

ACTIVITY 6

(a) **Averaging method**

		£	£
6 April 2021 – 5 April 2022 (official interest rate 2%)			
$\frac{35,000 + 16,000}{2} \times 2\%$			510
Less: Interest paid			
6 Apr 2021 – 31 May 2021	£35,000 × 1.75% × 2/12	102	
1 Jun 2021 – 30 Nov 2021	£31,000 × 1.75% × 6/12	271	
1 Dec 2021 – 5 Apr 2022	£16,000 × 1.75% × 4/12	93	
			(466)
			44

(b) **Precise method**

		£
6 Apr 2021 – 31 May 2021 (2 months)	£35,000 × 2/12 × 2%	117
1 Jun 2021 – 30 Nov 2021 (6 months)	£31,000 × 6/12 × 2%	310
1 Dec 2021 – 5 Apr 2022 (4 months)	£16,000 × 4/12 × 2%	107
		534
Less: Interest paid (as above)		(466)
		68

Daniel will choose to be assessed on the lower figure of £44. HMRC can assess the precise method but are only likely to do so if it gives rise to a materially higher assessment.

MULTIPLE CHOICE QUESTIONS

1 The correct answer is C.

The value of the benefit is 20% of the market value when it was first provided. As the computer was not available until 1 October 2021, the benefit must be time apportioned. It is therefore calculated as follows:

(£4,300 × 20% × 6/12) = £430

2 The correct answer is D.

D is the correct answer because all of the others are taxable benefits for 2021/22.

Childcare facilities run by the employer (who must be responsible for finance and management) at the workplace or at other non-domestic premises are not a taxable benefit. The exemption includes facilities run jointly with other employers or local authorities and similar facilities for older children after school or during school holidays.

3 The correct answer is B.

The list price of £35,000 is reduced by Carla's capital contribution of £1,000. The correct calculation is therefore:

List price (£35,000 – £1,000)	£34,000
Relevant %	
15% + 4% (diesel) + 13% [120 – 55 = 65 /5]	32%
Taxable benefit	£10,880

The 4% diesel supplement applies, as the car does not meet the RDE2 standard.

4 The correct answer is C.

C is the correct answer because Leo's benefit is computed on the higher of:

- the annual value of the property (i.e. £12,750), or
- the rent paid by the employer (i.e. £32,000).

This figure is then reduced by any employee contribution (i.e. the rent paid by Leo).

The benefit is therefore (£32,000 – £12,000) = £20,000.

PRACTICE QUESTION

ADRIANNE

Employment income – 2021/22

	£	£
Salary		50,000
Bonus (Note 1)		10,000
Car (£25,000 × 25%) (Note 2)	6,250	
Less: Contribution (£50 × 12)	(600)	
		5,650
Petrol (£24,600 × 25%)		6,150
Mobile phone (Note 3)		–
Medical insurance (Note 4)		250
Credit card (Note 5)		2,500
Loan (£16,000 × 2%)		320
Suit (£800 × 20%) (Note 6)		160
Less: Subscriptions		(400)
Employment income		74,630

Notes:

1 The bonus is taxed on the date it is received, not when earned.

2 The percentage is 25% (15% + (105 – 55)/5). The payments for the car by ABC Ltd are not relevant – the car benefit includes all costs of running the car except petrol.

3 The benefit of private use of one mobile phone is exempt.

4 The benefit of the medical insurance is the cost to the company.

5 The payment of the annual fee and interest is not a taxable benefit.

6 When an asset is made available to an employee, the benefit is 20% of the market value when first provided.

CHAPTER 11

ACTIVITY 1

Class 1A contributions for 2021/22 are:

	£
Income tax benefits	
Car (£26,000 × 35%)	9,100
Fuel (£24,600 × 35%)	8,610
Medical insurance	720
	18,430
Class 1A NICs at 13.8%	2,543

ACTIVITY 2

BILL

	£
Class 2 NICs	
(£3.05 × 52 weeks)	159
Class 4 NICs	
(£50,270 – £9,568) × 9% (maximum)	3,663
(£51,850 – £50,270) × 2%	32
	3,695

MULTIPLE CHOICE QUESTIONS

1 The correct answer is B.

Class 1 employee contributions: (£31,608 – £9,568) × 12% = £2,645

Benefits are not liable to class 1 contributions. They are liable to class 1A which is payable by the employer.

2 The correct answer is D.

D is the correct answer because Anastasia is liable to pay:

- Class 2 contributions and class 4 contributions in respect of her trading profits and
- Class 1 employer's contributions as a result of employing Patrice.

3 The correct answer is A.

A is the correct answer because class 1 employee contributions are not payable on either exempt benefits (the employer pension contributions) or taxable benefits (i.e. the company car).

No deduction is made for allowable expenses in arriving at the earnings figure.

PRACTICE QUESTIONS

CLARE (1)

Clare will pay:

1 Flat rate class 2 contributions in respect of her self-employed business.

Class 2 NICs

(£3.05 × 52 weeks)	£159

2 Class 4 contributions in respect of her self-employed business based on her tax adjusted trading profits, as they are in excess of £9,568.

Class 4 NICs	£
(£50,270 – £9,568) × 9% (maximum)	3,663
(£54,000 – £50,270) × 2%	75
	3,738

CLARE (2)

1 Class 1 employee contributions are levied on the assistants. However, it is Clare's responsibility to deduct the NICs from the assistants' salaries and pay them to HMRC along with the class 1 employer's contributions on the 19th of each month, (22nd if she pays electronically).

The contributions are based on her assistants' salaries of £15,000 and bonus of £5,000.

In 11 months the assistants receive £1,250 (£15,000 ÷ 12), and in December they receive £6,250 (£1,250 + £5,000).

Note: The monthly limits must be used,
i.e. £797 (£9,568 ÷ 12) and £4,189 (£50,270 ÷ 12).

Employee class 1 NICs (each)	£
(£1,250 – £797) = £453 × 12% × 11 months	598
(£4,189 – £797) = £3,392 × 12% × 1 month	407
(£6,250 – £4,189) = £2,061 × 2% × 1 month	41
	1,046

2 Class 1 employer's contribution, as she is an employer.

The monthly employer's threshold is £737 (£8,840 ÷ 12).

Employer's class 1 NICs (each)	£
(£1,250 – £737) = £513 × 13.8% × 11 months	779
(£6,250 – £737) = £5,513 × 13.8% × 1 months	761
	1540

Total NICs payable **to HMRC in 2021/22**	£	£
Class 1 employee NICs (£1,046 × 2)		2,092
Class 1 employer's NICs (£1,540 × 2)	3,080	
Less: Annual employment allowance (max £4,000)	(3,080)	
		0
		2,092

CLARE (3)

Class 1A contributions based on the taxable employment benefit arising from the provision of a company car to the personal assistant.

Taxable company car benefits for class 1A purposes:

	£
Car benefit	
15% + 4% (diesel) + ((100 – 55)/5) = 28% × £13,500	3,780
Private fuel provided (28% × £24,600)	6,888
Taxable benefits for class 1A	10,668
Employer's class 1A NICs	
(£10,668 × 13.8%)	1,472

Note that the 4% diesel car supplement applies as the question states that the car does not meet the RDE2 standard.

CHAPTER 12

ACTIVITY 1

The rent taxable is the rent **received** during 2021/22. Rent of £1,250 (£5,000 × 3/12) was received on 1 July 2021, 1 October 2021, 1 January 2022 and 1 April 2022. The total rent received during the tax year is therefore £5,000.

Expenses **paid** during 2021/22 are deductible.

	£	£
Rent received		5,000
Expenses paid		
Redecoration	200	
Repairs – not paid until 2022/23	0	
		(200)
Taxable property income for 2021/22		4,800

ACTIVITY 2

	£	£
Rent received (£3,600 × 11/12)		3,300
Expenses		
Replacement furniture relief	1,200	
Insurance paid	480	
Drain clearance	380	
Redecoration (not paid until 2022/23)	0	
Mileage allowance (100 miles × 45p)	45	
		(2,105)
Taxable property income for 2021/22		1,195

The replacement furniture relief is limited to the cost of an equivalent item and cannot include the improvement element.

ACTIVITY 3

	Property 1 £	Property 2 £	Property 3 £
2020/21			
Income	1,200	450	3,150
Less: Expenses	(1,850)	(600)	(2,800)
	(650)	(150)	350
Total			(450)
Property income assessment (loss c/f £450)			0
2021/22			
Income	800	1,750	2,550
Less: Expenses	(900)	(950)	(2,700)
	(100)	800	(150)
Total			550
Less: Property income loss b/f			(450)
Taxable property income			100

ACTIVITY 4

Taxable property income for 2021/22

	£
Premium	10,000
Less: 2% × (21 – 1) × 10,000	(4,000)
	6,000

Note: The remaining £4,000 is subject to capital gains tax; however, this is not examinable.

MULTIPLE CHOICE QUESTIONS

1 The correct answer is A.

A is the correct answer because of the following:

	£
Rent received (1 June 2021 to 1 April 2022 inclusive)	
(£600 × 11 months)	6,600
Less: Repainting windows	(800)
Replacement of kitchenware	(700)
Taxable	5,100

2 The correct answer is D.

	£
Premium received	50,000
Less: 2% × (45 – 1) × £50,000	(44,000)
Premium taxable as rental income	6,000
Rent received in 2021/22	10,000
Taxable property income	16,000

3 The correct answer is B.

An allowable deduction is available for the purchase of new and replacement furniture and fittings in a furnished holiday letting.

£1,800 + £1,600	£3,400

No deduction is available for the brought forward property loss, as it does not relate to furnished holiday lettings.

PRACTICE QUESTION

GITA

Taxable property income for 2021/22

	£	£
Rent due for year ended 5 April 2022		
(£1,600 + £2,040 + £2,060+ £1,820 + ((£350 x 5) + £2,100) + £2,400)		13,770
Less: Expenses		
Insurance (£280 + £220 + £340 + £150 + £150 + £140)	1,280	
Advertising	450	
New dishwasher	0	
Replacement furniture and furnishings - carpets	700	
Roof repairs	10,000	
Computer	500	
Approved mileage allowance (2,000 × 45p)	900	
		(13,830)
Net loss for the year carried forward to offset against future property income		(60)

Notes:

1 On the cash basis rent is taxed when it is received. Therefore, the rent received in advance is taxed in full in the tax year 2021/22 and there is no taxable income for the month's rent that was not received.

2 Capital expenditure on assets provided for use in a residential property (e.g. dishwasher) is not a deductible expense. However, there is tax relief for the replacement of such assets (e.g. replacement carpets) under replacement furniture relief.

3 Although the question refers to a new roof for No 25, it is reasonable to assume that there was one there already and the expenditure is deductible as a repair.

4 Capital expenditure on assets used in running a property business (e.g. computer) is an allowable deduction.

5 Capital expenditure on cars is not an allowable deduction. Gita has chosen to use the approved mileage allowance in respect of her motoring expenses. Alternatively, she could have claimed capital allowances of £432 (£12,000 × 18% × 2000/10,000) in the tax year 2021/22.

6 It is not necessary to consider profits and losses on each property individually.

CHAPTER 13

ACTIVITY 1

	£
NS&I investment account – 31 December 2021	812
Gilts – 1 June and 1 December 2021	400
Bank interest – received 30 September 2021	400
	1,612

MULTIPLE CHOICE QUESTIONS

1 The correct answer is C.

Proceeds from NS&I savings certificates are exempt income and profits on the sale of shares are subject to capital gains tax and not income tax.

2 The correct answer is C.

Glennys is taxed on interest income actually received in the tax year. The ISA interest income is exempt. Her taxable interest income is therefore £900.

PRACTICE QUESTION

Schedule of taxable income

Income	Non-savings income	Savings income	Dividends
	£	£	£
Trading income	25,000		
Building society interest		495	
NS&I account interest		250	
Bank interest		280	
UK dividends (amount received)			6,090
	25,000	1,025	6,090

Dividends from an ISA and interest from NS&I Savings Certificates are exempt.

CHAPTER 14

ACTIVITY 1

TERESA

Income tax computation – 2021/22

		£
Net income		60,290
Less: PA		(12,570)
Taxable income		47,720
Income tax:		
	£	£
Non-savings income – basic rate	37,700 × 20%	7,540
Non-savings income – higher rate	10,020 × 40%	4,008
	47,720	11,548

ACTIVITY 2

DAVE

Income tax computation – 2021/22

Deductions (e.g. personal allowance) should be made firstly from non-savings income, then savings income and finally dividend income.

	Non-savings income	**Savings income**	**Dividend income**	**Total**
	£	£	£	£
Employment income	40,035			40,035
Interest		1,000		1,000
Dividends			10,000	10,000
Total income				51,035
Less: PA	(12,570)			(12,570)
Taxable income	27,465	1,000	10,000	38,465

Income tax:	£	£
On non-savings income – basic rate	27,465 × 20%	5,493
On savings income – nil rate	500 × 0%	0
On savings income – basic rate	500 × 20%	100
On dividend income – nil rate	2,000 × 0%	0
On dividend income – basic rate	7,235 × 7.5%	543
	37,700	
On dividend income – higher rate	765 × 32.5%	249
	38,465	
Income tax liability		6,385

Note: The 0% starting rate of tax on savings income is not applicable here, as non-savings income exceeds £5,000.

Dave is a higher rate taxpayer (i.e. taxable income is greater than £37,700 but less than £150,000) so he is entitled to a savings income nil rate band of £500.

Dave is also entitled to a dividend nil rate band of £2,000.

ACTIVITY 3

BERNARD

Income tax computation – 2021/22

	Non-savings income £	Savings income £	Dividend income £	Total income £
Employment income	50,690			50,690
Dividends			12,000	12,000
Interest		1,200		1,200
Total income				63,890
Less: PA	(12,570)			(12,570)
Taxable income	38,120	1,200	12,000	51,320

Income tax:	£	£
On non-savings income – basic rate	37,700 × 20%	7,540
On non-savings income – higher rate	420 × 40%	168
	38,120	
On savings income – nil rate	500 × 0%	0
On savings income – higher rate	700 × 40%	280
On dividend income – nil rate	2,000 × 0%	0
On dividend income – higher rate	10,000 × 32.5%	
	3,250	
	51,320	
Income tax liability		11,238
Less: PAYE		(7,800)
Income tax payable		3,438

ACTIVITY 4

ARIADNE

Taxable income 2021/22

	£
Employment income	130,000
Total income	130,000
Less: PA (W)	(5,570)
Taxable income	124,430

Working	£	£
Basic PA		12,570
Net income (Note)	130,000	
Less: Gross gift aid donation	(16,000)	
Adjusted net income	114,000	
Less: Income limit	(100,000)	
	14,000	
Reduction of PA – 50% × £14,000		(7,000)
Adjusted PA		5,570

Note: As there are no other sources of income, Ariadne's employment income = total income = net income

ACTIVITY 5

MARWA	Non-savings income	Savings income	Dividend income	Total
	£	£	£	£
Employment income	175,000			175,000
Dividends			36,000	36,000
Interest		2,240		2,240
Total income				213,240
Less: PA (Note)	0			0
Taxable income	175,000	2,240	36,000	213,240

Income tax:	£		£
On non-savings income – basic rate	37,700	× 20%	7,540
On non-savings income – higher rate	112,300	× 40%	44,920
On non-savings income – additional rate	25,000	× 45%	11,250
	175,000		
On savings income – additional rate	2,240	× 45%	1,008
On dividend income – nil rate	2,000	× 0%	0
On dividend income – additional rate	34,000	× 38.1%%	12,954
	213,240		
Income tax liability			77,672
Less: PAYE			(69,670)
Income tax payable			8,002

Note: Marwa is not entitled to any personal allowance as her income exceeds £100,000 by more than twice the personal allowance (i.e. > £125,140).

Marwa is also not entitled to any savings income nil rate band, as she is an additional rate taxpayer (i.e. taxable income exceeds £150,000).

All taxpayers are entitled to the dividend nil rate band of £2,000 regardless of the level of their taxable income.

ACTIVITY 6

Income tax payable – 2021/22

	Non-savings income	Savings income	Total
	£	£	£
Employment income – salary and benefits	47,410		47,410
Building society interest		1,960	1,960
Government stock interest		1,300	1,300
NS&I investment account interest		82	82
Total income	47,410	3,342	50,752
Less: PA	(12,570)		(12,570)
Taxable income	34,840	3,342	38,182

		£
Income tax:	£	£
On non-savings income – basic rate	34,840 × 20%	6,968
On savings income – nil rate	500 × 0%	0
On savings income – basic rate	2,429 × 20%	486
	37,769	
On savings income – higher rate	413 × 40%	165
	38,182	
Income tax liability		7,619
Less: PAYE		(6,932)
Income tax payable		687

Notes:

1 Interest received in an ISA is exempt from tax.

2 Funds from NS&I savings certificates are exempt.

3 Sekou's basic rate band is extended by the grossed up amount of the gift aid payment to £37,769 (£37,700 + [£55 × $\frac{100}{80}$]).

4 Sekou is entitled to a savings income nil rate band of £500, as he is a higher rate taxpayer i.e. taxable income exceeds £37,769 (extended basic rate band).

MULTIPLE CHOICE QUESTIONS

1 The correct answer is B.

B is the correct answer because a taxpayer's net earnings must be reduced by the personal allowance of £12,570 to arrive at taxable income upon which income tax is calculated.

In addition, the calculation of a taxpayer's income tax **liability** is before the deduction of tax deducted via PAYE. The question asked for liability not payable.

The correct figure is arrived at as follows:

	£
Net earnings	51,615
Less: PA	(12,570)
Taxable income	39,045

Income tax:	£
£37,700 × 20%	7,540
£1,345 × 40%	538
Income tax liability	8,078

2 The correct answer is C.

C is the correct answer as shown below:

	£
Dividend income	18,550
Less: PA	(12,570)
Taxable income	5,980
Income tax:	
On dividend income – nil rate (£2,000 × 0%)	0
On dividend income – basic rate (£3,980 × 7.5%)	299
Income tax liability	299

3 The correct answer is B.

False is the correct answer because taxable income is £25,430 (£38,000 – £12,570) which is less than £37,700. The bank interest therefore falls in the basic rate band and will be taxed at 0% on the first £1,000 and then 20% on the remaining £2,000.

4 The correct answer is C

	£
Salary	135,000
Dividend income	25,000
Taxable income	160,000

The remaining higher rate band is £150,000 – £135,000 = £15,000.

The dividends will be taxed as follows

£2,000 × 0%, £13,000 × 32.5% and £10,000 × 38.1%

5 The correct answer is A.

Interest under B is deductible in arriving at tax adjusted trading profits for the business.

Interest under C is not deductible as the shares are not in a close trading company (i.e. controlled generally by five or fewer persons) nor an employee controlled UK resident unquoted company.

Interest under D is not eligible for any tax relief.

6 The correct answer is D.

D is the correct answer as shown below:

	£
Non-savings income	51,650
Less: PA	(12,570)
Taxable income	39,080
£38,325 (W) × 20%	7,665
£755 × 40%	302
Income tax liability	7,967

Working

The basic rate band is extended by the gross gift aid donations:

£37,700 + (£500 × $\frac{100}{80}$) = £38,325.

7 The correct answer is C.

	£	£
Basic PA		12,570
Net income	110,700	
Less: Gross gift aid donation (£2,400 × $^{100}/_{80}$)	(3,000)	
Adjusted net income	107,700	
Less: Income limit	(100,000)	
	7,700	
Reduction of PA – 50% × £7,700		(3,850)
Adjusted PA		8,720

8 The correct answer is B.

Income received by a married couple on an asset held in joint names is automatically split 50:50, unless the couple elect, in which case, the split will be based on the actual ownership of the asset.

PRACTICE QUESTION

JOHN AND FIONA

John – Income tax computation – 2021/22

	Non-savings income	Savings income	Total
	£	£	£
Employment income	51,514		51,514
BSI		2,500	2,500
Bank interest		400	400
Total income	51,514	2,900	54,414
Less: PA	(12,570)		(12,570)
Taxable income	38,944	2,900	41,844

		£
Income tax:	£	
On non-savings income – basic rate	38,124 × 20%	7,625
On non-savings income – higher rate	820 × 40%	328
	38,944	
On savings income – nil rate	500 × 0%	0
On savings income – higher rate	2,400 × 40%	960
	41,844	
Income tax liability		8,913
Less: Income tax paid		
PAYE		(7,100)
Income tax payable		1,813

Note: The basic rate band is extended by gross gift aid: £37,700 + (£339 × $\frac{100}{80}$) = £38,124

John is entitled to a savings income nil rate band of £500 as he is a higher rate taxpayer (i.e. taxable income exceeds the extended nil rate band of £38,124).

Fiona – Income tax computation – 2021/22

	Non-savings income	Savings income	Total
	£	£	£
Employment income	10,340		10,340
BSI		7,500	7,500
Total income	10,340	7,500	17,840
Less: PA	(10,340)	(2,230)	(12,570)
Taxable income	0	5,270	5,270

	£
Income tax:	
On savings income – starting rate (£5,000 × 0%) (Note 1)	0
On savings income – nil rate (£270 × 0%) (Note 2)	0
Income tax liability/payable	0

Note 1: As there is no taxable non-savings income, £5,000 of savings income is taxed at 0% in the starting rate band.

Note 2: As Fiona is a basic rate taxpayer, she is entitled to a savings income nil rate band of £1,000. This covers the remainder of her taxable savings income, therefore it is all taxed at 0%.

CHAPTER 15

ACTIVITY 1

Income tax computation – 2021/22

	£
Employment income	43,000
Less: Occupational pension contribution (8% × £43,000)	(3,440)
	39,560
Property income	15,000
Total income	54,560
Less: PA	(12,570)
Taxable income	41,990

Income tax:

	£	£
On non-savings income	37,700 × 20%	7,540
	4,290 × 40%	1,716
	41,990	
Income tax liability		9,256

Note: Shaun is not taxed on his employer's contributions.

ACTIVITY 2

(a) **Maximum pension premium**

There is no maximum payment; however, tax relief is limited to 100% of earnings, i.e. £60,650.

However, a contribution of £60,650 would exceed the annual allowance of £40,000 – see section 4.1.

(b) **Income tax liability – 2021/22**

	Non-savings income	**Savings income**	**Total income**
	£	£	£
Trading income	60,650		60,650
Savings income		1,500	1,500
Total income	60,650	1,500	62,150
Less: PA	(12,570)		(12,570)
Taxable income	48,080	1,500	49,580

Income tax:	£	£
On non-savings income	47,700 × 20%	9,540
	380 × 40%	152
	48,080	
On savings income	500 × 0%	0
	1,000 × 40%	400
	49,580	
Income tax liability		10,092

Her basic rate band is extended by the gross personal pension contribution (i.e. £37,700 + £10,000 = £47,700)

Daphne is a higher rate taxpayer, as her taxable income exceeds the extended basic rate band, and therefore her savings income nil rate band is £500.

	£
Note: Daphne obtains tax relief of (£10,000 × 40%)	4,000
Basic rate retained by paying net: (£10,000 × 20%)	2,000
Higher rate saving: £10,000 × (40% – 20%)	2,000
	4,000

The actual payment made by Daphne to the pension scheme will be £8,000 (£10,000 × 80%).

MULTIPLE CHOICE QUESTIONS

1 The correct answer is C.

C is the correct answer because Isaiah is entitled to relief on the lower of his gross contributions of £27,500 (£22,000 × 100/80) and the higher of £3,600 or his relevant earnings (£70,000).

Relief is therefore available for £27,500 and as a higher rate taxpayer his basic rate band will be extended by the gross contributions made of £27,500.

2 The correct answer is D.

Contributions paid by an employer into a registered pension scheme are:

- tax deductible in calculating the employer's taxable profits, provided the contributions are paid for the purposes of the trade
- an exempt employment benefit for the employee
- added to the pension contributions paid by the employee to determine whether the annual allowance has been exceeded and an income tax charge levied.

However, the contributions paid by the employer are not deducted in calculating the employee's income tax, only employee's contributions are deducted in this way.

3 The answer is B.

	£	£
Basic PA		12,570
Adjusted net income (£119,500 – £10,000 – £2,400)	107,100	
Less:	(100,000)	
	7,100	
Withdrawal of PA – 50% × £7,100		(3,550)
Adjusted PA		9,020

PRACTICE QUESTIONS

1 STEVE

Income tax computation – 2021/22

	Non-savings income	Savings income	Total income
	£	£	£
Trading income	50,650		50,650
Savings income		10,000	10,000
Total income	50,650	10,000	60,650
Less: PA	(12,570)		(12,570)
Taxable income	38,080	10,000	48,080

Income tax:

		£
On non-savings income	38,080 × 20%	7,616
On savings income	500 × 0%	0
	7,520 × 20%	1,504
	46,100	
On savings income	1,980 × 40%	792
	48,080	
Income tax liability		9,912

Steve paid his personal pension contribution net of basic rate tax. Relief at the higher rate is given by extending the basic rate band by the gross premium (£37,700 + £8,400 = £46,100).

Steve is a higher rate taxpayer, as his taxable income exceeds the extended basic rate band and therefore his savings income nil rate band is £500.

2 Omar

Income tax computation – 2021/22

	Non-savings income £	Savings income £	Total income £
Trading income	39,690		39,690
Building Society interest		2,480	2,480
Gilt interest		12,300	12,300
Total income	39,690	14,780	54,470
Less: PA	(12,570)		(12,570)
Taxable income	27,120	14,780	41,900

Income tax:	£	
On non-savings income	27,120 × 20%	5,424
On savings income	500 × 0%	0
	14,080 × 20%	2,816
	41,700	
On savings income	200 × 40%	80
	41,900	
Income tax liability		8,320

Note: Omar's basic rate band is extended by the gross amount of the personal pension contribution, i.e. £37,700 + £4,000 = £41,700.

CHAPTER 16

ACTIVITY 1

The relevant amount of income tax and class 4 NICs is £8,000 (£7,300 + £700).

Payments on account are due for 2021/22 as follows:

31 January 2022 (£8,000/2)	£4,000
31 July 2022	£4,000

ACTIVITY 2

The balancing payment for 2021/22 is:

	£
Total tax payable	13,849
Less: Payments on account	(8,000)
Balancing payment due 31 January 2023	5,849

Payments on account are due for 2022/23 as follows:

31 January 2023 ((£8,300 + £800)/2)	£4,550
31 July 2023	£4,550

(Remember that you never make payments on account for CGT or class 2 NICs).

ACTIVITY 3

The answer is D.

The duty of confidentiality can be overridden if the client gives authority or if there is a legal, regulatory or professional duty to disclose.

MULTIPLE CHOICE QUESTIONS

1 The correct answer is A.

2 The correct answer is C.

The return for 2021/22 was due on 31 January 2023 and was therefore submitted more than six months late. A fixed penalty of £100 is imposed, plus a further 5% of tax due. As 5% of £470 (£23) is less than the minimum penalty of £300, the minimum will be imposed instead. The total penalties will therefore be £400 (£100 + £300).

3 The correct answer is A.

A is the correct answer because of the following calculation:

£	
2020/21 income tax liability	22,440
Less: PAYE	(2,400)
Income tax payable under self-assessment	20,040
Payment on account for 2021/22 (£20,040 × ½)	10,020

PRACTICE QUESTIONS

1 PAYMENT SCHEDULE

Schedule of payments:

31 January 2022	– payment on account of 2021/22 liability	£1,500 (£3,000/2)
31 July 2022	– payment on account of 2021/22 liability	£1,500 (£3,000/2)
31 January 2023	– balancing payment of 2021/22 liability	£1,632 (£4,632 – £3,000)
31 January 2023	– payment on account of 2022/23 liability	£2,316 (£4,632/2)
31 July 2023	– payment on account of 2022/23 liability	£2,316 (£4,632/2)

2 TAX RETURNS

(i) A paper return must be submitted by 31 October 2022.

(ii) An online return must be submitted by 31 January 2023.

(iii) Hanif can correct any errors on the return up to 31 January 2024.

CHAPTER 17

ACTIVITY 1

		£
Proceeds		20,000
Less:	Cost	(10,000)
	Improvement	(2,100)
Chargeable gain		7,900

No relief is available for the insurance as this is a revenue expense.

ACTIVITY 2

TOMOHARU

2021/22	£
Chargeable gains	12,000
Allowable losses	(8,000)
Net chargeable gains for the year	4,000

Net chargeable gains are covered by the annual exempt amount, therefore taxable gains are £Nil. No losses to carry forward to 2022/23.

2022/23

	£
Chargeable gains	14,900
Allowable losses	(2,000)
Net chargeable gains for the year	12,900
Less: Annual exempt amount	(12,300)
Taxable gains	600

Tomoharu is taxed on gains of £600 in 2022/23.

LIOR

2021/22

	£
Chargeable gains	4,000
Allowable losses	(4,000)
Net chargeable gains	0

Lior is unable to use her 2021/22 annual exempt amount since her gains are all covered by current year losses. She has losses of £3,000 (£7,000 – £4,000) to carry forward to 2022/23.

2022/23

	£
Chargeable gains	13,800
Allowable losses	(1,000)
Net chargeable gains for the year	12,800
Less: Annual exempt amount	(12,300)
	500
Less: Losses brought forward (2021/22)	(500)
Taxable gains	0

Lior used £500 of her losses brought forward, to reduce her taxable gains to £Nil. She still has losses of £2,500 (£3,000 – £500) to carry forward to 2023/24.

HARRY

2021/22

	£
Chargeable gains	5,000
Allowable losses	(5,000)
Net chargeable gains for the year	0

Like Lior, Harry wastes his 2021/22 annual exempt amount as all his 2021/22 gains are covered by current year losses. He has losses of £1,000 (£6,000 – £5,000) to carry forward to 2022/23.

2022/23	£
Chargeable gains	7,000
Allowable losses	(2,000)
Net chargeable gains for the year	5,000
Less: Annual exempt amount	(12,300)
Taxable gains	0

Harry's net chargeable gains for 2022/23 are all covered by his annual exempt amount. His losses brought forward from 2021/22 (£1,000) are thus carried forward to 2023/24 in full.

ACTIVITY 3

	£
Chargeable gains	18,000
Less: Allowable losses	(2,500)
Net chargeable gains for the year	15,500
Less: Annual exempt amount	(12,300)
Taxable gains	3,200

Capital gains tax liability for 2021/22

	£		£
Lower rate: remaining BRB (£37,700 – £36,090)	1,610	× 10%	161
Higher rate	1,590	× 20%	318
Taxable gains	3,200		
Capital gains tax liability			479

ACTIVITY 4

Capital gains tax liability for 2021/22

	Total	Other gains	Residential
	£	£	£
Residential property	15,000		15,000
Antique table	18,000	18,000	
Total gains	33,000	18,000	15,000
Less: AEA	(12,300)	–	(12,300)
Taxable gains	20,700	18,000	2,700
	£		£
Lower rate (other)	10,500	× 10%	1,050
Higher rate (other)	7,500	× 20%	1,500
	18,000		
Higher rate (residential)	2,700	× 28%	756
Taxable gains	20,700		
Capital gains tax liability			3,306

Working – Lisa's unused basic rate is £10,500 (£37,700 – £27,200).

ACTIVITY 5

Carlos Silva's capital gains supplementary pages tax return entries

Box 1	Carlos Silva
Box 3	1
Box 4	£275,000
Box 5	£255,000
Box 6	£20,000
Box 14	1
Box 15	£18,500
Box 16	£15,000
Box 17	£3,500
Box 23	1
Box 24	£10,000
Box 25	£18,000
Box 27	£8,000
Box 45	£3,200 (£20,000 + £3,500 – £8,000 – £12,300 = £3,200)
Box 47	£10,800 (£14,000 – £3,200)

ACTIVITY 6

Stanislav Ltd – Calculation of chargeable gains/allowable losses

		Vase	**Painting**
		£	£
Disposal proceeds		12,000	20,000
Less:	Allowable selling costs		
	(1% auctioneer's fees)	(120)	(200)
Net proceeds		11,880	19,800
Less:	Allowable expenditure		
	Cost of acquisition	(13,000)	(17,000)
Unindexed gain/(loss)		(1,120)	2,800
Less:	Indexation allowance (IA) (**Notes**)	–	(2,800)
Indexed gain/(loss)		(1,120)	–

Notes:

1 There is no IA available in respect of the vase, as the IA cannot increase a loss.

2 The IA on the painting is restricted, as the IA cannot create a loss.

MULTIPLE CHOICE QUESTIONS

1 The correct answer is B.

B is the correct answer because of the following:

	£
Proceeds	174,000
Less: Incidental costs of disposal	(3,480)
	170,520
Less: Cost	(129,600)
Chargeable gain	40,920

Note: The fees of £2,400 were incurred by the seller, not Peter.

2 The correct answer is B.

B is the correct answer, because the loss is utilised as follows:

	2020/21	**2021/22**
	£	£
Chargeable gains	10,000	17,000
Capital losses – CY	(10,000)	(1,900)
	0	15,100
Less: Annual exempt amount	0	(12,300)
	0	2,800
Less: Capital losses b/f	0	(2,800)
Taxable gains	0	0

Loss memo	£
2020/21 loss	(21,000)
Utilised 20/21	10,000
	(11,000)
Utilised 21/22	2,800
Carried forward	(8,200)

3 The correct answer is C.

C is the correct answer because of the following:

	£
Proceeds	330,000
Less: Cost (including incidental costs)	(252,500)
	77,500
Less: Indexation (0.316 × £252,500) (restricted)	(77,500)
Chargeable gain	0

Note: Indexation allowance cannot turn a gain into a loss.

PRACTICE QUESTIONS

1 VALENTINA

(a) **House**

		Gain/(loss)
	£	£
Net sale proceeds	68,350	
Less: Cost	(9,000)	
Less: Enhancement expenditure (garage)	(5,000)	
Chargeable gain	54,350	54,350

(b) **Alfa-Romeo vintage car**

Exempt asset			0
Total chargeable gains			54,350
Less: Annual exempt amount			(12,300)
Net chargeable gains			42,050
Less: Losses b/f			(2,191)
Taxable gain			39,859
Capital gains tax			
(£37,700 – £32,585)	5,115 × 18%		921
	34,744 × 28%		9,728
	39,859		10,649

2 STEEL LTD

		£	Gain/(loss) £
(a)	**House**		
	Net sale proceeds	68,350	
	Less: Cost	(9,000)	
	Less: Enhancement expenditure (garage)	(5,000)	
	Unindexed gain	54,350	
	Less: Indexation (0.607 × £9,000)	(5,463)	
	Chargeable gain	48,887	48,887
(b)	**Alfa Romeo car**		
	Exempt asset		0
	Total chargeable gains		48,887
	Less: Losses b/f		(2,191)
	Net chargeable gains (for inclusion in corporation tax computation)		46,696

Note: Indexation allowance is not available after December 2017

CHAPTER 18

ACTIVITY 1

	£
Disposal proceeds	6,600
Less: Cost	(3,200)
Chargeable gain	3,400

Marginal relief imposes a limit on the gain of:

5/3 × (£6,600 – £6,000) = £1,000.

Therefore, the chargeable gain is £1,000.

ACTIVITY 2

	£
Deemed sale proceeds	6,000
Less: Expenses of sale	(250)
Actual cost	(6,500)
Allowable loss	(750)

MULTIPLE CHOICE QUESTIONS

1 The correct answer is C.

C is the correct answer because the gain is calculated as follows:

	£
Proceeds	60,000
Less: Cost	
$£30{,}000 \times \dfrac{60{,}000}{(60{,}000 + 15{,}000)}$	(24,000)
	36,000
Less: Indexation allowance (until December 2017)	
0.047 × £24,000	(1,128)
Chargeable gain	34,872

2 The correct answer is D.

D is the correct answer because:

- The machine, although a wasting asset, is chargeable as it qualifies for capital allowances.
- The greyhound is a wasting chattel and therefore exempt.
- The painting is a non-wasting chattel and was sold for more than £6,000. The gain will be restricted using the 5/3 rule, however it is still chargeable.
- The land, although bought and sold for less than £6,000 is not movable property and therefore not a chattel.

3 The correct answer is D.

D is the correct answer because there is a disposal. If the proceeds are not used to replace the asset, then a normal gain/loss is computed.

PRACTICE QUESTIONS

1 MILANA

			Gain/(loss)
		£	£
(a)	**Sculpture**		
	Sale proceeds	6,500	
	Less: Cost	(3,900)	
	Chargeable gain	2,600	
	Gain cannot exceed (£6,500 – £6,000) × $\frac{5}{3}$		833
(b)	**One-tenth interest in racehorse**		
	Exempt as a wasting chattel		0
(c)	**Painting**		
	Insurance proceeds	35,000	
	Less: Cost	(11,000)	
	Chargeable gain	24,000	24,000
(d)	**Jade**		
	Sale proceeds	29,000	
	Less: Cost	(12,200)	
	Capital gain	16,800	16,800
	Net chargeable gains		41,633
	Less: Annual exempt amount		(12,300)
	Taxable gains		29,333
	Capital gains tax (£29,333 × 20%)		5,867

2 MAISIE

		£	Gain/(loss) £
(a)	**Icon**		
	Deemed sale proceeds	6,000	
	Less: Cost	(6,300)	
	Allowable loss	(300)	(300)
(b)	**Plot of land**		
	Sale proceeds of 3 hectares	8,000	
	Less: Cost of 3 hectares		
	$£2,000 \times \frac{8,000}{8,000 + 20,000}$	(571)	
	Chargeable gain	7,429	7,429
	Net chargeable gains		7,129
	Less: Annual exempt amount		(12,300)
	Taxable gains		0

CHAPTER 19

ACTIVITY 1

The value of the XYZ plc shares is 240p (½ × (230p + 250p)

ACTIVITY 2

JAPER LTD

The share pool

	No of shares	Unindexed cost £	Indexed cost £
10 October 1990 – purchase	300	600	600
Indexed rise (£600 × 0.529)			317
			917
11 August 2006 – purchase	585	2,160	2,160
	885	2,760	3,077
19 November 2021 – sale			
Indexed rise to December 2017 (£3,077 × 0.396)			1,218
			4,295
Sale of shares	(885)	(2,760)	(4,295)
	0	0	0

	£
Sale proceeds	8,379
Less: Unindexed cost	(2,760)
Unindexed gain	5,619
Less: Indexation allowance (£4,295 – £2,760)	(1,535)
Chargeable gain	4,084

Note: The indexation allowance is not available after December 2017

MULTIPLE CHOICE QUESTIONS

1 The correct answer is B.

B is the correct answer because the share identification rules for individuals match shares in the following priority:

- Shares acquired on the same day as the disposal – not applicable here.
- Shares acquired in the following 30 days

  – 100 shares acquired on 5 January 2022.
- Shares in the share pool

  – 300 of the shares acquired on 6 April 2007 and 14 February 2011.

2 The correct answer is B.

B is the correct answer because the shares are valued as follows:

½ × (260p + 276p) = 268p

PRACTICE QUESTION

GORE AND BLOOD

The disposal of 1,500 shares is matched as follows:

(i) 280 shares acquired on 20 December 2021 (within 30 days after the disposal)

(ii) 1,220 shares from the share pool

	No of shares	Cost £
8 March 2008 purchase	1,000	5,000
7 May 2011 purchase	500	3,050
	1,500	8,050
11 December 2021 sale (1,220/1,500 × £8,050)	(1,220)	(6,547)
Share pool c/f	280	1,503

Gain computations

		£	Gain/(loss) £
(i)	Sale proceeds £10,484 × $\frac{280}{1,500}$	1,957	
	Less: Cost	(2,060)	
	Allowable loss		(103)
(ii)	Sale proceeds £10,484 × $\frac{1,220}{1,500}$	8,527	
	Less: Cost	(6,547)	
	Chargeable gain		1,980
	Total net chargeable gains		1,877

CHAPTER 20

ACTIVITY 1

Chargeable and exempt periods of ownership

		Non-occupation (chargeable months)	Actual/ deemed occupation (exempt months)
1 April 1998 – 30 June 1998	(resident)	–	3
1 July 1998 – 30 Sept 2000	(absent – any reason)	–	27
1 Oct 2000 – 30 Sept 2001	(absent – employed abroad)	–	12
1 Oct 2001 – 31 Jan 2002	(absent – any reason)	–	4
1 Feb 2002 – 30 June 2002	(resident)	–	5
1 July 2002 – 30 April 2021	(absent – see tutorial note)	226	–
1 May 2021 – 1 Feb 2022	(final 9 months)	–	9
		226	60

Total period of ownership (226+60) = 286 months.

Exempt element of gain is thus: 60/286.

Polina's chargeable gain is:

	£
Gain	200,000
Less: PRR relief	
(60/286 × £200,000)	(41,958)
Chargeable gain	158,042

Note: After Polina left her residence to move to Newcastle, she never returned. Therefore she did not meet the condition of actual residence both before and after the period of deemed occupation.

In contrast, the exemption for the final nine months of ownership has no such restriction, and was thus still available.

ACTIVITY 2

Jonas has made a disposal in June 2021 as follows:

	£
Market value of asset	40,000
Less: Cost	(35,000)
Chargeable gain before reliefs	5,000
Less: Gift holdover relief	(5,000)
Chargeable gain	0

Sandra has allowable expenditure to set against a future disposal, calculated as follows:

	£
Market value of asset acquired	40,000
Less: Gift holdover relief	(5,000)
	35,000

MULTIPLE CHOICE QUESTIONS

1 The correct answer is C.

C is the correct answer because the gain on the sale of the original warehouse can be rolled over against the cost of the new warehouse as follows:

	£
Gain on sale of warehouse	290,000
Less: Rollover relief	(255,000)
Chargeable gain = proceeds not reinvested (£550,000–£515,000)	35,000

2 The correct answer is C.

C is the correct answer because Martha's period of occupation includes actual occupations (i.e. two years from 1 January 2010 to 1 January 2012) plus any periods of deemed occupation as follows:

1 April 2021 – 1 January 2022 being the last 9 months of ownership. There is no requirement to reoccupy the property for this period of deemed occupation to apply.

No part of Martha's absence can be a deemed period of occupation as she did not reoccupy the property.

3 The correct answer is A.

A is the correct answer because rollover relief is available for the purchase of qualifying assets purchased within 12 months before and 3 years after the sale of the original factory.

However, property let out to tenants (i.e. not used in Leo's business) does not qualify for rollover relief, nor does movable (rather than fixed) plant and machinery (i.e. the forklift truck).

PRACTICE QUESTIONS

1 HINA

(i)	6 Apr 1999 – 5 Oct 2009	–	actual occupation
(ii)	6 Oct 2009 – 5 Oct 2013	–	deemed occupation (4 years allowed due to location of workplace)
(iii)	6 Oct 2013 – 5 Oct 2016	–	deemed occupation (3 years absence allowed for any reason)
(iv)	6 Oct 2016 – 5 Oct 2020	–	non-occupation – chargeable
(v)	6 Oct 2020 – 6 July 2021	–	deemed occupation (last 9 months – includes one month in which the property was occupied)

2 HOPE

(a) **2021/22**

	£
Disposal of hydraulic lift:	
Net sale proceeds	35,000
Less: Cost	(27,450)
Chargeable gain before reliefs	7,550
Less: Roll-over relief (all proceeds reinvested)	(7,550)
Chargeable gain	0

Note that if this is Hope's only disposal during 2021/22, rollover relief should not be claimed, as the gain will be covered by the annual exempt amount.

(b) The cost of the new land for future capital gains purposes is

	£
Purchase price	60,000
Less: Gain rolled over	(7,550)
Allowable cost	52,450

(c) Since the replacement asset is a depreciating asset, the gain is not rolled over and deducted from the cost of the replacement but instead, is deferred until the earliest of:

1 May 2031 (10th anniversary of the acquisition of the lift)

2 the date of disposal of the lift

3 the date the lift ceases to be used in any of Hope's businesses.

CHAPTER 21

ACTIVITY 1

(a) 12 months from 1 October 2020 to 30 September 2021

(b) 3 months from 1 October 2021 to 31 December 2021.

ACTIVITY 2

Holl Ltd: Taxable total profits for the year ended 31 March 2022

	£
Adjusted trading profit	1,433,000
Less: Capital allowances	(60,000)
Tax adjusted trading profit	1,373,000
Interest income	25,000
Property income	15,000
Total profits	1,413,000
Less: QCD relief	(4,000)
Taxable total profits	1,409,000

ACTIVITY 3

Oak Ltd: Taxable total profits	**Year ended 31 March 2022**	**3 months ended 30 June 2022**
	£	£
Trading profit (W1) (12:3)	1,059,104	264,776
Less: Capital allowance (W2)	0	(255,800)
Tax adjusted trading profit	1,059,104	8,976
Interest income (£20,900/£22,720 × $\frac{3}{12}$)	20,900	5,680
Property income (£10,000 × $\frac{3}{12}$)	0	2,500
Chargeable gain	0	16,000
Total profits	1,080,004	33,156
Less: QCD relief	(3,000)	–
Taxable total profits	1,077,004	33,156

Workings

			£
1	**Adjusted profit per question**		1,383,880
	Less:	Patent royalties	(30,000)
		Loan note interest (£48,000 × $\frac{15}{24}$) (Note)	(30,000)
			1,323,880

2 **Capital allowances**

		£
3 m/e 30 June 2022:	AIA (max) £1,000,000 × 3/12	250,000
	WDA (£350,000 – £250,000) × 18% × $\frac{3}{12}$	4,500
	Super deduction (£1,000 × 130%)	1,300
		255,800

Notes:

1 In the 15 months to 30 June 2022, two payments of loan note interest have been paid. Hence, the £48,000 relates to 24 months and has to be reduced to 15 months by multiplying by 15/24.

2 The property income received relates to the year to 31 March 2023, only 3 months of which falls within this period of account.

MULTIPLE CHOICE QUESTIONS

1 The correct answer is B.

B is the correct answer because the long period of account is divided into two accounting periods, the first for the 12 months ended 31 March 2022 and the second for the remaining 2 months to 31 May 2022.

2 The correct answer is C.

C is the correct answer because for corporation tax purposes, there is no adjustment to capital allowances as a result of private use of assets by employees. The allowances are computed as follows:

3 months ended 31 March 2022	£
Car with high emissions	18,000
WDA at 6% × 3/12	(270)

3 The correct answer is A.

A is the correct answer because of the following calculations:

	£
Adjusted trading profits	56,000
Less: Capital allowances (W)	(18,800)
Tax adjusted trading profits	37,200
Bank interest receivable	3,000
Taxable total profits	40,200

Note: Dividends received are not subject to corporation tax.

Working

		Main pool	**Allowances**
		£	£
TWDV b/f		26,667	
Additions – AIA	14,000		
Less: AIA	(14,000)		14,000
		0	
WDA at 18%		(4,800)	4,800
TWDV c/f		21,867	
Total allowances			18,800

Note: The lorry is second-hand so does not qualify for 130% super deduction, but does qualify for AIA.

PRACTICE QUESTIONS

1 SPRINGVALE LTD

Taxable total profits computation for year ended 31 March 2022

			£
Tax adjusted trading profit (W1)			77,905
Interest income:	Bank deposit interest	359	
	Loan note interest receivable	1,200	
			1,559
Chargeable gain			51,160
Total profits			130,624
Less: QCD relief			(3,800)
Taxable total profits			126,824

Workings

(W1) **Tax adjusted trading profit**

	£	£
Net profit per accounts		43,163
Director's remuneration		0
Depreciation		44,400
Loan note interest payable		0
Entertaining		420
Donation to national charity		3,800
Patent royalty payable		0
Salaries and wages		0
Rent and business rates		0
Audit fee		0
Trade expenses		
Gifts of drinks		320
Loan note interest received	1,200	
Bank deposit interest received	359	
Dividend received	400	
Capital allowances (W2)	12,239	
		(14,198)
Tax adjusted trading profit		77,905

(W2) **Capital allowances**

	£	Main pool £	Special rate pool £	Allowances £
TWDV b/f		15,544		
Additions:				
Not qualifying for AIA:				
Car			16,250	
Qualifying for super deduction				
Lathe (1,200 × 130%)	1,560			
Plant (2,000 × 130%)	2,600			
Plant (3,520 × 130%)	4,576			
	8,736			
Super deduction	(8,736)			8,736
	0			
Disposal proceeds		(1,500)		
		14,044	16,250	
WDA × 18%/6%		(2,528)	(975)	3,503
TWDV c/f		11,516	15,275	
Total allowances				12,239

Notes:

1 The private use of a car has no effect on capital allowances. The sales director will be taxed on the private use as an employment benefit.

2 The dividend received is not liable to corporation tax.

3 Interest paid is allowed on an accruals basis as a trading expense (as the loan has a trading purpose). The legal fees in connection with the issue of the loan note are also an allowable trading expense as the loan note has a trading purpose.

2 SUPERSCOFF PLC

Corporation tax computation: 12 months ended 31 March 2022

	£
Tax adjusted trading profit (W1)	1,241,832
Interest income – bank deposit interest	1,200
Property business profits (W2)	3,710
Chargeable gain	798
Total profits	1,247,540
Less: QCD relief	(500)
Taxable total profits	1,247,040

Workings

(W1) Tax adjusted trading profit

		£	£
Net profit per accounts			1,191,040
Add: Salaries and wages			0
Rates, light and heat			0
Travelling expenses			0
Entertaining customers			4,750
Advertising			0
Depreciation			27,800
Director's remuneration			0
General expenses:	Trade subscription		0
	Donation to Oxfam		500
	Fine		250
Loan note interest paid			0
Dividend paid			31,950
			1,256,290
Less: Bank deposit interest		1,200	
Dividends received		6,000	
Rent received		1,460	
Profit on investments		798	
			(9,458)
			1,246,832
Less: Capital allowances			(5,000)
Trading profit			1,241,832

(W2) Property business profits

	£
Rent (on accruals basis)	4,000
Less: Letting expenses	(250)
Agent's fee	(40)
Property business profits	3,710

Note: The cost of installing a new shop front is a capital expense and so is not deductible.

3 AMOS LTD

Capital allowances

	AIA	FYA	Main pool	Special rate pool	Allowances
	£	£	£	£	£
TWDV b/f			11,400	6,750	
Additions:					
No AIA/FYA:					
Car				22,500	
AIA and FYA:					
Thermal insulation	1,800,000				
AIA (max)	(1,000,000)				1,000,000
		800,000			
Disposal proceeds (lower than cost)			(1,200)	(6,350)	
			10,200	22,900	
WDA × 18%			(1,836)		1,836
WDA × 6%				(1,374)	1,374
FYA at 50%		(400,000)			400,000
				400,000	
TWDV c/f			8,364	421,526	
					1,403,210

CHAPTER 22

ACTIVITY 1

	£
Oboe Ltd	
Taxable total profits	2,100,000
FY2020/FY2021	
Corporation tax liability (£2,100,000 × 19%)	399,000

ACTIVITY 2

	£
Tax adjusted trading profit	1,480,000
Chargeable gain	80,000
Taxable total profits (TTP)	1,560,000
Corporation tax on taxable total profits £1,560,000 × 19%	296,400

Ash Ltd's profits (i.e. TTP) exceed £1,500,000 and the company is therefore a large company for tax payment purposes. Assuming that profits also exceeded the threshold in the previous accounting period then Ash Ltd must pay tax by instalments for the year ended 31 March 2022.

Ash Ltd must pay instalments of £74,100 (£296,400 ÷ 4) on 14 October 2021, 14 January 2022, 14 April 2022 and 14 July 2022.

ACTIVITY 3

Clent Ltd's corporation tax return entries

Box 330	2021
Box 335	£370,160
Box 340	19%
Box 345	£70,330
Box 430	£70,330
Box 440	£70,330

MULTIPLE CHOICE QUESTIONS

1 The correct answer is A.

Roberts plc is large (i.e. has profits > £1,500,000) for the year ended 31 March 2022. Therefore, instalments payments would normally be expected.

However, Roberts plc was not large for the previous accounting period and therefore (given its profits do not exceed £10m) will not have to pay instalments for the year ended 31 March 2022.

Roberts plc's corporation tax liability is payable by 9 months and 1 day after the end of the accounting period, i.e. by 1 January 2023.

2 The correct answer is D.

D is the correct answer because the corporation tax liability is computed as follows:

Year ended 31 March 2022	£
Tax adjusted trading profits	330,000
Less: CAs (£57,778 × 18%)	(10,400)
Trading profit	319,600
Interest income	9,000
Taxable total profits	328,600
Corporation tax (£328,600 × 19%)	62,434

Note: Dividends received are not taxable income for a company.

PRACTICE QUESTION

DREW PLC

Corporation tax computation – year ended 31 March 2022

	£
Tax adjusted trading profit before interest payable	531,250
Less: Interest payable on trade related loans (£1,000 + £300)	(1,300)
Trading profit	529,950
Interest income (W)	2,100
Chargeable gain	1,000
Total profits	533,050
Less: QCD	(500)
Taxable total profits	532,550
CT liability (£532,550 × 19%)	101,184

Working

Interest income

	£
Bank deposit interest receivable (£2,000 – £640 + £890)	2,250
Less: Non-trade related interest on late paid corporation tax	(150)
Interest income	2,100

CHAPTER 23

ACTIVITY 1

Prepare taxable total profits computations for all three periods. The loss may be carried back against total profits of the 12 months before the year to 31 December 2022 but no earlier. Hence, no loss can be offset against profits of the year ended 31 December 2020.

Underneath the taxable total profits computation prepare a loss memorandum, showing how the loss has been relieved, and any loss remaining carried forward.

This loss memorandum is essential in an examination question, as it shows the reasoning behind the reliefs claimed.

Lily Ltd:

Taxable total profits computation for the three years ending 31 December 2022

	Year to 31 Dec 2020	**Year to 31 Dec 2021**	**Year to 31 Dec 2022**
	£	£	£
Tax adjusted trading profit	18,000	20,000	0
Less: Loss relief – PY	0	(20,000)	0
Total profits after loss relief	18,000	0	0
Less: QCD relief	(2,000)	0	0
Taxable total profits	16,000	0	0
Unrelieved QCD relief		1,000	2,000

Loss memorandum	£
Loss for y/e 31 December 2022	100,000
Less: Loss relief:	
y/e 31 December 2021	(20,000)
Loss available to carry forward	80,000

ACTIVITY 2

Remember that current year and carry back claims are all or nothing claims against total profits (before QCDs). Contrast this with a claim to offset carried forward losses against total profits (before QCDs), where the amount of the claim can be specified, so that it could be restricted to protect relief for QCDs.

Languish Ltd:

Taxable total profits computation for the three years ending 31 March 2023

	Year to 31.3.21	Year to 31.3.22	Year to 31.3.23
	£	£	£
Tax adjusted trading profit	50,000	0	22,500
Interest income	5,000	4,000	500
Total profits	55,000	4,000	23,000
Less: Loss relief	(55,000)	(4,000)	(20,000)
Less: QCD relief	0	0	(3,000)
Taxable total profits	0	0	0
Unrelieved QCD relief	2,000	1,000	

Loss memorandum	£
Loss for y/e 31 March 2022	85,000
Less: Loss relief:	
y/e 31 March 2022	(4,000)
y/e 31 March 2021	(55,000)
y/e 31 March 2023	(20,000)
Loss available to carry forward	6,000

Note: The amount of the carry forward loss relief claim in the year ended 31 March 2023 has been restricted to preserve relief for the QCDs, which would otherwise be wasted. It would not have been beneficial to offset an amount to fully reduce the total profits as this would have used £23,000 of the loss but not saved any tax.

ACTIVITY 3

Tulip Ltd: Taxable total profits for the four years ended 31 March 2022

	Year ended			
	31 March 2019 £	**31 March** 2020 £	**31 March** 2021 £	**31 March** 2022 £
Tax adjusted trading profit	8,000	5,000	19,000	0
Property business profits	6,000	6,000	6,000	6,000
Interest income	1,500	1,000	1,200	1,400
Chargeable gains	0	2,000	0	1,900
Total profits	15,500	14,000	26,200	9,300
Less: Loss relief		(8,500)	(26,200)	(9,300)
	15,500	5,500		0
Less: QCD relief	(500)	(500)	0	0
Taxable total profits	15,000	5,000	0	0
Unrelieved qualifying charitable donation			500	500

Loss memorandum		£
Loss for year ended 31 March 2022		44,000
Less:	y/e 31 March 2022	(9,300)
	y/e 31 March 2021	(26,200)
	y/e 31 March 2020	(8,500)
		0

Notes:

1 The layout should be filled in with the various sources of income.

2 The loss for the year ended 31 March 2022 is dealt with. It is relieved against total profits of the current year and then carried back against total profits of the preceding year.

3 Since Tulip Ltd ceased trading, the loss can be carried back for up to three years on a last in first out basis. Note that the claim is against total profits and cannot be restricted to prevent wastage of the QCDs.

ACTIVITY 4

Year ended	31 March 2021		31 March 2022
	Original	**Revised**	
	£	£	£
Trading profit	200,000	200,000	0
Interest income	20,000	20,000	20,000
Total profits	220,000	220,000	20,000
Less: Current year loss relief			(20,000)
Less: Carry back relief		(220,000)	
	220,000	0	0
Less: QCDs	(1,000)	wasted	wasted
Taxable total profits	219,000	0	0
Corporation tax payable			
£219,000 × 19%	41,610		
£0 × 19%		0	
	41,610	0	

Corporation tax repayable (£41,610 – £0) = £41,610. Note that the tax saved is not the same as the loss carried back at 19% (i.e. £220,000 × 19% = £41,800). This is because relief was given for the QCD in the original computation but is wasted in the revised computation.

Loss memorandum		£
Loss for year ended 31 March 2022		250,000
Less:	y/e 31 March 2022	(20,000)
	y/e 31 March 2021	(220,000)
Loss carried forward as at 1 April 2022		10,000

MULTIPLE CHOICE QUESTIONS

1 The correct answer is D.

D is the correct answer because the loss is set off against total profits before QCDs (which are wasted) in the current year and then total profits before QCDs in the preceding 12 months. A current year claim must be made before a carry back claim, as follows:

	£
Trading loss	240,000
Utilised: Current year offset	(6,000)
Carry back claim	(104,000)
Available to carry forward	130,000

2 The correct answer is C.

C is the correct answer because a claim to carry back the loss must be made within 2 years of the end of the accounting period in which the loss arose.

PRACTICE QUESTIONS

1 SWANEE LTD

(a) **Computation of trading loss y/e 31 March 2022**

		£	£
Trading loss per accounts			(96,000)
Add:	Depreciation	10,800	
	Entertaining	1,200	
			12,000
			(84,000)
Less:	Capital allowances (£22,222 × 18%)		(4,000)
Trading loss			(88,000)

(b) **Relief for trading loss**

	Year ended 31 March 2021	2022
	£	£
Tax adjusted trading profit	40,000	0
Interest income	2,000	3,500
Chargeable gain	0	14,500
Total profits	42,000	18,000
Less: Loss relief	(42,000)	(18,000)
Taxable total profits	0	0

Loss memorandum

		£
Loss y/e 31 March 2022 (a)		88,000
Less: Relief	y/e 31 March 2022	(18,000)
	y/e 31 March 2021	(42,000)
Loss carried forward		28,000

Any remaining losses can be carried forward and set against future total profits.

2 FLOUNDER LTD

	Year to 31 Dec 2017	Year to 31 Dec 2018	Year to 31 Dec 2019	Year to 31 Dec 2020	Year to 31 Dec 2021
	£	£	£	£	£
Trading profit	20,000	27,000	30,000	13,500	0
Less: Capital allowances	(3,800)	(7,200)	(5,400)	(4,050)	0
Net trading income	16,200	19,800	24,600	9,450	0
Interest income	900	1,000	1,200	1,300	1,400
Total profits	17,100	20,800	25,800	10,750	1,400
Less: Loss relief	0	(20,800)	(25,800)	(10,750)	(1,400)
Taxable total profits	17,100	0	0	0	0

	£
Trading loss y/e 31 December 2021	(75,000)
Less: Capital allowances	(6,600)
Available loss	(81,600)

Loss memorandum

Loss y/e 31 December 2021	81,600
Less: Relief	
y/e 31 December 2021	(1,400)
y/e 31 December 2020	(10,750)
y/e 31 December 2019	(25,800)
y/e 31 December 2018	(20,800)
y/e 31 December 2017 (cannot carry back more than 36 months)	0
Loss remaining unrelieved	22,850

CHAPTER 24

ACTIVITY 1

Cat Ltd is liable to registration from 1 April 2022 because supplies for the 30 days from that date are expected to exceed £85,000. The company must notify HMRC of its liability to register by 30 April 2022 (i.e. 30 days from 1 April 2022) and is registered with effect from 1 April 2022 (i.e. the beginning of the 30 day period).

Note: Cat Ltd does not make taxable supplies during the period 1 January 2022 to 31 March 2022. The future registration test does not apply to traders that are not making taxable supplies so that a liability to registration cannot arise during this period.

ACTIVITY 2

	Item	VAT-inclusive cost £	Input tax recoverable £
1	Car to be used by the managing director 60% for business and 40% privately.	16,600	0
2	Delivery van	17,500	2,917
3	Staff party – staff were each allowed to bring a guest. Half the cost is estimated to be for these guests.	630	53
4	Entertaining UK customers and suppliers	526	0
5	Entertaining overseas customers	150	25
6	Car to be used as a pool car (i.e. available for all employees and kept at the business premises)	11,475	1,913
7	Lease costs for the quarter for a car that will be used 80% for business use and 20% privately by the Sales Director	960	80

ACTIVITY 3

(a) **£25,000 deposit**

The basic tax point is the date of despatch, 30 November 2021. However, as the deposit was paid before the date of despatch, this is the actual tax point, i.e. 16 November 2021.

(b) **The balance of £75,000**

As an invoice was issued within 14 days of the basic tax point, this is the actual tax point, i.e. 12 December 2021.

MULTIPLE CHOICE QUESTIONS

1 The correct answer is A.

A is the correct answer because the normal tax point of 14 June (i.e. the date the goods are made available to the customer) is overridden as the cash was paid earlier (on 10 June). As the cash was paid earlier, the 14 day invoice rule is irrelevant.

2 The correct answer is D.

D is the correct answer because the flat rate scheme percentage is applied to the full VAT-inclusive turnover, including all standard, zero-rated and exempt supplies. Expenses are not taken into account in calculating the VAT under this scheme.

£132,000 × 9.5% = £12,540

PRACTICE QUESTIONS

1 KITE LTD

Kite Ltd is liable to register for VAT at the end of any month if the value of taxable supplies in the previous 12 months exceeds £85,000. Kite Ltd's taxable supplies exceeded the registration limit by the end of July 2021: (£29,000 + £57,100 = £86,100). It was therefore required to notify HMRC by 30 August 2021. Registration was effective from 1 September 2021 or an earlier agreed date.

2 CART LTD

VAT return – Quarter ended 31 March 2022	£	£
Output VAT		
Sales:		
Standard-rated (£228,000 × 20%)		45,600
Zero-rated		0
Input VAT		
Purchases and expenses (£71,280 – £960) × 20%	14,064	
Impairment losses (£4,000 × 20%)	800	
Machinery (£42,300 × 1/6)	7,050	
		(21,914)
VAT payable		23,686

Notes:

1 Input VAT on business entertaining cannot be reclaimed.

2 Relief for an impairment loss cannot be claimed until six months from the time that payment is due. More than 6 months has elapsed from the invoice due for payment on 10 August 2021 at the end of the quarter ended 31 March 2022 and therefore relief can be claimed for this impairment loss.

3 Input VAT on motor cars not used wholly for business purposes cannot be reclaimed.

INDEX